MAGILL'S
SURVEY
OF
AMERICAN
LITERATURE

REFERENCE

MAGILL'S SURVEY OF AMERICAN LITERATURE

Volume 6

Steinbeck–Zindel

Indexes

REFERENCE

Edited by
FRANK N. MAGILL

Marshall Cavendish Corporation
New York • London • Toronto • Sydney • Singapore

Published By
Marshall Cavendish Corporation
2415 Jerusalem Avenue
P.O. Box 587
North Bellmore, New York 11710
United States of America

Copyright © 1991, by Salem Press, Inc.
All rights in this book are reserved. No part of this work may be
used or reproduced in any manner whatsoever or transmitted in
any form or by any means, electronic or mechanical, including
photocopy, recording, or any information storage and retrieval system, without written permission from the copyright owner except
in the case of brief quotations embodied in critical articles and
reviews. For information address the publisher.

∞ The paper used in these volumes conforms to the American
National Standard for Permanence of Paper for Printed Library
Materials, Z39.48-1984.

Library of Congress Cataloging-in-Publication Data
Magill's survey of American literature. Edited by Frank N. Magill.
     p. cm.
  Includes bibliographical references and index.
  1. American literature—Dictionaries. 2. American literature—
Bio-bibliography. 3. Authors, American—Biography—Dictionar-
ies. I. Magill, Frank Northen, 1907.
PS21.M34 1991
810.9′0003—dc20
ISBN 1-85435-437-X (set)   91-28113
ISBN 1-85435-443-4 (volume 6)   CIP

Second Printing

PRINTED IN THE UNITED STATES OF AMERICA

CONTENTS

JOHN STEINBECK

Born: Salinas, California
February 27, 1902
Died: New York, New York
December 20, 1968

Principal Literary Achievement

Concerned with such universal themes as the meaning of life and death, Steinbeck, 1962 recipient of the Nobel Prize in Literature, employed realism to explore the lives of common people.

Biography

Salinas, California, over the hill from Monterey and close enough to Big Sur that John Steinbeck's mother was able to teach there, has long had the climate to grow some of the most profitable crops in the United States. When Steinbeck was born there in 1902, that part of the central California coast, some one hundred miles south of San Francisco, was quite untouched by the kind of industrial civilization that had grown up in the East, from which Steinbeck's family had come.

The father, John Ernst Steinbeck, born in Florida, had followed his parents to Hollister, California. He was a miller and served for eleven years as treasurer of Monterey County. In 1890, he married Olive Hamilton, a teacher. The Steinbecks had four children, of whom John, their third, was the only boy. He showed an early literary bent; his favorite pastime was reading, and his favorite book was Sir Thomas Malory's *Le Morte d'Arthur* (1485).

Steinbeck contributed to the school newspaper at Salinas High School, from which he was graduated in 1919, after which he entered Stanford University as an English major. He attended Stanford in a desultory manner from 1920 until 1925 but left without a degree. A contributor to several campus publications during his years there, Steinbeck was particularly affected by his creative writing teacher, Edith Ronald Mirrielees, for whose book, *Story Writing* (1962), he wrote the preface.

In the fall of 1925, Steinbeck went to New York City, working first as a day laborer. Before long, through the intervention of an influential uncle, Steinbeck had a twenty-five-dollar-a-week job on the New York *American*, where he had an undistinguished career as a reporter. Urged by an editor from the Robert McBride Publishing Company, Steinbeck produced a collection of short stories. When the publisher rejected the collection, a discouraged Steinbeck shipped out as a deckhand

on a steamer going to California via the Panama Canal. He found work as a care-taker at a remote Lake Tahoe resort, benefiting artistically from the isolation the job assured. He wrote three novels, none ever published. In 1929, however, his novel about English pirate Henry Morgan, *Cup of Gold*, was published by McBride. Appearing only two months before the stock market crash of 1929, it sold few copies.

In 1930, Steinbeck married the first of his three wives, Carol Henning, and moved to Pacific Grove, California, where they lived in a modest house provided by Stein-beck's family, who also gave them twenty-five dollars a month on which they could live decently during the Great Depression. Steinbeck met marine biologist Ed Rick-etts, who remained his closest friend for the rest of Rickett's life, in the same year.

For his next book—and for most of his subsequent ones—he turned to a Califor-nia setting and theme. Brewer, Warren & Putnam published *The Pastures of Heaven* in 1932. Before the book could be bound, however, the publisher failed. Despite this, Steinbeck earned more than four hundred dollars in royalties from it, more than his first book or his third book, *To a God Unknown* (1933), brought him. Neither book sold enough copies to cover the $250 advance he had received for each.

In 1934, the year in which Steinbeck's mother died, the *North American Review* accepted the first two sections of *The Red Pony* and two short stories, one of which, "The Murder," was selected to appear in the O. Henry Prize Stories volume for 1934. It was in 1935, however, that Steinbeck's star began to rise significantly, with the publication of *Tortilla Flat*, a latter-day Arthurian legend with Danny as King Arthur and his boys as Danny's knights.

A number of publishers rejected *Tortilla Flat*, thinking its frivolity inappropriate for the mood of the depression era. Pascal Covici, however, liked Steinbeck's writ-ing. When he called his agent to ask whether Steinbeck had any new manuscripts for him to read, he was sent *Tortilla Flat*, which he published, thus beginning a literary relationship that lasted through Steinbeck's years of greatest celebrity. *Tortilla Flat* did not fare well with the critics, but the public liked it; Steinbeck's future was assured. Steinbeck helped people to see that there is more to life than money.

Of Mice and Men followed in 1937 and was a Book-of-the-Month Club selection, assuring a minimum of ten thousand sales. In the same year, Steinbeck visited a camp for migrant workers. This visit led to his most celebrated work, *The Grapes of Wrath*, published in 1939. *Sea of Cortez* followed in 1941. The next year, Steinbeck and Carol divorced, and in 1943, he married Gwen Conger, with whom he had two sons before their divorce in 1948, the same year in which Ed Ricketts was killed in an accident. *Cannery Row*, titled for the sardine factory area of Monterey, was well received in 1945, as was the novella *The Pearl* in 1947. In 1947, *The Wayward Bus* was rejected by the public. Steinbeck continued to write, but he never again attained the level of artistry he had reached in *The Grapes of Wrath*.

When he was awarded the Nobel Prize in Literature in 1962, the academic estab-lishment was not overjoyed, although his faithful public, recalling the work he had produced between 1935 and 1947, was less negative in its judgment. The Nobel pre-sentation speech cited the impact of *The Grapes of Wrath*, but it also noted, among

Steinbeck's later work, *Travels with Charley* (1962) and *The Winter of Our Discontent* (1961). Steinbeck died in New York in 1968. In 1974, his boyhood home in Salinas was opened as a museum and restaurant. A collection of his papers is in the Steinbeck Collection at San Jose State University, whose Steinbeck Room attracts numerous scholars.

Steinbeck's close friendship with Ed Ricketts, enduring for almost two decades until Rickett's death in 1948, had a profound effect upon the author. Ricketts was a deeply philosophical man. Steinbeck trusted him and valued his judgment to the point that he had him read all of his manuscripts or read them aloud to him. Ricketts' judgments were not always valid—he liked *The Wayward Bus*—but were necessary to Steinbeck. Ricketts got Steinbeck to think about nature in ways that he never had before. Steinbeck began to take on the philosophical colorations of his friend and went so far as to include Ricketts' essay on nonteleological thinking, which had been circulating privately among Ricketts' friends since the 1930's, in *Sea of Cortez*.

Steinbeck wrote largely to please himself, and in so doing he often pleased vast audiences of readers as well. Seldom did he please the critics, however, after their vigorous acceptance of *The Grapes of Wrath*. Possibly this is because literary criticism was largely an enterprise of Easterners or of people educated at Eastern, often New England, schools. Their anti-California bias was seldom if ever expressed, but it arguably existed at the subconscious level.

Steinbeck resisted the inroads that the importunate tried to make upon his time. To protect his privacy, he moved away from California in 1945, buying a townhouse on the Upper East Side in New York City, where he continued to live until his death.

Analysis

Although John Steinbeck's first novel, *Cup of Gold*, is not much like his later work in theme, setting, or style, it supplies hints of themes that were to pervade his later work. The book is much influenced stylistically by the medieval legends with which Steinbeck had grown familiar during his boyhood. The protagonist of the book, Henry Morgan, is a brigand, a rugged individualist who is as much a nonconformist as Danny is in *Tortilla Flat*. Those two protagonists, each from a drastically different background than the other, would have understood each other and sympathized with the other's outlook.

In his next two books, *The Pastures of Heaven* and *To a God Unknown*, Steinbeck discovered the direction that most of his future books would take. He wrote about the central California agricultural areas in which he had grown up, and, in the latter book, he also experimented with symbolism stimulated by his early reading of medieval literature. The characters in these books are memorable as individuals, but they clearly represent universal types as well.

As promising as *The Pastures of Heaven* was, it was not a commercial success. The beginning of Steinbeck's widespread national acceptance came with *Tortilla Flat*, which might not have been published at all had Pascal Covici not read Steinbeck's two preceding books and been favorably impressed by them. In *Tortilla Flat*, Steinbeck transplants the medieval legend of King Arthur and his knights to the Monterey Peninsula, where Danny and his jolly band of *paisanos* lead lives of immediate gratification and satisfaction.

The Eastern establishment that essentially dominated literary criticism at that time did not always know how to handle Steinbeck's setting—California was the last frontier to the New York critics of the day—and many of them were appalled at the frivolousness and irresponsibility of Steinbeck's characters in the book. What shocked them most, however, was that Steinbeck made no value judgments about his characters. Rather, he presented them and let his readers make of them what they might.

The public accepted Danny and his boys because they represented to an economically depressed society an escape from the constraints that society had placed on many of its citizens. Danny and company lived outside those constraints. In *Tortilla Flat*, one finds the quintessential Steinbeck, the Steinbeck flexing his muscles before writing his great classic, *The Grapes of Wrath*. Steinbeck's greatest strength was his understanding and respectful depiction of people on the fringes of society.

It is important to remember that Steinbeck is not one with the people about whom he writes. They are from the other side of the tracks, but Steinbeck throws no stones. He embraces them appreciatively, not with the sense that he wants to be one of them, but with a genuine respect for them as they are. In his best work, it is this disinterested, objective, yet warm presentation that entices readers. If one thinks in terms of dichotomies, American novelist Henry James would be at one extreme in depicting human beings, Steinbeck at the other.

This explains in part Steinbeck's frequent rejection by the critics. The professionals who wrote about his work had essentially been brought up in the Henry James tradition; they had lived their lives either in the Eastern establishment or outside it trying to break in. Steinbeck disoriented and threatened some of them. As a result, Steinbeck's writing has not received the serious and objective critical evaluation it deserves.

If Danny and his boys are a sort of lost generation transplanted to the central California coast—and they do at times put one in mind of the characters in Ernest Hemingway's *The Sun Also Rises* (1926) in that they are searching for the same universal answers that Hemingway's characters are—they are also prototypes for characters such as George and Lenny in *Of Mice and Men*, Tom Joad in *The Grapes of Wrath*, Kino in *The Pearl*, and others who live on the fringes of society.

Steinbeck's visit to a migrant worker's camp in 1937 helped to focus his energies and to give him a cause about which to write. *The Grapes of Wrath*, probably the most significant socio-literary document of the Depression era, was Steinbeck's masterpiece. Using the simple and direct language and the casual syntax that characterizes his best writing, he captured a crucial era in American history by showing the way the Great Depression and the dustbowls of the Midwestern United States affected one family, pawns in a game so huge that they did not always realize there was a game.

Steinbeck became the darling of the Marxist critics when he published *The Grapes of Wrath* in 1939, but mostly for political reasons rather than for artistic ones. When his subsequent books failed to evince the social indignation of *The Grapes of Wrath*, the academy virtually abandoned Steinbeck and often made unfeeling, superficial judgments about his work because it had failed to meet their preconceived political expectations. Steinbeck was accused of being an intellectual lightweight and of having sold out—turning his back on his principles once he had secured his future. Actually, he had simply moved his cast of characters into new situations and shaped them to those situations, although not with consistent success. Even in the much—and justifiably—maligned *The Wayward Bus*, Steinbeck was experimenting with a milieu created by imitating and modernizing the kind of microcosm with which Sebastian Brant had worked in his long medieval poem, *Das Narrenschiff* (1494; *The Ship of Fools*, 1507).

Steinbeck's work is almost wholly antiestablishment, but gently so. Every good story must have opposing forces, friends and enemies to keep the conflict moving. Steinbeck knew who his friends were: simple people such as George and Lenny, Danny and his friends, the Joad family, Kino, Jody in *The Red Pony*, Mack and the boys in *Cannery Row*.

He had a little more trouble in deciding who the enemies were. He solved the problem, as many writers before him had, by keeping the enemy large, rich, and generalized. Upton Sinclair had taken on the impersonal giant of a meat industry in *The Jungle* in 1906; Frank Norris made the banks and the railroads the main enemies of society in *The Octopus* (1901), and *The Pit* (1903); Jack London had used greedy goldrush speculators the same way in *The Call of the Wild* (1903). Steinbeck found his enemies in faceless bureaucracies, unfeeling governments, and grasping banks in whose clutches the good people were held helplessly. The best they could do was to squirm a little and perhaps deal with the situation with the wry humor that characterizes Danny and his jolly cohorts.

Work remains to be done in assessing the artistry of John Steinbeck. His style reflects a mixture of influences as diverse as the Bible, the novels of Fyodor Dostoevski, Leo Tolstoy, Guy du Maupassant, Thomas Hardy, and other English and Continental writers, and of the medieval texts that he found so appealing during his childhood. Steinbeck was an uneven writer, but at his best, he was superb.

OF MICE AND MEN

First published: 1937
Type of work: Novel

The story of two men, one retarded, whose symbiotic relationship ends when George must kill the retarded Lennie.

The original manuscript of *Of Mice and Men* suffered a fate that gives writers nightmares: When Steinbeck and his wife were out one night, their dog, Toby, tore the first half of the finished manuscript to shreds. It was Steinbeck's only copy, so he had to rewrite half of the book. Steinbeck gave the dog meager punishment and said that he had a certain respect for the beast's literary judgment.

The book is one of Steinbeck's warmest. Lennie, a migrant ranchhand, is re-tarded. George, also a migrant ranchhand, travels with him and looks after him. The story opens and ends on a riverbank off the main road, separated from the world of machines and impersonal technology. It is to this place that George tells Lennie to return in case of trouble. As in many of Steinbeck's novels, this riverbank and the cave in which Lennie suggests that he and George might live away from the world are a back-to-the-womb motif.

Lennie is large and strong. He likes soft, furry things. He likes them so much that he sometimes crushes the life out of them accidentally in showing his affection. He keeps mice in his pocket, but they do not survive his attention. Lennie lives on dreams. He longs for the day that he and George will own a little land and a house, a place where they can hide from a world that Lennie does not understand and that George does not trust. George and Lennie are different from the other ranchhands because they have each other. They conceive of a future and harbor dreams because they think that they will always be together. Their symbiotic relationship humanizes some of the other ranchhands with whom they work.

The ranch owner's son, Curley, however, is not among those humanized by George and Lennie's presence. Curley has his own problems. He is a lightweight fighter, a combative sort who resents being small but resents even more people who are larger than he. Lennie is a perfect target for his aggressions. He provokes Lennie into a fight in which he bloodies Lennie's nose, but Lennie crushes Curley's hand.

Curley's other major problem is that he is newly married to Candy, a woman of whose fidelity he is quite unsure. Candy goes to a local dance hall on a Saturday night and makes advances to Lennie. Lennie's fondness for soft, furry things makes him vulnerable. He strokes Candy's hair to the point that she becomes alarmed and panics. When she does, Lennie breaks her neck.

Doing as he has been told, Lennie returns to the safety of the riverbank. He asks George to recite for him the details of how they will stay together, buy a small spread, and live out their lives happily. George, realizing that Curley will capture Lennie and make him die painfully for what he has done, puts a bullet through Lennie's head as Lennie looks out into the distance, where he envisions the future George is reciting to him.

The novel was unique in that it consisted largely of dialogue and was written so that it could also, with almost no adjustments, be acted on stage. Its popularity, particularly its acceptance as a Book-of-the-Month Club selection, surprised Steinbeck, who did not look upon the book as very significant. The original title, *Something That Happened*, reflects Steinbeck's objectivity in presenting his story; he makes no moral judgments about George and Lennie nor about the other ranchhands.

THE RED PONY

First published: 1937 (enlarged, 1945)
Type of work: Novella

The story of how Jody Tiflin moves from boyhood to adulthood.

Steinbeck, in Baja California in 1937, let it be known that he was writing a children's book, referring to what was to grow into *The Red Pony*. The first three of the four interconnected stories that make up *The Red Pony* were published in *The Long Valley* (1938). In 1945, Steinbeck added the final story, "The Leader of the People," to make the collection long enough to be published as a separate entity. The novella is not a children's book in the conventional sense; it is more accurately described as a *Bildungsroman*, a book that chronicles the education of a boy growing to manhood.

Jody Tiflin is about eleven years old. He learns some harsh lessons in life, although living on his parents' farm in the warm Salinas Valley provides him with an idyllic childhood. Jody's first disillusionment comes in "The Gift," when the horse he has been given—the fulfillment of any boy's dream—is drenched in a rainstorm that Billy Buck, the family's farmhand, has assured the boy will not come. The horse, Gabilan, catches cold and, despite all efforts to save it, dies. Billy Buck, who had been Jody's hero, is now diminished in his eyes, first because he promised fair weather when Jody took the horse out and then because Billy could not save the stricken animal.

Jody comes face to face with a second harsh reality relating to death in "The Great Mountains," the second story in the cycle. Gitano, an ailing old Chicano who was born on the Tiflin ranch before they owned it, walks onto the property and asks to be permitted to stay there until he dies. Carl Tiflin, ever practical and not a sympathetic character as Steinbeck depicts him, will not permit this, and the next morning Gitano rides off dejectedly—but not before he has stolen an old rapier that has been in the Tiflin family for generations.

In the third story, "The Promise," Jody is given his second horse, a newborn colt that needs care because its mother died in delivering it. Billy Buck had no choice but to kill her in order to save the colt, so, although Jody is pleased that this new life belongs to him, he grieves at the trade-off that accompanied the gift.

The last story, "The Leader of the People," is about the visit that Jody's maternal grandfather pays to the ranch. Jody adores the old man and dotes on his stories about the days when he was leader of a wagon train. Carl Tiflin hates those stories as much as Jody loves them, and he deplores the old man's visits because he knows they will be filled with reminiscences about an age in which he has little interest. The old man had a "westering" spirit, but that spirit, which helped Americans to conquer its last geographical frontier, is no longer necessary. The frontier has been conquered. Carl

Tiflin must get on with his work, and he turns his back on the past that helped him to reach the point at which he finds himself.

This story ends with Jody listening to his grandfather, who confides in him that he fears the new generation no longer has the spirit of which he speaks. Jody, quite tellingly, listens and then asks his grandfather if he would like some lemonade, indicating that, for the first time, the boy is showing a sensitivity to someone else's feelings. Jody is moving toward manhood.

The Red Pony builds on Steinbeck's notion that nature is unrelenting and mysterious. Mere humans cannot thwart it any more than they can control it. When Jody's Gabilan becomes food for the vultures, Steinbeck does not suggest that commiseration is the proper emotion. It is part of the natural cycle. Living things feed on living things as inevitably as humans die.

THE GRAPES OF WRATH

First published: 1939
Type of work: Novel

The saga of the Joad family as they leave the Oklahoma dustbowl during the Depression to find a new life in California.

In *The Grapes of Wrath*, Steinbeck vents his anger against a capitalistic society that was capable of plunging the world into an economic depression, but he does not exonerate the farmers who have been driven from the dustbowls of the Midwestern and Southwestern United States. He deplores their neglect of the land that resulted in the dustbowls, which helped to exacerbate the Great Depression.

The book is interestingly structured. Interspersed among its chapters are frequent interchapters, vignettes that have little direct bearing on the novel's main narrative. These interchapters contain the philosophical material of the book, the allegories such as that of the turtle crossing the road. As the animal makes its tedious way across the dusty thoroughfare, drivers swerve to avoid hitting it. One vicious driver, however, aims directly for it, clearly intending to squash it. Because this driver's aim is not accurate, he succeeds only in nicking the corner of the turtle's carapace, catapulting it to the side of the road it was trying to reach. Once the dust settles and the shock wears off, the turtle emerges and continues on its way, dropping as it does a grain of wheat from the folds of its skin. When the rains come, this grain will germinate; this is Steinbeck's intimation of hope.

As the narrative opens, Tom Joad has been released from a term he is serving in the state penitentiary for having killed someone in self-defense. On his way home, he falls in with Jim Casy, a former preacher down on his luck. Jim's initials can be interpreted religiously, as can much of the book. When Jim and Tom get to the farm where the Joads were tenant farmers, they find the place deserted, as are the farms around it, now dusty remnants of what they had been. Tom learns that his family has sold what little it owned, probably for five cents on the dollar, and headed to the promised land, California. En route, they pause to rest up at a relative's place and to work on the antique truck they had bought secondhand for the trek west. Tom and Jim catch up with them there, and they all leave—an even dozen of them—for the land in which they have placed their future hope.

The chronicle of the slow trip west, reminiscent of the turtle's arduous creep across the parched road, is recorded in such realistic detail that the reader is transported into a world peopled by hobos, stumblebums, the dispossessed, the disenchanted, and the dislocated—all of them pushing ahead to the jobs they believe exist for agricultural workers in California. Death haunts the motley band, threatening the elderly and those who are weak. The grandfather dies of a stroke the first night out; his wife dies as the family crosses the Mohave Desert. Noah, the retarded son, wanders off and is not heard from again. Ahead, however, lies hope, so the Joads bury their dead and keep going.

The land of their hearts' desire, however, proves to be no Garden of Eden. The dream of a future that will offer hope and security quickly develops into a nightmare. Tom's sister, Rose of Sharon, loses her baby and, lacking funds for a funeral, prays over it and sets it adrift in the rushes beside a river, much as Moses was set adrift in the bullrushes. Tom gets into trouble with the police, but Jim surrenders in his place and is taken away.

By the time Tom and Jim meet again, Jim is a labor agitator, and, in an encounter with the police, he is killed and Tom is injured. The Joads hide Tom in their shack, then sneak him into a farm. There he takes up Jim's work as a labor organizer.

As the rains come and flooding occurs, the Joads, who are encamped beside a river, endure floods that ruin their old truck. Having no place to live, they go into a decrepit barn, where a boy and his starving father have sought shelter. Rose of Sharon, having lost her baby, nourishes the starving man with the milk from her breasts, thereby saving his life. One is reminded again of the turtle and of the grain of wheat it deposits in the desiccated soil.

The Grapes of Wrath is a bitter tale of humans against nature and against a brutally exploitive society, but it is also a tale of nobility, of self-sacrifice, and ultimately of hope. It often offends the sensibilities, but life frequently offends one's sensibilities, and in that respect this novel is like life. It is a polemic, but it is more detached and objective than many critics have given it credit for being.

CANNERY ROW

First published: 1945
Type of work: Novel

A rollicking story of how the characters of Monterey's Cannery Row plan and give a birthday party for one of their friends.

Around the sardine factories of Cannery Row in Monterey, California, lived those who worked only when they had to, preferring to talk, fight, drink, and be lazy. These are the characters of Steinbeck's *Cannery Row*, who have been compared to the rogues depicted in English artist William Hogarth's engravings and in the picaresque novels of the eighteenth century.

Monterey is only a whisper away from Pacific Grove, where Steinbeck and his wife lived in the early 1930's. The two worlds, however, are continents apart ideologically. Pacific Grove developed as a Methodist campground. One could not buy liquor there, and the sidewalks were deserted not long after sunset. Three miles away, Monterey's bars stayed open almost until dawn. The population of each town was unique, although the communities were virtually adjacent.

Mack presides over a band of derelicts who live from one drink to the next, one fight to the next, and one day to the next. If earlier picaresque protagonists lived their irresponsible lives in ways that advanced them socially and economically, Mack's boys do not. Their progress is strictly horizontal. They live by bartering, borrowing, stealing, and conning Lee Chong, the Chinese merchant. They are the street people of an earlier age, although some of them have shacks to retreat into when they must. One of them, Malloy, lives sometimes in a huge boiler that his wife has decorated with chintz curtains.

The novel has only a loosely defined forward momentum. Mostly its characters drift laterally rather than move forward, as is quite appropriate. The motivating factor, the element that makes the novel justifiable, is that this assortment of undistinguished humanity is working together toward an outcome: getting a present to give Doc—a marine biologist modeled on Ed Ricketts, who runs a small business supplying biological specimens to commercial distributors—at a surprise birthday party they are planning for him. They have already arranged for the liquor. One of them has taken a temporary job as a bartender, enabling him to save the dregs of people's drinks in large containers. This accumulation of leftovers constitutes their liquor supply.

The boys scour the community, gathering Doc's birthday present, which is to consist of all kinds of specimens he can sell: cats, rats, frogs, dogs, anything biological enough to qualify. They invite everyone from the row to the party, including Dora, the local madam, and her girls. The climax of the novel comes in the hilarious fight that breaks out as the crowds gather and their spirits intensify. At the end of the novel, nothing has changed. The characters will go on living exactly as they have, ever good natured, drifters who drift within the limited precincts of Cannery Row.

As he did in *The Grapes of Wrath*, Steinbeck uses interchapters to comment on the main thrust of the novel and to set it into a philosophical context. In these interchapters, one finds the strong influences of Ed Ricketts' nonteleological philosophy, which was fully explained in *Sea of Cortez*.

THE PEARL

First published: 1947
Type of work: Novella

A simple Mexican Indian finds the pearl of the world and it all but destroys his life.

The Pearl, which its author calls a parable, was first published as "The Pearl of the World" in *Woman's Home Companion* in 1945. It was published as a novel and released as a film under the title *The Pearl* in 1947. In parables, characters exist outside and beyond their individual identities and are shaped to represent universal types.

Steinbeck's story came from a folk story he had heard and related in *The Log from the Sea of Cortez* (1951). The story, purported to be true, was of a simple Mexican peasant boy who had found a pearl near La Paz at the tip of Baja California; the pearl was so large that the boy was convinced he would never have to work again, that he could stay drunk forever, and that he could have his pick of women and then buy his eternal salvation after all his sinning by purchasing masses. His dream turned sour when opportunists and thieves, some of whom threatened his life, beset him. So frightened and disenchanted was this simple Indian boy that he eventually threw his great pearl back into the sea whence it came.

Steinbeck creates as his Indian peasant Kino, an unwed father whose chief concerns are to marry Juana, the mother of his child, Coyotito, in a church wedding and to provide for his family and for Coyotito's education. In short, Kino aspires to middle-class values to which the first readers of the story in *Woman's Home Companion* could easily relate.

Kino and Juana revel in the excitement that surrounds Kino's finding the pearl, but their elation soon turns into distrust. The brokers, through whom Kino must sell the jewel if he is to profit from it, conspire to cheat him, saying that the pearl is so big that it has no commercial potential. Kino has to hide the jewel, but while he sleeps, thieves try to rob him of it. The doctor who would not treat Kino and his family when they had no money now comes unctuously to them, proffering the best of services, to be paid for when the pearl is sold.

As the drama of Kino's situation unfolds, Kino, essentially peace-loving, is forced to kill three men and, worst of all, his adored Coyotito is killed by pursuers who shoot recklessly and blow off Coyotito's head. The pearl comes to represent all that is bad in life, all that is, in the eyes of this superstitious peasant, unlucky. Finally, at Juana's urging, Kino, like the Indian boy in the original legend, heaves the jewel into the sea. He has made nothing from his find. He has lost a great deal that is precious to him.

On an allegorical level, Kino's pearl is much like Santiago's marlin in Ernest Hemingway's *The Old Man and the Sea* (1952). It is a symbol of all the strivings of humankind. Dreams keep people going, offering them future hope even if the present is bleak. Steinbeck, however, like Hemingway after him, implies that human nobility comes from striving rather than from attaining.

EAST OF EDEN

First published: 1952
Type of work: Novel

An ambitious and convoluted saga of the Trasks, residents of the Salinas Valley, and of human cupidity.

East of Eden is the most uncharacteristic book in the Steinbeck canon. It is a complicated—at times convoluted—book that tries to accomplish more than it finally can. In his attempt to juggle three themes, Steinbeck at times fumbles, leaving his readers confused.

On the one hand, Steinbeck is attempting to write a documentary about the Salinas Valley, which comes to represent the nation as a whole. He seeks to accomplish this by directing his attention to two complicated families, the Hamiltons and the Trasks. Upon this situation, he superimposes, quite heavy-handedly, a modern redaction of the biblical story of Cain and Abel—Caleb and Aron in the novel.

Adam Trask and his half-brother, Charles, live together in Connecticut as the story opens. They get along, but some rivalries exist. Adam detests his father, although he gets along with his stepmother, Charles's mother. The father has a strong militaristic bent and dreams of having a son in the Army. He hand-picks Adam for this honor, leaving Charles, who adores his father, feeling rejected. In frustration, Charles beats Adam badly. After spending five miserable years in the service, Adam reenlists for another tour of duty. When it ends, he returns home to find that his father is dead. He and Charles inherit enough to make them rich. They live together in a harmony that is sometimes disturbed by violent fights.

Meanwhile, Cathy Ames is coming of age in Massachusetts. She is a confusing woman, beautiful and lovable on the surface but inherently evil in ways that few people can see. She sets fire to her parents' house, and both of them are killed in the blaze, leaving Cathy free to escape from a home she has found oppressive. She plants clues to suggest that she, too, died in the fire and runs away, becoming mistress to a man who operates a brothel.

When their relationship sours, he takes her into the wilderness and beats her badly, leaving her there to die. She manages to get to the nearest house, which is where the Trask brothers live. They take her in and nurse her back to health. Charles divines the evil that lurks beneath Cathy's prepossessing exterior. Adam is innocent of such feelings, and he marries Cathy. She drugs him on their wedding night and steals into Charles's room, where she seduces him.

The brothers' relationship is strained by Cathy's presence, although Adam is not aware of his wife's duplicity. He decides, over his wife's protests, to go to the Salinas Valley to farm. He buys one of the best ranches in the area, and Cathy is soon delivered of twin sons. Unknown to Adam, they are Charles's offspring. Before names have been picked for them, Cathy shoots and wounds Adam, then flees to a bawdy house in Salinas, where she works under the name of Kate. The owner of the brothel, Faye, grows fond of Kate and decides to leave her everything she has in her will. After the will has been drafted, Kate arranges for Faye's murder and comes immediately into her money.

Meanwhile, Adam is so disconsolate at his wife's defection that he has not named the twins. Finally, goaded by his neighbor, Sam Hamilton, and several friends, he names the boys Caleb and Aron. Steinbeck interjects at this point a conversation about Cain and Abel so that there is no question about his artistic intention.

Sam, who knows more about Kate than do the other principals in the novel, is aging and knows he cannot live forever. He is fully cognizant of Kate's past and knows that she has turned Faye's brothel into one in which sadism is the chief lure. He tells Adam what he knows, and Adam visits Kate. She tries to seduce him, but not before informing him that the twins are Charles's sons, not his.

Meanwhile, the two boys grow up to be quite different. Aron is blond and lovable, although quite staunch and adamant in his beliefs. Caleb, dark-haired and intelligent, is solitary but has the makings of a leader. Neither knows that Kate is alive until Aron falls in love with Abra Hamilton, Sam's daughter. She eventually reveals this information to Aron, who now realizes that his father has not been forthright with him. He does not seek to meet his mother. The story is further complicated because, at this time, Adam devises a plan for shipping lettuce to New York, iced so that it would survive the journey. When the venture collapses, Adam loses a large amount of money, causing Aron considerable embarrassment; he does not take well to failure in people, especially in his father.

Finally, Aron manipulates things so that Caleb finishes high school early and goes to college. Caleb has learned from Abra of Kate's existence, and he follows his mother about until she notices him and they talk. She hates him, feeling threatened by him. When he finishes college, Caleb goes into the bean business with Sam Hamilton, and the two become rich because they can meet some of the food shortages brought about by World War I.

Caleb, always unsure of his father's love, tries to buy it by giving Adam money to help him recover from the loss he had on the lettuce venture. Adam, too proud to accept the money, virtually throws it back at him. To assuage his hurt, Caleb now takes Aron to meet Kate, who is intimidated by Caleb. She writes a will in which she leaves everything to Aron and shortly afterward commits suicide.

Aron, unable to cope with all that has happened, joins the Army. Sent to France to fight in the war, he is killed. News of his death brings on a stroke that will kill Adam. Caleb blames himself for Aron's death, but as Adam nears death, at the urging of Lee, his Chinese servant, he gives Caleb his blessing and dies. Steinbeck attempted more than he could handle in this book; he was trying to produce something of epic proportions, but his greatest skill lay in working within more narrowly defined parameters.

Summary

John Steinbeck criticism has been generally less informed and more prejudiced than that accorded to other American writers of his stature. Current opinion supports the contention that Steinbeck will not weather well and that he will be forgotten long before contemporaries of his such as William Faulkner and Ernest Hemingway.

Further evaluation, however, may well prove the prophets incorrect. Steinbeck speaks to the general reader in ways that few American authors have. He has imbibed much of the storytelling style of medieval writers, and the folk elements that make his work appealing to a broad range of readers may be the elements that help his reputation to survive.

Bibliography

Benson, Jackson J. *The True Adventure of John Steinbeck: Writer*. New York: Viking Press, 1984.

DeMott, Robert. *Steinbeck's Reading: A Catalogue of Books Owned and Borrowed*. New York: Garland, 1984.

French, Warren. *John Steinbeck*. Rev. ed. Boston: Twayne, 1975.

Owens, Jack. *John Steinbeck's Re-Vision of America*. Athens: University of Georgia Press, 1985.

Timmerman, John H. *John Steinbeck's Fiction*. Norman: University of Oklahoma Press, 1986.

R. Baird Shuman

WALLACE STEVENS

Born: Reading, Pennsylvania
October 2, 1879
Died: Hartford, Connecticut
August 2, 1955

Principal Literary Achievement

A meditative poet whose work drew from both European and American traditions, Stevens blended poetry and philosophy in his exploration of the relationship between the real and the imagined worlds.

Biography

Wallace Stevens was born on October 2, 1879, to Garrett and Margarethe Stevens in Reading, Pennsylvania. His father's law practice was sufficient to support the large family, which included Stevens' older brother, younger brother, and two sisters, but not as well as Garrett Stevens would have wished. Constantly working to supply his family's needs, he transferred to the young Wallace Stevens his sense that a man's primary responsibility was to do well materially and support his family adequately. His mother, a strongly Christian woman who belonged to the Dutch Reformed church, provided her son with a respect for religious faith (though as a young man he rejected the practice of her religion) and a sense of the spiritual.

Growing up in Reading near the end of the nineteenth century, Stevens took part in all the activities available to the relatively privileged child. His earliest letters (home from summer camp in his teen years) show his powers of observation, his penchant for intellectual and word games, and his precocious and extensive reading. In 1897, he enrolled in Harvard College as a special student and tried to reconcile his father's wish for him to be a lawyer with his own desire (or even compulsion) to write. The excitement of the Harvard intellectual atmosphere caught him up: He took classes from Irving Babbitt, had long conversations with George Santayana, and wrote poetry for the Harvard literary magazine. In 1900, he allowed his own inclinations to rule in defiance of paternal demands and went off to New York to become a journalist.

Although he worked both for *The New York Tribune* and as a free-lancer, he was not able to support himself comfortably through journalism. After some months of struggle, he enrolled in New York Law School. The year he finished his law studies and was admitted to the bar, 1904, was also the year he met his future wife, Elsie

Moll. With his father's prudence, he waited for years to marry her until he had enough money saved from his first position (with the legal staff of American Bonding Company) for their support. They were married on September 21, 1909.

The early years of Stevens' marriage he spent establishing himself financially while doing some writing; living in New York gave him access to the New York literary and artistic scene, with its salons and the electrifying presence of innovative artists such as Tristan Tzara and Marcel Duchamp. His first poems were published in *Trend* in 1914 and were followed by others in other small journals, including the fledgling *Poetry*. Stevens joined the Hartford Accident and Indemnity Company in 1916 and spent the rest of his life with the firm; he also moved to Hartford that year. Having set himself up financially, he did so artistically in 1923 with the publication by Alfred A. Knopf of *Harmonium*, his first collection.

The rest of Stevens' life was a classic success story, despite the indifferent reviews of the first collection that may have contributed to the long silence following it. After his daughter, Holly Bright Stevens, was born in 1924, Stevens turned his attention to solidifying the position of his family. He was promoted to vice-president of Hartford Accident and Indemnity in 1934, a position he held until his death. In 1935, his collection *Ideas of Order* was published by Alcestis Press; it was republished by Knopf a year later. A leftist review of Stevens which criticized him for being out of touch with the realities of the Depression resulted in two collections that attempt to justify the existence of art in hard times. *Owl's Clover* was published in 1936; *The Man with the Blue Guitar and Other Poems* came out in 1937.

His later years underscored the divisions in his life between work and art, Hartford and New York, and public and private life. His daily office work continued even as he became more and more widely known as a poet. *Parts of a World* was published in 1942, and in 1945 he was elected to the National Institute of Arts and Letters. His grandson Peter was born in 1947, the same year that saw publication of *Transport to Summer*. The prestigious Bollingen Prize was awarded him in 1949, and in 1950 Knopf published *The Auroras of Autumn*, to be followed by *The Necessary Angel: Essays on Reality and the Imagination* in 1951 and *The Collected Poems of Wallace Stevens* in 1954. In 1955, the year of his death, he received both the National Book Award (his second) and the Pulitzer Prize. His later poems show a metaphysical drift, away from the proclaimed antireligion stance of such early poems as "Sunday Morning," and his death on August 2, 1955, was apparently preceded by a conversion to the Roman Catholic church during his last illness.

Analysis

In 1954, the year before his death, Wallace Stevens was asked to define his major theme for a contributor's column. His clear, direct statement might have been taken from almost any of his earlier critics' analyses. His work, he said,

> suggests the possibility of a supreme fiction, recognized as a fiction, in which men could propose to themselves a fulfillment. In the creation of any such fiction, poetry

would have a vital significance. There are many poems relating to the interactions between reality and the imagination, which are to be regarded as marginal to this central theme.

From his earliest work in *Trend* and *Poetry* to the last few poems before his death, Stevens explored the relationships between the mind and the world, sometimes setting the greater value on the imagination, verging on Romanticism, and sometimes on the actual. His final position is an attempt to balance or reconcile the two.

Stevens' first poems tend to glorify the imagination. In their energetic mental gymnastics, the poems of *Harmonium* astound by their virtuosity and their intellectual energy. It is these poems that prompted Stevens' earliest critics to call him a "dandy." Beneath the glittery surface of these early poems, however, is the first elaboration of the dynamic that would occupy him for a lifetime: the nature of the struggle between mind and world, as mind seeks to encompass and world resists.

The *Harmonium* poems return to several central propositions, including the failure of religion to satisfy the mind in the contemporary world, the split between man's consciousness and unconscious nature, and the need for imagination to somehow replace the failed gods. The problematic role of the imagination is expounded in the various poems. The difficulty is that the mind must not simply transform reality into whatever it desires or thinks should be, but it must enhance the world's own reality through creative perception. The overall theme of Stevens' work might be described as a search for an aesthetic for his time, one which would fill the spiritual vacuum of contemporary lives. (Later in the poet's work, the aesthetic and the spiritual merge.) "The Comedian as the Letter C" traces the stages of discovery and disillusion in the travels of the naïve truth-seeker; this early long poem explores how the mind grapples with reality and is finally consumed by it. This collection is dominated by images of the tropical and exotic, and its techniques include Poundian Imagism and orientalism.

His second collection, *Ideas of Order*, deals with the same themes, but the meditative component becomes stronger, while the imagery becomes less dense and physical. The opening poem abandons the southern paradise of *Harmonium* for a tougher northern landscape; this move north represents Stevens' desire for more involvement with the real: "My North is leafless and lies in a wintry slime/ Both of men and clouds, a slime of men in clouds," he says. The negative or at least critical reviews of *Ideas of Order* caused him to engage even more directly with the realities of the Depression that his critics accused him of neglecting; his next collections, *Owl's Clover* and *The Man with the Blue Guitar*, are essentially apologies for art in troubled times. He develops also his theories of heroism and the heroic, a preoccupation perhaps originally linked to questions of World War I, but which remains a major issue throughout the collections of his middle period.

After these collections come his most sustained discursive poems on the relationship between mind and world. His later poems describe an energetic search for a world both imagined and real, and they reflect reading of philosophy as well as poetry and poetics: His description of the grasp for experiential truth parallels the phenomenological theories of Edmund Husserl, Martin Heidegger, and other philosophers. The poems illustrate the irony of creative perception: to perceive anything is to impose an order on it and so limit it. These limitations must then be recognized as falsifications and swept away so that reality may be reinvented afresh. Thus the mind is constantly creating and de-creating the world, and to keep this reinvention in force is the creative artist's joy and taxing duty.

His last collections are preoccupied with the search for a poetry to replace religion, poetry as what he called "the supreme fiction." For Stevens, the act of creation, not the product, is the art. His poetry is concerned with the way the mind engages with reality to perceive and thus represent it. The ultimate poetry itself, as he indicates in "Notes Toward a Supreme Fiction," must be abstract, must change, and must provide pleasure. (Originally he had planned a fourth section for this long poem, "It Must Be Human.") His very last poems tend toward the mystical, raising the possibility that the truth so long sought may also be looking for the seeker: "Presence of an External Master of Knowledge" suggests this, as do some sections of "The Rock."

Stylistically, Stevens' work is powerful in its use of images of the sacred to describe the endeavors of the imagination. The tone of Stevens' work is often both exalted and elegiac: It is an elegy for the lost metaphysic, and it exalts and ennobles the search for a replacement. The later poems in particular are declamatory, using rhetorical balances and antitheses to build to a powerful conclusion that is, in his own words, "venerable and articulate and complete." His earliest poems are sometimes rhymed, sometimes blank verse, and sometimes melodic free verse. As he developed his rhetorical, meditative style, he drifted toward a form of three-line stanzas of flexible blank verse. This form allowed him to develop theory discursively and illustrate it at once. A major characteristic of Stevens' work is the tentativity of his conclusions; "as" and "as if" appear frequently, as he approaches a position and then retreats from its finality. Although Stevens' work is filled with references to incompleteness, fragmentation, and inconclusiveness, its power and its appeal to succeeding generations of poets and readers comes in part from the sense that the entire work is a single poem. Stevens at first intended to call his volume of collected poems *The Whole of Harmonium*; its "notes" form a letter and its parts cohere.

SUNDAY MORNING

First published: 1915 (expanded version, 1922)
Type of work: Poem

The faded promises of Christianity should be replaced by full participation in this world; one can reclaim one's own godhead by accepting that the only permanence is change.

"Sunday Morning" is an exploration of the position that religious piety should be replaced by a fully lived life. Part of the poem was published in 1915, but the whole was not printed until *Harmonium*. In its final form, the poem is a series of ten fifteen-line stanzas of blank verse. The argument of the poem is just that: an argument between a woman, who feels guilty about not going to church and enjoying "coffee and oranges in a sunny chair" instead, and another voice, presumably that of the poet, which tries to persuade her to give up her attachment to dead things and dead ideas. The focus alternates from what is happening in her mind—her objections and preoccupations—and his answers to her.

The woman is interrupted in her enjoyment of the "complacencies of the peignoir" by reflections on death and religion that remind her that the pleasant particulars of the moment are only transitory. Then the other voice asks, "Why should she give her bounty to the dead?" No divinity is worthwhile if it comes "only in silent shadows and dreams." One should worship where one lives: within and as part of nature. The woman should accept her own divinity as part and reflection of nature.

The woman's interlocutor then thinks about the development of godhood, from Jove, who was fully inhuman, through Christ, who was partly human, to the new god appropriate to the present, who would be wholly human. With a fully human god, heaven and earth would merge. The woman thinks about this before asking, more or less, how this system can explain away death. He responds that life is more eternal than anything promises of immortality could provide:

> There is not any haunt of prophecy,
>
> . . . .
>
> Nor visionary south, nor cloudy palm
> Remote on heaven's hill, that has endured
> As April's green endures; or will endure
> Like her remembrance of awakened birds
> Or her desire for June and evening.

The woman, though, is interested in personal immortality, which the speaker claims would not even be desirable, since, in the poem's most famous line, "Death is the mother of beauty." There is no ripeness without rot, and change, not stasis, brings fulfillment. The speaker imagines a static Paradise and the boredom that it would bring.

He then considers a possible symbol for the new perspective that life in the world would bring; it would not be a religion exactly, but a religion substitute. A sun-worship image presents itself, the sun being the symbol of the real, of natural force. The men would dance naked to the sun, an image of energetic life-expending and celebrating. The woman finally accepts the speaker's proposition hearing

> A voice that cries, "The tomb in Palestine
> Is not the porch of spirits lingering,
> It is the grave of Jesus, where he lay."

Accepting the "unsponsored" and isolated ("island") human situation, she recovers her freedom to live as part of the natural world, described in the conclusion in terms reminiscent of Romantic poet William Wordsworth:

> Deer walk upon our mountains, and the quail
> Whistle about us their spontaneous cries;
> Sweet berries ripen in the wilderness.

Human beings are like the pigeons of the closing lines, whose lives are indecipherable but beautiful in their vulnerability:

> casual flocks of pigeons make
> Ambiguous undulations as they sink,
> Downward to darkness, on extended wings.

The woman has progressed from an exaggerated seizing of experience to submission to it, and the change shows a growth in understanding. Stevens returns to the theme of this poem again and again throughout his poetic career.

ANECDOTE OF THE JAR

First published: 1919
Type of work: Poem

Placing an object in the midst of a landscape rearranges the landscape.

Perhaps the most frequently anthologized of Stevens' poems, "Anecdote of the Jar" reflects Stevens' preoccupation with appearances or surfaces. "The world is measured by the eye," he said in one of his many aphoristic comments, and this difficult poem plays with the issues of what the eye measures and how. The poem's interpretation is far from agreed upon, as any identification of the jar (art? technology? any single point of reference?) tends to limit the poem unacceptably.

The poem's twelve lines describe the placement of a "jar"—a mason jar, as one critic suggests? a vase?—on a hill in Tennessee; once placed, the jar reorders the landscape. "It made the slovenly wilderness/ Surround that hill." The description suggests the distortions of the landscape in the curved sides of a plain glass jar. The new order is only that, a new order; it is not beauty. The jar takes over the scene: "It took dominion everywhere." Yet it is "gray and bare." The double negative in the last two lines causes confusion: "It did not give of bird or bush,/ Like nothing else in Tennessee." If the jar itself is read as the subject of the last line, the statement is clarified, but one might ask whether such a grammatical wrench is acceptable.

Read with as few limitations as possible, the poem suggests that adding an artifact or a point of focus compels a new interpretation of any scene. Moreover, there is a certain arrogance in making such rearrangements: "I placed a jar in Tennessee" has a casual affrontery to it, as the jar placer assumes the right to a whole state. Perhaps "I placed a jar in Tennessee" may even be read as "Eye placed a jar in Tennessee." Whatever the jar is or represents, it has made order out of chaos or "slovenly wilderness." Yet which is better—disorder or gray, bare order? If the order is not artistically preferable to the wilderness, if the net change is not a gain, what the jar represents is finally irrelevant.

Many of the *Harmonium* poems deal with changes wrought by the imagination upon reality, and these changes may alter things for the better, if the imagination is a true or honest creative perception, or for the worse, if (as in "The Ordinary Women") the imagination is limited by preconceived clichéd interpretations. "Anecdote of the Jar" is an example of perception as imagination with little judgment of its product. Only the process is defined.

TEA AT THE PALAZ OF HOON

First published: 1921
Type of work: Poem

The imagination may construct a separate reality which consists of its own being.

Although many of the poems of *Harmonium* preach a yielding to reality, "Tea at the Palaz of Hoon" is an exception. Hoon is a vaguely Eastern potentate who creates a world from his mind and takes pleasure in inhabiting it.

"Hoon" may suggest "hero-moon"; in Stevens' early poems, moon and sun translate very roughly into imagination and reality. Hoon speaks about his sense of self and world, which is virtually solipsistic—he concludes that the self is the only reality. He is enclosed in trappings of royalty, "in purple." His majesty, even his divinity, is recognized by the world in which he moves: Ointment is sprinkled on his beard, and hymns are sung. The second part of the poem, however, explains the source of the recognition: "Out of my mind the golden ointment rained,/ And my ears made the blowing hymns they heard." He is enclosed in his self-made world, creator of his own landscape:

> what I saw
> Or heard or felt came not but from myself;
> And there I found myself more truly and more strange.

The solipsistic world is not limited and limiting, as one might expect. Rather, to live in a world of one's own making results in a rediscovery, or reinvention, of self.

Yet one cannot conclude that Stevens is advocating solipsism in this poem. The persona of Hoon represents an extreme position on the scale of relations between imagination and reality; Stevens explores the world of a mind given over wholly to the imagination. Moreover, the speaker insists on the primacy of the imagined world, rather than the merely demonstrated. "Not less was I myself," he claims in the first stanza, and "I found myself more truly" in the last line.

This poem anticipates his later comfortable style of three-line sections. It approaches iambic pentameter, often Stevens' preferred meter, in most of the lines, but does not use rhyme. Like others of Stevens' earlier, more formal poems (including "The Emperor of Ice Cream"), it is divided into two rhetorical parts; in this poem, the first part poses questions about the origin of Hoon's world and the second answers them.

THE EMPEROR OF ICE-CREAM

First published: 1922
Type of work: Poem

The only way to evade the proposition that death cancels out life is to live fully in the present.

A poem that Stevens once described as his favorite, "The Emperor of Ice-Cream" so puzzled its first readers that an ice-cream company wrote to Stevens about it, asking whether the poem was in favor of ice cream or against it. Ice cream suggests the evanescent pleasures of life; one could answer, then, that the poem is for it.

This poem is set up as a counterpoint between a scene of a funeral and images of enjoyment. The first lines suggest a sensual celebration, as cigars, "concupiscent curds," and "wenches" are mentioned. Yet the temporary quality of all this is suggested by the lines, "let the boys/ Bring flowers in last month's newspapers." The flowers are vivid blooms of the day, but last month's news is only history, fit to wrap flowers in. "Let be be finale of seem,/ The only emperor is the emperor of ice-cream," the first of the poem's two sections concludes. That is, one should accept whatever seems to be as what is, including flowers and history. One should not attempt to put prefabricated interpretations on life; rather, accept it in its transience and enjoy its vivid delights.

The second section presents a dead woman who, although she was poor (since she had a "dresser of deal"—deal being cheap wood—and it was moreover "lacking three glass knobs") still managed to adorn her impoverished life. She embroidered figures on her plain sheets, giving them life and color. (The "fantails" she embroidered may be either birds or goldfish.) The sheets she embroidered should be her epitaph. The poem suggests: Let each one take pleasure in the world commensurate with his or her ability to enjoy, because there is no other world. The final line echoes, "The only emperor is the emperor of ice-cream."

The poem is memorable for its double focus—the impoverished death on the one side and the wild sensual celebrations on the other. The doubleness of the poem is underscored by the two-stanza division with the shared last line, as well as by the single rhyme in the poem that concludes each section.

THE IDEA OF ORDER AT KEY WEST

First published: 1934
Type of work: Poem

Art, or the imagination, changes life by reordering the world and intensifying the human experience of it.

"The Idea of Order at Key West" is a discursive poem reflecting upon the work of the imagination and the relationship between the real and the imagined worlds. The poem's form is iambic pentameter with some irregular end rhymes. It begins with an unidentified woman singing beside the sea: "She sang beyond the genius of the sea." "She" is the imagination, and her voice does not change the reality it represents: "The water never formed to mind or voice." These two, then, woman and water, mind and world, are separate. Yet it would seem that reality, too, has some sort of guiding principle or spirit, a "genius." Her song does not change or "form" reality, which has its own inhuman "cry."

The second section of the poem reiterates and redefines the separation between the two: The water's sound is reflected in her song, but "it was she and not the sea we heard." She is singing in words; reality speaks its own language, that of "the grinding water and the gasping wind."

She is the "maker," and the sea is merely "a place by which she walked to sing." The listeners ask, "Whose spirit is this?" They wish to know what, or who, this secret voice, the imagination that is at the center of human nature, is. The answer is that the voice is not merely reality, "the dark voice of the sea," for if it were, the human listeners would not understand it, "it would have been deep air." Nor is the sound only humans' readings of reality, "her voice, and ours, among/ The meaningless plungings of water and the wind." Rather, her voice is the human understanding of the real—the only entrance point to it. The imagination is neither mind nor world, but an act of perception that is also a blending point:

> She was the single artificer of the world
> In which she sang. And when she sang, the sea,
> Whatever self it had, became the self
> That was her song, for she was the maker.

Neither embroidery nor simple reflection, the imagination becomes a force that penetrates and incorporates.

The last two sections are addressed to "Ramon Fernandez." Stevens insisted that Ramon Fernandez was simply a made-up name and was not an allusion to the French critic by that name who was then popular, but since Stevens owned books by Fernandez, one might perhaps discount that claim. In any case, the speaker asks Fernandez (if the critic, an analyst of the imagination and its products) why the song, once ended, has reordered the world. Leaving the sea, the speaker turns back to the town and sees that the "lights in the fishing boats at anchor there" have "mastered the night and portioned out the sea,/ Fixing emblazoned zones and fiery poles." Reality has been changed by the "lights"—image suggesting consciousness/imagination— to something of intense and personal meaning.

The concluding five lines reach an emotional pitch seldom found in Stevens, as he defines the impulse of the artist/maker as a "blessed rage for order." Creative perception is necessary; it is "blessed." It is an internal imperative; it is a "rage." Moreover, it is not reality that is being ordered, finally, but words: "The maker's rage to order words of the sea." This self-defined goal is also a destiny. The words are of the "fragrant portals, dimly-starred," suggesting a mystic birth; they are "of ourselves and of our origins." As the definitions become more spiritual or mythic ("ghostlier demarcations"), the poetry too becomes more acute ("keener sounds"). The end of this poem may suggest that humankind's deepest, most spiritual need is for the imaginative, and that, moreover, there is a point at which mythmaking becomes discovery.

OF MODERN POETRY

First published: 1942
Type of work: Poem

Tradition and convention no longer produce poetry in modern times; poetry must be reenvisioned as the mind's act of self-creation.

One of the most frequently anthologized of Stevens' poems, "Of Modern Poetry" is another poem which attempts to define art for a fragmented world in constant flux. Poetry is now a search, whereas it used to be a method. In the past, "the scene was set; it repeated what/ Was in the script." That is, convention and tradition defined poetry, and each poem was a modification of a pattern. Now, Stevens says, the conventions no longer apply.

The contemporary poem must reflect the world, speak its speech; it must "face the men of the time and . . . meet/ The women of the time." War, the current state of affairs, must have a part in it. Most important, it must find "what will suffice," a phrase repeated twice in the poem. The search for "what will suffice" amounts to a search for satisfaction, a solace for the mind's pain of isolation. It must in fact express the mind to itself, so that it becomes the internal made visible. The actor must speak words that "in the delicatest ear of the mind" repeat what it desires to hear.

The imagery so far has been of the theater, but when the method of this new poetry is described, philosophy and music are interwoven with theater images to give the impression of an art that is plastic and fluid. The actor becomes "a metaphysician in the dark," suggesting a thinker concerned with first and final causes but lacking the light of any received structure for his meditations. He is, moreover, "twanging an instrument," creating a music that is "sounds passing through sudden rightnesses." These vibrations are the mind's own pulsations made audible to it.

The poem concludes by returning to the subject matter of modern poetry, which can be any action in which the self is expressed: It "may/ Be of a man skating, a woman dancing, a woman/ Combing." The subject is not the important issue, however, for the real poem is the act of creating poetry; modern poetry is finally "The poem of the mind in the act of finding/ What will suffice." This poem twists and turns in an attempt to catch a glimpse of its own creation. It is about itself: Modern poetry, and this work defining it, are self-reflexive. The poem is the creation of poetry and not the product.

This poem contains germs of the ideas that Stevens will develop and elaborate in "Notes Toward a Supreme Fiction," in which he claims that poetry must be abstract, must change, and must give pleasure.

CHOCORUA TO ITS NEIGHBOR

First published: 1947
Type of work: Poem

The heroic man that is humankind's most central dream is half imagined, half real.

A poem that illustrates Stevens' growing preoccupation with the hero and the nature of heroism, "Chocorua to Its Neighbor" features a mountain discussing the man-myth. "Chocorua" consists of twenty-six five-line stanzas of blank verse, and it develops the definition of the heroic through images from alchemy. The creation of the hero, then, is a mystical process, like the transmutation of the base metals into gold. Like alchemy, the creation of the hero is really a process of self-refinement.

The poem begins with an indication of the mountain's perspective. The mountain has the detachment of distance, of objectivity, of largeness. Armies and wars are perceived as mass movements of numbers, not as individual soldiers in combat. A war is "A swarming of number over number, not/ One foot approaching, one uplifted arm."

Nevertheless, there is a "prodigious shadow" which represents humankind, visible on the mountain. He is "the self of selves" who is represented (in section 5) as a quintessence, or alchemical fifth essence, through references to the four elements of earth, air, fire, and water and to the "essay," a vessel for the transmutation. The figure is "the glitter of a being," half perceived, the blue "of the pole of blue/ And of the brooding mind"—that is, half real, half imagined. This figure speaks, explaining "the enlarging of the simplest soldier's cry/ In what I am, as he falls." That is, mythic man gives meaning to an individual life. The soldier's death has its significance because of this central man.

The man-myth doubts his own reality in section 12, but then grows "strong" from new reflections in 13. Essentially he draws his power from his source, which is human beings' desire for his existence, for something outside themselves which would dignify their lives. He now ponders the fact that there is a galaxy of figures of myth—the captain, the cardinal, the mother, "true transfigurers fetched out of the human mountain." That the human mind has produced such beings that in some sense exist is the proposal of this poem, which then summarizes its implications about the process of creation in a section that could stand for Stevens' whole aesthetic:

> To say more than human things with human voice,
> That cannot be; to say human things with more
> Than human voice, that, also, cannot be;
> To speak humanly from the height or from the depth
> Of human things, that is acutest speech.

This man, this self-creating creation, is true poetry or "acutest speech." True poetry does not speak with a voice of elements beyond human experience, nor does it speak with some inhuman wisdom of human concerns. Rather, it is the human voice speaking of and within the range of human lives.

The rest of the poem explores the nature of the shadow-myth-hero. He is constantly in flux, constantly re-becoming and reinvigorating the space he inhabits: "where he was, there is an enkindling, where/ He is, the air changes and grows fresh to breathe." He is not "father"—that is, he is not an authority figure to impose his views from above—but "megalfrere"—brother and equal. He is the "common self"; moreover, he is the "interior fons. And fond." He is the spring, the baptismal well, the basis of the self, and although he is "metaphysical metaphor," he is "physical if the eye is quick enough."

He is, then, both imagined and real, brought into existence by the intensity of the human need for him. The mountain concludes its meditation by recognizing the greatness of this presence—a human figure greater than nature, enlarged by his consciousness of himself.

This poem was written during that period of Stevens' career in which his preoccupation is imagining the hero; this figure is heroic in his imaginings, in his representation of the collective imagination. As his poetics developed, Stevens turned more and more to the poetic act itself as subject. His last poems verge on an alchemical transformation of world into mind; those poems, difficult and demanding, are not usually found in more general anthologies.

Summary

  Stevens' lifetime search for a contemporary aesthetic, one that could satisfy the mind by filling the hole left by the lost metaphysic, sustains his poetry. His early work sets up a persuasive symbolism for the dialogue between reality and the imagination, using the repeated images of Florida and the North, summer and winter, sun and moon. His later work, in its careful analysis of experience for clues to "being," provides a poetic parallel to phenomenology in philosophy. His eclectic use of techniques and ideas from other arts as well as both European and American poetry gives his work a sophistication perhaps unmatched among other American poets of his generation.

Bibliography

Baird, James. *The Dome and the Rock: Structure in the Poetry of Wallace Stevens.* Baltimore: The Johns Hopkins University Press, 1968.

Bloom, Harold. *Wallace Stevens: The Poems of Our Climate.* Ithaca, N.Y.: Cornell University Press, 1977.

Doggett, Frank. *Wallace Stevens: The Making of the Poem.* Baltimore: The Johns Hopkins University Press, 1980.

Hines, Thomas J. *The Later Poetry of Wallace Stevens.* Lewisburg, Pa.: Bucknell University Press, 1976.

Kermode, Frank. *Wallace Stevens.* London: Oliver & Boyd, 1960.

Leggett, B. J. *Wallace Stevens and Poetic Theory.* Chapel Hill: University of North Carolina Press, 1987.

Richardson, Joan. *Wallace Stevens: The Early Years.* New York: William Morrow, 1985.

_____. *Wallace Stevens: The Later Years.* New York: William Morrow, 1988.

Vendler, Helen. *On Extended Wings: Wallace Stevens' Longer Poems.* Cambridge, Mass.: Harvard University Press, 1969.

_____. *Wallace Stevens: Words Chosen Out of Desire.* Knoxville: University of Tennessee Press, 1984.

Janet McCann

ROBERT STONE

Born: Brooklyn, New York
August 21, 1937

Principal Literary Achievement
Working in a tradition of political and social satire, Stone explores man's individual heart of darkness as a reflection of national darkness.

Biography

Robert Stone was born in Brooklyn, New York, on August 21, 1937, the son of Gladys Catherine Grant, an elementary school teacher of Scots-Irish origins and schizophrenic tendencies, and C. Homer Stone, who fled domestic responsibilities during Stone's infancy. Young Stone read with puzzlement and then appreciation the works of Thomas Carlyle, Fyodor Dostoevski, Franz Kafka, John Dos Passos, Joseph Conrad, and F. Scott Fitzgerald. After time in an orphanage and in a series of Catholic schools, he clashed with the Marist Brothers at Archbishop Malloy High School over his drinking and his militant atheism, quit school before high school graduation, and in 1955 joined the United States Navy as a member of the amphibious force of the Atlantic Fleet. The experiences of his childhood clearly influenced his interest in the rootless, the psychotic, the irresponsible, and the hypocritical. His service as a radioman and then as senior enlisted journalist on Operation Deep Freeze Three in Antarctica prepared him to write credibly of military life, language, and style.

While attending New York University from 1958 to 1960, he worked as a copy boy, caption writer, and then editorial assistant for the *New York Daily News*. On December 11, 1959, he married social worker Janice G. Burr. The Stones dropped their conventional life and migrated to New Orleans, where Stone worked at menial jobs (in a coffee factory, on the docks, and as a radio actor, a merchant marine seaman, and a census taker) and where his daughter was born at Charity Hospital (a son, Ian, was born later). Stone read his own poetry to jazz accompaniment in a French Quarter bar and moved with the beatnik crowd, including LeRoi Jones and Gregory Corso. His experiences in that city and in the deep South during a time of sit-ins and struggles against segregation provided material for his first novel, *A Hall of Mirrors* (1967).

The Stones returned to New York City, where they became friends with Jack Kerouac and others of the emerging bohemian scene, but moved on to California when

Stone received a Stegner fellowship in creative writing at Stanford University. His Northern California (Menlo Park) life led to an experimentation with psychedelic drugs and a friendship with Ken Kesey, whose Merry Pranksters' bus he joined in its 1964 cross-country trip. (He later referred to them as very much like a group of fraternity boys out for a good time.) Kesey's La Honda hideaway provided a prototype for Dieter's mountain fortress in *Dog Soldiers* (1974). During this period of involvement with the drug culture, Stone began to evolve the values that became the moral heart of the books which followed: a sense of the ambiguity of motives and of the transitory nature of moral perception.

He wrote for the *National Mirror* in New York City from 1965 to 1967, then freelanced between 1967 and 1971. A Guggenheim Fellowship paid his way to London, England, but then, as correspondent for the *London Ink* and later the *Manchester Guardian*, he traveled to Saigon, South Vietnam, where he spent two months gathering material for his second novel. Of this experience he says, "I found myself witnessing a mistake ten thousand miles long, a mistake on the American scale." He then moved on to Hollywood, California, where he unsuccessfully fought changes in the title and in the character of Marge in the film version of *Dog Soldiers* (the film was released as *Who'll Stop the Rain?* in 1978). Next he began a teaching career as a writer-in-residence at Princeton University from 1971 to 1972. Later, as an associate professor of English and a writer-in-residence, he taught at Amherst College, Massachusetts, between 1972 and 1978, taking time out in the mid-1970's to travel to Central America three times, once by bus. There he went scuba diving, listened to all the stories he could about that area of the world, and began his third novel. He visited Honduras and Costa Rica, but he was particularly fascinated by Nicaragua under the Somozas and attended a party at the presidential palace in Managua— "just beyond the effective mortar distance from the nearest habitation."

His teaching has been itinerant: at Stanford University in 1979, at the University of Hawaii, Manoa, from 1979 to 1980, at Harvard University in 1981, at the University of California at Irvine in 1982, at New York University from 1983 to 1984, at the University of California at San Diego in 1985, and at Princeton again thereafter. His fourth novel grew out of his experiences with the Hollywood motion picture scene. He retains his friendship with Kesey, writes short stories and articles for popular journals, and has begun a fifth novel, this one set in New England. Samuel Beckett and Jorge Louis Borges are his favorite writers. His family is a strong stabilizing force in his life; they have called Northhampton, Massachusetts, home for many years.

Analysis

Robert Stone, called "a beat-generation Carlyle" by Thomas Sutcliffe and "the strongest novelist of the post-Vietnam era" by Walter Clemons, writes as an American romantic, intrigued by the exotic and the far away, by worlds that promise wealth or adventure but that prove sadly disappointing. In these alien locales, he finds American truths as his characters pursue the American Dream in New Orleans, Vietnam,

Southern California, Central America, and Mexico; failing to accept responsibility and acting unwisely, they have their wealth or dreams of success turn into ashes, their personal lives disintegrate, and their nightmares overcome them. Dieter, in *Dog Soldiers*, claims to have "succumbed to the American dream," which he defines as "innocence" and "energy," and describes his friend Ray Hicks as "trapped in a samurai fantasy—an American one" of "the Lone Ranger" or "the great desperado" who "has to win all the epic battles singlehanded." Later Dieter claims that his mountain retreat is "[t]he last crumbling fortress of the spirit" as the world breaks down into "degeneracy and murder": "We're in the dark ages." His final line sums up part of the message in all Stone's novels, a message Stone interprets as "an act of affirmation."

Stone's strength as a writer has been his ability to render truly the obsessions of the baby boom generation and the tragedy of their excess. He has been brilliant at capturing generational zeitgeists, the feeling and spirit of each of a series of benchmark decades. In the 1960's he produced *A Hall of Mirrors*, a sharp, satirical look at romantic pessimism in the face of racial prejudice and right-wing extremism. In the 1970's he captured the naïve cynicism of failed upper-middle-class idealists and their involvement in romanticized drug-dealing and gun-running plots—during the war in Vietnam in *Dog Soldiers* and during a would-be Latin American revolution in *A Flag for Sunrise*. *Children of Light* depicts the selling out in the 1980's of the dreams of the 1960's. Therein potential artists, novelists, and actors have lost their vision and given in to crass commercialism, a reflection of a criticism often made in the 1980's. Thought provoking and emotionally engaging, his works relate the individual to the trends of his or her time and raise questions about responsibility and choice. His characters are self-destructive men and women who pay the price of national and personal ignorance and irresponsibility. *A Flag for Sunrise* ends with the idea that "[a] man has nothing to fear . . . who understands history," yet Stone's characters continually fail to understand history in any of its contexts. Converse, in *Dog Soldiers*, says, "I don't know what that guy did or why he did it. I don't know what I'm doing or why I do it or what it's like. . . . Nobody knows. . . . That's the principle we were defending over there [Vietnam]. That's why we fought the war." His blindness about motive and reason is quintessential Stone.

Stone's novels define the romantic illusions of the trend-setters of the 1970's and 1980's. His characters attempt to toy with outlaws, but in a bourgeois setting; the mafiosi, the drug-dealers, the gunrunners, and the revolutionaries often prove too violent and unpredictable to be tamed. Like the French student poster in 1968, Stone suggests, "We are all undesirables," afloat morally and emotionally. His characters are cynical drifters in some way at odds with the law or the government; they are "students of the passing parade" (*Dog Soldiers*). His priests have lost their vocations and have turned to whiskey and a wishful humanism to compensate; his nuns seek a political commitment and martyrdom that will help them overcome the boredom and the doubts of their calling; his professors muse on universal meaning but have difficulty coming to terms with simple daily decisions of right and wrong. His characters shift with the prevailing winds; caught up in movements beyond their understanding, they continually betray one another without guilt and without self-knowledge. They are rootless wanderers of mind and world—sometimes violent, often at the end of their tether. William Shakespeare's line could well be said of each of them: "[H]e hath ever but slenderly known himself."

Many of his characters are burnt-out figures, at one time extremely competent but now pulled down in an inevitable spiral by irresponsible incompetents. There is a sense of a cultural breakdown, of misplaced dreams, of the despair that comes from losing hope. Often Stone sets up a dangerous fool, and someone gets killed or hurt as a result. His characters contemplate or commit suicide: Geraldine Crosby in *A Hall of Mirrors*, Marge in *Dog Soldiers*, Holliwell and Naftili in *A Flag for Sunrise*, and the neurotic actress, Lee Verger, in *Children of Light*. Stone's characters ask one another what they are worth and find the answer to be depressing: "A little cinder in the wind, Pablo—that's what you are."

Often there is a truth-telling speech; therein the main character tells his audience what he really thinks, but either no one hears or they hear only what they want to hear. In *A Flag for Sunrise*, the drunken and insulting Holliwell attacks Uncle Sam and exported American popular culture as a moneymaking conspiracy to pander to the ignorant and the vulgar abroad and warns Latin Americans that in the end "Mickey Mouse will see you dead," and he adds further insult when he suggests that American popular culture is no worse and is in some ways better than what was originally there. In *A Hall of Mirrors*, Rheinhardt, in an ironic parody of reactionary prose, claims that a napalm bomb dropped in Vietnam is a "bomb with a heart," the heart of "a fat old lady on her way to . . . the world's fair," innocent and motherly and pursued by a fiendish black with rape in his heart—his words are like an outrageous jazz riff played upon American fears and obsessions. His audience, however, hears nothing of his maunderings as it goes about its riot.

Stone has been influenced by Conrad, whom he quotes at the beginning of *Dog Soldiers* about man's "Heart of Darkness," and he notes through Hicks that "The desires of the heart . . . are as crooked as a corkscrew." Stone is interested in the grammar of dominance, power plays, accommodation, and victimization. His imagery repeatedly connects man to fish and a bleak bottom-of-the-ocean competition—the food chain as metaphor. He captures a sense of cosmic menace—the unseen terror of the deep—in nihilism and conflict: race wars in *A Hall of Mirrors*, Vietnam and drug wars in *Dog Soldiers*, crazed killers and guerrilla warfare in *A Flag for Sunrise*, and war against inner demons in *Children of Light*.

Stone's style is expressionistic and often surreal, yet his fiction is also firmly rooted in a solid sense of place. The third-person point of view often reflects the febrile imaginings of one of the central characters, with a resulting exaggeration of mood through intense emotion. Holliwell, for example, skin dives down the sheer wall of an offshore reef, and his sensitivity toward what may or may not be a killer shark or other undersea creature (or perhaps even the watery grave of a murdered girl) transforms a casual outing into a symbol of psychological and philosophical evil, the "lower depths" where "sharks" await the adventurous. This fine scene is typical of Stone's method. As Stone says in *Modern Fiction Studies*, "fiction refines reality and refracts it into something like a dream [serving] to mythologize . . . in a positive way a series of facts which of themselves have no particular meaning."

Yet Stone's settings are also drawn with a sharp realism. New Orleans, Saigon, Southern California, Central America, and Mexico are all recognizably real places, locations one can visit and identify. It is perhaps this contradictory nature of Stone's style that has attracted filmmakers to his novels and yet has marred the two books transmuted to the screen, *A Hall of Mirrors* and *Dog Soldiers*. Paul Newman, Joanne Woodward, and Anthony Perkins could not save *WUSA* (1970), the film version of *A Hall of Mirrors*, from critical and popular disdain, and even Rheinhardt's wonderful drunken speech scene is tame and flat. Similarly, Nick Nolte, Michael Murphy, and Tuesday Weld could not rescue *Who'll Stop the Rain?* from being an interesting and provocative failure. The considerable strengths of both films lie in the "exteriors" they share with their respective novels—the images of the New Orleans French Quarter, lakefront, and municipal auditorium in the first book and of Dieter's mountain retreat in the second. What is lacking is the gripping force of character created by Stone's prose, the sense of solidarity and identification he induces between reader and characters that are diverse and often fairly unattractive. Melodrama traditionally asks its audience to connect with heroic figures so perfect that the audience would like to become them; it is no mean trick to bring one into the skin and psyche of the Reinhardts, Hicks, Holliwells, and Walkers. One guesses that Stone's novels will never make great films, since they rely so heavily on the writer's skill with prose. If Stone is right in "The Reason for Stories" that the purpose of fiction is to "expand human self-knowledge" and decrease "each individual's loneliness and isolation," then he is indeed teaching a sympathy for the "losers" of the world, the self-damned and marginal people normally ignored by mainstream fiction.

At the sentence level, Stone's prose reflects the same mixture of expressive emotion and realistic description delineated above. Stone has a journalist's sharp eye for detail and for short, intense dramatic scenes, a poet's ear for dialogue, and an English teacher's sense of the subtle nuances of language and the importance of a complex interplay of images and scenes that gain weight and meaning from the interlocking patterns. To these he adds imaginative drive and a vision of the "convolutions and ironies of events."

A HALL OF MIRRORS

First published: 1967
Type of work: Novel

Three down-and-out characters, suffering and self-destructive, face the racism and fanatical right-wing extremism poisoning American society in the 1960's.

1920 *Magill's Survey of American Literature*

Winner of the William Faulkner Award for best first novel and filmed as *WUSA* in 1970, *A Hall of Mirrors*, as Stone himself says, takes the United States as its subject and has built into it "all . . . [Stone's] quarrels with America," but most particularly right-wing "exploitation of the electronic media." Some have called it a story of the dark night of the American soul. Its title comes from Robert Lowell's poem, "Children of Light," in which the puritan children of light become the corrupted, evil children of night, "the Serpent's seeds," and the whole world is inverted into a hideous hall of mirrors where "candles glitter," a reflected image of "might-have beens." Thus, "the children of the night" in this novel, three rootless drifters undermined by illusions, must face a perverted potential, distorted and tainted; one of them, Rheinhardt, even turns the reference into a play on vampires and Dracula and a bloodsucking world where all is not as it seems.

Once a brilliant classical clarinetist, now a failure and an alcoholic, Rheinhardt is down and out in New Orleans and is happy to espouse any cause to be taken on as the rock disc jockey of a right-wing radio station, WUSA, whose motto, "The Truth Shall Make You Free," is perverted by the reality of its racist message. Rheinhardt's refrain is "I am not dead . . . I am—but hurt. Defend me friends, I am but hurt." Stone calls him his "scapegoat" and "alter ego." The second "child of the night" is a lonely, abused, and scarred country girl, a West Virginian, Geraldine, who seeks love but finds only bitter alienation ("they're about to lay me low" becomes her refrain and later, to Rheinhardt, "you done undermined me, love"). She is ignorant and down-and-out, but decent, and her affair with Rheinhardt only brings her more pain and disillusionment. The third "child of the night" is Morgan Rainey, an idealistic but ineffectual social worker, pursued by childhood nightmares of blacks tarred and feathered. He takes a room in the same rundown building as Rheinhardt and Geraldine as he helps conduct a supposed "welfare" census, but he finds that every positive act results in pain and injury and leaves him "feeling broken" (though it is those affected by his misguided attempts to help who are truly broken).

The novel captures the conflicts and obsessions of the South in the 1960's. M. T. Bingamon, a power-hungry right-wing demagogue, exploits the racist fears of poor whites aided by Brother Jensen, alias Farley the Sailor, a con man, philosopher, and supposed missionary, head of the Living Grace Mission. Rheinhardt and Rainey become pawns in Bingamon's power plot. The final third of the novel is an apocalyptic "Armageddon," a nightmarish description of the violent, fanatical, racist, "patriotic" rally that the station sponsors and of the ensuing riot, which leaves nineteen dead. Rainey is grievously wounded and Geraldine, picked up for vagrancy, finds herself unable to face the cold metallic solitude of her jail cell. At the end Rheinhardt, a misfit and a drifter, is on his way out of town, a survivor who finds the battle and its losses endless. Rheinhardt, Geraldine, and Rainey's hall of mirrors reflects an American nightmare in which civilization proves a false image, actions produce unintended results, and man wanders confusedly without direction.

Rheinhardt's ironic, drug-inspired speech about American innocence sums up the illusions that Stone's novel negates:

The American way is innocence. In all situations we must and shall display an innocence so vast and awesome that the entire world will be reduced by it. American
innocence shall rise in mighty clouds of vapor to the scent of heaven and confound the
nations!

Stone's characters have lost their innocence and their Garden of Eden, and instead
blindly and mistakenly pursue their self-interests.

DOG SOLDIERS

First published: 1974
Type of work: Novel

An ex-marine smuggling drugs from Vietnam, seeking love, "the real thing,"
and a drug buyer, finds death, betrayal, and ambiguity.

Winner of the National Book Award for Fiction in 1975 and filmed as *Who'll Stop
the Rain?* in 1978, *Dog Soldiers* depicts the ongoing effects of the Vietnam War
back home, where heroin has become an obsession and it is hard to tell friend from
enemy. Its title derives from a passage in Joseph Conrad's *Heart of Darkness*, re-
phrased by Ernest Hemingway, about grimly soldiering on, leading a dog's life, but
staying alive. Despite its initial scenes in Vietnam, however, *Dog Soldiers* concentrates not on combat but on the impact of the war on the moral certainties, loyalties,
and conscience of the civilian United States, where, as Stone later said, "all sorts of
little bills were coming up due for payment." The novel argues that the Vietnam War
most affected values back home, infecting the survivors with greed and corruption
summed up in the heroin underworld. Stone calls the 1970's "a creepy, evil time"
and *Dog Soldiers* his reaction to it.

John Converse, a talented but tainted journalist on assignment to Vietnam, schemes
with an acquaintance, Charmian, to smuggle three kilograms of pure heroin home
from Vietnam for a $40,000 profit. To do so he enlists the aid of ex-Marine Ray
Hicks, a friend but also "probably a psychopath" and therefore usable. What Converse does not realize is that he has been set up from the beginning—after he handles the smuggling, the heroin is to be stolen from him.

Consequently, when Hicks contacts Converse's wife, Marge, a ticket girl for a
pornographic cinema and a drug addict, he finds himself waylaid by hoods, and he
and Marge must flee for their lives. When Converse arrives home, he is threatened,
tortured, and then forced (by circumstances and by his ruthless father-in-law, Elmer
Bender) to deal with a less than honest federal "regulatory" agent named Antheil.
As Hicks and Marge are relentlessly pursued across Southern California, they meet
an array of fringe characters from Hicks's past, characters that make Hicks conclude, "It's gone funny in the states." During this flight, Hicks becomes almost as
obsessed with Marge as with the heroin and is unwilling to leave her behind to speed

up his escape. Hicks, with his cold eyes and cruel face, envisions himself a serious man, a modern samurai with a worthy illusion, riding the wave till it crashes. Their final encounter is with Hicks's past mentor and Zen master, Dieter, a onetime drug advocate turned guru of the apocalypse, who lives in a mountain compound near the Mexican border.

In the final shootout between Hicks and federal agents, Dieter bombards the countryside with sounds of Vietnam battles blasted out over loudspeakers as if the war itself continued on the homefront. After a confused battle scene during which Hicks misunderstands Dieter's attempts to free him from heroine, Hicks discovers an escape route but is badly wounded when he returns to rescue Marge and help reunite her with her husband. Despite this rescue, the self-centered, amoral Converse, dreaming of personal profit at the expense of friendship and loyalty, attempts to renege on his agreement to meet Hicks in the desert on the far side of the mountains and then dumps the heroin to save himself. The moral ambiguity of the conflict continues as the crooked federal agent, Antheil, confiscates the drugs for his own profit. Hicks has said, "I'm just doing what everybody else is doing," and, in a world where the U.S. Army destroys elephants as "enemy agents," all perversities prove possible. The war's by-product, heroin, corrupts and destroys, and Stone demonstrates that its end result is nightmare and death—"a chain of victims"; both war and drug reduce man to less than human, destroy his dreams, and annihilate his values.

A FLAG FOR SUNRISE

First published: 1981
Type of work: Novel

Americans abroad precipitate or are caught up in events that they will never fully understand but which will either consume or transform them.

An ambitious novel set in the fictional Central American country of Tecan, *A Flag for Sunrise* attacks United States interference in the economy, politics, and culture of Latin American countries. Its title derives from Emily Dickinson's question, "Sunrise, hast thou a flag for me?"—an unspoken plea by Stone's characters as they pursue something beyond themselves, a new vision to salute tomorrow. The novel continually draws parallels with the horrors and fiascoes of Vietnam through the memories of the central observer, Frank Holliwell, onetime Central Intelligence Agency operative, now a wandering professor.

By exploring the fate of Americans whose lives become entangled in Tecanecan politics, Stone sums up the diverse motives that draw Americans into conflicts which he believes are none of their business and which they only vaguely understand: the self-righteous commitment of the bored and frustrated Roman Catholic nun, the beautiful and naïve Sister Justin Feeney; the curiosity of the burned-out drifter, anthropologist Frank Holliwell, a would-be romantic, who finds that he only feels alive when involved in the mystery of conflicts in the threatening and oppressive tropics; and the aggressive paranoia of Pablo Tabor, a demented killer who runs guns to Tecanecan revolutionaries. CIA agents, a Gnostic whiskey priest, a crazed Mennonite, journalists, an international jeweler, and resort developers suggest the multiplicity of reasons that have led to U.S. involvement in countries such as Nicaragua and El Salvador. At the same time, Stone convincingly examines the internal weaknesses of such countries that make chaos and political expediency normal.

The basic plot lines move the separate lives of different characters inexorably toward one another and toward death. The nun, ordered to close her failed mission and to return to the United States, yet "hungry for absolutes," volunteers to care for the revolutionary wounded and, after a very brief moment of glory, finds herself senselessly battered to death by a crazed Tecanecan lieutenant, who feels justified in wiping out hippies and Communists but is disturbed by Sister Justin's final words: "Behold the handmaid of the Lord." Pablo, after a rampage of killing, is convinced he has finally found his destiny in the ancient Indian place of sacrifice, a field of blood called "the place of the skull," where hideous ancient bloodlust still takes its toll. The toll is exacted through a lunatic Mennonite who murders children, through armed warriors destroying one another in the name of fleeting political affections, and through CIA interference in local concerns. Holliwell finds himself "alone and lost, in utter darkness without friend or faction . . . a frightening place—the point he had been working toward since the day he had come south . . . his natural, self-appointed place." When Holliwell and Pablo find themselves alone together on a small boat, illusions are stripped away, the animal in man dominates, and what Holliwell had thought an aberration of nature proves normal. Like Faust, he looks to the sunrise, "where Christ's blood steams in the firmament! One drop of blood will save me," but the blood shed there reveals only "another victim of ignorance and fear," with mankind "the joke on one another."

The outsiders, as Holliwell discovers, have "no business down there." Only the revolutionaries seem to know what they are doing, and they are betrayed, tortured, and killed. Stone's final image of the world is the cold, hostile environment of the sea: at times delicate and beautiful, but always predatory—the cold, gray, unfeeling monsters of the deep always at hand and always feeding.

CHILDREN OF LIGHT

First published: 1986
Type of work: Novel

Degraded and disillusioned by the Hollywood dream, an actress and screenwriter undergoing mid-life crises seek unsuccessfully to recapture the romance and idealism of their youth.

The title, *Children of Light*, is uttered by Lee Verger, who is referring to herself and her lover, Gordon Walker. Verger is an actress of unfulfilled promise who has an incredible presence and intensity that are enhanced by her "dark, blue saintly . . . secret eyes." She and Walker are of the film generation, sitting in darkness and staring at the lighted screen, which becomes their only reality. Walker, once a Shakespearean actor and now a Hollywood writer, creates a screenplay of Kate Chopin's *The Awakening* (1899), and, after his wife's desertion, comes to Bahia Honda, Mexico, to see it in production. His real interest, however, is seeing his old flame, Lee Verger. Verger, in turn, projected by her screen role into the marital and personal conflicts of Chopin's Creole character Edna Pontellier, acts out that talented woman's terrible stress as her own reality, giving up her medical treatment because it interferes with her acting, driving away her psychiatrist husband with her schizoid psychic projects, puzzling over the trauma, inner conflicts, and turmoil that would lead the fictive character to suicide, and merging with that character as she enacts the suicide/drowning first for the camera and then in private for herself and her lover. The image is like that of Plato's cave allegory: The reality is elsewhere; the shadows on the screen are but projections of light, distorted and fake.

As "children of light," Verger and Gordon cannot distinguish between true relationships and those projected in their art. The film world around them is a schizophrenic one of pretense, masks, and lies. Walker, the nihilist, remembers his role of King Lear as the most intense and meaningful time of his life, for he could lose himself in the mad King's vision of reality, rave against the elements, and triumph on stage; Verger, who is at heart more of an idealist, turns back to her role of Rosalind as that projected image which best captures what she would like to be, but is not. Unlike those roles, in which the microcosm of the stage provided a philosophy and a solid base for understanding character and act, the "real" Walker and Verger have lost touch with their inner reality and have buried themselves in drugs, fantasies, sex, and a wealthy life-style that leaves them restless, unhappy, and unfulfilled. Alienated from their marital partners, their children, and their art, they have for too long sought escape in cocaine and alcohol, and their bodies and minds are bearing too heavily the weight of this bitter solace.

Verger's smile quivers "between drollery and madness" as she faces the emptiness and degradation of Hollywood success and struggles to please director, producer, and press and to deal with sexual advances, blackmail, and threats while attempting to make this one film her triumph over the mundane and the vulgar. For Walker, recapturing his bittersweet past romance with Verger and reenacting the days when they were young and fearless together can help him recapture a sense of who he was and what he can still be. When the couple escape to the distant mountain of their past, their would-be religious epiphany (complete with storm, stigmata, and Gadarine swine) turns to muck. Verger, like the mad Ophelia, understands the degree of her alienation from Walker, but she is no longer able to cope with the harshness of that reality and yields to her "immortal longings"; she is a broken person for whom nothing remains. Walker, in contrast, ever the survivor—no matter the cost—returns to family and home and shoddy career. A woman has the final say: "Men have died from time to time and worms have eaten them, but not for love."

Stone denies that this novel is an attack on film-making *per se* and argues instead that it is a political study of how the United States works, with Hollywood's pretenses and self-delusions merely reflecting the larger dishonesty of American culture.

Summary

Stone believes that his culturally sophisticated but streetwise stories abet "the awareness of ironies and continuities" and show people that "being decent is really hard and that we carry within ourself our own worst enemy." His rootless characters, hooked on alcohol, drugs, greed, or egocentricity, become intertwined, usually in sets of three, and engage in various forms of sophistry, rationalization, equivocation, and indifference. Whether passionate or withdrawn, they are corrupt and vulnerable, their lives a juxtaposing of daily banality and exotic nightmare. His true villains are casual, feckless individuals who act without thinking or feeling, who use the loyalty and affection of others, and who survive at the cost of destruction and death. The cold and ruthless survive and the sentimental perish; moral ambiguity prevails.

Bibliography

Epstein, Joseph. "Robert Stone: American Nightmares." In *Plausible Prejudices: Essays on American Writing*. New York: W. W. Norton, 1985.

Jones, Robert. "The Other Side of Soullessness." *Commonweal* 113 (May 23, 1986) 305-308.

Kagueuzian, Maureen. "Interview with Robert Stone." *TriQuarterly* 53 (1982) 248-258.

Moore, L. Hugh. "The Undersea World of Robert Stone." *Critique: Studies in Modern Fiction* 11, no. 3 (1969): 43-56.

"Robert (Anthony) Stone." *Current Biography* 48 (January, 1987): 42-47.

Ruas, Charles, "Robert Stone." In *Conversations with American Writers*. New York: Alfred A. Knopf, 1984.

Schroeder, Eric James. "Two Interviews: Talks with Tim O'Brien and Robert Stone." *Modern Fiction Studies* 30 (Spring, 1984): 135-164.

Stone, Robert. "The Reason for Stories: Toward a Moral Fiction." *Harper's Magazine* 276 (June, 1988): 71-77.

Andrew Macdonald
Gina Macdonald

HARRIET BEECHER STOWE

Born: Litchfield, Connecticut
June 14, 1811
Died: Hartford, Connecticut
July 1, 1896

Principal Literary Achievement

Stowe is widely recognized as the most important writer of antislavery fiction; she shaped the genre for future antislavery writers.

Biography

Harriet Beecher was born in Litchfield, Connecticut, on June 14, 1811, the seventh child of Lyman and Roxana Foote Beecher. Two years after her mother's death in 1816, her father married Harriet Porter of Portland, Maine. Lyman Beecher, a minister in the tradition of eighteenth century preacher Jonathan Edwards, who had attempted to put life into old Calvinism, dominated the household when he was not out saving souls. Daily family worship and religious instruction shaped the lives of all the Beecher children. All seven brothers who reached maturity became ministers according to their father's wishes, and the girls in the family were expected to marry ministers. Because of her father's sole focus on his sons' mental and intellectual preparation as future ministers, Harriet often felt neglected. Even on family activities, such as gathering and stacking firewood, Lyman Beecher was known to say that he wished she were a boy.

When Harriet was attending Litchfield Female Academy, she wrote her first essay, on the question, "Can the immortality of the soul be proved by the light of nature?" It was to be read with those of the older pupils at the next exhibition. This experience of success, along with the pleasure of expressing herself freely to an extent hardly possible within her family, with so many older people holding the floor, awakened her love for writing when she was eleven.

After the death of her fiancé, Harriet's eldest sister, Catherine, opened Hartford Female Seminary together with her sister Mary. When Harriet was twelve, she was placed in the seminary under her sisters' care; as soon as she was old enough, she too had to assist with the teaching, a task that was a burden to her and that she did not enjoy. Catherine Beecher, who had devoted her life to female education, was

said to possess the same doctrinary personality as her father, and life under her care was not a happy experience for Harriet.

In 1832, nine of the Beechers reunited and moved to Cincinnati, then the border settlement to the West. While her father was excited about the possibility of converting the West, Harriet perceived Cincinnati to be simply an uncouth town. Catherine founded and was running the Western Female Institute, and Harriet had to fall in line again, much against her own wishes. Her unhappiness became so severe that she fell ill repeatedly from the drudgery of her work and the depression accompanying it. It was there that she first visited a plantation in neighboring Kentucky and was introduced directly to issues of slavery, because in Cincinnati there were many freed and fugitive slaves.

She soon met Calvin Ellis Stowe and his wife Eliza, who became a good friend. After Eliza's death, Harriet consoled the widower, meeting with him more and more frequently until, on January 6, 1836, she found herself marrying him—without feeling much emotion. Soon her days were filled with caring for her six children who survived childhood, the last born in 1850. Constant financial problems prompted her to support the family by writing, and she published her first writings in the *Western Monthly Magazine*. She was contributing sketches to the New York *Evangelist*, *The Ladies' Repository*, and *Godey's Lady's Book*. Amid the household clutter and noise, she wrote her stories, mostly domestic fiction, later collected in *The Mayflower* (1843). The parlor was reserved for Mr. Stowe, who was annoyed at intrusions upon his studies. In 1850, Calvin Stowe received an appointment to Brunswick College in Maine and moved his family to New England.

After the political climate toward slavery changed and the seizure and return of fugitive slaves to their owners was even preached from Boston pulpits, Harriet Beecher Stowe, despite a long New England winter, a chaotic household, and the fact that she was exhausted from yet another birth and nursing a child, set out to write an antislavery story after being given an advance of one hundred dollars. She began poring over antislavery literature. Her main source of information was probably Weld's *American Slavery as It Is* (1839), a collection of excerpts from legal documents, advertisements, and statements from slave holders. *Uncle Tom's Cabin* first appeared as a serial in the *National Era* (the first installment on June 5, 1851), and when it appeared in book form in 1852, fifty thousand copies were sold within eight weeks; within a year, a million copies were sold in England and America combined. Her second antislavery novel, *Dred: A Tale of the Great Dismal Swamp*, followed in 1856.

There never seemed to be enough time for Harriet Beecher Stowe to consider writing as art. Writing books seems to have been a substitute for the pulpit of her male minister family—a means for a moral end, not an end in itself. *The Minister's Wooing* (1859) has a religious theme that was well received during the years of public distress that accompanied the financial panic of 1857. *The Pearl of Orr's Island* (1862) is dominated by a longing nostalgia for the primitive Puritan society.

In 1862, in anticipation of her husband's retirement, Stowe moved once more to the city of Hartford, where she had a large house built that would force her for the next ten years to write at a furious pace in order to keep up with the bills. After 1870, her daily load was lightened somewhat. The large, expensive house in Hartford was sold and a smaller one, cozy and adequate, was purchased. The Stowes spent the winters in Florida between 1869 and 1884. In 1873, Stowe published *Palmetto Leaves*, sketches describing her winter residence in Florida. Another novel, *Poganuc People*, with autobiographical undertones, was written for serialization in the *Christian Union* and appeared in book form in 1878. After her husband's death on August 6, 1886, Stowe began writing her testament with her son Charley's help. Until her death on July 1, 1896, she lived once again near her father's house in Litchfield, Connecticut, surrounded by her family.

Analysis

Harriet Beecher Stowe began her writing career with small sketches and stories that earned her a modest place among the minor writers. They were examples of the domestic fiction popular in many of the magazines of the time, especially in ladies' magazines and gift annuals. The characteristic elements of the sketch, with its looseness in plot and characterization, is also employed in her longer stories. Her stories and sketches are informed by personal details owed to her own experiences and to her New England background, which yielded a rich element of local color to her works.

Another earmark of most of her mature writing is also already apparent in her early sketches: the need to participate in the moral debates of her time. With her story "Let Every Man Mind His Own Business," collected in *The Mayflower*, she hoped to contribute to the temperance crusade.

Another important theme, the pathetic death of a perfect child, which stands at the core of *Uncle Tom's Cabin*, was already apparent in "Uncle Tim" and "Little Edward."

Her habit of writing sketches for magazines or periodicals that paid by the page, which she could write between her housekeeping chores, shaped her style. She did not cultivate the copybook English of the *Godey's Lady's Book* but wrote as she thought and talked. Because she stuck closely to topics that concerned and interested her, there was a naturalness and almost a colloquial quality about her style. Because she was always pressed for time, she never rewrote passages, corrected punctuation and grammar, or practiced the time-consuming task of stylistic refinement. Content for her was decidedly more important than form. She considered herself the lucky recipient of inspiration, and very often she transformed visual images directly into literary text, which is thus descriptive and lacking the proper qualities of plot.

UNCLE TOM'S CABIN

First published: 1851-1852
Type of work: Novel

Tom, a slave, is separated from his family and sold to a plantation in the South, where he loses his life because of the abuses of his brutal owner.

Uncle Tom's Cabin was Harriet Beecher Stowe's first novel. Initially printed by installments in the *National Era*, an antislavery weekly published in Washington, D.C., from June 5, 1851, to April 1, 1852, it was a best-selling book of previously unheard of proportions. It was an instant success and soon acquired fame in many parts of the world. Yet it is not easy to make a clear judgment of the merits of *Uncle Tom's Cabin*. Those who exclude works that cater to the taste of the masses from the realm of high culture have difficulty describing its artistry in positive terms. Moreover, Stowe has been criticized for her depiction and characterization of blacks, which led to numerous stereotypical and trivial imitations on the stage, in almanacs, in songs and poems, and even in paintings. Her depiction of women has often been objectionable to modern sensibilities, because her women seem to be restricted to moral issues as they play themselves out in the domestic sphere. Underlying her portrayal of blacks and women is an acceptance of the power of Christianity that is alien to modern readers. These three interwoven issues, the place of women and blacks and the role of Christianity, are at the core of the novel and make it a central literary and political document of the American experience in the 1850's.

If one accepts the standards set by male writers of the American tradition, which depicted masculine confrontation with nature, as exemplified in the frontier myth of the American male, Stowe's novel seems naïvely visionary, lacking in complex philosophical content, overly melodramatic, and awkwardly plotted. It was earmarked as a book for women and children. It was not until critics such as Jane Tompkins reexamined the novel that Stowe's efforts to reorganize society from a woman's point of view came to be recognized.

The book appeared amid a growing controversy over race and religion. The author wrote in reaction to the Compromise of 1850, which admitted California to the Union as a free state, abolished the slave trade in Washington, D.C., organized the new Mexico and Utah territories without prohibiting slavery, and enacted the Fugitive Slave Law, which forced Northerners to assist in returning fugitive slaves to their owners. Although Stowe was hardly the first to point to slavery's destruction of both black and white families, her novel presented a very effective fusion of the sentimental novel with the rhetoric of an antislavery polemic.

Tom, a broad-chested, strong slave who lives with his wife and children in a small hut near the house of his master in Kentucky, is sold by his master against the will of the master's wife in order to pay off debts. He is sold "down river" and expects the worst: to work on a Southern plantation. On the boat, he meets Evangelina (Eva), a perfect, angelic child. In her character, the tradition of children in sentimental literature and the ministerial leader of evangelical social reform are combined into a childlike female Christ figure. She persuades her father, Augustine St. Clare, to buy Tom, and he is bought as Evangelina's playmate and keeper. Evangelina dies and makes her father promise to free his slaves, but before he signs the papers, St. Clare dies and thus inadvertently sets in motion Tom's demise. Tom is sold to Simon Legree, who tortures and finally kills Tom because he is unwilling to betray two fellow slaves, Cassey and Emmelina, who fled from their brutal, sexually abusive master. Tom's death is a direct result of his aggressive nonviolence, and makes him a black Christ figure. Numerous subplots and their respective characters depict various aspects and views of slavery and miscegenation.

Summary

Uncle Tom's Cabin was so captivating and moving to its readers that the more subversive attacks on white male hegemony went largely unnoticed. Furthermore, positing the spiritual superiority of women and blacks was not enough to disrupt the status quo. Coupled with the lack of a clear and intellectually convincing argument for the moral and intellectual identity between the races and genders, the focus on the religious vision of Christ as mother overshadows the book's possible political impact. By postulating the moral and spiritual superiority of the two suppressed groups, women and blacks, instead of a vision of equal adulthood, Stowe marred the political impact of the book.

Bibliography

Adams, John R. *Harriet Beecher Stowe.* New Haven, Conn.: Yale University Press, 1963.

Gosset, Thomas F. *Uncle Tom's Cabin and American Literature.* Dallas: Southern Methodist University Press, 1985.

Kirkham, E. Bruce. *The Building of Uncle Tom's Cabin.* Knoxville: University of Tennessee Press, 1977.

Sundquist, Eric J., ed. *New Essays on Uncle Tom's Cabin.* Cambridge, England: Cambridge University Press, 1986.

Wagenknecht, Edward. *Harriet Beecher Stowe: The Known and the Unknown.* New York: Oxford University Press, 1965.

Wilson, Forrest. *Cruasader in Crinoline: The Life of Harriet Beecher Stowe.* Philadelphia: J. B. Lippincott, 1941.

Karin A. Wurst

GLENDON SWARTHOUT

Born: Pinckney, Michigan
April 8, 1918

Principal Literary Achievement
Swarthout's gritty, realistic novels set in the Southwest explore themes that transcend the common perception of the Western genre, revealing characters who triumph personally even as they suffer defeat.

Biography
Glendon Swarthout was born in Pinckney, Michigan, on April 8, 1918, the son of Fred H. and Lila (Chubb) Swarthout. He was reared and educated in Michigan, taking his A.B. in 1939 from the University of Michigan in Ann Arbor. His studies and his marriage to Kathryn Vaughn in 1940 were interrupted by the outbreak of World War II. Swarthout served in the infantry from 1943 to 1945, earning the rank of sergeant and two battle stars. After the war, he returned to his wife and to university study, this time at Michigan State University, in East Lansing, completing his M.A. in 1946. Swarthout then accepted a teaching fellowship at Michigan State. The Swarthouts were at the University of Maryland between 1948 and 1951. In 1951, he returned to Michigan State to accept an associate professorship in English and pursue a course of study leading to the Ph.D., which he completed in 1955. From 1951 to 1959, he was an associate professor of English at Michigan State; in 1959, the Swarthouts moved to Tempe, Arizona, where Swarthout served as a lecturer in English at Arizona State from 1959 to 1963.

Despite the demands of a successful academic career, Swarthout has been a consistently prolific and acknowleged novelist, dramatist, and writer of short stories with fifteen novels to his credit. *Where the Boys Are* (1960), *They Came to Cordura* (1958), *Bless the Beasts and Children* (1970), and *The Shootist* (1975) have been produced as motion pictures. Swarthout's first novel, *Willow Run* (1943), written before his stint in the infantry, established him as a writer of promise. *Willow Run* received a largely favorable review in *The New York Times Book Review*. The reviewer, Rose Feld, wrote, "Swarthout's conception of his novel is an interesting and ambitious one and his book . . . has definite rhythm and vitality." Heady praise indeed for a first novel by an aspiring twenty-five-year-old writer.

After the war, Swarthout managed to keep his career as a writer alive even though he had undertaken advanced studies while supporting his family; he published short

stories in such respected periodicals as *Cosmopolitan, Esquire, Collier's*, and *The Saturday Evening Post*. His efforts as a writer of short stories culminated in 1960 when he won an O. Henry award for excellence in short fiction. The completion of his doctoral studies made it possible for him to turn again to the novel. The publication of *They Came to Cordura* in 1958 brought him wide recognition and financial reward. This work was critically acclaimed and was translated into a film of the same name starring Gary Cooper. The publication of this novel marked the beginning of Swarthout's commercial success as a novelist and as a novelist whose work translates easily to the screen.

Swarthout published ten novels from 1960 to 1979, the most successful of these and the best-known to the public being *Bless the Beasts and Children* and *The Shootist*, the latter becoming the acclaimed vehicle for John Wayne's last film. Swarthout's novels of the West appeal not only to aficionados of the western but also to audiences as diverse as the temporal and geographic settings of his works. He has twice been the recipient of the Western Writers of America Spur Award, in 1976 for *The Shootist* (1975) and in 1988 for *The Homesman* (1988). Swarthout has also collaborated with his wife, Kathryn, on six books for children and young adults, a partnership that one might suppose has had a tempering effect on the streak of cynicism that sometimes pervades his darker works.

If one measures Glendon Swarthout's career by financial success, critical acclaim, professional recognition, or academic success, it can be said that he has fulfilled the American Dream. He has been the recipient of numerous awards, among the most prestigious being the Hopwood Award in Fiction, the O. Henry Award, the National Society of Arts and Letters Gold Medal, and two Spur awards from the Western Writers of America. More important, he has produced a body of literature that has brought pleasure and insight to a generation of readers.

Analysis

With the exception of *Where the Boys Are*, set in Fort Lauderdale, Florida, Glendon Swarthout's novels take place either in Michigan, where he was born and reared, or in the more spacious landscape of his adopted home in the West. Moreover, the novels tend to mirror the landscape: The ones set in the East are somewhat cribbed and confined in theme, whereas the broader backdrop of the West seems to liberate his prose and the scope of his thematic concern. His first novel, *Willow Run*, written in 1943, just before Swarthout's own entry into World War II, reflects a United States going to war. The novel follows the story of six workers in a bomber plant who, united by ride sharing, manage to damage one another's lives during a graveyard shift filled with misunderstanding, jealousy, and violence. Much of the characterization is weak, and there are some dreadfully loose ends; however, much of Swarthout's basic promise is in evidence. *Willow Run* begins to reveal Swarthout's eye for detail, his empathy for the vulnerable, and his basic affirmation of individual dignity.

His second novel, *They Came to Cordura*, reflects Swarthout's fascinations with the testing of courage and the physical and psychic landscape of the West. Again, Swarthout juxtaposes individual effort against the dynamic of a group. Five American soldiers involved in the bloody expedition ordered against Pancho Villa have been chosen to receive the Congressional Medal of Honor. The central character, Major Thorn, had exhibited cowardice in the face of the enemy. His disgusted commanding officer assigns Thorn to select recipients for the Medal of Honor and escort them to Cordura for an awards ceremony—as an added humiliation, he is designated to make the presentations. Swarthout handles what could have been simply melodrama with understanding and skill. The journey to Cordura proves to be full of physical and emotional pitfalls. Thorn wonders what facet of character separates the cowardly from the brave, his cowardice from the seemingly careless courage of the hero. As it turns out, the heroes are far from noble and their bravery under fire was nothing if not serendipitous. Moreover, Thorn discovers in himself the courage that he thought was absent. Swarthout's own experience as an infantryman during World War II gives this work a ring of authenticity. Moreover, the novel fully establishes Swarthout's gift as a gripping storyteller.

When Swarthout shifts from telling a good story to social criticism, he loses narrative momentum and his characters tend to become stereotypes; *Welcome to Thebes* (1962) and *The Cadillac Cowboys* (1964) are illustrative of these flaws. The former follows the adventures of Sewell Smith, a down-and-out writer seeking material for a pulp novel. Motivated as much by malice as greed, Smith discovers that an eighth-grade nymphet has been dispersing her charms to the town worthies. Delighted to have the opportunity to settle old scores and pick up a little extortion money, Smith sets about ruining people's lives. The novel has a morbid fascination, but it is difficult to care about people who are essentially shallow and preoccupied with themselves. The characters in *The Cadillac Cowboys* suffer from equally truncated development. The corruption of the plain, honest cowhand into a rich urban bumpkin is the stuff of television comedy. Moreover, what purports to be a satire is interspersed with long passages on the destruction of the environment. As much as one might sympathize with Swarthout's passion and point of view, the reader would be better advised to turn to Joseph Wood Krutch or Edward Abbey.

Swarthout manages to interweave social criticism, character development, and storyline successfully in *Bless the Beasts and Children*, a novel that may very well stand the test of time. Here he is at his very best; the reader shares his anger and disgust with a society that makes victims of the innocent—the beasts and children. Swarthout does not stop to preach. Instead, he tells of the plight of the buffalo that are about to be slaughtered by so-called sportsmen and of the mission of a group of misfit boys who are out to save them. Nevertheless, by the close of the novel, it is clear that he sees deep flaws within American society.

Swarthout has the unusual ability to involve his readers with idiosyncratic characters who are often the outcasts and misfits of a society that demands they be different. Paradoxically, his best creations are some of the most flawed characters. John Bernard Books, however, the dying gunman of *The Shootist*, is a vivid exception.

Books is a man who represents his time and place and who has outlived his circumstances. He stands tall and lives by a personal code of honor. In short, as a representative of the rugged individualism of the American frontier, he is everything that modern America is not. Books faces the circumstances of his dying with dignity and courage. When those who would seek to profit from his death move in like eaters of carrion, Books beats them at their own game. Books is not for sale, but Swarthout seems to suggest that most things in the twentieth century are.

Swarthout's most successful foray into humor is *The Old Colts* (1985), which picks up the story of Wyatt Earp and Bat Masterson when they meet again in the New York City of 1916. They encounter the likes of Damon Runyon, the bard of Broadway (whose Sky Masterson of *Guys and Dolls* (1932) was, in fact, patterned on Bat, then a newspaperman and gambler in New York), Jimmy Walker, the dandy governor of New York, Arnold Rothstein, the flamboyant gangster, and Teddy Roosevelt. After geriatric escapades among the urban folk, Wyatt and Bat head for Dodge City, a town more worthy of their talents.

In *The Homesman*, Swarthout turns once again to individuals who are tested by the rigors of frontier life, a life frequently crueler to the women than to the men. Faced with isolation, hunger, and the illness and death of children, many women broke down, escaping from misery into madness. When this occurred, a homesman had to be appointed to escort the broken women home. This is the story of an unlikely couple yoked together by necessity. Mary Bee Cuddy, moved by the dementia of her best friend, offers to escort four women to meet the Ladies Aid Society in Iowa, from there to be returned to their families. Cuddy must team up with the reprobate George Briggs. The story of Cuddy and Briggs is central, but the flashbacks to the lives of the women who have gone insane is told with gripping power. Swarthout demonstrates again that he is able to enlist compassion for the broken, for the victims of life who, despite their personal plights, manage to affirm human worth.

Swarthout is most effective when he sticks to storytelling and abandons rhetoric. There is a repressed anger in his novels that sometimes leads him to preach or become vitriolic, and his humor tends to be heavy-handed. On the other hand, when he moves beyond social ciphers, he creates characters that engage a reader's mind and heart. Moreover, he is willing to risk writing novels that take a moral stance; at his best, he tells a good story that has a point.

BLESS THE BEASTS AND CHILDREN

First published: 1970
Type of work: Novel

A group of troubled adolescents undergoes a rite of passage at an Arizona summer camp that specializes in turning boys into cowboys.

In *Bless the Beasts and Children*, Box Canyon Boys Camp becomes a microcosm for American society; a process of "natural selection of age and cruelty and regionalism and kindred interest" divides the boys of the camp into a ranked tribal structure. The boys strive to outdo one another and to usurp the place of those higher in the social order, either by excelling in the weekly competition or by stealing the totem of another tribe. Each tribe has its special totem: the Apaches, a mounted buffalo head; the Sioux, the head of a mountain lion; the Comanches, the head of a black bear, and so on, down to the tribe of the lowest social order, designated the Bedwetters, whose totem of shame is an enameled chamber pot. The Apaches is the tribe of winners, of the biggest, toughest, and most competent boys. Swarthout writes, "Incentive was thus inherent in the system, as it was in the American way of life." Because of their prowess in weekly competition, these boys retain their rank and the special privileges that go with it. The camp staff and the indifferent or desperate parents of the boys believe that this competitive system will bring about the onset of masculine maturity. Within this specially created hothouse for the development of the American male, Swarthout selects the most unlikely and apparently the least likeable group for an adventure that takes them from self-loathing and infantile rage to an awakening to the promise of their own lives.

When the Bedwetters watch the annual shooting of buffalo, conducted by the Arizona Game and Fish Department to thin the herd, they are horrified by the slaughter they witness. Swarthout is relentless in presenting a description of the helplessness of the semi-domesticated beasts and the gleeful joy the "shooters" take in bringing a hideous death to the confused and terrified animals. The incompetent marksmanship creates a bloody shambles that both shocks the reader and traumatizes the boys who watch in numbed horror.

Under the halting leadership of John Cotton, the oldest of the frequently pathetic boys in the Bedwetters, the group has begun to emerge from the private world of fear and hostility into which they had withdrawn. On a subconscious level, they recognize themselves in the innocent beasts led to the slaughter. Indeed, the story opens in the middle of Cotton's nightmare in which he and the others are the buffalo who are being led to slaughter, and in that dream Cotton recognizes his mother as one of the shooters. This shattering dream serves to merge the personal and private world of the boys with the mindless destruction encountered in the adult world of their parents. Their witnessing the killing of the buffalo returns them to desperate isolation. Only when the younger of the Lally brothers, "Lally 2," embarks on the impossible mission of returning to the buffalo range and freeing the buffalo, are the boys again brought together by a purpose outside themselves, independent of their special weaknesses.

Thus, the stage is set for high adventure: The boys must escape the confines of the camp, travel across half of northern Arizona, free the buffalo penned up for the next day's shooting, and return to camp without getting caught. The task is impossible, but the boys are gavanized into action by their need to rescue the buffalo and an image of themselves as heroes: "They were mad for western movies. They doted on tales told with trumpets and ending in a pot of gold, a bucket of blood, or a chorus of the national anthem." What follows is indeed an adventure, but more important, the Bedwetters must overcome the obstacles they encounter from within.

The narrative technique Swarthout employs juxtaposes the events of the storyline with events from the past that reveal the damaged and broken lives the children have led and how they have become what they are. This is some of Swarthout's most effective and poignant writing. For one reason or another, these boys have been abandoned emotionally, orphaned by their parents' insensitivity, selfishness, and immaturity. Unloved and isolated, they must work together to carry out their task. Each boy finds something of value in himself. Teft, the perpetual juvenile delinquent and thief, turns his talent to "borrowing" a car; Lally 2 has a special way with animals; Shecker, the fat boy, is strong enough to break the wire on the bales of hay, and Cotton binds them together with dauntless courage when a turn of events seems to make their mission to free the thirty remaining buffalo impossible. The love that they failed to find at home they find in each other. The boys initially find themselves united by their misery and fear, then by the odd ferocity of John Cotton's protection and acceptance, and finally by a shared sense of purpose, triumph, and tragedy.

The triumph of misfits over a callous social order is not uncommon thematic material, but Swarthout manages to avoid the pitfalls of stereotypical villains; there are no wicked oil executives, slimy politicians, or ruthless militarists. Rather, it is the structure of society itself that has made the children victims. Swarthout seems to suggest that if the innocence of the beasts and children means their destruction, then the society at large is trapped in a box canyon of its own making.

THE SHOOTIST

First published: 1975
Type of work: Novel

When a gunman discovers that he is dying of cancer, he chooses to meet death on his own terms.

The Shootist is as much a story of the end of the Old West as it is the story of John Bernard Books, the last famous living gunman, whose passing will mark the end of an era. On January 22, 1901, the day of Queen Victoria's death, Books rides into El Paso, Texas, to consult a doctor he trusts, only to discover that he is dying of cancer of the prostate—inoperable, incurable, and unimaginably painful. Books cannot move on; he has come to the end of the road in El Paso, but clearly he is an unwanted anachronism. The town, represented by Marshall Thibido, would be more comfortable if Books had picked another place to die. Like the marshall, the citizens are both fearful and fascinated by Books, royalty in his own right, a living legend of a bygone era.

Books has rented a room from Mrs. Bond Rogers, a widowed woman who is struggling to make ends meet by taking in boarders. She is unaware of the reputation of her houseguest, who in self-parody tells her he is William Hickok, United States Marshal of Abilene, Kansas; however, her son knows that Hickok has been dead for more than two decades, and he recognizes the famous custom-made .44 Remingtons carried by the legendary shootist J. B. Books. The interplay between these characters as Books moves toward death gives the narrative depth and dimension.

Bond Rogers finds herself both attracted to and repelled by Books—repelled by the violence he brings to her home and attracted by his courage in the face of an adversary against whom he cannot prevail. As the word spreads that Books is in El Paso and that he is a dying man, he is plagued by parasites and reputation hunters. When a couple of would-be assassins try to ambush Books in bed, there is a shootout that results in the bloody death of Books' assailants and the flight of the widow Rogers' remaining tenants. She upbraids Books for being a vicious killer, but Books points out, quite reasonably, that they were in the process of trying to kill him. She struggles with the ambivalence of her feelings and with her fear that Books will become a terrible model for her son Gillom, who already is showing signs of becoming one of the local toughs.

Books becomes remorseful for the trouble that he has brought to the Rogers' home. In an effort to make up for the lost revenue, he cleverly takes advantage of those who would seek to profit from his death. The undertaker who offers Books a free funeral in hopes of making money from putting the corpse on display finds that Books is wise to his game. Books charges him a fee for the privilege of conducting his funeral. He sees through the photographer's offer of a free portrait as well, charging him a fee for the photograph, which he is bound to copy and sell. He feels more kindly toward a second-hand man who is more candid about his motive for the purchase of his last effects. Swarthout's cynicism is relentless, as a tenderly remembered lover from Books's past pays him a visit with an offer of marriage. It turns out that she has been offered a deal to have a book written in her name—or, rather, in the name of J. B. Books's widow. Even the preacher hopes to capitalize on Books's plight. He offers him salvation for a signed statement of repentance, for he would be the preacher who saved the soul of J. B. Books, killer and sinner extraordinary. The shallow opportunism of the denizens of the new age is in painful contrast to the often ruthless Books who lives by a Spartan code: "I will not be laid a hand on. I will not be wronged. I will not stand for an insult. I don't do these things to others. I require the same from them."

When Books presses Doc Hostetler into revealing the awful agony awaiting him, Hostetler tells Books that he will go out screaming no matter how brave he is, unless he is lucky enough to slip into a coma. Hostetler plants the seed of suicide, but Books chooses another way. Marshal Thibido had warned him that El Paso was full of toughs who would like to make a name for themselves by being the man who killed J. B. Books. Books sends a separate invitation to three of the worst of El Paso's citizens to meet him at the Constantinople Saloon: Pulford, a gambler who prides himself on having shot a man through the heart at a distance of more than eighty feet; Serrano, a cattle thief, killer, and molester of children; and Cobb, an impotent punk who hurts prostitutes. These are to be his adversaries in a final confrontation; John Bernard Books does not plan to die alone.

Throughout the novel, Books has taken grim comfort from the newspaper reporting Queen Victoria's death that he purchased as he entered El Paso. He wryly observes that it is a newspaper that he has had time to read. He perceives a parallel between his passing and the passing of an era that will later come to be known as Victorian, but he is not vain enough to think that his life has been important. As he steps through the swinging doors of the Constantinople, he takes satisfaction in the thought that even though his life did not amount to much, his death will be remembered for some time, for there is still a lot of John Bernard Books left to kill.

The Shootist reveals Swarthout at his narrative best. The action is suffused with dark humor and the revelation of characters who are both interesting and complex. Books does not prove to have a heart of gold, but he does stand above those who seek his end. His ruthlessness, flamboyance, and flinty integrity are a part of the age in which he lived.

Summary

Robert Browning's famous admonition that "man's reach should exceed his grasp" is applicable to Swarthout's central thematic concerns and perhaps to his work as well. His most successful novels employ characters who find themselves facing seemingly insurmountable obstacles. Pitted against overwhelming circumstances, they come to discover their inner strengths and weaknesses. The outcome of their efforts to prevail over forces greater than themselves is less significant than how they meet the challenge. These are the ingredients of tragedy that fundamentally affirm the human condition. When Swarthout succeeds, he succeeds in an important way; when he fails, it is usually not because the task is too small.

Bibliography

Appel, Benjamin. "The Mystery of Courage." *The Saturday Review* 41 (February 6, 1958): 30.

Conner, John W. Review of *Bless the Beasts and Children*. *English Journal* 61 (1972): 41-42.

Dempsey, David. "Scapegrace's Homecoming." *The New York Times Book Review*, June 17, 1962, p. 24.

Feld, Rose. "Building a Bomber." *The New York Times Book Review*, May 30, 1943: p. 18.

"Glendon (Fred) Swarthout." In *Contemporary Literary Criticism*. Vol. 35, edited by Daniel G. Marowski. Detroit: Gale Research, 1985.

Levin, Martin. Review of *The Cadillac Cowboys. The New York Times Book Review,* February 19, 1964: p. 30.

Nelson, Nancy Owen. Review of *The Homesman. Western American Literature* 24 (1989): 70-71.

Nordyke, Lewis. "Outbreak of Courage." *The New York Times Book Review,* February 9, 1959, p. 4.

Oberbeck, S. K. "High Noon." *Newsweek* 85 (February 3, 1975): 64.

Richardson, Maurice. *"Where the Boys Are." New Statesman* 60 (1960): 534-541.

David Sundstrand

HENRY DAVID THOREAU

Born: Concord, Massachusetts
July 12, 1817
Died: Concord, Massachusetts
May 6, 1862

Principal Literary Achievement

With *Walden* and his other nature writings, Thoreau advocated environmental awareness; as a Transcendentalist, he urged all individuals to develop their fullest potential; as a social critic, he challenged materialism and conformity and formulated the doctrine of civil disobedience.

Biography

Many of Thoreau's writings are autobiographical, for he thought that the poet's noblest work was his life. Henry David Thoreau was born on July 12, 1817, in Concord, Massachusetts, the third of four children of John and Cynthia Thoreau. The family name is French, and Henry's paternal grandfather was a Protestant emigrant from Jersey, an island in the English Channel. His maternal grandfather was a Congregationalist minister. Thoreau was baptized David Henry but later reversed his first two names. His father, a quiet, subdued person, after failing as a shopkeeper, moved to Boston to teach school but returned to Concord when Henry was six and began to manufacture lead pencils. His mother was more energetic; active in community affairs and considered one of the most talkative persons in Concord.

Though a village of some two thousand people, Concord was full of intellectual ferment, being the home of Ralph Waldo Emerson and Bronson Alcott (and later, of Nathaniel Hawthorne). To it came many literary people attracted to Emerson's Transcendentalism. After attending the Concord Academy, Thoreau went to Harvard College and was graduated in 1837. While there, he heard Emerson lecture and read Emerson's "Nature," which became a seminal book for him. In the spring of 1837, Thoreau met Emerson in person, and the neighbors became friends and associates. Thoreau joined an informal group of Transcendentalists who met at Emerson's house.

At Thoreau's commencement, Emerson had given his lecture "The American Scholar," urging intellectual independence from Europe and advocating physical activity as much as book learning, and he apparently thought Thoreau best exemplified this concept. A jack of all trades, Thoreau was skilled with tools; an expert surveyor; a practical scientist in botany, zoology, ornithology, mineralogy, astronomy, and an-

thropology; and "could outwalk, outswim, outrun, outskate, and outboat most of his contemporaries," according to his biographer Walter Harding. Thoreau built boats and houses and invented tools, machines, and techniques that made the Thoreau pencils the best in America. Emerson, by contrast, was absolutely unhandy, even at making minor repairs, and, for all his talk of nature, was not an outdoorsman and confined himself to walks in his orchard.

After graduation, Thoreau worked for a while in his father's pencil factory, invented a superior method of mixing graphite, and began to lecture at the Concord Lyceum. In 1838, he and his brother John reopened the Concord Academy, where Thoreau was a popular and innovative teacher who took his students on frequent field trips and immersed them in local human and natural history. He stopped teaching because he would not flog students, but he later did a good deal of tutoring. In 1839, the Thoreau brothers took a boating trip on the Concord and Merrimack rivers that became the subject of Thoreau's first book. Both brothers proposed marriage to Ellen Sewall, who rejected them both.

When the Concord Academy closed in 1841 because of John's tuberculosis, Thoreau moved into Emerson's house as resident handyman for two years. There, he had access to Emerson's library, with its extensive collection of Oriental philosophy and literature. Thoreau rejected the Oriental myths as superstition but appreciated the Eastern values of spirituality, meditation, and solitude. He also began to publish poems and essays in *The Dial*, the Transcendentalist magazine. In 1842, Thoreau met Hawthorne, then living in Concord's Old Manse, who later used him as a model for the faunlike Donatello in *The Marble Faun* (1860). That year, John Thoreau died of tetanus, and the grieving Henry developed identical symptoms that were purely psychosomatic. Recovering, he took a position on Staten Island in New York as tutor to the children of Emerson's brother, but, homesick for Concord, he returned home after a few months and resumed working in the family pencil factory.

In 1845, Thoreau built a one-room cabin on the shore of Walden Pond on land owned by Emerson. Aside from some visits and excursions, he lived there alone for two years, two months, and two days. During his time at Walden, he was imprisoned for a night in 1846 for refusing to pay the state poll tax. In 1847, Thoreau left the Walden cabin when he was invited to take care of Emerson's house and family while Emerson lectured in Europe. The following year, Thoreau began his own career as a lecturer, though he listed his profession as surveying. His first book, *A Week on the Concord and Merrimack Rivers*, written while he was at Walden, was published in 1849 but sold poorly. That year, he took the first of three trips to Cape Cod, and the next year, he made an excursion to Quebec. During the 1850's, he gathered a vast store of data on botany, zoology, and ornithology during his daily walks in the woods, donated specimens to museums, became a member of the Boston Society of Natural History, did pioneer work on pollens, and wrote a paper on "The Succession of Forest Trees" that made important discoveries about forest management. Emerson, for whom nature (and much else) was almost entirely an abstraction, objected to Thoreau's detailed work in natural history, but it is precisely this vivid detail that makes Thoreau seem more meaningful today than Emerson. Thoreau practiced the self-reliance about which Emerson merely talked. Even Emerson acknowledged, "Thoreau gives me, in flesh and blood and pertinacious Saxon belief, my own ethics. He is far more real, and daily practically obeying them, than I." Emerson gave lip service to abolition, but Thoreau was the most active conductor on the underground railroad in Concord and wrote the militant "Slavery in Massachusetts" (1854). By 1850, Emerson had become estranged from Thoreau, who called their relationship "one long tragedy" in which the older writer had patronized the younger.

In compensation for the loss of Emerson's friendship, Thoreau became friends with Louis Agassiz and got to know most of the leading American writers of his day, including Walt Whitman, the Alcotts, Henry Wadsworth Longfellow, Henry James, Sr., and Horace Greeley, who regularly promoted his work. During the 1850's, Thoreau took several trips to the Maine woods and to Cape Cod. In 1853, he published Parts of "A Yankee in Canada" in *Putnam's Monthly*; in 1854, he published his masterpiece, *Walden: Or, Life in the Woods*, and in 1855, he published his first Cape Cod essays in *Putnam's Monthly*. In 1857, he met John Brown in Concord and became a champion of his militant abolitionist activity. When his father died in 1859, Thoreau took over the family pencil factory, while continuing to give frequent lectures and to defend John Brown, executed for his raid on Harpers Ferry.

In 1855, Thoreau had contracted tuberculosis, perhaps from too much exposure in the woods. For seven years, he fought the disease; in 1861, he visited Minnesota in a vain attempt to improve his health in a drier climate, but he died at the age of forty-four in 1862. Posthumous publications include numerous essays, including *The Maine Woods* (1864), *Cape Cod* and *Letters to Various Persons* (1865), *A Yankee in Canada* and *Antislavery and Reform Papers* (1866), and his *Journal* (1906).

Analysis

Thoreau is a major figure in the American Transcendental movement and in what F. O. Matthiessen calls the American Renaissance of the 1840's and 1850's, when American literature came of age. Undogmatic and unsystematic, Transcendentalism was in part a heritage from Puritanism but in larger part a rebellion against it. Its American leader was Emerson, who resigned from his Unitarian ministry because even it was too dogmatic for him. Transcendentalism rejected organized religion, biblical authority, and original sin in favor of pantheism and a belief in the daily rebirth of God in the individual soul. An eclectic faith rather than a systematic philosophy, it derived in part from Platonic idealism, German mysticism, French utopianism, and the Hindu scriptures. Part of the Romantic movement's reaction against the Age of Reason, it stressed the instinct rather than the intellect. As Thoreau wrote, "We do not learn by inference and deduction and the application of mathematics to philosophy, but by direct intercourse and sympathy."

At first Thoreau was Emerson's disciple, but soon he became his own man. Emerson complained that Thoreau had no new ideas: "I am very familiar with all his thoughts," Emerson wrote, "they are my own quite originally drest." Formulating new ideas did not interest Thoreau. Emerson wrote largely in abstractions, but Thoreau did not care for abstract ideas and theorizing, stating, "Let us not underrate the value of a fact; it will one day flower in a truth." His friend Ellery Channing said that "metaphysics was his aversion." Thus F. O. Matthiessen observes that "Thoreau does not disappear into the usual transcendental vapour." Thoreau had to test his ideas by living them and then communicating his experiences instead of declaiming abstractions. "How can we expect a harvest of thought who have not had a seed time of character?" he asked. His actions were not entirely original; Alcott had earlier refused to pay his poll tax, and Stearns Wheeler had lived in a shanty on Flint's Pond, but they did not write about these experiences in the pithy way Thoreau did, nor did they offer his profound criticism of materialism, which prevented people from realizing their own potential. Thoreau insisted that "if one advances confidently in the direction of his dreams, and endeavors to live the life which he has imagined, he will meet with a success unexpected in common hours" and will thus transcend his lower self and his society. Doing so requires what Emerson called self-reliance, which Thoreau exemplified in his own life, writing that "If a man does not keep pace with his companions, perhaps it is because he hears a different drummer. Let him step to the music which he hears, however measured or far away."

Thoreau is the United States' first and best major writer on nature as well as one of its most trenchant social critics. His vivid, pithy prose is ultimately richer than Emerson's abstractions, and although his verse is usually second-rate, his prose poetry has made him one of the great artists of American literature.

A WEEK ON THE CONCORD AND MERRIMACK RIVERS

First published: 1849
Type of work: Essay

The contemplation of nature reveals the unity of nature and man and provides a health not found in diseased society.

Thoreau's first book, *A Week on the Concord and Merrimack Rivers*, is the account of a two-week boat and hiking trip he made with his brother John in 1839. Shortly thereafter, Thoreau sold the boat to Nathaniel Hawthorne. Thoreau worked on the manuscript for ten years, intending it, after John's death in 1842, to be a tribute to him. Thoreau wrote most of the work while living at Walden (writing it was part of the "private business" he planned to transact there) but continued revising it for two more years. Despite its being promoted by Emerson, publishers would not print it unless the author underwrote the cost. James Munroe & Co. printed a thousand copies but bound only 450. Despite generally favorable reviews at home and in England, the book did not sell, and Thoreau, stuck with the unsold copies, lamented in 1853, "I have now a library of nearly nine hundred volumes, over seven hundred of which I wrote myself." A second edition came out posthumously in 1867, with additions and corrections, and the book has remained in print ever since.

In part, the work is an elegy to Thoreau's brother, who, in the elegiac tradition, is never named. Following an introductory essay, there are seven chapters—one for each day of the week. About 40 percent consists of travel narrative; the rest is a combination of essays, poems, anecdotes, quotations, translations, philosophical observations on life and nature, and numerous digressions. James Russell Lowell complained that so little of it is about the trip itself, noting, "We were bid to a river party—not to be preached at."

Carl Bode somewhat agrees with Lowell, noting that "[t]he scholar is much more apparent than the traveler, for the original narrative has been weighted down with learned allusions and quotations." While the book does contain many of Thoreau's philosophical musings, however, it is by no means all preaching. Thoreau celebrates the sounds and silences, the light and shadows, of the natural world. Drifting along in their boat, he and his brother find a freedom like that of Huckleberry Finn on his raft. There are word paintings of the river and the landscape through which it flows that make it a verbal correspondence to some of the landscape paintings of the time. Thoreau celebrates the variety and vitality of nature and wildlife, "such healthy natural tumult as proves the last day is not yet at hand." He presents part of what he elsewhere calls "The Natural History of Massachusetts" in his incisive picture of river birds, fish and fishermen, trees and wildflowers. As Robert Frost would later, Thoreau often details a scene of nature and then draws a moral or philosophical reflection from it. A neo-Platonist, he sometimes sees "objects as through a thin haze, in their eternal relations," wondering "who set them up, and for what purpose." At times, "he becomes immortal with her [nature's] immortality." Yet he also has a Darwinian awareness of the suffering in nature, the tragic end of creatures of the wild. Sometimes he recounts historical vignettes called to mind by passing locations. The book lacks the unity of *Walden* but anticipates it in many of Thoreau's concerns—a mystical relationship with nature and the life spirit, a love for wildness in nature and independence in people, and the belief that people can redirect their lives in simpler and more fulfilling ways.

WALDEN

First published: 1854
Type of work: Extended essay

By living alone in the woods, Thoreau set an example of how to simplify and enrich one's life.

In 1845, when he was twenty-seven years old, Thoreau built a one-room cabin on Emerson's land in the woods on the shore of Walden Pond, less than two miles from

Concord. He borrowed an axe, bought the boards from an Irish railroad worker's shanty, and erected a ten-by-fifteen-foot building. He moved into his new abode on the symbolic date of Independence Day. There he lived austerely, working about six weeks a year growing beans and doing odd jobs, living on a simple diet, and spending less than nine dollars for food during the first eight months. His plan was to simplify his life, to "live free and uncommitted," working about six weeks a year in order to have the remaining forty-six weeks free to read, write, live in intimate relationship to nature, "affect the quality of the day," and demonstrate the Transcendental belief in "the unquestionable ability of man to elevate his life by a conscious endeavor." He summed up his experiment by writing:

> I went to the woods because I wished to live deliberately, to front only the essential facts of life, and see if I could not learn what it had to teach, and not, when I came to die, discover that I had not lived. . . . I wanted to live deep and suck out all the marrow of life, to live so sturdily and Spartan-like as to put to rout all that was not life, to cut a broad swath and shave close; to drive life into a corner, and reduce it to its lowest terms, and, if it proved to be mean . . . to get the whole and genuine meanness of it, and publish its meanness to the world; or if it were sublime, to know it by experience, and be able to give a true account of it.

Feeling that most people live hurried, complicated "lives of quiet desperation," "frittered away by detail," he urged them to simplify. Citing the case of an Indian craftsman whose baskets people would no longer buy, Thoreau set an example for poor students and for would-be artists, who fear being unable to make a living by their writing, painting, music, or sculpture. Believing that many people were enslaved too much by working at unfulfilling jobs to provide themselves with material objects, he showed that if they will do with less, they can find the freedom to pursue their heart's desire. Like Thomas Carlyle, the English Transcendentalist friend of Emerson, Thoreau urged people to lower their denominator—to enrich the spiritual quality of their lives by reducing their dependence on the material by choosing "the vantage point of what we should call voluntary poverty," for "a man is rich in proportion to the number of things which he can afford to let alone."

Walden functions on several levels. As autobiography, it resembles Walt Whitman's "Song of Myself" (1855), for like Whitman, Thoreau wrote, "I should not talk so much about myself if there were anybody else whom I knew so well." Leon Edel places *Walden* among the literature of imaginary voyages. On the autobiographical and documentary level, it has affinities with Robinson Crusoe's solitary and self-reliant life on his island; its documentary detail also resembles Herman Melville's accounts of South Seas culture and of whaling, while on another level, it is like the voyage of the *Pequod* in his *Moby-Dick* (1851) as a quest for ultimate spiritual reality. Emerson complained of Thoreau's fondness for leading huckleberry parties, and as a "drop-out" from "this chopping sea of civilized life," Thoreau resembles Huckleberry Finn fleeing from "sivilization," the Walden cabin and Huck's raft both symbolizing freedom from conformity. As a work of social criticism, *Wal-*

den challenges the abuses of capitalist materialism, for Thoreau observes that wage slaves such as the Fitchburg railroad workers laboring sixteen hours a day in poverty have no freedom to develop the artistic and spiritual side of their lives. Full of close observation of the seasons, of flora and fauna, *Walden* is finally a testament to the renewing power of nature, to the need to respect and preserve the environment, to a belief that "in wildness is the salvation of the world"—a statement that has become a doctrine of the Sierra Club.

Thoreau never expected his readers to follow his example and live alone in a one-room hut. Such a life would make marriage difficult if not impossible (indeed, Thoreau remained a bachelor). He himself stayed at Walden only long enough to prove that his experiment could work, after which he returned to Concord. In some ways, *Walden* is misleading. In form, it consists of eighteen essays loosely connected, in which Thoreau condenses his twenty-six-month sojourn at Walden into the seasons of a single year. In addition, he draws upon experiences there before and after his residence at the pond. Thoreau was not as solitary, austere, or remote as *Walden* suggests. Walden was not a wilderness, nor was Thoreau a pioneer; his hut was within two miles of town, and while at Walden, he made almost daily visits to Concord and to his family, dined out often, had frequent visitors, and went off on excursions. Thoreau did not expect his readers literally to follow his example but to find applications to their own lives so that they can live more freely and intensely, with their eyes and ears more keenly attuned to the world around them, whatever it may be, and with their spirit closer to the life force behind nature.

CIVIL DISOBEDIENCE

First published: 1849
Type of work: Essay

When a law is unjust, it is the just person's duty to refuse to obey it.

Thoreau wrote "Civil Disobedience," first entitled "Resistance to Civil Government" when it was published in the periodical *Aesthetic Papers*, in response to questions about why he had gone to jail. As an abolitionist, he had objected to the Massachusetts poll tax and refused to pay it as a protest against slavery. When the Mexican War broke out in 1846, he protested against it as an aggressive war of conquest aimed in part at adding new slave territories to the nation, and for this reason as well, he refused to pay the tax. For several years, the authorities ignored Thoreau's nonpayment, but in July of 1846, Concord constable Sam Staples ordered Thoreau to pay up; when he still failed to comply, Staples arrested him on July 23 or 24 and imprisoned him in the Middlesex County jail. That evening some unknown person paid Thoreau's fine, but Staples kept Thoreau in jail until after breakfast and then released him. Emerson called Thoreau's action "mean and skulking, and in bad taste," and there is an apochryphal story that Emerson, visiting Thoreau in prison, asked, "Henry David, what are you doing in there?" to which he replied, "Ralph Waldo, what are you doing out there?" Bronson Alcott, however, called Thoreau a good example of "dignified noncompliance with the injunction of civil powers."

In the essay, Thoreau argues that laws, being manmade, are not infallible, that there is a higher divine law, and that when those laws conflict, one must obey the higher law. Hence slavery, no matter how legal (and it remained legal until 1865), was always unjust in its violation of the integrity and divine soul of the enslaved. So long as the American government upheld slavery, Thoreau said, one "cannot without disgrace be associated with it. I cannot for an instant recognize that political organization as my government which is the slave's government also." Carrying to extreme the logic of the Declaration of Independence, Thoreau argues in effect that each individual should declare independence from unjust laws, that citizens must never surrender their conscience to the legislator, and that "[i]t is not desirable to cultivate a respect for the law, so much as for the right." Most people, he feared, served the state as soldiers do, like unthinking machines.

He does not, however, argue for violent revolution; he advocates nonviolent resistance. (Later, Thoreau contradicted himself in three essays championing John Brown, who endorsed and practiced violence.) The disobedient must be prepared to accept punishment if necessary: "Under a government which imprisons any unjustly, the true place for a just man is also a prison." Thoreau concludes:

> The authority of government . . . must have the sanction and consent of the governed. It can have no pure right over my person and property but what I conceded to it. . . . There will never be a really free and enlightened State until the State comes to recognize the individual as a higher and independent power, from which all its own power and authority are derived, and treats him accordingly.

This doctrine has always been repellent to authoritarians of the far right and left, who tolerate no dissent and have had protesters beaten, imprisoned, and even killed. In the seventeenth century, Governor John Winthrop of the Massachusetts Bay Colony reproved his constituents for daring to criticize him, calling them naturally depraved and maintaining that the authorities are instituted by God and that to criticize them constitutes treason and atheism. In *Billy Budd* (1924), Herman Melville satirically presented the authoritarian military point of view when Captain Vere insists that those in uniform must obey without question: "We fight at command. If our judgments approve the war, that is but coincidence. . . . For that law and the rigour of it, we are not responsible. Our vowed responsibility is in this: That however pitilessly that law may operate, we nevertheless adhere to it and administer it." Vere's is the defense of all war criminals—that they were only carrying out orders and cannot be expected to disobey. The rationale behind war crimes trials, however, is that even the military are subject to a higher law.

Civil disobedience is at least as old as Socrates, who preferred to die rather than yield to an order to stop asking questions that embarrassed the authorities, to whom he said, "I shall obey God, rather than you." The Christian martyrs who refused to deny their God and worship Caligula, Nero, or some other depraved Roman emperor were practicing civil disobedience. All abolitionists, members of the Underground Railroad, and those who refused to obey the Fugitive Slave Act were practicing civil disobedience, as was Huckleberry Finn when he resolved to defy his upbringing and "go to hell" to rescue his best friend, a runaway slave. History and literature are full of examples. Gandhi was an admirer of Thoreau and adopted his policy of nonviolent resistance to oppose racism in Africa and imperialism in India. In turn, Dr. Martin Luther King took nonviolent resistance from Gandhi.

In fact, the United States government's system of checks and balances sometimes requires its citizens to break the law, for the only way to challenge the constitutionality of an unjust law is to break it and get a test case, as Dr. King and his followers repeatedly did. Dr. King was frequently imprisoned and called a criminal for violating local laws that instituted racial discrimination, but he believed in the higher law of the Constitution and wrote, "Words cannot express the exultation felt by the individual as he finds himself, with hundreds of his fellows, behind prison bars for a cause he knows is just." During the Vietnam War, an increasingly large number of people protested that the war was unjust, and many of draft age refused to serve in the armed forces and went to prison or into exile rather than be forced to kill or be killed in Vietnam. The government's position was that they were cowards or traitors, but a majority of the population came to agree with the protesters.

One problem with Thoreau's doctrine is that it is not always easy to determine whether a law is just or unjust. Thoreau never intended the indiscriminate breaking of laws; civil disobedience applies only in cases of fundamental moral principle. Not all individuals are necessarily right in defying the government. For example, during the Civil Rights movement of the 1960's, some Southern governors defied court orders, arguing instead that segregation was the will of God. Frequently it is liberals who endorse civil disobedience, but in the late 1980's, members of the conservative Iran-Contra conspiracy defended their breaking of laws and lying to Congress on the grounds that they were serving a higher law. Similarly, opponents of abortion have argued that a higher law requires them to break laws that prohibit them from harassing proponents of abortion. Thus the debate continues; through it all, Thoreau's essay remains one of the most potent and influential ever written.

JOURNAL

First published: 1906
Type of work: Journal

For twenty-four years, Thoreau recorded his thoughts and observations in his private journal.

From October 22, 1837, when he was twenty years old, until November 3, 1861, when he was suffering his fatal illness, Thoreau kept a journal. Biographer Walter

Harding considers it "his major literary accomplishment," though its length of nearly 2 million words, fourteen volumes, and more than seven thousand printed pages makes it less accessible to the reader than *Walden* and the other shorter works that Thoreau polished for publication. A fifteenth lost volume was discovered and published in 1958. Leon Edel, who values the journal less than Harding does, calls it "discursive, sprawling, discontinuous" and complains that it is "aloof" and impersonal, with too much matter-of-factness and too little humor and feeling.

Much of the journal consists of his reflections on nature during his daily walks and comments on his reading. In it, Thoreau often considers the problem of writing and revision as well as his observations of nature and of his neighbors in and around Concord. In his published writings, Thoreau often seems more solitary than he really was, and it is the journal that comments on his friends, his activities in Concord, and the considerable variety of people he encountered and talked with on his daily walks or who visited him at Walden. From the journal, Thoreau mined much of the material for his lectures and the writings published during his lifetime. To it he confided many of his most intimate thoughts. As he put it, "From all the points of the compass, from the earth beneath and the heavens above, have come these inspirations and been entered duly in the order of their arrival in the journal. Thereafter, when the time arrived, they were winnowed into lectures, and again, in due time, from lectures into essays." Some of his excursions never made it into essays and are recounted only in the journal, which is invaluable as autobiography and as a supplement to the works that he prepared for publication. Readers reluctant to plow through all fifteen volumes might instead took at *The Heart of Thoreau's Journal*, edited by Odell Shepard in 1927, or at *Men of Concord*, edited from the journal by F. H. Allen in 1936 and illustrated by N. C. Wyeth.

Summary

Attacked by hostile critics such as James Russell Lowell for his nonconformity, Thoreau in some ways anticipated what came to be called the "counterculture." Despite his criticism of a materialistic society, he did not "propose to write an ode to dejection, but to brag as lustily as chanticleer in the morning, standing on his roost, if only to wake my neighbors up" to the Transcendental belief that they can elevate themselves to a fuller, simpler, more intense life. America's greatest nature writer, Thoreau is a forefather of John Muir, Edward Abbey, and Aldo Leopold. Politically, he influenced William Morris and leaders of the British labor movement in the late nineteenth century. Leo Tolstoy called *Walden* one of the great books, and Robert Frost wrote that it "surpasses everything we have in America." Frank Lloyd Wright spoke of its positive impact on American architecture, and President John F. Kennedy spoke of "Thoreau's pervasive and universal influence on social thinking and political action." Thoreau unquestionably wrote one of the indispensable classics of American literature.

Bibliography

Cavell, Stanley. *The Senses of "Walden."* New York: Viking Press, 1972.

Cook, Reginald L. *Passage to "Walden."* Boston: Houghton Mifflin, 1949.

Harding, Walter. *The Days of Henry Thoreau*. New York: Alfred A. Knopf, 1966.

Harding, Walter, and Michael Meyer. *The New Thoreau Handbook*. New York: New York University Press, 1980.

Krutch, Joseph Wood. *Henry David Thoreau*. New York: William Sloane, 1948.

Shanley, James Lyndon. *The Making of "Walden."* Chicago: University of Chicago Press, 1957.

Robert E. Morsberger

MARK TWAIN

Born: Florida, Missouri
November 30, 1835
Died: Redding, Connecticut
April 21, 1910

Principal Literary Achievement

Twain is considered one of America's greatest novelists and one of the world's greatest writers of juvenile and comic literature.

Biography

Mark Twain was born Samuel Langhorne Clemens in Florida, Missouri, on November 30, 1835. His father and mother both came from old Virginia families. His father was trained as a lawyer; somewhat feckless and unsuccessful in business, he moved slowly westward, involving himself in land speculation. In 1839, the family had reached Hannibal, Missouri, a small town on the Mississippi River not far from St. Louis, and it was here that Twain spent his early childhood and developed his love of the great river. His father died when Twain was twelve years old, and he left school to learn the trade of printing, which his brother had entered before him. He spent several years as a roving journeyman printer, working as far east as New York City, but in 1857, he was taken on by Horace Bixby, who trained him as a Mississippi riverboat pilot, a trade he practiced until the Civil War. He spent a short time in a Confederate volunteer unit, but left it after a few months. The war wrecked the Mississippi River traffic, so in 1862 he joined his brother, Orion, in Carson City, Nevada, where his brother had a government job. He drifted into silver mining and eventually back to journalism with the Virginia City *Territorial Enterprise*. It was in 1862 that he first adopted the pen name Mark Twain. Later, he was in newspaper work in San Francisco, where his work as a writer of short sketches and stories was encouraged by Bret Harte.

He was developing a minor reputation as a humorist and lecturer in the mid-1860's, but it was the publication of "The Celebrated Jumping Frog of Calaveras County" in 1865 in the New York *Saturday Press* that brought country-wide attention. He had a further success with a series of comic articles about a trip to Hawaii, commissioned by the Sacramento *Union* in 1866, and from then on he was able to make a living on the lecture circuit. The first major work to come out of this was *The Innocents Abroad* (1869), which was received with considerable praise, tem-

pered by some criticism of his Western lack of polish and discretion. His experience as a Mississippi pilot and his wandering life as a printer, writer, and jack-of-all-trades gave him the raw material for a successful career as a writer and a lecturer; in 1870, he was able to marry Olive Langdon of Elmira, New York, the daughter of a respected member of the Eastern establishment. In 1870, he became joint owner and editor of the Buffalo, New York, newspaper the *Express*, but two years later he sold his interest, having lost a considerable amount of money in the project. He withdrew from newspaper work to Hartford, Connecticut, where he was to spend the rest of his life and where he settled seriously into his career as a novelist. Some critics have suggested that this entrance into genteel social life affected the power of his work, but it is after this date that *The Adventures of Tom Sawyer* (1876), *The Adventures of Huckleberry Finn* (1884), and, indeed, all of his major novels were to be written.

He was never to forget his past, and his greatest book, *The Adventures of Huckleberry Finn*, and his greatest nonfiction work, *Life on the Mississippi* (1883), are directly related to the time and place of his early experiences as a child and a young man. However long he remained away from the Midwest, he was never to lose his allegiance to it, and the somewhat rough-cast quality of his humor, which is often seen as an integral part of his literary gift, has a rural, Western tang to it which no amount of New England gentility could ever expunge.

It is probably fair to say that his best work was done by the end of the 1880's. Certainly it is true that his work after that time becomes much more pessimistic, and the publications of the 1890's are his least read, and certainly least popular, titles, although he continued to write into the new century. The reasons for the change from comic happiness to work of misanthropic gloom are complicated. There were always occasional moments of cruelty in his work from the beginning, and he could be satirically sharp, as he showed as early as *The Innocents Abroad*. There clearly is a quantitative increase in human stupidity and violence from work to work through the period prior to 1890. *A Connecticut Yankee in King Arthur's Court*, published in 1889, if still ripe with the richness of invention that was one of his gifts, is a much more violent book than anything he had produced previously, and it rejects the happy ending of many of his early novels. So the tendency was there, and the works leading through the period between the late 1860's to the beginning of the 1890's show as interesting pattern of slowly increasing seriousness and pessimism.

In the 1890's, his life outside literature added to the problem. He lost a large amount of money early in the decade in a business proposition. His own health began to fail, and the ill health and eventual deaths of his two daughters and his wife plunged him into unmitigated sorrow through the 1890's and into the early years of the twentieth century. The literature produced in this period clearly reflects not only his increasing pessimism as he grew older but also the unimpeded run of bad luck and personal sorrow which he experienced up to his own death in 1910. This is the Twain known in the main to the critics; it does not detract from his reputation as one of the great comic writers or from his reputation as the writer of, perhaps, the best book ever written about the joys of being a young boy, free at last on the great river.

Twain did, however, write a considerable amount of material during the 1890's. His financial difficulties hardly allowed him to stop working, and he spent a lot of time both in America and internationally on the lecture circuit, amusing audiences. *Following the Equator* (1897) reveals his feelings about the experience of appearing publicly as the smiling, professional humorist at a time when his personal life was so unhappy. The book that is best known from this period is *The Tragedy of Pudd'n-head Wilson* (1894), and it carries the stamp of his deepening pessimism. He wrote a further handful of books, continuing to publish into the twentieth century, but the gloom was undiminished in all of his later work. He died in 1910, having lost his wife in 1904, as something of an enigma, a man of sometimes fierce misanthropic impulses who had begun his career as the sunniest of men.

Analysis

Mark Twain's general reputation as one of the most admired, and possibly the most beloved, writer in America is based, in the main, upon the work he published before 1890. After that time, the work takes on a much darker hue. *The Tragedy of Pudd'nhead Wilson*, published in 1894, though still a book of some comic mishap, marks the obvious pessimism that was to pervade his work until his death. Indeed, some materials left unpublished during his lifetime, such as *The Mysterious Stranger*, published posthumously in 1916, bear very little resemblance to the sunny idealization of *The Adventures of Tom Sawyer*.

He was, however, always more than simply a comic entertainer, and it should be remembered that as early as *The Innocents Abroad*, he responds to human error, on occasion, with quick satiric thrusts that remind one of eighteenth century English satirist Jonathan Swift. *The Adventures of Tom Sawyer* is reasonably free from such tonal darkening, but *The Adventures of Huckleberry Finn* certainly is not, and in order to appreciate fully the greatness of that novel, it is necessary to go beyond a sense of triumph in Huck's conversion to an outright defender of Jim to an under-standing of the kind of world which threatens both the slave and the boy. The confi-dence men, completely insensitive to the pain they cause, may be an obvious example of Twain's sense of evil in the world, but that does not circumscribe the way in which he suggests that human cruelty is gratuitously omnipresent—not simply among the rogues, but in the center of society. Jim's greatest enemy is a spinster woman of scrupulous moral and religious credentials, simply because he is black.

In *The Prince and the Pauper* (1881) and *A Connecticut Yankee in King Arthur's Court*, which start out looking like amiable fairy tales, cruel acts of physical vio-lence are dwelt upon in detail and go far beyond the ignorant "horseplay" of the rural citizens who simply do not know any better in his earlier works. It is, there-fore, unwise to simplify the tonal range of his work. If he is most often seen as a humorist, and often as a romantic, especially about boys and life on the Mississippi, he is often more than that; in *The Adventures of Huckleberry Finn*, his best work, tonal and intellectual range is very wide indeed, leaning strongly toward serious concern about human conduct. There are ideas in that novel that Twain wants to disturb his readers quite as much as they bother Huck. Perhaps an ambition to become a writer of ideas was there from the start.

In his early work he seemed to touch the core of late nineteenth century popular humor, giving Americans what they felt was the best part of their character in stories of good-natured, slightly skeptical, occasionally vulgar trickery. Twain had an eye for hypocrisy, self-interest, and pomposity, however, and his main characters, if sometimes less clever than he himself was, could not be fooled for long, even if they could be misled initially out of innocence. He certainly could have played it safe and been satisfied with a minor, lucrative career as a funnyman, but *The Innocents Abroad* showed that he could sustain a larger literary shape and, more important, that he had some things to say about human nature which could not be satisfied in the short comic story.

The other, perhaps greater, gift, was to show up in *The Adventures of Tom Sawyer*, where Twain emerges fully formed as a writer of children's fiction. The success of that work might have satisfied a lesser man and led him into a long career of repetition of the same kind of sweet-natured appreciations of childhood. *The Prince and the Pauper* looks by its title to be in that pattern, but it is loaded with comment about human stupidity and cruelty.

The Adventures of Huckleberry Finn, finally out in 1884, shows a further refinement and has been recognized not simply as one of the finest juvenile novels, not simply as a book of social comment, but as one of the greatest books of American fiction. He was never to write a better book, but he did not rest with it. *A Connecticut Yankee in King Arthur's Court* was to show that he had not abandoned his ambition to write the novel of ideas, opposing old English inequities against the ideals and practices of a nineteenth century American and giving himself the opportunity to create political theory.

What has to be recognized in Twain's work, beyond the singular success of *The Adventures of Huckleberry Finn*, is his range—not only in his richness of fictional embellishment, but also in his way of using material to make moral points with very little preaching. He can be, on too many occasions, a bit heavy-handed (surprisingly enough, when he is being funny), and the late twentieth century sensibility may find him a bit ponderous, even "corny." He can, however, be very sly and very smart. Sometimes the ideas get out in front of the fiction; this is often the case when he lets himself be personally moved by the subject. Yet he possesses a lively, quicksilver way of moving in and out of moral problems without much preaching, and he usually keeps the tale in the forefront of the work written before the dark days of the 1890's.

THE CELEBRATED JUMPING FROG OF CALAVERAS COUNTY

First published: 1865
Type of work: Short story

Jim Smiley, an obsessive gambler, meets his match when he bets that his trained frog, Dan'l Webster, can outjump any other frog in a Northern California mining area, Calaveras County.

Mark Twain, who had made his living as a Mississippi riverboat pilot before the Civil War and had gone on to be a printer, a journalist, and a sometime prospector, could hardly have imagined that his comic tale "The Celebrated Jumping Frog of Calaveras County," which appeared originally under the more modest title "Jim Smiley and His Jumping Frog," was to change his life forever and establish him in a career which was to lead to him becoming one of America's greatest writers.

Certainly the tale itself is moderately amusing, but it seemed to catch the imagination of the American reader, and Twain was to follow it up with equally artful stories and lecture tours which were to make him well-known some time before the artistic success of *The Adventures of Tom Sawyer* and *The Adventures of Huckleberry Finn*. Part of the reason for the success of the story lies in its moderation, its seeming lack of artfulness. Good-natured, garrulous old Simon Wheeler tells the story to the unsuspecting Mark Twain, who is, in fact, trying to find out about an entirely different man, the Reverend Leonidas W. Smiley. What he gets is a rambling, disjointed, ungrammatical tale of Jim Smiley, who sometime back in 1849 or 1850, had provided the locals with entertainment with his antics as a gambler.

Style is a strong element in the power of the tale. Twain sets himself up as the straight man for the dead-panned raconteur, who, once he gets started is impossible to stop, and Twain (the character) provides part of the amusement in his indignation; his letter to A. Ward (which is the exterior framing device for the story) is a complaint to the effect that Ward (probably Artemus Ward, who was himself a popular humorist) had deliberately misled Twain, knowing that the surname "Smiley" would trigger the long reminiscence in Wheeler. The style of the first paragraph of the letter has a kind of prim formality about it, and the sophisticated facility of an educated writer barely able to suppress his grudging suspicion that he has been made the fool. This style of fastidious restraint continues, but when Wheeler begins to speak, the prose relaxes into a homey, genial vulgarity and sly wit which immediately establishes the old man as a master teller of tall tales. Whether the story is true hardly matters; its real power lies in the telling. The way in which the "fifteen-minute nag" fumbles her way to the finish line and the look that Andrew Jackson, the bull-pup, gives to Smiley after the defeat by a dog without hind legs are examples of how skilled Twain was in writing cleverly without seeming to be writing at all.

He shows equal skill in the dialogue between Smiley and his supposed victim. The repetitions, the grammatical errors, the misspellings to indicate accent, and the wary rejoinders have a seamlessness about them which gives them an air of authenticity, of improvisational vivacity, which is part of Twain's charm as a comic writer. The story's success lies in Twain's ability to make it sound like the real thing: the loose-tongued babble of an old man who has caught another innocent fellow by the ear. Twain, the victim, twice-bitten (once by Ward and once by Smiley's narrator, Simon Wheeler), can only get away, if good-naturedly, by running for cover. The story's secret is not the trick it describes, but the structure and use of style.

Beyond its technical cleverness, however, the popularity of the story lay in large part in the fact that Twain refrains from patronizing his unlettered inhabitants of Calaveras County. Smiley may have been fooled this time, but he is usually the victor and is likely to rebound. His proposed victim is to be congratulated on his quickness of mind; Simon Wheeler may be a bit long-winded, but he tells a good story. If anyone is made to look the fool, it is Twain, the aggrieved letter writer, whose proper way with grammar has not made him any less susceptible to a harmless practical joke. The story's tone, in fact, is one of generosity and good nature. The joke is ultimately on Twain, and he takes it well.

It was this kind of happy tomfoolery in the early stories, with the acceptance of rural America as a place not without its own kind of bucolic silliness and occasional quick wit, which readers and audiences liked about the young writer and performer. The tougher, sharper Twain was yet to come.

THE INNOCENTS ABROAD

First published: 1869
Type of work: Travel literature

> Mark Twain accompanies a group of affluent Americans on a tour of Europe and the Near East and reports on the sights and sounds and the comic and satiric confrontations between the Old and the New Worlds.

It must have seemed a clever idea to send a popular young comic journalist on a tour with a boatload of prominent citizens in order to record, as *The Innocents Abroad* did, the day-to-day experience of Americans having a good time in the exotic old countries. When the book came out, however, the reaction was not entirely favorable. Twain had not only confirmed what every American already knew—that Europe was terribly run down and was greedy for the dollars of rich Americans—he also suggested that the Americans often made fools of themselves—and quite as often were downright vulgar, thereby confirming what Europeans already knew about America.

Obviously someone had misjudged Mark Twain when he was sent on the trip. His career as a literary figure was in its infancy, and he had yet to write a novel, but there was surely sufficient evidence in his newspaper work and in his short stories that he had a gift for satire that was barely controlled, and that he was not quite as refined in his literary conduct as might have been expected from an East Coast journalist. He was, in short, not always as fastidious in his work as might have been expected, and this book, certainly one of the funniest (and sometimes satirically savage) works in the travel genre was to offend at the same time that it added to his reputation as a writer of promise.

The book can also be seen as an interesting anticipation of a theme that Twain is to use over and over again: the confrontation between liberal, nineteenth century ideas of politics and society with the old, sometimes savage conservatism of the old world. The latter problem is to be used in *The Prince and the Pauper*, where the concern for humanity and for fair treatment of citizens is manifested in the conduct of both the prince and the pauper, but it becomes even more central in the later work *A Connecticut Yankee in King Arthur's Court*, in which a nineteenth century American finds himself in a position of power and attempts to put his ideas about society, politics, and commerce into action—with sometimes comic, but often dangerously disastrous, results.

Most obvious, and perhaps most enjoyable from an American point of view, are Twain's astringently funny comments upon the limitations of European civilization. He sees how quick the Europeans and the Near Eastern citizens are to take advantage of the Americans, who are open and generous in their curiosity. He has an amusing running joke about guides who may change throughout the tour but have a kind of obvious sameness in their determination to make a meal out of the Americans; they give very little in return, usually because they hardly have any idea what they are talking about. He is weakest, as he freely admits, in dealing with the art and architecture of the old countries, and he is often surprisingly insensitive, revealing himself as vulnerable to the charge that he is occasionally as stupidly stubborn as his fellow travelers. Yet that revelation gives the book a credibility which helps to keep it from becoming a tedious listing of constant complaint. It often breaks out into first-class description, particularly if Twain is moved by a scene, but its main line is that of slippery comic comment upon the discomfort of travel.

The Near East, in particular, fires the greatest enthusiasm in Twain, and some of the most pungent complaint, caused in part by the difficulties of travel in the barren landscape. The Christian history of that area is most interesting to Twain and his fellow travelers, but Twain, who usually maintains a pose of amused indifference, is enraged by the commercialization of the biblical sites. From early in the tour there is a line of anti-clerical comment which can become sharply splenetic, particularly if the Roman Catholic church is involved.

Twain's reaction to the tawdry, profit-making manipulation of the Christian mystery was enjoyed by his American readers, but he was not afraid to suggest that Americans on the road could also be less than admirable. He could be sharply disdainful of how his fellows flashed their money, their fractured French, and, particularly, their hammers, chipping away at any monument, however sacred, that might come under their hands. Much of this is funny, and that was expected of Twain, but it can involve a strong satiric bite; Twain can be irascible. He refuses to stay within the confines of the genial, romantic idea of what a travel book "should" be. He is often very good at showing what the foreign landscape looks like, but what really interests him is how human beings live and what the political, social, and physical implications are of the long histories of great civilizations, now less powerful and somewhat tattered and torn. Most to the point, he is fascinated by how people respond to tourists, how the experience seems to bring out the worst in both parties. He plays fair here, revealing that if the natives are often on the cheat, the Americans, acting thoughtlessly and sometimes stupidly, just as often deserved to be fleeced.

THE ADVENTURES OF TOM SAWYER

First published: 1876
Type of work: Novel

Tom Sawyer, the town's bad boy, experiences disapproval, love and hate, and imaginary and real adventure, and he ends up the town hero and a boy of property.

The Adventures of Huckleberry Finn is Twain's finest study of a boy's character and his best novel, but it is *The Adventures of Tom Sawyer* which is the more popular boy's tale with the public. Its simplicity, lack of psychological density, and single-minded celebration of the joys of childhood are the reasons for its attraction and the affection with which it is remembered by adults who have not read it for years and never intend to read it again. It is the American dream of ideal childhood written with unmitigated joy.

Much of its success lies with Tom, a child of lively curiosity with a mildly anarchic personality and an imagination fueled by reading (and often misreading) everything from fairy tales to the classics. He is also a boy capable of disarming affection. His relationship with Aunt Polly, swinging as it does between angry frustration and tears of loving joy, is one of the memorable child-adult confrontations in literature. For all of his strutting imitations of maleness, he has no inhibitions in his courting of Becky Thatcher. Twain has a rather crude way with feelings, but in Tom he found a character who acts out his emotions with a comic bravado that often saves the book from falling into sentimental excess.

The Tom Sawyer confidence tricks are part of the folklore of American life. The famous fence-painting game has developed a life of its own that goes beyond the novel, and Tom's systematic accumulation of those yellow tickets awarded for memorizing passages of the Bible leads to one of those lovely moments of exposure that fall regularly into Tom's life of precarious mischief. Beyond the individual incidents of comic chicanery, however, the novel has a strength which is often not noticed since it is carried on with such ease: It has a complicated plot that comes seemingly out of nowhere and increases in dramatic energy from its inception until the very end. The chance encounter of Tom and Huck which leads to the visit to the graveyard for the purpose of trying out a new method for curing warts leads them right into witnessing Injun Joe's murder of Doctor Robinson. Terrified by possessing a secret which they do not want, they vow to keep quiet, even after Muff Potter, a stupid, drunken companion of Injun Joe, is accused of the murder. Tom's failure at love when Becky finds out that he had another girlfriend, his depression over the murder, and his feeling that he can do nothing right lead him to run off with Huck, but only to a nearby island, and the boys are thought to have drowned. The tale becomes complicated further as Tom returns to his own funeral and manages to get away with his nonsense, but the murder still hangs fire. Add to that the trial, the hunt for the pirates' treasure, the discovery of Injun Joe, the picnic, Tom and Becky's misadventure in the cave, and the discovery of the hidden money, as well as the uproar that is caused in the town and the happy ending, and the reader has a deftly organized example of how adventure literature works at its very best.

At this stage in his career, Twain was most interested in telling the tale and in turning the simplicities of universal childhood play-acting into a tale of intrigue and heroism. What he never does, and this may be part of the secret of the novel's success, is expect Tom or his companions to do anything that might not be credible. Everything that happens is probable (if unlikely to happen). More to the point, Tom is not a morally perfect character. He is hardly the ideal child: He is superstitious, he is often ignorant, boastful, and devious, and he is slow to come to Muff Potter's defense. He does, eventually, do the right thing, however, even in the face of the fact that he is still terrified of Injun Joe. What Twain has brought into children's literature is the flawed, unfocused moral sensibility of the American boy who only wants to have fun, but who has in some mysterious way—through breeding, through education which he ignores and religion which he despises, through social contacts which he finds boring, and through a natural, if embryonic, fineness of character— the capacity ultimately to act with courage and firmness. Do not count on him being changed forever, however; one suspects that Tom is still susceptible to getting in and out of trouble for a long time to come.

The careful reader of *The Adventures of Tom Sawyer* will be able to watch the structure—the way Twain pulls the threads together; the way he puts on the dramatic pressure, then releases it, and puts it on again; the way seemingly separate occurrences come together in surprising ways and lead to the marvelous and dangerous discovery in the caves. Tom and Huck are rich boys, but they are not yet tamed, as Huck will prove in his own novel in which Tom once again spins a marvelous yarn of sheer comic trickery. The novel may have the requisite happy ending necessary in juvenile fiction, but here is a slight opening left—in Huck's reluctance to settle down—which will allow Twain to go on to a more ambitious fiction.

THE PRINCE AND THE PAUPER

First published: 1881
Type of work: Novel

In the last days of English monarch Henry VIII, a London beggar boy and the crown prince, Edward, change roles by chance, then attempt to undo the error.

In *The Prince and the Pauper*, Twain brought together several of his literary interests. His interest in old European civilization, which had begun so successfully in his travel book *The Innocents Abroad* and had been essayed again in *A Tramp Abroad* (1880), is here focused on England, with emphasis upon life in London. (He will come back again to the theme in *A Connecticut Yankee in King Arthur's Court*, which also returns to the idea of taking the novel back into the past.) The novel does not forget the part of his literary gift that is most celebrated: his interest in boys and how they cope in situations which are not without serious consequences. Twain also had wider ambitions for the novel, and he makes use of it to comment upon politics, social problems, and the relations between children and parents or, as often is the case in his books, surrogate parents.

The book is directly related to the fairy tale genre, and it starts simply enough with the unusual, but not impossible, idea that a London street urchin, who looks surprisingly like Prince Edward, is taken into the palace by the prince. They innocently change clothes and the prince goes off to chide the guard who had mistreated his new friend, only to be thrown out on to the street despite his claim that he is the prince. Then the real trouble starts, both for him and for Tom Canty, the beggar boy, for whom the danger is less physically obvious but potentially serious if he is discovered to be an imposter. Twain then begins an interleaved narrative of the adventures of the two boys, both determined to get back their identities. However much they protest, they fail to impress and are considered mad. Tom, sensing how precarious his situation is in the palace, goes about accumulating as much knowledge as he can about how he ought to act, hoping to wait out the absence of the prince. His task is complicated by the death of the king and the subsequent need for the prince to take a serious role in governing the country even before he is crowned. Pleased in part by the comforts of his position, he brings his native intelligence and his guile to bear on the problem, but he is determined eventually to clear the matter up.

The prince's situation is much more difficult. Tom's brutal father catches up with him and, mistaking him for Tom, proceeds to give him his daily beating. The prince is always less flexible than Tom, and he never admits to anyone that he is not the royal child; indeed, he is determined to play the ruler even in rags. Only the chance help of Miles Hendon, a gentleman-soldier home from the wars, protects him, and even Hendon has difficulty keeping the prince out of trouble. Hendon thinks he is mad, but he likes the boy and is prepared to be patient with him, hoping that in time, he will be drawn out of his madness by kindness.

Both boys, caught in radically different situations quite beyond their former experience, respond admirably, if the prince is always somewhat less agile in dealing with problems than Tom. All the obvious problems of rags and riches are displayed, sometimes with comic intent, but often with serious concern. Twain uses the switched identities for purposes beyond the study of character or comic confusion; Tom, champing at the boring nature of political duties (in a way that reminds one of Huck Finn's dislike of civilized life), is, nevertheless, aroused sufficiently to go beyond the pleasures of his position, and he begins to intrude upon the laws slowly, tempering their harshness, but doing so with a care which does not alarm his courtiers.

Edward, out in the country, confronted by the harshness and violence of common life, can do little to help the unfortunate, but his reactions to a world he did not know existed are as civilized in their own way as Tom's, and he is determined to do something about the lot of the common people, particularly the cruel penal laws, if he gets out of the mess alive—which is quite often shown as unlikely.

The parallels between the two, then, go beyond their physical resemblance. They are lively, strong-willed, imaginative boys who at the beginning of the novel are captives. Tom is terrorized by his criminal father; Edward, if in an obviously comfortable position, lives a sequestered life in the palace, dominated by the dying Henry VIII. Tom dreams of a life of royal power and plays that game with his mates in the slums, and he is given his chance. Edward is also given his chance to meet his subjects, sunk in the squalor of poverty, class privilege, and legal savagery. Both are freed of their fathers, one dying, the other disappearing into the criminal world forever, possibly also dead. What they do with their chance is central to the most serious themes in the book. What could have been simply a charming fairy tale becomes, as *The Adventures of Huckleberry Finn* is to become later, a study of boys becoming men.

LIFE ON THE MISSISSIPPI

First published: 1883
Type of work: Travel literature

A loosely organized, partly autobiographical story of Mississippi riverboat life before and after the Civil War.

Life on the Mississippi is Mark Twain's happiest book. Written early in his career, before the difficulties of his personal life had a chance to color his perception, and filled with reminiscent celebration of his time as a boy and man as an apprentice and as a Mississippi riverboat pilot, it is a lively, affectionate tribute hardly muted by the fact that the world of the romantic pilots of the Mississippi had disappeared forever during the American Civil War and the development of the railroads.

It is a great grab-bag of a book; it starts formally enough, with a sonorous history of the river that reveals how much Twain feels for the phenomenon of the Mississippi (which will appear again in *The Adventures of Huckleberry Finn*), but swiftly falls into rambling anecdotes, comic turns, and tall tales. It has, as is often the case in early Twain, a weakness for elephantine humor of the unsophisticated, Midwestern rural stripe, but the obvious happiness that marks the tonality of the book manages to keep it going despite its regular habit of floundering in bathos.

The book could well have descended into an amusing shambles had it not been used to tell the very long, detailed, and sometimes hilarious story of the riverboat pilots and of how Twain as a young boy wheedles his way onto the "Paul Jones," where Mr. Bixby, the pilot, agrees to teach him the Mississippi from New Orleans to St. Louis for five hundred dollars, which Twain is to pay him out of his first wages as a pilot. These passages are some of the best action writing done by Twain, and they anticipate the kind of exciting river narrative that is so important in *The Adventures of Huckleberry Finn*. Beyond the action, however, is Twain's ability to relate the minute-by-minute excitement of learning how to handle the great boats in their perilous journeys up and down a river that changed so rapidly, hour by hour, that charts were of no practical use; the pilots had to learn to read the river, night and day, with a sensitivity that was hidden behind the hard-drinking, tough-talking braggadocio of men who possessed a high skill, improvisatory intuition, and sheer nerve. Twain obviously fell in love with the river and with its pilots, and the whole book is a joyful exercise in telling it once and for all, since it had, at the time of printing, been lost forever. Mindful of this, Twain was determined to get it down in all its detail, and he follows the trade from its height, when the pilots were kings, through the battles to unionize as a defense against the owners, to the eventual falling away of the trade during the war period.

There is a kind of broken-backed structure to the work caused, in part, by the fact that chapters 4 to 17 originally appeared in *The Atlantic Monthly* in serial form; these, together with three further chapters, are concerned with Twain's career on the river. These were not sufficient to make a book, so the second half was added, with Twain, now the celebrity writer, touring the river and the cities along its banks. This later material is not all bad, but it has nothing like the dramatic focus or energy of the earlier chapters, and there is a feeling that Twain is sometimes at pains to pad it, despite the success of the anecdotes. The twenty-two years that separate the latter Twain from the early adventures of the boy Clemens take much of the immediacy out of the book, even when Twain tries to praise the improvements that engineering science has imposed on the river. There is a feeling that his heart is not really in it, and the latter half of the book has a melancholy air about it that Twain does not fully acknowledge, but which haunts the book's conclusion. Twain, the businessman, saw the profit; Clemens, the old pilot, saw the loss.

It could be argued, however, that there is a kind of structural propriety about the book, divided as it is between Twain's early life on the river and his return many years later to discover the changes not only to his beloved river but also to the Mississippi region in general. It is certainly true that this latter material best illustrates the function of the book as a travel document, since Twain catalogs the changes in the river and in the towns along its banks. The decades that had passed between the events of the first half and the second reveal how quickly Midwestern America was catching up with the East and how the village and town landscape was giving way to small cities.

THE ADVENTURES OF HUCKLEBERRY FINN

First published: 1884
Type of work: Novel

Huckleberry Finn, tired of well-meaning people trying to civilize him, takes to the Mississippi on a raft and discovers that he has a runaway slave along for the ride.

The Adventures of Huckleberry Finn may at first have seemed to Twain to be an obvious and easy sequel to *The Adventures of Tom Sawyer*, but this book, begun in the mid-1870's, then abandoned, then taken up again in 1880 and dropped again, was only ready to be published in 1884. It was worth the delay, since it proved to be Twain's finest novel—not merely his finest juvenile work, but his best fiction, and a book which has taken its place as one of the greatest novels written in the United States. In some ways it is a simpler novel than *The Adventures of Tom Sawyer*; it has nothing like the complication of plot which made that earlier novel so compelling. Huck, harassed by the Widow Douglas and her sister, Miss Watson, who only wanted to give him a good home and a place in normal society, and by his brutal father, who wants to get his hands on the money that Huck and Tom had found in *The Adventures of Tom Sawyer*, decides to get away from it all, and he runs away. This time, he does not have the tempering influence of Tom Sawyer, who was prepared to run away to a nearby island but could not resist going home for his own funeral. Tom is only an occasional renegade, eager for the romance, but not the long-term reality of rebellion. Huck is of tougher stuff, and he intends to go for good. No better indication of this is to be seen than in the simple fact that Tom tries to smoke but does not have the stomach for it; Huck does not play at it. He is a real smoker and a real rebel—or so he thinks.

Kidnapped by his father and held captive by him, he revels at least in the freedom of the barbaric world without soap, water, or school, but he manages to get away, leaving a trail which suggests that he has been murdered, and heads for an island in the Mississippi as a start on his attempt to get away from his father and from the well-meaning sisters who would turn him into a respectable citizen. He is on his way to leave all of his troubles behind him.

It is at this point that Twain adds the complication which is to be central to the ascent of this novel from juvenile fancy to the level of moral seriousness. Huck discovers that Jim, Miss Watson's Negro slave, has also run away, having overheard her plans to sell him to a Southern farmer, Jim, whose wife and children have already been separated from him and sold to a Southern owner, is determined to escape to the free Northern states, work as a free man, and eventually buy his family out of bondage. Huck is determined to help him but is also unnerved by his concern for Jim's owner. Jim is property before he is a man, and Huck is deeply troubled, surprisingly, by the thought that he is going to help Jim, not only because he sees it, in part, as a robbery, but more interestingly, because he sees his cooperation as a betrayal of his obligation to the white society of which he is a member. Huck, the renegade, has, despite himself, deeply ingrained commitments to the idea that white men are superior to Negroes, and for all his disdain for that society, he is strongly wedded to it. This is going to provide the psychological struggle for Huck throughout the novel. Even when the two move on, driven by the news that in the town a reward has been posted for Jim, accusing him of murdering Huck, Huck carries a strong sense of wrongdoing because he is helping Jim to escape—not from the murder charge, which can be easily refuted, but from his mistress, who clearly owns him and may do with him what she will.

Nevertheless, they set off on the raft, which is wedded archetypally to the Ulyssean ship and may be seen as the vehicle for Huck to find out who he is and what kind of man he is likely to become. The pattern is a common one in the history of fiction, and Twain weds it to another common structure, the picaresque, which has a long history in the novel, and in which the main characters, traveling through the country, encounter trials and tribulations that test their wits and ultimately their moral fiber. Twain tends to open this pattern up to include examples of human behavior that do not necessarily have any influence on Huck and Jim but rather that indicate Twain's pessimism about human nature in general. The Grangerford-Stephenson feud, for example, shows the kind of virulent stupidity that can obsess even relatively civilized human beings. The Duke and the King, however, who take Huck and Jim over and use them (and anyone else they can deceive) for profit without concern of any kind, reveal a much deeper strain of human degradation, which anticipates the inhumanity that is to become even more common in Twain's later works. Huck fears these men but is reluctant to make a clean break from them, though it is fair to remember that they watch him and Jim very closely. The ultimate betrayal comes when Huck, who has let their confidence games be played out in several communities, draws the line when they try to defraud a family of three daughters of their inheritance. The Duke and the King manage to escape without discovering that Huck has revealed their plan; not dismayed by their loss, they start their fraudulent games again, committing their most thoughtlessly cruel act by turning Jim in for the reward.

This is the point of no return for Huck. Jim—ignorant, superstitious, and timid, but loyal and devoted to Huck—has, on the long trip down the river, shown over and over that he is a man of considerable character, despite his color, and despite his disadvantaged life as a slave. Huck, in turn, discovers that however much he tries to distinguish Jim as other than an equal, however much he is bothered by his determination to see Jim as a lesser being than the white man, he cannot ignore his growing concern for him nor his deepening affection and respect for the way in which Jim endures and goes on. Disgusted by the unfeeling barbarity of the King and the Duke, Huck leaves them and sets out to free Jim.

Here the novel returns to the less dangerous world of Tom Sawyer, since it turns out that Jim's captors are, in fact, Tom Sawyer's aunt and uncle. Huck passes himself off as Tom in order to get to Jim, who is being kept in a farm outhouse. With the arrival of Tom himself, who passes himself off as his brother Sid, the fun begins, as Tom, as wildly romantic as ever, plots to free Jim the hardest way possible. From this moment on the novel can be said to fall away from the power that has been explored in Huck's battle to come to terms with his loyalties to society, to his own race, and, most important, to Jim. That battle has been won when Huck decides to save Jim. All works out well in the end. Huck and Tom admit their elaborate joke; Jim is found to have been freed by his mistress; and Aunt Sally, Tom's aunt, thinks she might have a try at settling Huck down. Huck has other ideas.

All this horseplay on the farm is irrelevant, if pleasingly so, to the real strength of the novel, which lies in the journey down the mighty Mississippi on which Huck Finn learns to care for someone, and perhaps more important, throws off that least valuable influence of society upon him: its belief that white men are superior to black men and have a right to treat them as property. Huck, in a sense, comes to the end of this novel as the most civilized white man of all.

A CONNECTICUT YANKEE IN KING ARTHUR'S COURT

First published: 1889
Type of work: Novel

A nineteenth century Yankee foundry superintendent, hit over the head with a crowbar, wakes up in King Arthur's Camelot and promptly decides to bring ancient England up to date.

A Connecticut Yankee in King Arthur's Court can be seen as looking both backward and forward in the career of Mark Twain. It is a further version of the historical fantasy that he used in *The Prince and the Pauper*, in which the commonly accepted inhumanities of late medieval life were exposed to civilized, liberal ideas which were not to have much support for some centuries to come. It also looks forward to the bleaker, more deeply pessimistic work which was to be so common in the Twain canon in the 1890's. Some of that savagery had been shown in *The Prince and the Pauper*, but in this book there is a predominating line of outright cruelty.

Surprisingly enough, Twain's hero, Hank Morgan, the enlightened nineteenth century man of science and democracy, is not without a tendency to violence; he may be on the right side, but he is no romantic. He does not intrude on the gratuitous cruelty of King Arthur's world unless he can do so safely, and he is often inclined to make his way with force in ways which would make any nineteenth century reader somewhat cautious about praising him. This change from the hero or heroes of reasonably romantic character is a mark of the darkening nature of Twain's artistic sensibility, and it is a long way from the fairly minor misconduct of a Tom Sawyer or a Huck Finn. Hank Morgan may want to civilize a vicious, savage, ignorant popu- lace, but he has in himself disturbing inclinations to what, in the twentieth century, would be recognized as a fascist zeal for power, if strongly tempered by his desire to bring an entire civilization out of the Dark Ages and into the nineteenth century in one lifetime.

In his previous work with the idea of confronting the modern sensibility with the ignorance of the past (which begins with his nonfiction account of Americans on tour in Europe in *The Innocents Abroad* and continues in *The Prince and the Pauper*), there was still room for the comic and the satiric to operate, although the latter book had a serious tonality. This book, however, is almost completely bereft of comic effects, and its satire has a hectoring shrillness which suggests that Twain no longer finds the idea of human frailty—however fictional or, at least, long since dead and buried it may be—amusing. It is a very dark book and one which, signifi- cantly, does not have the happy ending which draws *The Prince and the Pauper* back into the fairy tale genre with a kind of Dickensian sweetness, with the villains pun- ished and the good people living happily ever after. No such resolution is available in *A Connecticut Yankee in King Arthur's Court*, which ends in destruction of the dream.

Along the way, however, Twain's abundant imagination is used with great skill, not only to tell an interesting tale but also to provide him with the opportunity to make his points about superstition, religion, and politics with an earnestness which constantly forces the reader to realize that this is not simply an excursion into fancy: The structure of fantasy is used to make serious comments upon man's stupidity, and particularly upon his stubborn refusal to learn, his timidity, and his tendency to respond to authority with sheeplike devotion. Hank Morgan is not simply trying to get through an unfamiliar situation with some vestige of moral integrity intact, as was often the case with previous Twain characters, including Huck Finn. He sees this accident as a chance to anticipate history, to eliminate hundreds of years of pain and suffering, and to bring Camelot kicking and screaming (as it surely does) into the enlightened nineteenth century.

The richness of incident, particularly the various ways in which Hank Morgan ad- justs the scientific knowledge he possesses to the limited resources of the Arthurian times, manages to rise above the gloom of the novel, and the battle between Morgan and Merlin has a kind of comic energy that is expected in Twain's work. How his baby comes to be called "Hello, Central" reminds readers of his earlier, happier works. The center of the novel is not in the fantasy, the trickery, or the adventures, however; it lies in Hank Morgan's character. Just as *The Adventures of Huckleberry Finn* ultimately finds its real quality in the development of Huck's personal set of moral standards, this novel gets its strength from Hank Morgan—at first bemused, then outraged, then seizing and working his way through to the dream. In the battle to civilize, Twain is able to make Morgan his mouthpiece for his own concerns about society, sometimes without breaching Morgan's character, although the shrill, repetitive attack upon the clergy sometimes is more didactic than artistically appropriate. It is, however, another example of the way Twain makes obviously simple literary forms work in more than one way, and it possesses tonal range which, if sometimes excessive, indicates how ambitious and daring he can be. This book may have a title suitable for a child's bookshelf, but the book is a rough and powerful attack upon human nature, ancient and modern.

Summary

Mark Twain showed that literary art of international reputation could be made from the simplicities of rural American life and that the comic representation of that life did not necessarily have to patronize the actions and ideas of simple people trying to lead decent lives in a country still physically and intellectually unformed. He made Americans proud of his celebration of childhood innocence and childhood character and aware of the physical beauty and the psychological greatness of its Midwestern landscape.

He also showed that a comic writer need not eschew serious ideas and that the imagination of a writer of adventure literature could be used to consider serious human themes.

Bibliography

Anderson, Frederick, ed. *Mark Twain: The Critical Heritage.* New York: Barnes & Noble Books, 1971.

Bellamy, Gladys Carmen. *Mark Twain as Literary Artist.* Norman: University of Oklahoma Press, 1950.

Gibson, William M. *The Art of Mark Twain.* Oxford, England: Oxford University Press, 1976.

Smith, Henry Nash, ed. *Mark Twain: A Collection of Critical Essays.* Englewood Cliffs, N.J.: Prentice-Hall, 1968.

Stone, Albert E. *The Innocent Eye: Childhood in Mark Twain's Imagination.* New Haven, Conn.: Yale University Press, 1961.

Wagenknecht, Edward. *Mark Twain: The Man and His Work.* Norman: University of Oklahoma Press, 1967.

Charles H. Pullen

ANNE TYLER

Born: Minneapolis, Minnesota
October 25, 1941

Principal Literary Achievement
Tyler is admired for her skillful, sympathetic creations of extraordinary characters who courageously fight the wars of everyday existence.

Biography

Anne Tyler was born in Minneapolis, Minnesota, on October 25, 1941, the oldest child and only daughter of Lloyd Parry Tyler, a chemist, and Phyllis Mahon Tyler, a social worker, who later became the parents of three boys. During Anne's childhood, the family moved frequently, living in Quaker communes at various locations in the Midwest and the South and finally settling for five years in the mountains of North Carolina. As the oldest child and only girl in a large, active family, Anne Tyler recognized the feminine capacity for leadership, which is emphasized in many of her novels. Furthermore, both within the family and within the larger context of the commune, she became aware of the tension between two human needs—one for privacy, solitude, and personal freedom, the other for membership in a group, as a defense against indecision and loneliness. By nature, though warm and sympathetic, Tyler has defined herself as an extremely private person. Obviously, in her childhood, she became aware of the difficulties encountered by people such as herself when they are thrown into a group which demands that the primary allegiance be to the group rather than to the individual identity.

After she graduated at sixteen from a secondary school in Raleigh, Tyler entered Duke University, majoring in Russian. When she picked up the enrollment card for her freshman composition class, she became the first student of a new English teacher, Reynolds Price, who was himself only twenty-five but was already a promising novelist, experimenting with new ideas and new narrative techniques. Price recognized Tyler's talent and worked with her on her writing. The importance of this early tutelage, from a novelist whose *The Surface of Earth* (1975) would later be called by some critics one of the major American novels of the twentieth century, cannot be overestimated. Tyler, however, was not yet ready to commit herself to a writing career. Instead, although she continued to write, Tyler concentrated on her studies in Russian.

In 1961, after only three years, she graduated from Duke with a Phi Beta Kappa

key and moved to New York City, where she spent a year taking graduate courses in Russian at Columbia University. The following year she was back in North Carolina, where she had accepted a position as Russian bibliographer for the Duke University library.

In 1963, Tyler married Taghi Modarressi, a psychiatrist from Iran. While she was looking for a job in Montreal, Quebec, Canada, she wrote her first novel, *If Morning Ever Comes* (1964). Although critics found it unsatisfying as a whole, lacking in character and plot development, they did see evidence of considerable talent in the book, pointing out Tyler's comic gift and her effective handling of dialogue, both of which may well have derived from her reading of Eudora Welty, who, along with Reynolds Price, was a major influence on her work. Tyler's second book, *The Tin Can Tree* (1965), was much like the first—promising, interesting, but somehow unformed.

During her time in Montreal, Tyler held her last outside job, as assistant to the librarian at the McGill University Law Library in Montreal. In 1967, Tyler and her husband moved to Baltimore, Maryland, which was to be their permanent home and the setting of many of her works. At this time, she developed her highly disciplined work habits, dividing her time between writing and her family, which by now included two daughters.

With the publication of *A Slipping-Down Life* in 1970, it was clear that Anne Tyler had discovered how to combine realistic scenes into a novel whose complex characters would grow and change as the story progressed. This novel and *The Clock Winder*, which followed it in 1972, were praised by critics; however, it was not until the mid-1970's, when the best-selling authors Gail Godwin and John Updike publicly called attention to her works, that Tyler began to attract a large following. At the same time, her plots were developing the complexity which critics had found lacking in her early works. In *Celestial Navigation* (1974), Tyler skillfully moved from one point of view to another, interweaving the stories of half a dozen characters, all of whom were part of the novel's thematic pattern.

The steadily increasing importance of Tyler's works is indicated by the fact that *Morgan's Passing* (1980), her eighth and perhaps her bleakest novel, was nominated for the National Book Critics Circle award and the American Book Paperback Fiction Award and received the Janet Heidinger Kafka Prize. The novel which followed, *Dinner at the Homesick Restaurant* (1982), received the PEN/Faulkner Award for fiction and was nominated for the National Book Critics Circle fiction award, the American Book Award for fiction, and the 1983 Pulitzer Prize.

The works which followed, including *The Accidental Tourist* (1985) and *Breathing Lessons* (1988), have added to Tyler's reputation as well as to her general popularity. Her life still follows the pattern established in 1967; because she is an intensely private person, she does not teach, lecture, or make public appearances, and she prefers to avoid interviews, which she says have always been a disappointment to her. Instead, she spends her time with her family or with her writing. Her books, she believes, can speak better for her than any casual conversation.

Analysis

One reason that the works of Anne Tyler are so fascinating is that they are difficult to classify. Although she was born in Minnesota, has specialized in Russian,
and is married to an Iranian, Tyler herself is considered a Southern writer because
her works are set in the South—the early ones in North Carolina, where she spent
her adolescence and attended college, the later novels in Baltimore, Maryland, where
she has lived for more than two decades. Tyler does not fit the pattern of most
Southern writers, however, whose characters, often like the authors themselves, are
usually an integral part of rural communities where their families have lived for
generations. Although the sense of place is important in Tyler's novels, her emphasis is on the present. Instead of a rural home which a family has occupied for
generations, her locale is more likely to be a house in Baltimore—perhaps rented,
perhaps occupied for a generation.

Yet Tyler is certainly in the Southern tradition in that she emphasizes the importance of the community. For example, in her second novel, *The Tin Can Tree*, Tyler
traces the ways in which the accidental death of one young girl affects not only her
closest relatives but also the entire community in which she lived. The effect of the
tragedy on this large group of interrelated people is confined, however, to the present
and to the projected future; there is no conjecture as to patterns established in the
past, as is found in so much Southern fiction.

The protagonists in many Southern novels are interesting precisely because they
either refuse to accept community standards—rejecting racism, for example—or
because, like the lawyer Atticus Finch in Harper Lee's *To Kill a Mockingbird* (1960),
they represent the principles which the community professes but which, in practice,
it betrays. Tyler's protagonists are not members of the establishment who are either
rebels or idealists; they tend to be eccentrics who are in flight from their societies for
no particular reason other than the fact that they possess boundless energy and unre-
strained imaginations.

The energetic protagonist appears in a rather peculiar form in Tyler's first novel, *If
Morning Ever Comes*. At the beginning of the story, Ben Joe Hawkes is in law school
in New York City. Unfortunately, his imagination betrays him: he cannot forget the
household of women he has left behind in North Carolina, women he is sure cannot
manage without him. Desperately worried, Hawkes leaves law school and goes home.
There, when he finds that the women are all doing very well, he feels quite un-
necessary and falls into inertia. He apparently will have the energy to move on with
his own life only when he knows that a female is truly dependent on him. Fortunately, he finds an available sweetheart from his high school days and takes her to
New York with him, where one assumes he can now be dependent on her dependence.

By the time Tyler wrote *A Slipping-Down Life*, she had arrived at the peculiar
combination of imagination, rebellion, energy, and even frenzy that marks many of
her most interesting characters and often the protagonists in her later novels. Teenager Evie Decker loathes her school, her town, and her dull life. Her rebellion has

been shown by withdrawal: She has spent most of her life hiding in her own home, merely dreaming of escape. When she falls in love with a rock musician, however, she suddenly has considerable energy. One can only call it a kind of madness when she carves his name on her forehead, thus becoming a local celebrity. It is clear that Evie intends to follow her musician out of the community and into a more exciting world. If at the end of the story Evie is moving back to her old home instead of heading for Hollywood, it is only because the situation has changed. She has a new baby, and she now desires the security of living in a home she owns. Evidently she now has an outlet for her energy.

Energetic, imaginative characters such as Evie Decker never fit easily into a community which, like most groups of people, values the comfortable virtues of moderation, conformity, and predictability. In every human being, Tyler suggests, there are two conflicting human tendencies. On the one hand, there is the desire for attachment, which draws Evie first toward her rock musician and eventually back to her own house, and which pulls the protagonist of *The Accidental Tourist* toward his childhood home, where his sister and his brothers continue to live in a tight little unit. It brings both the law student of *If Morning Ever Comes* and the long-lost Caleb of *Searching for Caleb* (1976) back to the families with whom they never did feel particularly comfortable. On the other hand, there is also the need for privacy, for solitude, for possessing one's own soul, so strong in the author herself; it may drive one inward, like the artist recluse in *Celestial Navigation*, or outward into eccentric actions such as those of the protagonist in *Morgan's Passing*, who flees from his demanding, overwhelmingly female family into disguise and a fantasy world he can control.

Because her characters keep veering from one direction to the other as one, then another, of the two needs becomes dominant, and because sometimes, like Evie, her characters finally return to the same place where they began, Tyler's novels have been called unsatisfyingly circular in plot. In all except perhaps the first two novels, however, Tyler is so skilled in tracing the development of character that although the place may be the same, its inhabitants are clearly very different people. It is this emphasis on character which makes her readers ignore the fact that most of her incidents, though amazing and often amusing, are not earthshaking. When the protagonist of *Breathing Lessons* slams her newly repaired car into a Pepsi truck, or even when the protagonist of *Morgan's Passing* poses as a doctor and delivers a baby, the real interest lies in the motivations of some characters and the reactions of others. Thus, if Tyler's later novels are no longer accused of formlessness, it must be emphasized that their unity derives less from plotting than from the creation of compelling characters. Tyler's greatest achievement is her skill in deferring to those characters. As an author she effaces herself, moving among her characters and reproducing their thoughts and their conversations as they rush headlong toward self-discovery.

SEARCHING FOR CALEB

First published: 1975
Type of work: Novel

A ninety-three-year-old man determinedly seeks his half-brother, who disappeared sixty years before.

Searching for Caleb is unique among Tyler's novels in that it is a detective story. The first scene in the book takes place on a train from Baltimore to New York City, where Daniel Peck and his granddaughter, Justine Peck, hope to find some news of Daniel's half-brother Caleb Peck, who has been missing for sixty years. Caleb is finally found, thanks to a detective the family has hired; however, it is typical of Tyler's circuitous plotting that at the end of the story Caleb once again leaves the Peck family, with whom he had never been comfortable.

The conflict in *Searching for Caleb* is typical for an Anne Tyler novel. The community which demands conformity is the Peck family. As Duncan Peck, the black sheep of the family, says, the Pecks have dug a moat around themselves so that from their castle they can judge and disapprove of the rest of the world. From the time of their birth, Peck children are indoctrinated with rules of behavior. Pointing out to his cousin Justine Mayhew that she is wearing a hat only because it is a Peck practice, the observant Duncan lists all the family customs, such as wearing English riding boots and refusing to develop cavities, and all the family prejudices—against golf, plastic, and emotion, for example. So extensive a code can, like the moat that Duncan mentions, effectively keep non-Pecks at a distance.

It is Justine who develops most during the novel and who, therefore, should be considered the protagonist. Once she has accepted Duncan's view of the Pecks and, incidentally, married him, Justine becomes one of Tyler's energetic heroines, whose principle of life seems to be, "When in doubt, change." Since Duncan, too, is both imaginative and energetic, given to undertakings which begin with great promise and, unfortunately, soon bore him, thus ensuring their failure, it is perhaps as well that Justine can live the life of a gypsy, packing up the suitcases, giving away the cats, and moving on at a moment's notice.

Justine cannot completely forget her Peck upbringing, however, and near the end of the novel she almost succumbs. For her, Duncan offers to settle down, take a job in Baltimore, and live like the rest of the Pecks. Interestingly, it is not merely her love for him that changes Justine's original decision. It is also the feedback she gets from the Pecks, who seem less than enthusiastic about the possibility. Evidently, she discovers, the adult Pecks like to have one branch of the family living extravagant, colorful lives, just as the young Peck cousins had been delighted to have one of their number behaving like the outrageous Duncan. Both Caleb's second disappearance and Justine's arrangements for her family to travel with a carnival, then, are necessary for the existence of the fixed lives of the rest of the Pecks. In this exploration of her theme, Anne Tyler has illustrated the fact that in order for a community to remain healthy, there must be individuals who refuse to follow its rules; perhaps, too, if individuals are to know the joys of rebellion, there must be Pecks, providing rules for them to defy.

DINNER AT THE HOMESICK RESTAURANT

First published: 1982
Type of work: Novel

A dying woman looks back on her marriage and her stormy family life.

Dinner at the Homesick Restaurant begins with Pearl Cody Tull's deathbed reflections and ends with her funeral. Like *Searching for Caleb*, this novel revolves around an unconventional family in which the mother is a central figure. While the source of Justine's energy is that of her husband, whom she imitates and even exceeds, the source of Pearl's is her misery at having been unaccountably deserted by the husband whom she dearly loved. Pearl's excesses come not from joy in freedom but from anger because she is imprisoned in a life she did not choose.

At thirty, Pearl had been facing spinsterhood. Then she met a loud, brash salesman six years her junior who admired her ladylike behavior and had the power to persuade her that anything in the world was possible. Beck Tull and Pearl hastened into marriage. Eventually, they had three children. When the oldest was entering his teens, Beck disappeared, and it was then that Pearl became almost demented. Somehow she could never tell the children that Beck was never coming back. Trapped in her lie, overburdened by responsibility, and often financially desperate, she would suddenly be overcome by rage, striking out at the very children she had so desired and making much of their childhood a nightmare.

Because of their mother's peculiarities, the Tull children are isolated from the community; however, unlike the eccentric Pecks in *Searching for Caleb*, they cannot take delight in their own independence. Unfortunately, because no one ever explains to them either their father's absence or their mother's furies, they come to see life as dangerous and irrational, and as they grow to adulthood, in different ways they all try to find some kind of security.

The oldest child, Cody Tull, is particularly burdened. Convinced that one of his pranks must have caused his father to leave, Cody has a profound need to control his life so that no such event will ever occur again. His choice of profession is typical of Tyler, who even in tragic stories can amuse her readers with her imaginative but unfaltering logic: Cody becomes an efficiency expert. Unfortunately, he cannot organize his own emotions as well as he can structure a factory. Jealous of his brother's success with his own girlfriends, Cody marries a highly unsuitable girl simply because she is his brother's fiancée.

Jenny Tull, too, seeks the rationality which her childhood denied her. The highly intelligent and completely organized Harley Baines seems perfect for her; however, after she marries Harley, Jenny discovers that his most well-developed faculty is the critical one, and she finds herself constantly under fire. Clearly, she had looked for intellect in a partner when she should have emphasized commitment. Through her pediatric practice, she meets a desperate widower with children of his own, and the household they set up together, though as hectic and unpredictable as that of her childhood, is extremely happy because it is founded on love, not on anger.

It is Ezra Tull, however, the middle child and his mother's favorite, whose dreams of a harmonious family life are reflected in the book title. After Ezra becomes the owner of a restaurant where he has long been working, he changes its image and its name. "The Homesick Restaurant" is intended to cater to everyone who, like Ezra, associates food with the security of a loving family. Ironically, every time Ezra brings the family together for a fine meal, they quarrel and someone walks out. The only meal which is ever completed is the funeral feast after Pearl's funeral, when the missing Beck Tull, who had stormed out, consents to return and finish his meal with the family he had deserted.

The excuse Beck gives for his action, which caused so much pain to four people, is that Pearl could see his faults and he could not bear it. Although Tyler will never glorify conformity for its own sake, in *Dinner at the Homesick Restaurant* she makes it clear that unloving, irresponsible egotism such as Beck's cannot be justified, whatever the claims of the individual.

THE ACCIDENTAL TOURIST

First published: 1985
Type of work: Novel

A travel writer who hates to travel learns to accept the unexpected and in the process takes control of his own life.

Of all Anne Tyler's characters, Macon Leary, the protagonist of *The Accidental Tourist*, is undoubtedly the one most obsessed with routine. A travel writer who hates to travel, he has developed guides for other travelers who want to reproduce their home environment as much as possible when they are abroad. His life has been based on the assumption that he could outwit chance simply by planning carefully. Unfortunately, at the beginning of the novel, his only child has been killed in a random crime at a fast-food store, and, unable to cope with the death, Macon's wife Susan has left him.

Macon's first impulse is to order his household; however, his efforts at efficiency are less than successful, and he ends up with a broken leg. With considerable relief, he moves into the orderly household which his sister runs for their two brothers. The portrait of the four Leary children, all of whom have now returned home, symbolizes the security that Macon feels now that he has moved back into the unchanging past. It seems that conformity will win over the chaos which Macon so dreads.

Somewhat earlier in the story, however, Tyler has introduced one of her energetic women, Muriel Pritchett, a veterinarian's assistant with a young son and a mind of her own. Before long, Muriel is training Macon's aggressive dog and bringing Macon himself into her disorderly, fascinating world, where the unexpected is cherished. Finally, Macon must choose between returning to Susan, whose very body is comfortably familiar, and moving ahead in an adventuresome life with Muriel, where his only certainty will be her good nature.

In *The Accidental Tourist*, several characters move back and forth between individualism and conformity, disorder and order. For example, Rose Leary, who is responsible for keeping the family home untouched by time, falls in love with Julian Edge, Macon's boss, a breezy, confident person who carries her away from what might seem to be a dull life. Julian has not reckoned with Rose's appetite for order, however, and before long, she has returned to the family home and her old life. Only Macon's inventiveness saves the marriage; remembering the chaos of Julian's office, he suggests that Julian beg her help in getting it under control. Julian himself is finally the convert to conformity; the man who, Tyler says, never even consulted a consumer magazine before buying something, moves into the Leary household and happily takes part in their routine.

Two of the characters, Alexander Pritchett, Muriel's son, and Susan Leary, Macon's wife, are deeply troubled at the beginning of the novel. Allergic to everything, enthusiastic about nothing, Alexander evidently bears the burden of feeling unwanted by his father and perhaps also of his mother's eccentricity. He lacks something—the company of men, his mother thinks, but it may be a feeling of family structure as well. The turning point for Alexander comes in a scene which illustrates Tyler's subtle blend of humor and pathos. Macon decides to show Alexander how to repair a faucet; furthermore, he insists that the boy do it himself. When he has succeeded, Alexander smiles for the first time. It is obvious that Alexander has a need for order which his mother cannot fulfill but which Macon can.

In the grief-stricken, gloomy Susan Leary who is introduced in the first chapter of *The Accidental Tourist*, it is hard to imagine the high-spirited girl whom Macon married. It is not surprising that the father and mother of the murdered boy cannot share their feelings with each other. What is surprising is the turn that Susan takes later in her life. After she has gone to Paris with Macon, it seems that their marriage has been patched up; however, the once mercurial woman now seems to be clutching order and pattern. When Susan starts to plan every detail of their trip together, Macon realizes that he must return to Muriel, who saves that kind of bossiness for the dogs she is training. At the end of the novel, everyone except Susan has learned to live in tension between order and disorder, conformity and individualism.

BREATHING LESSONS

First published: 1988
Type of work: Novel

During a one-day automobile trip on the way to a funeral, a couple recall and strengthen their twenty-eight-year marriage.

If *Dinner at the Homesick Restaurant* and *Morgan's Passing* are Tyler's darkest works, *Breathing Lessons* is one of her most optimistic. Even though many of the misadventures in all of her works are comic, in those earlier works one cannot escape the suggestion that life consists mostly of missed opportunities. In *Breathing Lessons*, on the other hand, one feels that nothing is lost, that everything can be renewed, repaired, or redeemed.

The renewal which is central in *Breathing Lessons* is the twenty-eight-year marriage between Maggie and Ira Moran. At first glance, Maggie and Ira would seem completely unsuited to each other. Ira is rational and precise. His heroine is advice columnist Ann Landers, who personifies common sense. Maggie, on the other hand, has contempt for logic. Compassionate, ebullient, and friendly as a puppy, she moves through life as if it were a festival. In fact, that is one of the things that so annoys Ira. She does not take life seriously, he thinks; she acts as if it were all a practice for something else.

The action of *Breathing Lessons* takes place in a single day, during which Maggie, impulsive as usual, insists on going to Deer Lick, Pennsylvania, in order to attend the funeral of her girlhood friend's husband. Throughout that day, Maggie and Ira squabble, revealing their irreconcilable differences, draw apart, then forgive each other, remember how charming those differences have always been, and come back together. On the way to the wedding, for example, Maggie has an accident, forgets the road map, and stops to befriend people all along the way. When Ira quite understandably becomes annoyed, Maggie insists on getting out of the car. Even when Ira returns for her, things are not quite back to normal. When the friend shows some old pictures, however, Maggie gets sentimental, Ira remembers that it was her confidence about life that attracted him to Maggie in the first place, and the two start making love in an upstairs bedroom of the widow, who discovers them and promptly kicks them out.

This same ebb and flow is evident in Maggie's relationship with her daughter-in-law, Fiona Moran, who is now separated from her husband, Jesse Moran, who has not yet found himself. After Maggie persuades Ira to make a side trip to see their grandson, she decides to bring Fiona and Jesse together; with the help of a few blatant lies she drags Fiona and the child back to Baltimore. Throughout this adventure, Ira is appalled. He never did think that the marriage would work—but then, he is married to the same energetic, illogical woman who once recklessly pursued a purse snatcher for the sake of a few dollars. Maggie never calculates odds. She is hardly discouraged when Fiona and Jesse quarrel and part once again. The conclusion of the novel suggests that Tyler can see some victories for energetic, well-meaning, if disorderly characters such as Maggie. The widow apologizes, Ira once again falls under Maggie's spell, and undaunted, Maggie secretly begins to plan another campaign.

Summary

Although Anne Tyler's plots may seem as circular as life itself, with her characters often moving back to the place from which they came, the characters are changed by the events through which they have moved. Tyler's great gift lies in the creation and sympathetic treatment of these characters, who in their interactions produce scenes of comedy and even of farce.

Although Tyler's characters and their actions may seem extreme, the theme they illustrate rings true: Every human being must try to harmonize such opposites as individuality and conformity, emotion and reason, and energy and restraint. Some of her novels suggest that such reconciliation is almost impossible; others indicate that the possibility exists, that energy and love can do what reason can never accomplish.

Bibliography

Betts, Doris. "The Fiction of Anne Tyler." In *Women Writers of the Contemporary South*, edited by P. W. Prenshaw. Jackson: University Press of Mississippi, 1984.

Gilbert, Susan. "Anne Tyler." In *Southern Women Writers: The New Generation*, edited by Tonette Bond Inge. Tuscaloosa: University of Alabama Press, 1990.

Morrow, Mark. *Images of the Southern Writer.* Athens: University of Georgia Press, 1985.

Robertson, M. F. "Anne Tyler: Medusa Points and Contest Points." In *Contemporary American Women Writers: Narrative Strategies*, edited by Catherine Rainwater and William J. Scheick. Lexington: University Press of Kentucky, 1985.

Updike, John. *Hugging the Shore: Essays and Criticism.* New York: Alfred A. Knopf, 1983.

Rosemary M. Canfield Reisman

JOHN UPDIKE

Born: Shillington, Pennsylvania
March 18, 1932

Principal Literary Achievement

Widely recognized as one of the most accomplished stylists and prolific writers of his generation, Updike has emerged as a novelist of major importance.

Biography

John Updike was born on March 18, 1932, in Shillington, Pennsylvania, the only child of Wesley and Linda Grace (Hoyer) Updike. His early years were spent in the Shillington home of his mother's parents, John and Katherine Hoyer. When John was thirteen, they moved to the old family farm in Plowville, ten miles outside of Shillington, where John's mother had been born. These were lean years for the family, which was supported only by his father's meager salary as a mathematics teacher at Shillington High School. Though poor, the family was well educated and had high aspirations for their son, who showed an early aptitude for art and writing. Influenced by *The New Yorker*, the youthful Updike was determined to become a cartoonist and writer for that magazine. His mother, who had literary aspirations of her own, became determined that John should go to Harvard University. Because of his good grades, Updike won a full scholarship in 1950 to Harvard, where he majored in English and was editor of the Harvard *Lampoon*. He was graduated with highest honors in 1954. He met his future wife, Mary Pennington, a Radcliffe student and daughter of a Unitarian minister, while he was a sophomore. They married in 1953 when Updike was a junior. In 1954, Updike published his first story in *The New Yorker*.

The Updikes spent a year during 1954-1955 at the Ruskin School of Drawing and Fine Art in Oxford, England, financed partly by a Knox Fellowship. The Updikes' first child, Elizabeth, was born during this time. After publishing four stories and ten poems in *The New Yorker* during that year, Updike was offered a position as *The New Yorker*'s "Talk of the Town" reporter. The Updikes settled in New York City; Updike wrote for *The New Yorker* until 1957, when he felt the need to leave the city to devote full time to his writing. In April, 1957, the Updikes moved to Ipswich, Massachusetts, where they lived for the next seventeen years. In 1958, his first book, a collection of poems called *The Carpentered Hen and Other Tame Creatures*, was published. In 1959, Updike published *The Poorhouse Fair*, his first novel, and a

collection of stories, *The Same Door*. His second child, David, was born in 1957. In 1959, Updike's second son, Michael, was born; in 1960, his last child, Miranda, was born. The Ipswich years saw Updike not only a prolific writer but also active in community affairs. He was a member of the Congregational church and the Democratic Town Committee.

It was during that same period—the late 1950's and early 1960's—that Updike faced a crisis of faith prompted by his consciousness of the inevitability of death. Updike's reading of the Danish philosopher and theologian Søren Kierkegaard and, especially, the Swiss neo-orthodox theologian Karl Barth helped him overcome this crisis and find a basis for faith. A preoccupation with the sense of death runs throughout Updike's fiction, as does an exploration of theological and religious issues.

Updike's work published in the 1960's established him as one of America's important serious writers. In 1960, he published *Rabbit, Run*, the first in a series of works about a middle-class man and his family set in a small city in Pennsylvania. He returned to this character at intervals of a decade, with *Rabbit Redux* appearing in 1971, *Rabbit Is Rich* appearing in 1981 and winning the Pulitzer Prize in Fiction and an American Book Award, and *Rabbit at Rest* appearing in 1990.

In 1962, Updike's second short story collection, *Pigeon Feathers and Other Stories*, appeared, and in 1963, another collection of verse, *Telephone Poles and Other Poems*, was published. His novel *The Centaur*, also published in 1963, earned for Updike the National Book Award and election to the National Institute of Arts and Letters; he was the youngest man ever to be elected. In 1966, *The Music School*, his third collection of stories, appeared.

In 1964-1965, Updike traveled to Eastern Europe as part of a cultural exchange program. A number of works reflect that experience, in particular *Bech: A Book* (1970) and *Bech Is Back* (1982). In 1973, Updike traveled, under State Department auspices, to Africa; his novel *The Coup* (1978) draws upon that experience. His 1968 novel, *Couples*, caused quite a stir because of its explicit treatment of adultery in a Northeastern suburb and became a best-seller. It gained for its author a cover story in *Time* and favorable treatment in *Life* as well as a large sum for the film rights. Over the years, Updike has also published collections of his essays and reviews—*Assorted Prose* (1965), *Picked-Up Pieces* (1975), *Hugging the Shore: Essays and Criticism* (1983)—that show Updike as a fine critic and cultural commentator.

In addition to the Rabbit novels and *Couples*, a number of Updike's novels focus upon love and marriage and its discontents. His own marriage ended in divorce in 1974. In 1977, Updike married Martha Bernhard. They now live in Georgetown, Massachusetts, a few miles from Ipswich, where his first wife, also remarried, still lives. Such story collections as *Museums and Women and Other Stories* (1972), *Problems and Other Stories* (1979), *Too Far to Go: The Maple's Stories* (1979), and *Trust Me* (1987) reflect Updike's concern for marriage in various stages of decline and difficulty. The novel *Marry Me*, published in 1976, but mostly written before 1968, also focuses upon a flawed marriage. The novels *A Month of Sundays* (1975), *Roger's*

Version (1986), and *S.* (1988) make up a kind of contemporary updating of Nathaniel Hawthorne's *The Scarlet Letter* (1850). *The Witches of Eastwick* (1984), attempts to explore love and marriage from a woman's perspective.

Analysis

Showing remarkable versatility and range, and meeting with both critical and popular success, John Updike's fiction represents a penetrating realist chronicle of the changing morals and manners of American society. His novels continue the long national debate on American civilization and its discontents, but perhaps what is most significant about his novels is their depiction of restless and aspiring spirits struggling within the constraints of flesh, of time and gravity, and of changing social conditions, to find something of transcendent value—all of them lovers and battlers. For Updike, as for many other writers, the conditions and possibilities of love are an index of the conditions and possibilities of faith and belief. As Updike writes in an essay: "Not to be in love, the capital N novel whispers to capital W western man, is to be dying."

Updike's versatility and range can be seen in terms of both style and subject. His first novel, *The Poorhouse Fair*, written when he was in his twenties, is cast twenty years into the future and explores the social and spiritual implications of an essentially antihumanistic socialism. The novel captures imaginatively the voices and experiences of octogenarian characters. In *The Coup*, Updike portrays the speech and sensibility of an American-educated, deposed African leader. In the Bech books— *Bech: A Book* and *Bech Is Back*—Updike creates the persona of an urbane, sophisticated Jewish-American writer in search of his muse. In the Rabbit novels, Updike penetrates the ever-changing world of the former basketball player Harry "Rabbit" Angstrom. In such novels as *The Witches of Eastwick* and *S.*, Updike explores the feminine sensibility. In *A Month of Sundays*, *Marry Me*, *Couples*, and *Roger's Version*, and in such short story collections as *Problems and Other Stories* and *Too Far to Go: The Maples Stories*, Updike has perhaps become the United States' supreme examiner of marriage and its discontents. Each work has a style commensurate to its subject. Updike has a fine ear for the nuances and cadences of human speech from all levels of social life. In addition, his descriptive passages are unequalled in capturing the detail and texture of modern life. For some critics, however, Updike is more style than substance, a prose too ornate, even baroque, densely littered with perception. Nevertheless, the richness and variety of his narratives reveal a writer with extraordinary talent.

Although generalizations do not do justice to the particularities of each Updike work, there is a major predicament experienced by nearly all of Updike's protagonists—a sense of doubleness, of the ironic discrepancy of the fallen creature who yet senses, or yearns for, something transcendent. Updike's characters are creatures moving between two realms but not fully at home in either. The four novels devoted to Rabbit Angstrom illustrate this fallenness in quest of transcendence; they also portray the substitute of sexuality for religious experience.

Updike has written short stories since the beginning of his career, and he continues to publish stories in such magazines as *The New Yorker, Esquire, The Atlantic,* and *Playboy.* He has published a number of collections of his stories, including *The Same Door, Pigeon Feathers and Other Stories, Olinger Stories: A Selection* (1964), *The Music School, Museums and Women and Other Stories, Problems and Other Stories,* and *Trust Me.* Updike's stories are often anthologized in literature textbooks. His stories are generally concerned with subtle states of mind and small events; seemingly insignificant details assume an importance that is somehow sensed but is difficult to explain.

David, the teenaged protagonist of "Pigeon Feathers," has his faith threatened by reading H. G. Wells's account of Jesus. David's loneliness as an only child living on a farm aggravates his alienation. Contemplating the horror of his death without resurrection, David seeks reassurance from his pastor, who cannot help. When trying to rid the barn of pigeons, David regains his faith in his own immortality by an epiphany of design—the intricacy and beauty of the pigeons' feathers convince him that he is of ultimate importance.

In the story "A & P," Updike captures well the foolish heroism of a youth. Sammy, a nineteen-year-old checker at a supermarket, defends three girls in swimsuits from the scolding of Lengel, the store manager. Sammy tells Lengel, "I quit," and walks out of the store, hoping for the girls' approval. They have already gone, however, and Sammy is left to contemplate "how hard the world was going to be to me hereafter." Yet Sammy's foolish gesture is admirable, even heroic, in its affirmation of vitality and beauty in a rather vulgar, convention-bound world.

In "Separating," Updike portrays well the pain of a family on the verge of divorce. The story describes Richard and Joan Maples trying to work out how the children are to be told of the impending separation. The description of the scene of revelation at the table rings painfully true. When the father tells the older son later, the son appears to take the news calmly. Yet when the father kisses him good night, the son asks the virtually unanswerable question: "Why?" Love, so often, is a painful longing for what has been lost, an irretrievable moment, an irrecoverable place.

As seen in both his nonfiction and his fiction, Updike is one of the most theologically sophisticated writers of his generation. He has read deeply in Christian theology, especially in such authors as Kierkegaard and Barth. It is Updike's theological convictions that constitute the basis for his critique of modern men and women and of American society. In an interview conducted in the mid-1960's, Updike declared that "without the supernatural, the natural is a pit of horror." In his long poem *Midpoint,* in Canto IV, Updike writes: "An easy Humanism plagues the land;/ I choose to take an otherworldly stand." His characters seek passage through a decaying world, one whose traditions are disintegrating and dissolving from the pressures of secularity and materialism. Updike's fiction explores the implications of a world that is essentially post-Christian. To stay the anxiety of death, to fill the emptiness of lost or abandoned belief, Updike's characters turn to sexuality, but they are frequently disappointed. In his story "The Bulgarian Poetess" (1966), Updike writes:

"Actuality is a running impoverishment of possibility." This captures well Updike's sense of human incompleteness, of the sense of discrepancy between the actual and the ideal. Problems, in such a world, are rarely, if ever, solved. Instead, they are endured, if not fully understood, though occasionally there are moments of grace and affirmation.

In his 1962 memoir entitled "The Dogwood Tree: A Boyhood," Updike speaks of his commitment "to transcribe middleness with all its grits, bumps, and anonymities, in its fullness of satisfaction and mystery." Updike continues to fulfill that commitment in a rich and vital fiction that explores what Updike calls the "Three Great Secret Things: Sex, Religion, and Art," subjects that form the substance of most of his fiction.

RABBIT, RUN

First published: 1960
Type of work: Novel

In the conformity of the 1950's in the United States, a troubled quester has nowhere to go.

Rabbit, Run, a novel of a former basketball star and his floundering marriage set in the late 1950's, was the first of what has become a series of four novels about the protagonist and his family; Updike has published one of them every ten years since 1960. Together the novels form a revealing chronicle of the complex changes occurring in American culture between the 1950's and the late 1980's. In Updike's hero, Harry "Rabbit" Angstrom, the reader sees one of the author's many lapsed creatures in search of renewal, of regeneration, of something to believe in. The destructiveness of the character's actions in the first novel reflects Updike's own intense religious crisis, experienced at the time he was writing the novel.

At twenty-six, Rabbit, who got his nickname from the way he twitches his nose, finds himself in a stultifying life. He has a job selling magic-peelers in a dime store and is married to Janice, a careless and boozy woman who is pregnant with their second child. Coming home with new resolve to change his life after a brief game of basketball with some children in an alley, Rabbit finds the mess of his marital life too much to overcome. Thus begins his series of recoiling actions from the stifling experiences of his present life. The novel captures well the sense of bottled-up frustration of the 1950's, a decade that put a premium on conformity and adapting to one's environment. Hence, like so many of Updike's protagonists, Rabbit is enmeshed in a highly compromised environment, one committed to the values of the marketplace and lacking in spiritual concerns. Like a latter-day Huck Finn, Rabbit bolts from a civilization that would deny him freedom and a sense of wonder. His movement can be viewed as a kind of spiritual survival tactic.

A quote from Blaise Pascal serves as an epigraph to the novel: "The motions of

Grace, the hardness of heart; external circumstances." Those three things, Updike says, describe human lives. They also describe the basic movements and conflicts in the Rabbit novels, indeed of most of Updike's fiction. Bewildered and frustrated, Rabbit wonders what has happened to his life. His disgust with his present life is deepened by his memories of when he was "first-rate at something" as a high school basketball star.

As some critics have noted, the novel is the study of a nonhero's quest for a nonexistent grail. Rabbit initially tries to escape by driving south, goaded by visions of fertility and warmth. After getting hopelessly lost, he returns to his hometown and seeks out Tothero, his old high school coach. Tothero sets Rabbit up with Ruth Leonard, a part-time prostitute, with whom Rabbit begins to live. Pursued by the do-good minister Jack Eccles, Rabbit resists returning to Janice. To Eccles, Rabbit claims that "something out there wants me to find it," though what that is he cannot say. When Janice goes into labor, Rabbit returns, feeling contrite and resolving to restore the marriage. For nine days, their life seems to be going well. When Janice refuses Rabbit's sexual advances, however, he bolts again and looks for Ruth. Feeling abandoned, Janice starts drinking heavily and accidentally drowns the baby. Rabbit returns to Janice again, but at the funeral he outrages the family by his claims of innocence. He runs again, returning to Ruth—who reveals that she is pregnant and demands that Rabbit divorce Janice and marry her. He refuses Ruth, and the novel ends with Rabbit running the streets, resisting all claims upon his commitment.

Rabbit's back-and-forth actions create much havoc and mark him as selfish and irresponsible in the America of the 1950's, a world offering little margin for the quest for the transcendent. In place of the old revelations of religion, Rabbit substitutes the ecstasy of sex, the deep mysteries of the woman's body. Failed by his environment and its various authority figures, Rabbit registers his revolt through movement, through a refusal to stand still and be taken over by the tides of secular culture.

RABBIT REDUX

First published: 1971
Type of work: Novel

In 1969, no longer in flight, Rabbit witnesses and experiences the racial and cultural upheavals of the times.

In *Rabbit Redux*, Rabbit believes that the whole country is doing what he did ten years earlier. Rabbit appears to have made his peace with the world and has settled down to fulfill his various obligations. He works as a typesetter in the same shop where his father has worked for more than thirty years. (He works at a trade, however, that will soon be replaced by a new technology.) In this novel, Rabbit is more a passive listener and observer than a searcher. The racial and cultural turmoil that he sees on television literally comes into his home, and Rabbit is forced to be a student of his times. Updike uses this rather feckless working-class man in small-city Pennsylvania as a foil to the upheavals sweeping the United States during the late 1960's.

The landing of Americans on the moon, which Rabbit, like millions of others, watches on television, is a fitting analogue or metaphor for the cultural shifts of the decade. The astronauts, pioneers of the new technology and exemplars of the centrifugal movement of the West, land on a barren satellite. The implication is that America's spiritual landscape is as barren as that of the moon. Americans have gone about as far as they can, and they must now return home and make the best of things here. The gravity of Earth cannot be escaped for long.

In *Rabbit, Run*, Rabbit left Janice for a mistress. In *Rabbit Redux*, Janice leaves Rabbit to live with her lover Stavros. Rabbit acquiesces to this affair and stays home to care for his son, Nelson. Through a strange set of circumstances—not wholly probable—Rabbit takes in Jill, a runaway flower child, and Skeeter, a bail-jumping Vietnam veteran and black radical. Rabbit's own living room becomes the place for Rabbit's encounter with the radical attacks upon America's values and policies. Skeeter's charismatic critiques of the American way of life challenge Rabbit's unquestioning patriotism and mesmerize him. As a consequence, Rabbit is helpless when disaster finally comes. His house is set on fire, probably by disgruntled neighbors; Jill is caught inside and dies in the fire. Rabbit helps Skeeter escape. Because of Stavros' heart condition, Janice gives him up to return home to Rabbit and Nelson. The novel ends with Janice and Rabbit together in a motel room asleep, in a sense rendered homeless by the forces of their time, over which they have little control.

In *Rabbit, Run*, Rabbit was a radical of sorts, a seeker for the transcendent in an entropic environment. In *Rabbit Redux*, Rabbit is a conservative, a defender of the American Dream and the war in Vietnam. He resents all the nay-sayers, the radicals who want to overthrow everything. He has a flag decal on his car window. In a sense, his patriotism has replaced his old religious quest for the supernatural. It is a shaky religion in a revolutionary time when all quests are quite this-worldly. Contrite because of the suffering his earlier quest produced, Rabbit has returned to the old rules precisely at the time most of the culture is repudiating them. Jill flees her upper-class world and seeks to overcome ego and materialism through drugs. Skeeter proclaims a radical black religion to rejuvenate an empty, "dollar-crazy" America. Janice seeks liberation through a lover. The burning of Rabbit's home represents the failure of all these quests—Jill dies, Skeeter flees, Janice returns home, and Rabbit's old dream is chastened. Significantly, it is Rabbit's sister, Mim, a Las Vegas call girl, whose visit home resolves the conflicts of the novel. Her unabashed worldliness and acceptance of an essentially empty world enable her to help the others find a way to live in the new American desert.

The novel sounds an apocalyptic note: What we sow, we reap. The "external circumstances" become overwhelming. The televised images of flame and violence come home to destroy, perhaps to purify, like an ancient holocaust or whole-burnt offering. Rabbit bears witness to a disintegrating United States, even as it puts a man on the moon. Janice and Rabbit sleep, perhaps to awake to a new sense of maturity and responsibility. At least they may awake to a new beginning, which still lingers as a key element of the American Dream.

RABBIT IS RICH

First published: 1981
Type of work: Novel

In a world "running out of gas," Rabbit comes into material success, only to see it threatened by his erratic son.

Rabbit Is Rich is a novel about a middle-aged man—a fitting image for the spiritual condition of the United States at the end of the 1970's. At forty-six, Rabbit is successful, but his expansive waistline reminds him of his declining energies as well as the encroachment of death. Updike updates Sinclair Lewis' novel, *Babbitt* (1922), about the ever-aspiring businessman George F. Babbitt. The remaining sparks of vitality in Rabbit seek to combat the forces of exhaustion that fill the novel. Indeed, the sense of things running down and images of falling dominate the book.

The novel is set during the summer and fall of 1979 and the first few weeks of 1980. In those last months of the Carter administration, America faces long lines at the gasoline pumps, high inflation rates, and the continuing stalemate over the American hostages in Iran. Rabbit is not worried, however, for he is a co-owner of Brewer's Toyota agency, since his father-in-law, Fred Springer, died in 1974. He and Janice have been living in the Springer house since their own house was destroyed by fire in 1969. Their son, Nelson, has been going to college at Kent State University. While Rabbit struggles with his son, he is haunted by the ghosts of his past—his dead daughter, his dead mother's voice, and memories of Jill and Skeeter. Rabbit imagines that they embrace him, sustain him, and cheer him on in the autumn of his life.

In the first two novels, Rabbit was out of step with his decade—in the complacent 1950's, he ran; in the frenetic 1960's, he watched. In *Rabbit Is Rich*, he is running again, but this time more in rhythm with the 1970's, Rabbit jogs, an activity in keeping with the fitness craze that grew in the decade. The novel begins with Rabbit thinking "running out of gas," a phrase which resonates at several levels. As a middle-aged man, Rabbit knows that his energies are diminishing. Because of the gasoline crisis, he sees America perhaps literally running out of gas. Spiritually, the phrase suggests a running out of the old dynamism that fed the American Dream. In 1979, the American satellite Skylab was falling out of orbit—another fitting metaphor for the crisis facing the Angstroms and America. Rabbit finds that his old desires and wants have shriveled. "Freedom, that he always thought was outward motion, turns out to be this inward dwindling." When asked if he has seen the film *Jaws II*, Rabbit responds in a way that reinforces the sense of entropy running throughout the novel: "D' you ever get the feeling that everything these days is sequels? . . . Like people are running out of ideas."

In his new prosperity, Rabbit plays golf at a new country club, goes to Rotary Club lunches, and reads *Consumer Reports*, the bible of his new status. Consumption is linked with sex as a way to fill the spiritual void of modern life. In a telling scene, Janice and Rabbit make love on top of their newly purchased gold Krugerrands. Ambiguously, sex represents both vitality and the void, the unfillable emptiness that constitutes death. Rabbit lusts after Cindy, the lovely young wife of one of their new country-club friends. Janice tells Rabbit: "You *al*ways want what you don't have instead of what you do." In a wife-swapping episode during the three couples' brief Caribbean holiday, however, Rabbit must take Thelma Harrison instead of Cindy and is introduced to anal sex (arguably an appropriate image of the sense of worthlessness pervading American culture in the 1970's).

Nelson's return home is like the visit of a nightmare, of something neglected or repressed that cannot be avoided any longer. He wreaks havoc within the family's affluent complacency. Like his father, but lacking Rabbit's grace and conscience, Nelson's quest for attention and for love leads him to wreck practically everything he touches. Nelson also brings home a girl pregnant with his child. A marriage is arranged and in January of 1980, Rabbit receives a grand-daughter, placed in his lap on the night of the Super Bowl. Perhaps at last Rabbit has the daughter he has longed for ever since Becky drowned and Jill died in his house in previous novels. He accepts his grand-daughter—"fortune's hostage, heart's desire"—who represents both the hope for his future and a reminder of his mortality.

Abandoning his wife, Pru, Nelson begins the cycle of irresponsibility and bad luck that plagued his parents twenty years earlier. At one point, Rabbit tells Nelson: "Maybe I haven't done everything right in my life. I know I haven't. But I haven't committed the greatest sin. I haven't laid down and died." The statement is a good summary of the character of Rabbit throughout the novels—a man of vitality, a lover of life, an embodiment of forces running counter to entropy and death.

THE CENTAUR

First published: 1963
Type of work: Novel

Through the creative blending of memory and myth, an artist-protagonist recovers the meaning of his father's life as a means to recovering his own vocation.

The Centaur draws heavily upon Updike's experiences growing up in Shillington, Pennsylvania, and pays homage to his father. In many ways, the novel is Updike's most complex work, involving a complex interweaving of the myth of Chiron the centaur with the story of an adolescent boy and his father in the winter of 1947. The novel is part *Bildungsroman*, a novel of moral education, and part *Künstlerroman*, a novel of an artist seeking his identity in conflict with society and/or his past. The nine chapters of the novel emerge as a collage, a narrative appropriate for the painter-narrator. Nearly thirty, Peter Caldwell, the artist-protagonist, is seeking to recover from his past some insight or understanding that might clarify and rejuvenate his artistic vocation. He reminisces to his black mistress in a Manhattan loft about a three-day period during the winter of 1947, fourteen years earlier.

Peter tells of his self-conscious adolescence, growing up an only child, living on a farm with his parents and Pop Kramer, his grandfather. His father is the high school biology teacher and swim coach, and his acts of compassion and charity embarrass the boy. On a mythic level, the father is depicted as Chiron the centaur, part man and part stallion, who serves as mentor to youthful Greek heroes. Chiron's life is sacrificial—he suffers for his charges, just as Peter's father suffered for (and often from) his students. Peter is eventually able to arrive at an understanding of his father's life and death, and he finds a clarification of his own lost vocation.

In the myth, Chiron sacrifices his immortality so that Prometheus may be free to live and to create. Peter interprets his father's life in the same sacrificial terms—his father, George, in effect gives his life for Peter. While the character of George seems obsessed with death, it is doubtful that he really dies. Rather, his sacrifice is his willingness to go on fulfilling his obligation to his family. Seeing his father's life in sacrificial terms, Peter, despairing over his failure to fulfill his artistic talent, asks: "*Was it for this that my father gave up his life?*" In this harsh reappraisal, Peter learns what he could not know as an adolescent about sacrificial love. He comes to see that love, guilt, and sacrifice are somehow inherent in the very structure of life. Telling the story and mythologizing his father's ordinariness reveal some truths about love to Peter. Such fatherly love liberates the son to resume his artistic vocation with courage.

The figure of the centaur captures well the recurring predicament of Updike's protagonists. The centaur embodies both the godly and the bestial; he is a creature conversant with both heaven and earth, yet not fully at home in either realm. Such a figure points to faith as the way to live with courage and hope.

COUPLES

First published: 1968
Type of work: Novel

In a secular, post-Christian culture, affluent couples in a Massachusetts suburb turn to sex and adultery as the new religion.

Couples created quite a stir when it was published because of its graphic and emancipated treatment of adultery. It was on the best-seller list for most of a year, and it led to favorable treatments of the author by *Time* and *Life* magazines. Despite the book's apparent sensationalism, the novel exhibits Updike's serious intent to explore the moral and spiritual consequences of a post-Christian world; the novel explores the question, "After Christianity, what?" To Updike, the novel is "about sex as the emergent religion, as the only thing left." Human sexuality seemed to be liturgy and sacrament of the new religion emerging in America in the 1960's— another end of innocence in a "post-pill paradise." The new religion does not truly assuage the anxiety of death, however; it leads instead to self-deception and disillusionment. Indeed, the cultic celebration of sex is the courting of disaster.

Set in the fictitious Massachusetts town of Tarbox, the novel focuses upon ten white, essentially upper-middle-class couples, most of whom have children and professional occupations. The time of the novel is from the spring of 1963 to the spring of 1964—from one season of rebirth to the next—between two pregnancies, one resulting in the birth of a child, the other in an abortion. The religion that the couples have made of one another dissolves into divorce and migration. The main sexual pilgrim in the novel is Piet Hanema, a thirty-five-year-old building contractor, who is plagued by death anxiety and still attends church. Fearing death without immortal life, Piet finds no consolation in his marriage to the lovely Angela, who accepts death as a natural part of the cycles of life. Piet's many infidelities in large part stem from his inner desperation for some sort of certainty. Piet's foil is dentist Freddy Thorne, who casts himself as the priest of the new hedonism, of sensuality. To Freddy, the body is all that there is and, hence, should be celebrated and indulged. The novel is filled with scenes of the couples' weekly gatherings at picnics, parties, and games. In the backdrop of their continuous fun and games are the growing crises in national and international affairs, but the couples have little interest in the news. Even on the night of Kennedy's assassination, they gather at Freddy's for a party. When it comes out that the assassin is a left-winger, one of the group comments, "He wasn't one of us."

The suspensiveness of Piet's adulterous activity is broken by the arrival of a new couple—Ken Whitman, a research biologist, and his pregnant wife, Foxy. Hired to redo their house, Piet is drawn to the very sensual Foxy, who shares his religious concerns. In Foxy, Piet finds what he lacks in Angela. After her baby is born, she gets pregnant by Piet, who goes to Freddy Thorne to arrange an abortion. For payment for the favor, Freddy asks for a night with Angela. When he gets Angela in bed, however, Freddy cannot perform; the priest of sex is impotent before the earthy and ethereal Angela. Both men, in getting what they think they most desire, lose something vital to their identities. The loss of Angela causes Piet's fall into the earthly, to the mortal flesh. In effect, *Eros*, physical love, defeats *Agape*, spiritual love. Piet's church is destroyed by a fire, which Piet construes as a divine judgment upon them all. Piet and Foxy marry and move to another suburb where they become simply another couple.

Couples shows that a certain light has gone out in the American landscape; death and decay haunt the imagination and spirit. Piet, as do the others, fails in the quest to find in the flesh what has been lost in the spirit. The church, given over to secularity and worldliness, fails them. The religion of sensuality leads to trivial and empty lives, a kind of death. Disappointment and disillusionment are the results of the failure of the new religion.

THE WITCHES OF EASTWICK

First published: 1984
Type of work: Novel

In the tumult of the late 1960's, three divorcées find a witchlike power in their friendship, encounter evil both outside and inside themselves, and end up remarried.

The Witches of Eastwick is a diabolical comedy—a novel that explores the uses and abuses of power in its diverse forms in an age of moral and social confusion and that resolves itself in marriage. Like *Rabbit Redux*, the novel is set during the first year or so of the Nixon presidency, an era of protest, discontent, and polarization. The place is a small town in Rhode Island called Eastwick. In *Rabbit Redux*, Updike portrays a rather powerless Rabbit as witness to cultural disintegration and moonlike spiritual barrenness in the context of the late 1960's. In *The Witches of Eastwick*, though written in the early 1980's, Updike goes back to the same polarized period but explores the female perspective and the emerging new feminist synthesis. As the power of patriarchy "wastes" itself in yet another war—this time the seemingly endless war in Vietnam—women are rediscovering the old goddesses, the old sources of unity, integration, and power. Yet, like Nathaniel Hawthorne, Updike shows that power unmindful of history and exploitative of nature constitutes an evil that produces death and guilt.

The "witches" of the title refer to three divorcées, Alexandra Spofford, Jane Smart, and Sukie Rougemont, who have become close friends, meeting each Thursday and speaking often over the telephone, and who have discovered the power of sisterhood as well as some ancient feminine powers. The term witch is meant to refer to free women and to imply the discovery of neo-pagan powers—an inner-direction, a sense of nature as sacred, a rejection of such dualisms as body and soul and of various political hierarchies. This hypothesis, represented by the three women, is challenged by the demonic figure of Darryl Van Horne, who takes them all as lovers and proves later to be a confidence man.

The novel is divided into three parts, "The Coven," "Malefica," and "Guilt," which suggest a progression from the women's newly found power and independence through an encounter with the demonic to a rediscovery of responsibility. In "The Coven," the portrayal of the three women shows their neo-pagan, feminist convictions, their various loves and work. Alexandra calls forth a storm that clears a beach. The women tend to speak of men in ways that infantilize them. Eastwick has ecology-conscious industry, "clean" technology, and marshes where egrets rest. Male dominance is characterized as constituted of science and technology, of machine systems. Alone and free, the women have found new powers, natural powers. This gender split raises the question of whether evil is the result of technology or of nature.

"Malefica" deals with the effects of Darryl Van Horne's presence on the women and the community. Reminiscent of some of Hawthorne's scientist characters, Horne comes in proclaiming to be a technologist doing research in polymers and solar energy. Taking over the old Lenox mansion, he fills in some of the fragile wetlands for his tennis court, adds an immense hot tub, and installs fancy stereo equipment. He argues with the liberal antiwar Unitarian minister, Ed Parsley, who later elopes with Dawn Polanski, a teenage war protester, to join the antiwar movement. Ironically, Ed Parsley blows himself up with a bomb he planned to use to bring about peace—another instance of the misunderstanding of power. The social do-gooder Felicia Gabriel, upon whom the women placed a minor curse, is killed by her frustrated husband, Clyde, who in turn commits suicide. At this point, the three witches remain caught in the solipsism of their philosophy, unable or unwilling to see or make connections between external, historical events and local events.

Like Updike's many male protagonists, the three women must come to grips with the reality of death before they can reconstitute a meaningful life. Falling for Van Horne's clumsy charms, the women develop a jealous rage when Van Horne chooses the young Jennifer Gabriel for his wife. The women use their powers to put a curse on Jennifer. When Jennifer dies, the women feel a terrible guilt, even though it is not clear that their curse causes the girl's cancer. The women begin to sense their participation in an evil act of creation, one that cannot be reversed by a simple change of course or inner state. Jennifer's death provides the occasion for Van Horne to give a sermon on the evilness of creation, in which he excoriates a cosmos saturated with invisible parasites plaguing human life. He then leaves town with Jennifer's brother, Christopher, suggesting Van Horne's possible homosexuality.

The three women are left with the need to reflect upon all that has occurred and their responsibility with it. They move to a sense of reality that includes both the external and the internal, to an awareness of evil that is both technological and natural. The women find their way into appropriate marriages, an act which is not meant to be seen as a capitulation to patriarchical tradition, but rather as an acknowledgment of their responsible connection with historical existence. In much of Updike's fiction, women and nature are associated (some of his male protagonists feel guilt because "women and nature forget"). *The Witches of Eastwick* complicates that formula by showing how guilt in the three women functions to open memory to full human responsibility.

Summary

John Updike is rightfully acclaimed as one of the most accomplished stylists and prolific writers of his generation. In both thematic seriousness and narrative range, Updike has produced a body of writing of the highest order.

Updike's fiction constitutes a serious exploration and probing of the spiritual conditions of American culture in the late twentieth century and reflects a vision of life informed by his protestant Christian convictions. Like the work of Hawthorne, in whose steps Updike ably follows, Updike's fiction continues the long conversation concerning the plight of innocence and its loss that has been so central to the American tradition. In a world no longer supported by traditional beliefs, Updike's fiction explores the possibilities of love as the basis for a gracious and responsible life.

Bibliography

Campbell, Jeff H. *Updike's Novels: Thorns Spell a Word*. Wichita Falls, Tex.: Midwestern State University Press, 1987.

Detweiler, Robert. *John Updike*. Boston: Twayne, 1984.

Greiner, Donald. *John Updike's Novels*. Athens: Ohio University Press, 1984.

Hamilton, Alice, and Kenneth Hamilton. *The Elements of John Updike*. Grand Rapids, Mich.: Wm. B. Eerdmans, 1970.

Hunt, George W. *John Updike and the Three Secret Things: Sex, Religion, and Art*. Grand Rapids, Mich.: Wm. B. Eerdmans, 1980.

Marble, Joyce B. *Fighters and Lovers: Theme in the Novels of John Updike*. New York: New York University Press, 1973.

Newman, Judie. *John Updike*. New York: St. Martin's Press, 1988.

Uphaus, Suzanne Henning. *John Updike*. New York: Frederick Ungar, 1980.

Vargo, Edward P. *Rainstorms and Fire: Ritual in the Novels of John Updike*. Port Washington, N.Y.: Kennikat Press, 1973.

Wood, Ralph C. *The Comedy of Redemption: Christian Faith and Comic Vision in Four American Novelists*. Notre Dame, Ind.: University of Notre Dame Press, 1988.

John G. Parks

GORE VIDAL

Born: West Point, New York
October 3, 1925

Principal Literary Achievement

As a principal literary figure in the post-World War II era, Vidal has achieved success as a novelist, short-story writer, essayist, playwright, and television and film scriptwriter.

Biography

Gore Vidal, named Eugene Luther Vidal at birth, was born on October 3, 1925, at the United States Military Academy, West Point, New York. His father, Eugene Vidal, was an instructor in the new science of aeronautics; he later founded airlines and in the 1930's was director of air commerce for President Franklin D. Roosevelt. Gore's mother, Nina, was the beautiful and socially prominent daughter of Oklahoma Senator Thomas P. Gore.

Soon after Gore's birth, his family moved to Washington, D.C., and lived with his grandfather. Senator Gore was blind; in exchange for young Gore's reading to him, the senator allowed his grandson to use his huge library. Gore began to educate himself at age five, when he could read and write. When the Vidal marriage ended in divorce in 1935, Nina married Hugh D. Auchincloss, a wealthy investment banker. Gore moved to the huge Auchincloss estate in Virginia, only a few miles from his grandfather Gore.

Young Gore grew up among the nation's political, economic, and journalistic elite. He attended good private schools with other young men from prominent families, spending the happiest three years of his life at Phillips Exeter Academy in New Hampshire. When he was graduated in 1943, during World War II, he immediately went into the Army. He never went to college but is considered one of the most learned literary figures of his generation.

Before he left the Army in 1946, Vidal finished writing his first two published novels, *Williwaw* (1946) and *In a Yellow Wood* (1947). These established him as one of the best of the young postwar writers. By 1954 he had published eight novels, but it was his third novel that would affect the rest of his life: *The City and the Pillar* (1948) dealt with homosexuality. Homosexuality was a shocking subject in 1948, made doubly so because Vidal made his protagonist a normal, all-American boy, not a bizarre or doomed figure, as such characters usually were in American fiction.

Vidal would himself be labeled homosexual, which would influence reaction to him in the literary and political world. Vidal does not believe that anyone is a homosexual or a heterosexual. He believes that all humans feel sexual desires for both males and females, but that most societies try to socialize their members into suppressing their desire for their own sex. Sexual acts are homosexual or heterosexual, Vidal says, but a person is neither.

His next few books were ignored, and Vidal found himself in financial trouble. In 1954, he began writing for television, in the so-called "Golden Age" when television broadcast many live dramas. He also became a Hollywood figure, writing screenplays, including *The Catered Affair* (1956) and, with Tennessee Williams, *Suddenly Last Summer* (1959). He wrote several plays, including two Broadway hits: *Visit to a Small Planet: A Comedy Akin to a Vaudeville* (1957) and *The Best Man: A Play About Politics* (1960). He also wrote three mystery novels under the name Edgar Box.

By the early 1960's, Vidal had built a secure financial base and had established himself as a well-known public figure. He was an outspoken social critic, and he offered a scathing indictment of United States leadership and policy. The turmoil produced by the Civil Rights movement, the Vietnam War, and the Watergate scandal made a large segment of the educated public receptive to his message. In 1960, Vidal ran for a seat in the House of Representatives; in 1982, he ran for the Senate. He did not win either race but ran more successfully than anyone thought he could.

In 1964, Vidal published *Julian*, a historical novel about a fourth century Roman emperor, Julian the Apostate, who had tried to stop the spread of Christianity. This was Vidal's first novel in ten years and was a critical and financial success. After this, Vidal turned out a succession of best-selling novels, including more historical fiction and such famous and controversial forays into popular culture as his novel *Myra Breckinridge* (1968).

Vidal remains a scathing critic of every aspect of American life. He lives much of each year in Italy, where he has an apartment in Rome and a beautiful villa overlooking the Bay of Salerno. He also retains a home in the United States, to which he returns periodically to make the talk-show circuit on television and to release his newest novel or book of essays.

Analysis

Great diversity in subject matter, narrative structure, and style characterizes Vidal's fictional work. His first eight novels, written before he was thirty years old, typically depicted young men in search of proper and fulfilling lives. Young men at war on a ship have to work out moral and ethical problems in a small group under stress; other young men examine the meaning of friendship and love; some are caught up in historical events, such as a revolution in Central America; some face the dilemma of choosing careers and life-styles. Young men who choose what appear to be secure positions or socially acceptable and conforming life-styles often find themselves destroyed. Vidal's message is that to live fully, one must defy social pressures and choose to live a life of personal freedom.

Author Ernest Hemingway greatly influenced Vidal's writing style, as he did most other young writers in the postwar years. Vidal's seventh and eighth novels were particularly important to his development. In *The Judgment of Paris* (1952), Vidal began to develop his own stylistic voice, marked by wit and irony. In the old myth, Zeus forces a young man, Paris, to choose the most beautiful among three goddesses. In Vidal's story, a modern young man confronts three women, each offering him a different gift: political power, knowledge, or love. He chooses love—not static, possessive love with one person but the stance of remaining open to love and friendship as he moves through life. In *Messiah* (1954), regarded by some as a small masterpiece awaiting discovery, Vidal took up a subject to which he would return in several future novels. *Messiah* is a journal narrated by an old man, Eugene Luther, who had helped found a new religion based on the teaching of John Cave. Cavesword had displaced Christianity. Figures in the book correspond to Jesus, Mary, Saint Paul, Martin Luther, and other religious figures. Vidal shows how the needs of the organized church suppress and distort the message of a religious founder such as John Cave (or Jesus Christ).

Lack of money during the ten years that followed *Messiah* forced Vidal to write for a mass audience on Broadway and in televison and films. He continued to explore the proper role of the individual in modern civilization, but he also learned to entertain and to lace his social criticism with biting satire and flashing wit.

In 1964, Vidal turned back to the novel and proved to be a master of historical fiction. *Julian* and *Creation* (1981) won applause from historians because of Vidal's fidelity to the historical record. Vidal turned his historical probing to the United States by writing a cycle of six novels, in order by the period covered: *Burr* (1973), *Lincoln* (1984), *1876* (1976), *Empire* (1987), *Hollywood: A Novel of America in the 1920's* (1990), and *Washington, D.C.* (1967). Vidal believes that the United States is a deeply flawed society, a garrison state that manages a worldwide empire, a society run by a small, wealthy, elite removed from any concern with the masses of American people. The genius of the American ruling class, he says, is that the people do not even know they have one.

In his historical cycle, Vidal studies this ruling class as it evolves over two centuries. He believes that the democratic promise of American society was lost at the very beginning of United States history. The founding fathers, such as George Washington, Thomas Jefferson, and Aaron Burr, he depicts as opportunists who built a nation not from some great sense of national purpose but to secure their fortunes and to gain political power. Lincoln is shown as a great man, but his greatness is in creating a centralized and unified nation, not in achieving the nation's proclaimed democratic promise. In *Empire* and *Hollywood*, set in the early twentieth century, the United States' rulers create an overseas empire which will serve as the foundation of the military-industrial complex. The nation's rulers use modern mass media, such as newspapers and films, to manipulate the people. The closing novel, *Washington, D.C.*, shows the emptiness of a John Kennedy-like politician whose only goal is to win power. Vidal typically provokes and angers readers, but he also edifies.

Vidal's historical fiction provides a foundation for understanding some of his "campy" literature: *Myra Breckinridge*, *Myron* (1974), *Kalki* (1978), and *Duluth* (1983). These are studies of sexuality—of the "heterosexual dictatorship," in Vidal's terms—the nature of religious movements, and the role of mass media, especially television and films, in shaping people's sense of reality.

JULIAN

First published: 1964
Type of work: Novel

In the fourth century, Roman Emperor Julian tries to stop the spread of Christianity.

Julian was Gore Vidal's first venture into historical fiction. History fascinates him, and he has read as widely in the field as most professional historians. Vidal adheres closely to the historical record, but as a novelist he can do two things that professional historians cannot: He can invent facts when the facts are not known, and he can ascribe motives to historical figures. In both cases, Vidal carefully invents facts and motives that seem most likely to have been true historically. Vidal intends to entertain, but he also intends to instruct: He gives a historically accurate portrait of Julian and explores with his readers the origins of Western civilization.

The novel opens in A.D. 380, seventeen years after Emperor Julian's death during an invasion of Persia. Two old friends of Julian, the philosophers Libanius of Antioch and Priscus of Athens, learn that the Emperor Theodosius has declared an end to toleration of Christian and non-Christian "heresy." Libanius has heard a rumor that Priscus possesses the only copy of a memoir written by Julian. He proposes that they publish the memoir to remind the world of Julian's previous attempt to stop the spread of Christianity. The novel, then, consists of Julian's memoir, interspersed with letters and comments by Libanius and Priscus, who were eyewitnesses to the events described by Julian. They "correct" his version of events and add their own perspective.

Julian (Flavius Claudius Julianus), born about 331, is a descendent of the Christian emperors Constantine the Great and Constantius II. Constantius kills all the other members of Julian's family to prevent any challenge to his authority. Julian saves himself by making sure he is not seen as a threat. He lives a secluded life, aiming first to be a priest and later studying philosophy with some of the greatest minds of his age.

Yet Julian loses his faith in Christianity, even though he has a religious mentality and personality. His friends say that at another time Julian might well have been a Christian saint. He leads a life of asceticism and, after his wife's death, maintains sexual celibacy. His faith breaks because he grows up in an age when church bureaucrats gain control of Christianity and rob it of its mystery by carrying on dry and learned battles over esoteric matters. They engage in political intrigues that neglect or distort Jesus' simple message of love. Julian is drawn to Jesus but detests the church that speaks in his name. As a young boy, Julian witnesses Christians beating and killing other Christians. He cannot square Christian violence and brutality with Jesus' message of peace and love. Simultaneously, he reads the works of non-Christian scholars, who teach pre-Christian Greek philosophy and religion.

Meanwhile, Constantius brings Julian out of seclusion to play a role in governing the huge Roman Empire. In A.D. 355, Constantius places Julian in control of the Roman provinces beyond the Alps. The young ascetic scholar proves to be a military genius and quickly wins the love of his troops. In 361, Constantius dies, and Julian becomes emperor.

As emperor, Julian proclaims religious toleration for both Christians and non-Christians. Julian says that he is going to punish Christians by forbidding them to do what they enjoy most—persecuting one another. He sacrifices to the old gods of Mt. Olympus and tries to revive the pagan temples and rituals. He lays plans to breathe new life into Hellenism, the civilization inherited from Greece. He also, Vidal believes, is captivated by Alexander the Great's vision of conquering the known world. Julian invades Persia and drives deep into the heart of that empire. He wins many victories but is killed—murdered, Vidal believes, by one of his Christian soldiers. "With Julian, the light went, and now nothing remains but to let the darkness come," says Libanius. Now nothing stands in the way of the spread of Christianity, and Western civilization enters a thousand-year decline, later called the Dark Ages.

One of Vidal's biographers asked two outstanding historians of the fourth century Roman Empire to evaluate *Julian*. The historians agreed that Vidal's work is probably the best portrait of Julian that exists. Vidal sees the era as crucial to the evolution of the West. If Julian had lived, Vidal believes, Christianity would be only one of several religions in our Western civilization.

WASHINGTON, D.C.

First published: 1967
Type of work: Novel

Political insiders vie for power and influence during the administrations of Presidents Franklin D. Roosevelt, Harry Truman, and Dwight Eisenhower.

With *Washington, D.C.*, Vidal began his cycle of six novels exploring American history. Vidal has said that he was born to be a writer but was trained to be a politician; he grew up in the environment he describes in *Washington, D.C.* The origins of the United States fascinate him, and he uses his historical novels to trace the evolution of the nation's history. Vidal keeps his focus on the elite, since he believes that the masses of people have little to do with shaping the course of American national history. He confronts one of the oldest and hardest questions that historians face: Do individuals (the "great" men and women) shape history, or do impersonal forces (such as the rise of nationalism or the intertwining of global economies) shape history and sweep individual leaders along with the tide? Vidal says, "A good ruler in a falling time falls, too, while a bad ruler at a time of national ascendancy rises," then adds, "But, men certainly affect events. . . . [T]he only moral life is to act as if whatever one does is of great moment."

Washington, D.C. moves through the years of the Great Depression, World War II, the beginning of the Cold War, the McCarthy period of anti-Communist hysteria, and the Korean War. It opens in July, 1937. A fictitious Southern senator, James Burden Day, has successfully led the fight to block President Roosevelt's attempt to pack the Supreme Court with supporters of his New Deal program. Day, who has similarities to Vidal's grandfather, Senator Gore, is being pushed for the presidency by anti-Roosevelt conservatives, and he wants to save the republic from F. D. R. He and the president represent two opposing principles, Day says: F. D. R. believes that government must do everything for the people, while he, Senator Day, believes it cannot do much more than it is doing if individuals are going to retain any sort of private freedom. Day is a decent, restrained man. He does not have much idealistic feeling for others, although "he tried, for he truly believed that one ought to be good." In his quest for the presidency, he is supported by his smart, cold assistant, Clay Overbury, and by Blaise Sanford, a ruthless newspaper publisher who wants to make someone—anyone—president. Burden Day has a major problem, however: He lacks money to run a campaign, since he has not used his office to enrich himself. Blaise introduces him to a man who represents oil interests. He offers Senator Day money in return for a favor that will benefit those interests. Day agrees, but in the contest for the presidency, Roosevelt outmaneuvers him and goes on to win the 1940 and 1944 elections.

Burden Day remains senator but finds himself on the periphery of power as Roosevelt and his successors, Harry Truman and Dwight Eisenhower, move the United States into a new arena as a world imperial power and leader of the so-called Free World during the Cold War with the Soviet Union. A central point in the mind of Day (and Vidal) is that the American empire is no different from any other empire. The republic, based on the ideal of a small government with limited power and on the dignity of the individual, is submerged within a militarized empire that operates on a global scale.

As an old man who has served in Washington since the days of Woodrow Wilson, Day decides in the early 1950's to run for one last term in the Senate. Clay Overbury, however, now the son-in-law of Blaise Sanford, uses his knowledge of the bribe to force his friend Day to withdraw from the race. Clay takes Burden's seat in the Senate. If Day is a decent, modest, flawed man, Overbury, with some similarities to John Kennedy, is an empty man without belief in friends, ideals, or issues. He only wants power. At the end, Clay has his power and Burden Day dies, perhaps by suicide. As Burden dies, he tells a ghostly vision of his father; "It has all gone wrong." Presumably he means that not only his life has gone wrong but the promise of the American republic has also been lost.

BURR

First published: 1973
Type of work: Novel

The activities of the founding fathers of the United States were aimed at gaining wealth and power for themselves, not at any idealistic concept.

Vidal's iconoclastic portrait of the American founding fathers in *Burr* would have shocked an earlier generation. In 1973, however, the United States had just emerged from the tumult of the civil rights revolution and was still torn by controversy over the Vietnam War and by the Watergate scandal that would soon force President Richard Nixon to resign from office. As one reviewer of *Burr* pointed out, to the millions of Americans who believed that the ancient verities of the Republic had become hollow, Vidal explained that they always had been. If many readers were surprised that Vidal's history was not what their teachers had taught them, his description of the founding fathers did not shock professional historians. As usual, Vidal had done excellent research and had based his work solidly in the interpretative tradition of such great American historians as Henry Adams and Charles Beard, as well as the young revisionist historians of the 1960's and 1970's.

Burr opens in 1833 and ends in 1840, four years after Aaron Burr's death at age eighty. It is narrated by Charles Schuyler, a twenty-five-year-old law clerk in Burr's office, who wants to give up the legal profession to be a writer. He is intrigued by Burr, a dark figure of the heroic period of American history, who is still very much alive and active. Burr is witty, cosmopolitan, and sophisticated. He is willing to talk to Charlie about the past. Meanwhile, several friends of Charlie are plotting against Vice President Martin van Buren, whom they expect to try for the presidency in 1836, after Andrew Jackson's second term in office. Van Buren's enemies see Charlie's project with Burr as a possible way to carry out their political schemes. They know that Burr and Van Buren had been close; in fact, there is a rumor that Van Buren is Burr's illegitimate son. If Charlie finds evidence of that in his research on Burr, they can use it to defeat Van Buren.

Burr provides Charlie with copies of his journal on the Revolutionary War, in which he was an officer, and dictates additional material to fill out his memoirs. Charlie is quickly captivated by the old man, who makes the famous figures of the past, his friends and acquaintances, come alive: George Washington, Thomas Jefferson, Benedict Arnold, James Madison, James Monroe, John Marshall, Alexander Hamilton, John Adams, Andrew Jackson, and many more. Burr had been a leader among the founding fathers, a man who sparkled even among that glittering elite. He was Jefferson's vice president and he assumed, as did many others, that he would someday be president. Yet he got in the way of powerful interests in New York, represented by Alexander Hamilton, and seemed to threaten the Virginia clique headed by Jefferson. Burr killed Hamilton in a duel. His political career in ruins, he went westward, probably with plans to break Mexico away from Spain. Perhaps he intended to become king of Mexico. Jefferson accused him of attempting to break up the union; he had Burr arrested and tried for treason. Despite pressure from Jefferson, however, Burr was not convicted.

Burr brings to life one of American history's important and neglected figures, but it does more. It entertains and titillates as Burr turns his irreverent wit against the holy figures of the past. Washington is a plump figure who has difficulty getting on a horse without splitting his pants. As a general, he displays "eerie incompetence"; he is a man of courage and will, not military ability. His real genius is for business and for political intrigue. Jefferson is a hypocrite who rattles on about inalienable rights yet denies them to slaves, Indians, women, and poor white men. He is an empire builder who doubles the size of the United States.

Burr is not an embittered old man who has nothing good to say about his contemporaries, however; he likes John Adams, James Madison, and Andrew Jackson. His point is that the founding fathers were like all political leaders: They were opportunistic men out for money and power. They did not create the United States out of some idealistic concern for the masses. When they wrote the United States constitution, they built a governmental structure designed to benefit themselves personally. Burr sees nothing wrong with that; he simply dislikes the hypocrisy with which many of his contemporaries, especially Jefferson, cloaked their intentions.

When Charlie Schuyler finishes his work with Burr, he loves the old man. He finds evidence that Burr is indeed Van Buren's father, but he does not use it; Van Buren rewards him with a government positon overseas. In a final twist, Charlie learns that Burr is his own father (a wish fulfilled), making Van Buren his big brother.

LINCOLN

First published: 1984
Type of work: Novel

Abraham Lincoln creates a new centralized and unified nation that goes far beyond the vision of the founding fathers.

Lincoln surprised some readers, who expected Gore Vidal to turn his inconoclastic wit on the Great Emancipator, as he had Washington and Jefferson. Instead, Vidal draws an admiring portrait of the Civil War president. In this long, rich study of Abraham Lincoln during the Civil War, Vidal describes the interwoven lives of a variety of people surrounding Lincoln in the war-besieged capital: Young John Hay, Lincoln's personal secretary (and later one of the greatest American secretaries of state); Lincoln's rivals for power in the Republican party, including wily Secretary of State William Seward and staid Secretary of the Treasury Salmon P. Chase; arrogant generals such as George McClellan, who struts prettily in his uniform but never gets around to fighting battles; and plotters determined to kill Lincoln, including young David Herold and actor John Wilkes Booth, who finally does assassinate the president. Vidal shows deep sympathy for the president's wife, Mary Todd Lincoln, so often portrayed as a horrible shrew, another burden for the beleaguered president to carry. Vidal presents Mary Lincoln as an intelligent and decent woman going insane.

Lincoln is the mystery. Vidal does not take the novelist's liberty of getting inside Lincoln's mind to show what he was thinking; he presents Lincoln only from an exterior viewpoint, as described and interpreted by those around him. Vidal emphatically rejects the popular view of Lincoln, the view largely shaped by poet and Lincoln biographer Carl Sandburg. The folksy, man-of-the-people figure presented by Sandburg was only a mask created by Lincoln, Vidal believes, to hide his real self. The real Lincoln was a cold, brilliant, ruthlessly determined man, a man who did not shrink from exercising dictatorial power during the Civil War crisis, becoming the most powerful president in American history.

In *Lincoln*, William Seward, another master of power and of masks, most clearly understands the president. Seward knows what later generations tended to forget: Lincoln did not step out of a log cabin directly into the White House. He had served in Congress and had been a successful railroad lawyer. Lincoln heads the Republican party, which Seward has helped create. This is not a party of backwoods farmers but of industrial capitalism. After the war starts, Seward tells Lincoln that he has a chance to re-create the republic and to achieve greatness. Lincoln, startled, freezes with attention. Seward says that he had looked at an old Lincoln speech, given when he was twenty-eight years old. Lincoln had mentioned Alexander the Great, Julius Caesar, and Napoleon. The founding fathers had gotten all the glory of great deeds, Lincoln said in his speech; those who came afterward, such as Lincoln himself, would be mere office holders. The founding fathers had left little room for an eagle or lion. Now, Seward implies, the war crisis gives Lincoln a chance to soar, to achieve greatness.

Lincoln understands one terrible fact. Despite the squabbling of Republican politicians and the incompetence of northern military leaders, if he can hold the nation together, the North will inevitably win. Since it has more people than the South, the South will run out of men before the Union does. Seward finally fully understands that "there had been, from the beginning, a single-minded dictator in the White House . . . by whose will alone the war had been prosecuted." Seward understands Lincoln's political genius: "He had been able to make himself absolute dictator without ever letting anyone suspect that he was anything more than a joking, timid backwoods lawyer."

Lincoln achieves his destiny. He leads the nation to victory and, like a hero in an ancient myth, is swept away at his moment of success. In 1867, while in France, John Hay meets Charles Schuyler, the narrator of *Burr*, who has not returned from overseas since 1837. Hay tries to explain to the curious Schuyler Lincoln's place in history. Lincoln had superseded Washington, Hay said, because he had led the greatest war in human history and had put the Union back together. More than that, he had created a new country not envisioned by the founding fathers, a unified, centralized power. He was the American Bismarck, Hay and Schuyler agree, referring to Otto von Bismarck, who was at that time creating a unified Germany.

Summary

Gore Vidal has proved to be the master of historical fiction in the post-World War II era. His concern with the nature of Western civilization and with the way people gain and use power has led him to explore history from sixth century B.C. Athens to modern Washington, D.C. Wit, irony, and deep pessimism about the human estate characterize his work.

Bibliography

Dick, Bernard F. *The Apostate Angel: A Critical Study of Gore Vidal.* New York: Random House, 1974.

Kiernan, Robert F. *Gore Vidal.* New York: Frederick Ungar, 1982.

Stanton, Robert J. *Gore Vidal: A Primary and Secondary Bibliography.* Boston: G. K. Hall, 1978.

Stanton, Robert J., and Gore Vidal, eds. *Views from a Window: Conversations with Gore Vidal.* Secaucus, N.J.: Lyle Stuart, 1980.

White, Ray Lewis. *Gore Vidal.* New York: Twayne, 1968.

Ziolkowski, Theodore. *Fictional Transfigurations of Jesus.* Princeton, N.J.: Princeton University Press, 1972.

William E. Pemberton

KURT VONNEGUT, JR.

Born: Indianapolis, Indiana
November 11, 1922

Principal Literary Achievement
Short story writer and novelist Vonnegut is noted for his satiric humor, social commentary, frequent use of science fiction, and increasingly postmodern techniques.

Biography
Kurt Vonnegut was born in Indianapolis, Indiana, on November 11, 1922, the son of Kurt and Edith Vonnegut. He was the youngest of three children. His ancestors had come from Germany in 1855. They were prosperous, originally as brewers and merchants, down to Kurt's grandfather and father, who were both architects, and they were prominent in the heavily German Indianapolis society. Then World War I left a residue of anti-German feeling in America and prohibitions on the use of the German language, dimming the family's pride and its cultural heritage. Prohibition brought an end to the brewing business, and the Great Depression of the 1930's left Vonnegut's father without work essentially for the rest of his life. Vonnegut writes frequently of the Depression and repeatedly portrays people who, like his father, are left feeling purposeless by loss of occupation.

At Shortridge High School, he wrote for the *Shortridge Daily Echo*. The rigor of writing daily to deadlines helped shape his habits as a writer. In 1940 he went to Cornell University in Ithaca, New York, where he majored in biochemistry and wrote for the *Cornell Sun*. By January, 1943, Vonnegut was a private in the United States Army. The following May, his mother committed suicide, an event of which he sometimes writes as having left him a "legacy of suicide." Soon thereafter he was sent to Europe, captured, and held as a prisoner of war in Dresden, Germany. There he experienced the event that forms the basis of his novel *Slaughterhouse-Five* (1969), the firebombing that virtually destroyed Dresden on the night of February 13, 1945.

After discharge from the Army, Vonnegut did graduate studies in anthropology at the University of Chicago. He also married his former high school sweetheart, Jane Cox. While a student, he once again worked at journalism as a police reporter for the Chicago City News Bureau. Vonnegut left Chicago without a degree, although in 1971 his novel *Cat's Cradle* (1963) was accepted in lieu of a thesis and he was awarded an M.A.

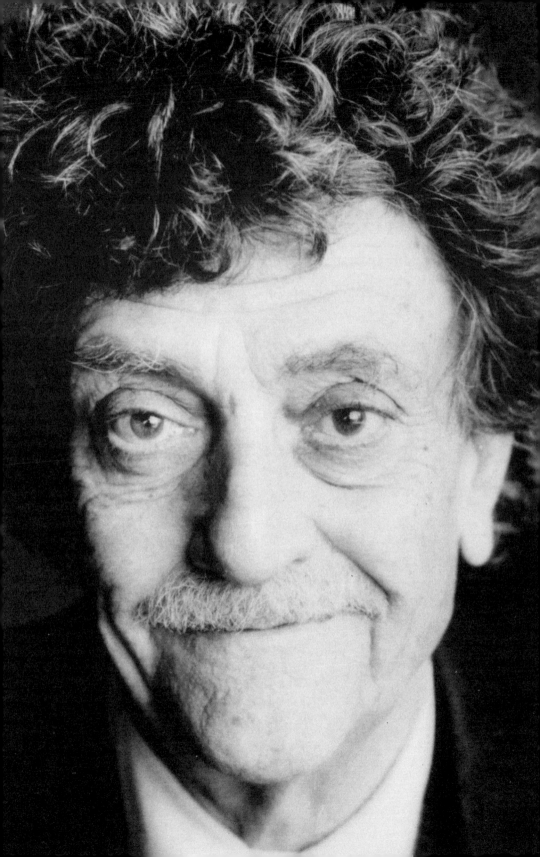

In 1947, Vonnegut moved to Schenectady, New York, where he worked as a public relations writer at the General Electric Research Laboratory. There he began writing fiction, and his first published short story, "Report on the Barnhouse Effect," appeared in *Colliers* in February, 1950. Encouraged by his success as a short story writer, he resigned from General Electric and moved to Provincetown, Massachusetts, to devote himself full time to writing. He continued to publish in popular magazines such as *The Saturday Evening Post, Ladies Home Journal, Colliers,* and *Cosmopolitan,* but he also placed stories in science fiction journals such as *Galaxy* and *Fantasy and Science Fiction Magazine.*

His first novel, *Player Piano* (1952), was reissued by Bantam in 1954 with the title *Utopia 14.* Largely because of his success with short stories, which often paid well, Vonnegut did not produce his second novel, *The Sirens of Titan* (1959), until seven years after *Player Piano.* Those first two novels, together with a number of the short stories, earned for Vonnegut identification as a science fiction writer, a label with which he was not always happy, because that genre was disdained in many quarters.

During this time, Vonnegut faced personal hardships. In October, 1957, his father died, and in 1958, his sister Alice was stricken with cancer. Days before her death, her husband, John Adams, was killed when his commuter train crashed from a bridge. After this double tragedy, Vonnegut adopted three of the four orphaned children, doubling the size of his family.

The 1960's began as difficult times, but then saw Vonnegut's gradual emergence to fame. Television dried up the magazine market for short stories, and he turned to the paperback market, first with a collection of short stories called *Canary in a Cat House* (1961), then with the novel *Mother Night* (1961). Neither achieved great sales. The next two novels, *Cat's Cradle* and *God Bless You, Mr. Rosewater* (1965), appeared in hardcover. In 1965, he went to teach at the Writers' Workshop at the University of Iowa, where he met other writers and critics who influenced him, particularly in encouraging him to enter his fiction more personally. This led to his adding a new and highly personal preface to the 1966 hardcover edition of *Mother Night*; in many of his subsequent works, such autobiographical introductions have become a popular feature.

In 1966 and 1967, Avon and Dell reissued all of his novels in paperback, and *Player Piano* and *Mother Night* were reprinted in hardcover. The coincidence of these events brought greater public attention to his work, and his fame began to build. A new collection of his short stories, *Welcome to the Monkey House,* appeared in 1968. Meanwhile, Vonnegut had won a Guggenheim Fellowship to revisit Dresden and research the event he had struggled to write about for years, the great air raid he had experienced. This led to *Slaughterhouse-Five*; the novel, and the film that followed it, brought Vonnegut broad popularity and financial security.

Success, however, brought its own difficulties. Having faced in fiction the event that had motivated so much of his writing, Vonnegut now struggled. He even considered abandoning the novel for other forms, writing the play *Happy Birthday, Wanda*

June (1970). A compilation from his works appeared as a teleplay called *Between Time and Timbuktu* (1972). His marriage to Jane foundered, and he moved alone to New York City. At last, in 1973, came another novel, *Breakfast of Champions*, different in form from his previous work and illustrated with his own drawings. It drew mixed reviews but achieved excellent sales, with a first printing of a hundred thousand copies.

In 1974 came the publication of a collection of essays, speeches, stories, and biography called *Wampeters, Foma, & Granfalloons (Opinions)*. Two more novels, *Slapstick* (1976) and *Jailbird* (1979), followed, in what Vonnegut has asserted was a difficult decade for him as a writer. He achieved a feeling of completion with *Slaughterhouse-Five*, he said, and found little that provided stimulation in the society of that period. By 1979, however, Vonnegut had remarried, to the photographer Jill Krementz, and adopted a baby daughter, Lily. Also in 1979 he had a return to the stage when his daughter Edith produced a musical adaptation of *God Bless You, Mr. Rosewater* in New York. He wrote the text of a children's Christmas story, *Sun Moon Star* (1980), illustrated by Ivan Chermayeff. *Palm Sunday: An Autobiographical Collage* (1981) was another collection, and it was followed by the novels *Deadeye Dick* (1982), *Galápagos* (1985), and *Bluebeard* (1987).

Having become a major figure in the American literary establishment, Vonnegut has been much in demand as a speaker, frequently using the title "How to Get a Job Like Mine" to embark upon a rambling and highly entertaining evening something in the manner of Mark Twain. He has also been much in demand for articles in magazines and even for advertisements—an ironic echo of his beginnings as a public relations writer for General Electric.

Analysis

Vonnegut has spoken of his experience of being in Dresden in 1945, when that city was firebombed and perhaps a hundred thousand lives were lost, as being an early motivation to write. Although it was not until his sixth novel, *Slaughterhouse-Five*, that he actually based a novel on that experience, the first five all point in that direction. Notably, there is an apocalyptic event involved in each of those novels. There is also the descent into an underground place—much as he went underground to survive Dresden—from which the protagonist emerges with a new view of the world. In this way, Vonnegut weaves together personal experience with the mythic pattern of descent (Jonah into the belly of the whale, Orpheus into the underworld) as prelude to rebirth, transformation, or new knowledge.

Other patterns discernible in Vonnegut's novels clearly draw on personal history. Vonnegut's father was a retiring person who, after his prolonged unemployment, became reclusive. The novels contain numerous father-son relationships where the fater is distant. Vonnegut's mother committed suicide, and he speaks frankly of his "legacy of suicide" and his proneness to depression. He repeatedly treats the themes of isolation, depression, mental illness, and suicide in his characters as manifestations of the stresses of society.

Vonnegut was very close to his late sister—in *Slapstick*, he speaks of her as the imaginary audience to whom he writes—and her death touched him deeply. Perhaps the early loss of the two women closest to him gave rise to a fear of entrusting love to women, as seen in the earlier fiction, where women frequently withdraw, die, or betray. Certainly a triangle of two men and a woman, reflecting his family structure of the two brothers and the sister, is repeated.

Apart from Dresden, Vonnegut speaks of the Great Depression as being the other shaping event in his life. It gives rise to his interest in socioeconomic topics such as how to achieve full employment, how to distribute the wealth of the nation equitably, how to preserve a sense of individual worth in an automated system, and how to ensure that technology is applied with thought for human needs. Novels such as *God Bless You, Mr. Rosewater* and *Jailbird* make issues of economics and ethics their main theme, and these issues make up one of the most persistent themes throughout Vonnegut's work.

Because his prewar education had a science emphasis, because his brother was a scientist, and because he worked for General Electric's Research Laboratories, his interest in science and technology was always considerable. In fact, he has said that he did not write science fiction but simply wrote about the world he saw, which was a technologically sophisticated one. He is the product of a generation that saw science produce the atomic bomb and hoped-for solutions such as the insecticide DDT prove poisonous. Science, technology, and the moral and ethical issues raised by their uses occupy a major place in Vonnegut's fiction.

As early as college, Vonnegut wrote antiwar columns, and that theme has endured—most conspicuously in *Slaughterhouse-Five*. Other recurrent themes bear on social issues: how to overcome individual loneliness in an indifferent urban society; the treatment of blacks, Indians, and women in American history; the plight of the homeless; and the inadequacy of the small nuclear family to deal with the stresses of contemporary life. He describes himself as being like a shaman who responds to and comments on the flux of daily life.

This description makes Vonnegut sound solemn, whereas he is for many first and foremost a comic writer. Much of his humor is satire, mocking the foibles of human behavior and ridiculing aspects of modern society. He sees himself in the tradition of previous satirists such as Voltaire, Jonathan Swift, and Mark Twain. This kind of humor is often barbed. At other times he is farcical, finding humor in odd-sounding words, ludicrous situations, comical names, oddly proportioned bodies, and almost anything that might provoke laughter. It is laughter, he sees, that helps people through many testing moments in life. Growing up in the Depression, he saw how the comedy of such comedians as Laurel and Hardy, W. C. Fields, and Jack Benny boosted public morale. Vonnegut has even described his books as being like mosaics, where each tile is a separate little joke.

A characteristic of the slapstick comedians such as Laurel and Hardy whom Vonnegut applauds is that they "bargain in good faith with destiny." They are decent people who honestly try and who naïvely expect fair return. Vonnegut sees most people as being like that, which is one reason why there are few villains in his books. Romantic love, he argues, is overestimated, but what is important is treating other people with "common human decency," a phrase he often repeats. That also may account for the kindly tone that persists in Vonnegut's fiction, however sharp the satire.

Stylistically, Vonnegut's work suggests the influence of his early work in journalism. There is little flourish, elaborate description, or prolonged psychological characterization. His prose is compressed, functional, and curt. In the middle novels, notably *Cat's Cradle* and *Breakfast of Champions*, exaggeratedly short sentences, paragraphs, and chapters are conspicuous.

Vonnegut's mature fiction also displays characteristics associated with "postmodernism," such as declaring its own fictionality, refusing to be consistent in form, and not trying to order a chaotic world. Such elements are seen in the chopped-up and shuffled chronology of *Slaughterhouse-Five*; Vonnegut's own appearance in *Breakfast of Champions* as the author, discussing what he will do next with the characters; his use of drawings and his mixing of history and fantasy in that same book; and his basing the world of *Deadeye Dick* on the characters and setting of his own previous *Breakfast of Champions*.

Those characteristics add up to a highly individualized style. This effect is heightened by the way in which Vonnegut enters many of his novels directly and personally. Often there is a character who seems partly autobiographical, standing for some aspect of Vonnegut: Billy Pilgrim, the soldier and prisoner of war in *Slaughterhouse-Five*, or the science fiction writer Kilgore Trout, for example. Frequently there is also an autobiographical preface or introduction in which Vonnegut talks about his life and how it relates to the present story. Hence the reader may sense an unusually overt connection between the fiction and the author when reading Vonnegut's work.

MOTHER NIGHT

First published: 1961
Type of work: Novel

A former American double agent comes to question whether he was really the Nazi he pretended to be.

Mother Night, Vonnegut's third novel, differs from its predecessors in having no emphasis on technology or use of a fictional future. It is the first to be written with a first-person narrator, which deepens the characterization of the protagonist and intensifies the soul searching, both on his part and the author's, that goes on in this novel. *Mother Night* is also the first of his novels to have an autobiographical introduction, added to the 1966 edition, in which Vonnegut ruminates about his own wartime experience and his being of German origin. He notes:

If I'd been born in Germany, I suppose I would have *been* a Nazi, bopping Jews and gypsies and Poles around, leaving boots sticking out of snowbanks, warming myself with my secretly virtuous insides. So it goes.

That thought illustrates the moral that Vonnegut sees in this novel: "We are what we pretend to be, so we must be careful about what we pretend to be."

The pretense in this story concerns Howard Campbell, an American playwright living in Germany with a German wife as World War II breaks out. Campbell is persuaded to remain in Germany, cultivate the Nazis, and become an American agent. He becomes increasingly successful as a Nazi propagandist, although his broadcasts contain coded information vital to the Allies. At war's end he is spirited back to New York because his secret role cannot be revealed and he is generally thought to be a Nazi. He is hunted by revengeful patriots and by admiring neo-Nazis and racists — and by the Israelis, to whom he eventually delivers himself.

Campbell's narrative is written in an Israeli prison as he searches himself for the answers to the question of whether he was really the Nazi he pretended to be or the secret spy, whether he did more to further Nazi crimes than he needed to, and what he would have done if the Germans had won. He had always believed that his propaganda was too ludicrous to believe and that he could remain detached from the horrors around him, yet the fact remained that many Nazis found him inspirational. What sustained Campbell during the war was the love of his actress wife, Helga Noth. They would retreat into a private world of love, defined by their big double bed, and become a separate "Nation of Two." That escape is denied only when Helga disappears while entertaining German troops.

Clearly this novel raises questions of the "good Germans" who never spoke out against the Nazis or their atrocities, and it probably looks back to the McCarthy hearings of the early 1950's, when the American government was involved in a "witch hunt" for suspected Communists. Almost certainly it reflects some doubts on Vonnegut's part about his own former role as a public relations person at General Electric. It also prompts its readers to ask themselves about those situations in which they may have believed they remained inwardly loyal to certain values while doing nothing publicly to oppose their violation. The novel takes a hard look at how people survive in such times as the Nazi reign, either believing themselves secretly aloof or escaping into narrow personal worlds, or by "schizophrenia" — simply obliterating a part of their consciousness.

In the end, Campbell commits suicide, condemning himself for "crimes against himself." He is unable to unravel the pros and cons of his public role; what he does know is that he betrayed his conscience and misused both his love for Helga and his integrity as a writer. The issue of a writer's integrity comes up in several of Vonnegut's novels, starting with *Player Piano* (1952). His writers frequently have to decide whether to compromise in order to achieve sales, for example, or determine what responsibility they bear for actions to which they may prompt their readers. Campbell goes from being a romantic playwright dealing in pure fantasy to a propagandist contributing to hideous atrocities. *Mother Night* also extends the moral issue to include everyone, inasmuch as they may try to author parts of their lives, create illusions for themselves, and manipulate others like characters.

Mother Night, especially with its added introduction, reflects Vonnegut's ruminations about Dresden and about the contradictions implicit in his being a German-American fighting against Germans, who then is nearly killed by the Americans; it reflects his concerns about the Allies' destruction of historic, nonmilitary Dresden and thousands of civilian lives in the name of a noble cause. It also shows him moving to a first-person voice, which enables him to explore directly the inner doubts such issues raise. The novel is especially compelling because its questions are not easy to resolve. Howard Campbell's dilemma is no easier for the reader to resolve than it is for him. He remains one of Vonnegut's most complete characterizations, the more haunting because the reader may think, on a smaller scale, that "there, but for the grace of God, go I."

CAT'S CRADLE

First published: 1963
Type of work: Novel

A careless scientific genius leaves his children crystals that turn all the world's water into ice.

Cat's Cradle is narrated by "Jonah," or John, who originally intends to write a book about the atomic bombing of Hiroshima called "The Day the World Ended." The book he ends up writing is the present one, which could have the same title, although it is about a different apocalypse. John sets out to interview "Newt," the son of the late Dr. Felix Hoenikker, one of the " 'Fathers' of the first atom bomb."

There are three Hoenikker children: Frank, the oldest, Angela, the tall musician daughter, and the diminutive Newt. The father has left each of his children a vial of crystals of ice-nine, a compound that turns water to ice at room temperature. Angela has used hers to buy a "tom cat husband" who turns out to be a United States agent, Newt has turned over his to a tiny dancer from the Bolshoi Ballet who is a Soviet agent, and Frank uses his to gain his position as chief adviser to Papa Monzano, dictator of the island of San Lorenzo, where most of the plot is set.

Also on San Lorenzo is a fugitive preacher named Bokonon, founder of a religion called "Bokononism," which has been invented as a placebo for the population of an island so destitute that no economic system can possibly help them. Bokononism is outlawed but practiced by virtually everyone on the island. Its tenets are contained in the Books of Bokonon, which begins, "All of the true things I am about to tell you are shameless lies." Vonnegut the former anthropology student obviously enjoys inventing this religion, parodying the way religions are shaped to fit the needs of particular times, places, and populations. He also has fun inventing the language made up of the dialect of San Lorenzo and the vocabulary of Bokononism. To Bokononists, nations are "granfalloons," lies are "foma," and one's inevitable destiny is one's "Zah-mah-ki-bo."

Ultimately, Papa Monzano uses his ice-nine crystals to commit suicide, thus starting the chain reaction that turns all the world's water to ice and dooms humanity. Those islanders not already killed join Bokonon in suicide. Jonah plans to write his story of "The Day the World Ended" before he, too, takes ice-nine.

While *Cat's Cradle* takes a view of religions that is at once spoofing and anthropologically valid, it also comments on the nature of fiction. In so doing, it draws analogies between preachers and writers. Both use words to persuade audiences of the truth of the visions of the worlds they create. Both, this novel seems to say, may be like the maker of the cat's cradle, who tells the child it sees the cat and sees the cradle, where there is only string. Bokonon makes a religion of a fiction, just as the writer makes up a plausible world out of words. Bokonon, however, admits his religion is "shameless," if helpful, lies. In *Cat's Cradle*, Vonnegut essentially does the same, prefacing it with the epigraph "Nothing in this book is true" and beginning with a borrowing of Herman Melville's opening of *Moby-Dick* (1851), possibly the most conspicuous sentence in American literature. He then spoofs serious fictional forms with 127 "chapters," each with its own joke title, made-up words, calypsos, and poems; a digressive, rambling plot; and a bizarre array of slapstick characters.

While *Cat's Cradle* typifies earlier Vonnegut with its ending in mass suicide and the end of the world, it is irresistibly comic and light in tone. In the previous three novels, Vonnegut had worked with recognizable forms—the dystopian novel in *Player Piano* (1952), the space opera with *The Sirens of Titan* (1959), and the confessional novel in *Mother Night* (1962). *Cat's Cradle* is strikingly different and shows the author emerging with a style that is uniquely his own. The blend of serious social commentary and irreverent lampooning, of cynicism and compassion, of caricature figures and staccato style, would become Vonnegut's trademark.

GOD BLESS YOU, MR. ROSEWATER

First published: 1965
Type of work: Novel

An alcoholic philanthropist tries to prove that his obsession with the needy does not mean he is insane.

God Bless You, Mr. Rosewater: Or, Pearls Before Swine is the story of a multimillionaire who, traumatized by a wartime experience, tries to compensate by treating the underprivileged with kindess and philanthropy. He seeks to enact the motto, "God damn it, you've got to be kind," which some have seen as the essence of Vonnegut. This proves to be difficult and complicated, however, in a society that equates riches with merit and morality, and poverty with sloth and undeserving.

Eliot Rosewater's egalitarian efforts cause universal doubt about his sanity, drive his wife to a breakdown, infuriate his father to the point of obsession, and eventually lead to his own mental collapse.

Vonnegut writes that a sum of money, the Rosewater fortune, is the central character of the novel. The distribution of wealth and its social and psychological consequences is certainly the novel's central theme. One can see the impact on Vonnegut's life of the Great Depression of the 1930's behind this novel. Through prolonged unemployment, his father became purposeless and reclusive, while his mother could never live in the style in which she had been reared, and she was anguished to the point of suicide.

A second major theme of this book is neurosis. Almost every character suffers some degree of mental affliction, often accompanied or caused by physical malaise. The craziness contributes to both the poignancy that occurs in this novel and the humor that dominates it, but through the wacky characters and events, Vonnegut examines troubling social issues that he sees pervading America: excessive wealth alongside dire poverty; attitudes that make the poor despised, even by themselves; purposelessness bred alike by unemployment and unearned riches; and the loneliness, depression, and suicidal complexes generated by such an economic and moral structure.

The trigger for Eliot Rosewater's neurosis seems to be that in the war he killed some German soldiers who were actually noncombatant volunteer firefighters. For Eliot, volunteer firefighters are the perfect symbolic saviors. Without pay, they will go to the point of risking their own lives to help anyone, regardless of who or what they are. His philanthropy seems an effort to atone for his mistake and to become a kind of social firefighter, rescuing those suffocating in the flames of the economic system. At first he tries giving money to charities, museums, and other causes but feels no satisfying consequences of his actions and sinks into alcoholism. He then moves back to Rosewater County, Indiana, his ancestral home, where he organizes fly hunts for the unemployed and dispenses aspirin, sympathy, and glasses of wine to the distraught. He becomes a slovenly slum saint, to the despair of his conservative, hygiene-obsessed senator father, while his wife Sylvia breaks down under Eliot's obsession with the needy and his neglect of her.

An avaricious attorney named Norman Mushari (first seen in *The Sirens of Titan*) tries to overturn Eliot's inheritance by proving him insane, but he is rescued by Kilgore Trout, Vonnegut's shabby science fiction writer who reappears in several novels and is perhaps his best-known character. Trout argues that Eliot is not insane—what he has done is to conduct a social experiment. "The problem is this," says Trout: "How to love people who have no use?" The answer, he says, is to find a way of "treasuring human beings because they are *human beings.*" That is what volunteer firefighters do and what Eliot has tried to do in a society in which such a response is rare.

Vonnegut once said in an interview that the Dresden firebombing was less of an influence on him than the Great Depression. True or not, he is certainly deeply concerned with the kinds of socioeconomic issues stamped in his memory in those years; this novel (and the later *Jailbird*) emphasizes those issues. It offers no easy answers, but its implications seem almost as religious as political and seem to owe as much to the Sermon on the Mount as to the political or economic theories of Karl Marx or John Maynard Keynes. At the end, Eliot is echoing biblical language and might be seen as a kind of modern saint or Christ figure. The novel asks what this acquisitive age would make of someone who advocated giving everything to the poor. Where limitless greed is condoned and approved, a new Christ would seem crazy unless a crafty Trout could help out.

God Bless You, Mr. Rosewater has some of Vonnegut's most interestingly developed characters. The interactions between Eliot, his father Lister, and his wife Sylvia are psychologically complex. The rest of the cast are caricatures, but they are just what is needed for the novel's moral commentary—and for the broad comedy that stops it from becoming too didactic.

At the point that Eliot's mind snaps, he imagines that he sees Indianapolis consumed by the Dresden firestorm. Other than the references to fires and firefighters, there is little other allusion to the apocalypse that is to dominate Vonnegut's next novel, *Slaughterhouse-Five* (1969). Yet the story of a man who returns from the war haunted and changed by what he has seen parallels the author's own experience and paves the way for his next protagonist, Billy Pilgrim.

SLAUGHTERHOUSE-FIVE

First published: 1969
Type of work: Novel

An American prisoner of war witnesses the firebombing of Dresden during World War II and time-travels to the planet Tralfamadore.

In full, the title, *Slaughterhouse-Five: Or, The Children's Crusade, a Duty-Dance with Death*, says much about Vonnegut's sixth novel. This is the novel in which Vonnegut confronts his traumatic experience of having been in Dresden when, on February 13, 1945, it was bombed by the Allies, producing a firestorm that virtually destroyed the city and killed perhaps as many as 130,000 people. He survived the raid in the underground meatlocker of a slaughterhouse, to spend the following days exhuming corpses from the ruins and cremating them. For him, Dresden becomes the symbol of the senseless horror of war, of humankind's self-destructive propensities, and of how events arbitrarily overrule the lives of individuals.

"The Children's Crusade" comes from the wife of a wartime buddy's having said, "You were just *babies* then!" Vonnegut reflects that they were indeed very young, and the soldiers in his novel are swept along as helplessly as the hapless children of the original medieval Children's Crusade, many of whom were in fact sold into slavery. "A Duty-Dance with Death" expresses Vonnegut's need to encounter in words his experience with death, to wrestle with its meaning—or rather, lack of meaning.

In *Slaughterhouse-Five*, the wartime experience is undergone by his protagonist, Billy Pilgrim. As his name implies, Billy is a kind of universal manchild going through the pilgrimage of life. In this way, Vonnegut is able to embody directly his personal experience in an autobiographical character, yet universalize its meaning through the use of an Everyman figure.

Similarly, Vonnegut speaks directly as himself in the first and last chapters and interjects periodically throughout, "That was I. That was me," permitting him both to express intensely personal emotions and to make detached editorial comment. He avails himself of the chance to be in the story and outside it, so that he can tell his personal experience and perhaps come to a cathartic cleansing of it. Yet Vonnegut does not entirely want to make sense of Dresden or to make his book an explanation. Dresden is for him an event without sense, and it becomes an emblem of the senseless and arbitrary in life. Those qualities are emphasized when the Germans shoot one of the American prisoners as a looter when he picks up a teapot from among the ruins. Such strict and arbitrary justice in the midst of the carnage is the crowning irony of the novel.

Part of Vonnegut's resistance to ordering and rationalizing the events of his story is to chop them up, fragment them, and displace them chronologically. Billy Pilgrim becomes "unstuck in time," which means that his mind constantly shifts between times and places, as, then, does the novel. Because the story recounts Billy's postwar life up to his death, and his adventures, real or imagined, on the planet Tralfamadore, there is considerable disjunction. The reader is jerked from a childhood memory to the war years to a middle-aged Billy (an optometrist) to the preacher Pilgrim's death, and from Ilium, New York, to Dresden to Tralfamadore.

The style of the novel emphasizes its disjunction. Each of the ten short chapters is divided into short segments, each of three or four paragraphs, which may themselves be no more than a sentence long. A fragment of one scene succeeds a fragment of another, not ordered by time, place, or theme, but hurled together almost as a collage. Looked at all together, however, the parts add up to a moving depiction replete with ethical implications and emotional impact, if shorn of the kind of direct moral summations Vonnegut supplies in *Mother Night*.

Slaughterhouse-Five sees the return of Kilgore Trout, Vonnegut's fictional science fiction writer, and also of Eliot Rosewater and Howard Campbell, so that, in part, the novel builds upon preceding ones. This is not the novel's only metafictional characteristic; it mixes fact and fiction, history and fantasy. It includes quotations from actual documents by President Harry Truman and Air Marshall Sir Robert Saundby and from the fictional Trout and Campbell as if equally authentic. There are quotations of all kinds, from mildly off-color jokes to the Serenity Prayer, scattered throughout the book. There is the world of Tralfamadore, presented right alongside the historical events of World War II.

An often-noticed trait of this novel is its repetition of the phrase, "So it goes." This occurs every time anything or anyone dies. The repeated phrase has annoyed some readers, who see it as inappropriately flippant. Its repetition drums home the amount of death there is in this story and in the world, constantly calling attention to that, while at the same time reflecting a weary recognition that the author can do little to change things.

Although *Slaughterhouse-Five* has earned an enduring reputation, much of its initial popularity was related to the climate of the times. In the late 1960's, protest of America's involvement in the Vietnam War was at its height. There was a large, receptive audience for an antiwar novel. The young, among whom Vonnegut was already popular, were intensely active politically. The legions of students who campaigned for antiwar presidential candidate Senator Eugene McCarthy in 1967 and 1968 were frequently called "the Children's Crusade" in the press, and that allusion in Vonnegut's subtitle was not missed by readers of the time.

Slaughterhouse-Five, then, is remarkable in its ability to evoke pathos and laughter together, to simultaneously voice antiwar outrage and philosophical acceptance, and to combine the story of personal experience with a broader social commentary. The novel's unique form, which enables it to accomplish so much, is the culmination of Vonnegut's experiments with narrative technique in the five preceding novels.

SLAPSTICK

First published: 1976
Type of work: Novel

A giant neanderthaloid twin becomes president and creates artificial extended families to end Americans' loneliness.

In the prologue to *Slapstick: Or, Lonesome No More!* Vonnegut writes, "This is the closest I will ever come to writing an autobiography." That may seem surprising, given that the protagonist is a seven-foot six-inch neanderthaloid with seven fingers on each hand and six nipples, but he clarifies his point by saying: "It is about what life *feels* like to me." He calls it "grotesque situational comedy," and that seems an apt description of the bizarre content of this novel. He also dedicates the novel to comedians Laurel and Hardy, who "did their best with every test." There is a lot of that spirit in the novel, too.

Wilbur Swain and his twin Eliza are born so abnormal that their parents send them to be reared in a distant, obscure mansion. While they learn to behave like idiots in public because that is expected of creatures who look like them, they are actually capable of great intelligence so long as they are together. Separated, they become dull. Yet separated they are for most of their lives. Wilbur goes on to become president on the campaign slogan "Lonesome No More!" (which is also the novel's subtitle). As president, Wilbur institutes a system of artificial extended families, wherein everyone is issued a new middle name by the government and thus inherits a whole set of new relatives of the same name. Wilbur, however, comes to preside over a country which, under the impact of variable gravity, the Albanian flu, and the "Green Death," is disintegrating into warring dukedoms and states. He ends his days living among the ruins of Manhattan.

The world of this novel is one of hyperbolic distortion. In that respect it is heightened slapstick, the world rendered in manic-depressive surrealism. Vonnegut has amused with invented religions before, but the Church of Jesus Christ the Kidnapped, whose believers constantly snap their heads to look over their shoulders in hopes of seeing their abducted savior, seems peculiarly suited to this novel, where so much of the humor is visual. Similarly, the Chinese experiments that vary gravity, so that on some days bridges collapse and elevator cables snap, while on others all men have erections and can toss a manhole cover like a discus, emulate the broad, often painful comedy of slapstick.

Vonnegut's "grotesque situational comedy" includes an impression of his personal life as well as the national. He speaks of how his sister Alice loved slapstick comedy and describes how, when she heard that her husband had been killed as she herself was dying of cancer, commented, "Slapstick." That situation, with both parents dying within days of each other in tragic circumstances and leaving four young children, is a good example of the kind of real-life grotesquerie that contributes to Vonnegut's vision in *Slapstick*. The close relationship of Eliza and Wilbur may be seen as a play on Vonnegut's closeness to Alice, whom he describes as still the imagined audience for most of his writing. Similarly, Wilbur's dependence on "tri-benzo-Deportamil" may be a slapstick rendition of the author's own use of antidepressant drugs at one point in his life.

"Lonesome No More!" is a slogan Vonnegut actually suggested that vice-presidential candidate Sargent Shriver might use during the 1972 election campaign. Believing that the large, extended family of relatives living in proximity has virtually ceased to exist in America and that the small nuclear family is incapable of fulfilling the same role, Vonnegut has argued seriously that other kinds of social groupings are needed to support the individual. When he went to Biafra during the Nigerian civil war, he was most impressed with how tribal families operated, and this experience gave rise to the artificial extended families presented in *Slapstick*. The idea is treated humorously and shown with limitations, but the problem of individual isolation and loneliness within American society is one Vonnegut has always taken seriously.

His return to the theme of love in this novel is also familiar. Eliza's argument that saying "I love you" to someone leaves them no option but the obligatory "I love you, too" echoes those exchanges in the same words and the same tone in *Player Piano*. Romantic love—and here, sibling love becomes erotic—remains volatile, emotional, and undependable. Vonnegut again reasserts the superiority of "common human decency," which treats others with respect and consideration. There are other reiterations from earlier work. The name Bernard O'Hare—actually that of a wartime buddy—is used again, and Norman Mushari reappears. There is even the reappearance of a boring Paradise. These "in jokes" become part of the humor of the novel.

Some of the humor has aroused criticism of *Slapstick* as being cavalier with serious issues and carelessly dismissive. The repeated, interspersed uses of "Hi ho" and "And so on" particularly draw ire. They are the words of a first-person narrator, however, and one who is frequently high on "tri-benzo-Deportamil" and having to describe cataclysmic events beyond his control. The phrases and the tone are as much an invocation of the slapstick films of Laurel and Hardy, to whom the book is dedicated, as are the caricatures and exaggerated actions.

That tone changes in the ending, where Wilbur has died and a third-person narrator takes over. The account of his granddaughter Melody's journey to share Wilbur's old age is a touching and affirmative one. Her act is one of family love, and the story of how she is helped along the way by other people, not only those of her extended family, and by birds and animals, is a warmly affirmative one. Closing the novel with *"Das Ende"* is Vonnegut's gesture to the large, close-knit, German-speaking family that once existed in Indianapolis, as described in the prologue.

GALÁPAGOS

First published: 1985
Type of work: Novel

The last survivors of the human race escape to the Galápagos Islands and evolve over a million years into furry amphibians.

Galápagos is narrated from a future one million years hence by the ghost of Leon Trout, son of Vonnegut's frequently used character, science fiction writer Kilgore Trout. Leon was beheaded while working as a shipbuilder, and his ghost inhabits a cruise ship bound for Guayaquil, Ecuador, to carry tourists to the Galápagos Islands. While the ship is awaiting its maiden voyage, the world economic system breaks down under the burben of global debt, and World War III is triggered. Those events, however, which contain typical Vonnegut warnings about current conditions, do not end the human race; what does is a corkscrew-like microorganism that destroys ovaries.

As order breaks down in the port of Guayaquil, ten people escape in the cruise ship. They reach Santa Rosalia, one of the Galápagos Islands. At this point there is only one male, the ship's captain, and the women include an Indianapolis schoolteacher who eventually becomes the mother of the new human race. She transmits the captain's sperm to six Indian girls and impregnates them. The male line survives in the baby of a Japanese woman. He is born furry as the result of a genetic mutation caused when his grandparents were caught in the atom bombing of Hiroshima.

Over the succeeding million years, as the descendants of these original survivors reproduce, they adapt to their largely marine life by developing flippers instead of hands and feet and smaller, streamlined heads. They also inherit the fur of the Japanese mutant ancestor. Thus they evolve as seal-like "fisherfolk."

Charles Darwin and evolutionary theory are major themes in this book, and evolution is even reflected in the form of *Galápagos*. The novel has fifty-two chapters, as the year has weeks. The first part of the book is called "The Thing Was," capturing the colloquial way to refer to complications in a narrative as well as alluding to the original form of the human animal. The second part's title is "And the Thing Became," recounting the adaptation to aquatic life. Having *Galápagos* narrated by the son of his fictional alter ego, Kilgore Trout, makes it seem as if the novel itself has evolved out of Vonnegut's own earlier fiction.

Vonnegut recognizes that evolutionary theory is often misunderstood and that it leaves unanswered questions. He points out that evolution is not simply an inevitable progression of constant improvement. Contingency often shapes the course of events, such as the occurrence of a new virus that destroys female reproductive organs or the mutation caused by the Hiroshima bomb. Moreover, evolution is not always toward the better. In the Irish elk, the deer family's defense mechanism of antlers was taken to such an extreme that it ultimately led to the extinction of the species.

Some of these ideas Vonnegut treats with typical humor. The convoluted development of the first part of the book, with its many characters, digressions, histories, and coincidences, creates its own kind of whimsical evolution into the main plot concerning the few who reach Santa Rosalia. The short chapters, chopped into subsections, end with suspenseful jokes. It is as if *Galápagos* itself, like evolution, is shaped not by grand design but by chance and coincidence.

One of the central ideas, comical but pointed, that the novel presents is that the huge human brain has become as burdensome an evolutionary step for humans as the Irish elk's huge antlers were. Humans' brains, with their capacity to invent, imagine, and hold opinions, have become their greatest enemies. One problem, Vonnegut posits, is that it has proved impossible for humans to imagine something that could happen without trying to make it happen, often with disastrous results. Similarly, opinions, not necessarily grounded in fact, become so firmly held that they drive humans to irrational acts. In *Galápagos*, then, Vonnegut reverses the general supposition that as people evolve to higher intelligence they improve. His fisherfolk develop flippers and lose the manual dexterity to make tools or weapons, and as their skulls shrink, their brains diminish and they become harmonious and content.

Implicit in *Galápagos*, despite its humor, are some grim warnings. Among the most obvious are warnings about the world economic situation, with its inequalities resulting in massive starvation and in debts that threaten the monetary system. There are warnings about the possibilities of accidental war, of conflict over "opinions," and of new viruses made dangerous by environmental damage to immune systems. Behind all these ideas, though, looms the overriding danger of what humans are themselves, here presented as the danger posed by their overlarge brains.

Galápagos is dominated by a positive tone, however, not only because of its humor but because it ultimately is affirmative about human decency. It is notably affirmative about females. While many of the males are impaired or incompetent, the women, particularly the central mother figure Mary Hepburn, cope, survive, and nurture. Even the ghostly narrator rejects his father's cynicism and his own tormented past to become reconciled. The epigraph, borrowed from Anne Frank, is appropriate: "In spite of everything, I still believe people are really good at heart."

Summary

Kurt Vonnegut has likened his role as writer in society to that of the canary in the old coal mines—to give alarm of danger. He has also spoken of himself as a shaman, responding to and speaking about what goes on in society. Yet he remains a comic novelist. His novels, as a result, are full of warning, social commentary, and, frequently, moral judgment, but in their humor and compassion escape heavy didacticism.

Vonnegut has evolved a distinctive individual style. His often fragmented, tragicomic renderings have struck a chord in the readers of his time.

Bibliography

Broer, Lawrence. *Sanity Plea: Schizophrenia in the Novels of Kurt Vonnegut*. Ann Arbor: University of Michigan Press, 1989.

Giannone, Richard. *Vonnegut: A Preface to His Novels*. Port Washington, N.Y.: Kennikat Press, 1977.

Klinkowitz, Jerome. *Kurt Vonnegut*. London: Methuen, 1982.

_____. *"Slaughterhouse-Five": Reforming the Novel and the World*. Boston: Twayne, 1990.

Klinkowitz, Jerome, and Donald L. Lawler, eds. *Vonnegut in America*. New York: Delacorte/Seymour Lawrence, 1977.

Klinkowitz, Jerome, and John Somer, eds. *The Vonnegut Statement*. New York: Delacorte/Seymour Lawrence, 1973.

Lundquist, James. *Kurt Vonnegut*. New York: Frederick Ungar, 1976.

Merrill, Robert, ed. *Critical Essays on Kurt Vonnegut*. Boston: G. K. Hall, 1990.

Pieratt, Asa B., Julie Huffman-Klinkowitz, and Jerome Klinkowitz. *Kurt Vonnegut: A Comprehensive Bibliography*. 2d ed. Hamden, Conn.: Shoe String Press, 1987.

Reed, Peter J. *Kurt Vonnegut, Jr.* New York: Thomas Y. Crowell, 1976.

Schatt, Stanley. *Kurt Vonnegut, Jr.* Boston: Twayne, 1976.

Peter J. Reed

ALICE WALKER

Born: Eatonton, Georgia
February 9, 1944

Principal Literary Achievement

Accomplished in several literary genres, Walker has achieved most recognition and notoriety for her innovative, Pulitzer Prize-winning novel, *The Color Purple*.

Biography

Alice Walker was born on February 9, 1944, in Eatonton, Georgia, the eighth and youngest child of Willie Lee and Minnie Grant Walker. Eatonton was a small, poor town, and the Walkers made their living by sharecropping cotton, a way of life that earned the family about three hundred dollars a year. Walker learned early the oppression of economic deprivation coupled with the Southern reality of white domination.

Despite adverse circumstances, Walker developed into a pretty, precocious child who excelled in school. Her self-image received a life-changing blow, however, when Walker was eight years old and her brother accidentally shot her in the right eye with a BB gun during a game of cowboys and Indians. Although rendered blind in that eye, Walker experienced more emotional trauma from the wound's disfiguring scar tissue. Her vivaciousness gave way to reticence as society responded to her scarred eye. Accustomed to admiration, Walker began to retreat emotionally and physically. She hung her head; although she turned to books for solace, she began to do poorly in school. She wrote her first poetry during this difficult period.

Six years after the accident, Walker visited her brother in Boston; he took her to a local hospital, where the hated scar tissue was removed. Walker's head came up, she made friends, and she became high school prom queen and class valedictorian. Although many years would pass before Walker could make peace with the injury, she ultimately came to attribute much of her inner vision to the suffering it caused. The experience of overcoming physical deformity, in some cases by its acceptance, is reflected in Walker's art.

Walker's education continued when she received a scholarship to attend Spelman College, a black women's school in Atlanta. Her mother gave her three practical gifts to take with her—a suitcase, a sewing machine, and a typewriter—all suggestive of a liberated, self-sufficient, artistic life. Walker's Spelman experience juxta-

posed freedom with restriction. Through her studies, she discovered the intellectual liberation inherent in education; simultaneously, she became active in the Civil Rights movement, which was particularly concentrated around Atlanta during her two years (1961-1963) at the college. Spelman itself advocated turning out "proper" young women and discouraged political activism among its students. The school's attitudes and the students' frustration with them are suggested by Meridian Hill's experiences at the fictional Saxon College in Walker's novel *Meridian* (1976).

Having had a taste of the larger world and desiring a less restricted involvement in it, Walker accepted a scholarship to Sarah Lawrence College, a prestigious women's college in Bronxville, New York. There, another traumatic event in her life led to a positive result. Between her junior and senior years, Walker became pregnant. Having entertained thoughts of suicide during her years of disfigurement, she once again contemplated taking her life and kept a razor blade under her pillow. Her immediate anguish was relieved when a friend found an abortionist for her. As her body recovered, she reclaimed her emotional health by incessantly writing poetry. She slid the poems under the door of teacher and poet Muriel Ruykeyser, who gave them to an editor at Harcourt, Brace and Jovanovich; the collection, *Once*, was published in 1968.

After Walker was graduated from Sarah Lawrence College in 1965, she worked for the welfare department in New York City and in voter registration projects in Georgia. In 1966, she received a writing fellowship and spent that summer working in civil rights programs in Mississippi, where she met and fell in love with Melvyn Rosenman Leventhal, a white civil rights lawyer. During the year they lived together in New York City, she published her first story, "To Hell with Dying," and her first essay, "The Civil Rights Movement: What Good Was It?" After their marriage on March 17, 1967, they moved to Jackson, Mississippi. Walker worked with Head Start programs and served as writer-in-residence at Tougaloo College and Jackson State University. During those seven years in the South, Walker and Leventhal's daughter, Rebecca Grant, was born, and Walker wrote her first novel, *The Third Life of Grange Copeland*, published in 1970 by Harcourt Brace Jovanovich.

In 1973, Walker left the South to accept temporary positions teaching at Wellesley College and the University of Massachusetts, Boston. Leventhal remained in Mississippi. In 1973, Walker published a second book of poems, *Revolutionary Petunias and Other Poems*, as well as a collection of stories entitled *In Love and Trouble: Stories of Black Women* and a children's biography, *Langston Hughes: American Poet*. *In Love and Trouble* won the Rosenthal Award of the National Institute of Arts and Letters in 1974.

Walker and Leventhal returned in 1974 to New York, where Walker went to work for *Ms.* magazine as a contributing editor. In 1976, the year her second novel, *Meridian*, was published, Walker and Leventhal were divorced. During this period, Walker wrote her third book of poems, *Goodnight, Willie Lee, I'll See You in the Morning*, and edited an anthology of work by Zora Neale Hurston entitled *I Love Myself When I Am Laughing . . . and Then Again When I Am Mean and Impressive*, both of which were published in 1979.

Following the divorce, Walker moved to San Francisco, then to a nearby farm. Her second book of short stories, *You Can't Keep a Good Woman Down*, was published in 1981 while she was living there. The characters of her third novel, *The Color Purple* (1982), could not develop in an urban setting, emerging fully only after Walker found a place to live that reminded her of rural Georgia. Heeding her creative instincts produced a novel that has given Walker fame, money, and literary recognition. *The Color Purple* won the Pulitzer Prize and the American Book Award, was on *The New York Times* best-seller list for six months, and was made into a popular, although somewhat controversial, film by Steven Spielberg.

In 1983, Walker published *In Search of Our Mothers' Gardens*, a series of essays concerning her life, literature, the Civil Rights movement, and black women, among other subjects. Her fourth book of poetry, *Horses Make a Landscape Look More Beautiful*, was published in 1984. Her second collection of essays, *Living by the Word: Selected Writings, 1973-1987* (1988) addresses global concerns as well as feminist and political issues and also contains excerpts from Walker's journal. Her fourth novel, *The Temple of My Familiar*, was published in 1989.

Analysis

Walker is at home in many literary forms, managing originality and innovativeness in whatever genre she chooses, be it poetry, essay, or long or short fiction. Walker identifies diverse literary influences as well: Zora Neale Hurston, Jean Toomer, Thomas Hardy, Flannery O'Connor, and the nineteenth century Russian novelists among them. Walker's style is characterized by clarity and experimentation. In particular, the language of her characters marked Walker early in her career as a careful listener and later as a medium through whom the characters speak.

Walker's experience with the novel form began with *The Third Life of Grange Copeland*, a straightforward, chronological novel. *Meridian* moved away from strict chronology, using vignettes as puzzle pieces. Those two novels show the conception of character and language development that bore unique fruit in *The Color Purple*. Using for that novel a common nonfiction form, a collection of correspondence, Walker functions as a medium through whom two sisters tell the novel, each in changing language that reflects her life's experience. *The Color Purple* epitomizes Walker's control of believable dialogue. Similarly, in *The Temple of My Familiar*, the characters share narration, which gives the effect of storytelling and reveals much of their personalities through their use of language.

The reader of Walker's work finds that the common thread binding the varied genres is Walker's genius of kneading the personal into the political, the unique into the universal. Most of the drama experienced by Walker's characters points to a larger issue. For example, her black female characters experience much in common with the larger black female population: the search for self-reliance and self-confidence, and the embrace of a black feminist stance referred to by Walker as "womanism."

Although Walker's characters do not function as autobiographical vehicles for her personal experience as a black woman in the South, neither are they homogenous composites. Walker strives not to sacrifice character for stereotype merely to fulfill an African-American or "womanist" agenda. Instead, she creates believable heroines. Ruth, Meridian, Celie, and Shug are made fine, in part, by their flaws; from their believable experiences, a light may be brought to bear on more universal truths.

Hand-in-hand with the recurring theme of the black woman's struggle in a white-dominated society is Walker's controversial representation of the black man and the black woman's struggle against him. In *The Third Life of Grange Copeland*, *Meridian*, and *The Color Purple*, black men react against their economic and social oppression by dominating their wives, lovers, and daughters. Walker has received criticism for these repeated "negative" portrayals, but she creates from a primary moral responsibility to what she believes to be the truth—part of that truth being that, through honesty, understanding and change come. Particularly in *The Third Life of Grange Copeland*, Walker dissects her black male characters' violence in an attempt to understand the frustrations and results of repressed anger. Not an apologist, Walker ultimately demands that black men assume responsibility for their actions.

The tension between black men and women usually takes precedence in Walker's fiction over the issue that, in large part, precipitates it: the oppression of blacks by whites. In the tradition of Zora Neale Hurston's fiction, Walker's black characters do not think about whites constantly. Walker focuses far more on the internal struggles of black people and the black community than on the relationship between the races. As Walker demands the assumption of responsibility by black men, so she commands all of her black characters to look to themselves, to find their inner strengths and talents and thereby improve their lives. This is not to say that civil rights issues and political activism do not play a role in Walker's fiction, only that civil rights must begin with personal growth and family relationships.

Ruth is introduced to the Civil Rights movement in *The Third Life of Grange Copeland*, but *Meridian*, in particular, portrays one woman's discovery of the sanctity of change offered by the Civil Rights movement. Meridian realizes that the best way she can help people is to put them before the movement that, to her, becomes a separate entity whose radicalism she cannot embrace; moral integrity overrides a political agenda.

The importance of the family unit is another theme on which Walker varies throughout her fiction and nonfiction. Given the dysfunctional marriages and relationships between black men and women presented in her work, the hope of sanctuary in the family may at first appear absurd. The contradictions fade, however, when Walker's broader definition of family is understood. In *The Third Life of Grange Copeland*, for example, Ruth and her grandfather form a family unit based on trust and reciprocity. In *The Color Purple*, the two sisters' faith in their relationship, even when separated by years and miles, takes them farther spiritually than God can; Celie's family expands to embrace Shug and even Albert. Slavery destroyed family relationships for the African American; Walker suggests reclaiming the family as an important element of black self-determinism.

Religion as a theme also appears in Walker's fiction and nonfiction, religion as a broad concept embracing self-determined redemption, as in the case of Grange Copeland, as well as Nettie's Christian missionary stance in *The Color Purple*. In the latter novel, Shug's belief that God is in everything allows Celie to begin to make peace with the heinous wrongs done to her. The idea of personal integrity and independence becomes a religious concept in *The Color Purple* and elsewhere in Walker's work. Walker's personal spiritual journey toward harmony with the earth's environment (involving becoming vegetarian) and with the universe is described and celebrated in *Living By the Word* (1989).

The concept of the ever-present capacity to change runs through Walker's life and work. The theme of change accompanies each of the already discussed themes: race, the oppressed and oppressive black male, "womanism," civil rights, the black family, religion, even the language by which Walker's characters express themselves.

THE THIRD LIFE OF GRANGE COPELAND

First published: 1970
Type of work: Novel

A black tenant farmer achieves integrity from a life of oppression, redemption through love and sacrifice.

The Third Life of Grange Copeland, Walker's first novel, is the chronological story of three generations of a black sharecropping family in the South. The novel addresses several issues that occupy Walker's career: the abuse of black women by their husbands and fathers, the Civil Rights movement, and the necessity of self-reliance and moral responsibility.

Grange Copeland begins his married life with Margaret as an optimistic sharecropper. By the time their son Brownfield is born, however, the white landowner's exploitation of Grange's labor, resulting in irreversible indebtedness, has spawned hopeless frustration. Grange's feelings of inadequacy precipitate a rage that finds misdirected expression in the abuse of his wife and son. He drinks heavily and begins a sexual relationship with a prostitute. When Margaret retaliates by having sex with white men, which results in a light-skinned baby, Grange abandons Margaret and the children, going North. Completely demoralized, Margaret kills the baby and herself, leaving Brownfield alone.

Brownfield determines not to work for the same white man who controlled his father, but even as he tries to break from Grange's behavior pattern, he unknowingly becomes involved with Josie, his father's mistress. This ironic situation takes a positive turn, however, when Brownfield falls in love with and marries Mem, Josie's educated niece. Walker explains in a later afterword to the novel that she named this character from the French word *la meme* for "the same," and Mem proves to be the same kind of victim Brownfield's mother was and that countless other black women have been.

Mem dreams of a middle-class life for them, and Brownfield believes, as did Grange, that working as a sharecropper will be a steppingstone to this better life. As was the case with his father, a growing family and indebtedness work against him. Mem's attractiveness and education, the very traits that drew Brownfield to her, become symbols of his failure, and he sets out to destroy her so she will be the ruined woman that he believes he deserves. Mem, no matter how Brownfield batters her, manages always to hold up her head and tries to improve their situation. Mem's persistent hope, a trait long gone from Brownfield, finally enrages him so much that he murders her.

Grange had returned from the North before that happened and made an effort to help his son and Mem, but Brownfield bitterly refused the atonement. After Brownfield murders Mem, Grange takes the youngest granddaughter, Ruth, to rear. The reader is told at this point in the novel that Grange's experiences in New York were no better than life in the South. The crisis of trying to save a drowning white woman, only to have her refuse his hand because it is black, proved a pivotal point for Grange. The woman's death triggers active hostility toward all whites, and having finally taken an indirect revenge against them, Grange feels renewed and vindicated. Purged from the old, defining victimization, Grange chooses sanctuary from whites and a self-determined life. He marries Josie, buys a farm, and vows to give Ruth a nurturing environment away from whites and the violence born of frustration.

Ruth matures into an independent young woman who, having been sheltered by Grange, does not share his bitterness toward society. Through the media and the local activities of civil rights workers, Ruth comes to believe in the possibility of social change. Grange humors Ruth's ideals, but he still cannot bear the thought of a white woman under his roof, civil rights worker or not.

Grange's greatest battle must still be fought on the home front when Brownfield is released from prison and seeks custody of Ruth, not because of love, but in rage against his father. A corrupt white judge gives Ruth to Brownfield, but Grange, having suspected the outcome, shoots his son in the courthouse to prevent Brownfield's sure destruction of Ruth. Grange and Ruth escape to the farm, where Grange prepares to defend his autonomy to the death. Educated, self-reliant, and full of a hope that Grange himself had lost, Ruth emerges the black woman that Margaret and Mem could have been.

Walker's novel delivers an ultimately hopeful message of the possibility of change through love and moral responsibility. Grange finds a productive way out of his anger by himself; his reclusive solution allows Ruth to reenter the world with the inner strength imperative to a black woman's survival. Walker's attempts to understand the reasons behind Grange and Brownfield's violence do not condone it; rather, the motives revealed serve to clarify the means to change it.

MERIDIAN

First published: 1976
Type of work: Novel

A young, black, single mother becomes involved with the Civil Rights movement, coupling self-determinism with a commitment to poor blacks in the South.

Walker's second novel, *Meridian*, explores one black woman's experience in the Civil Rights movement, the psychological makeup of which fascinates Walker more than the political and historical impact it had. *Meridian* exemplifies Walker's ability to combine the personal and the political in fiction. Whereas Walker's first novel, *The Third Life of Grange Copeland*, moves chronologically, *Meridian* is constructed of smaller "chapters" that make up the novel, as Walker has said, much as pieces of cloth compose a quilt.

Meridian Hill grows up in the South, marries a high school boyfriend, becomes pregnant, and has a son. She experiences mixed feelings about motherhood, often fantasizing about killing the baby. After her husband leaves her, Meridian lives in an emotional limbo, daydreaming and watching television—on which, one morning, she sees that the nearby house where the voter registration drives are organized has been bombed. She decides to volunteer to work with the movement, more out of curiosity about what the people are like than from any political ideology. One of the workers is Truman Held, a man with whom Meridian will have an ongoing, although stormy, relationship.

Because of her unusually high intelligence, Meridian is offered a scholarship to Saxon College, and when she discovers that Truman attends college in Atlanta, his potential proximity becomes a motivating factor in her decision to accept it. Against the protests of her mother, Meridian gives away her baby, believing that he will be better off with someone else, and leaves for Saxon College. As a former wife and mother, Meridian is not the socially preferred virginal Saxon girl. Much as Walker's own experience at Spelman proved paradoxical, so Meridian feels the pull of her former life, feminism, and the Civil Rights movement.

The world beyond Saxon seems to contradict itself as well. Truman becomes involved with a white exchange student, Lynne, a baffling development to Meridian. Walker's story explores the difficulties an interracial relationship encounters, the reactions it causes in families, friends, and society in general, and the confusion of a political statement with love.

Throughout Truman's fascination with Lynne and other white women, he periodically returns to Meridian for spiritual and physical comfort. One of those homecomings leaves Meridian pregnant, and she suffers the subsequent abortion alone, never telling Truman. Although Meridian ultimately reconciles spiritually with Truman, she must learn to love and accept him and Lynne in the act of letting them go.

Letting go becomes a discipline that Meridian perfects as her purpose matures. When the movement demands that she vow to kill for it if need be, Meridian cannot comply. She realizes her willingness to sacrifice and even die for the cause, but when she cannot say what the group wants to hear, Meridian lets them go. She returns to the South, where she lives a spartan life of emotional wealth, working for poor blacks in small, everyday ways. Such seemingly insignificant protests in fact come to define the Civil Rights movement for many people. Again, Walker extracts the political from the personal.

Meridian's almost saintly qualities magnify Walker's belief in the power of personal discipline. Meridian is not perfect, however; her physical maladies and her guilt concerning her mother and child combine effectively to cripple her until she determines to move toward a life of work with which she is morally comfortable. Only then does her strength return. By her example, Truman comes to see the power in her life and dedicates himself to similar work.

Meridian proclaims that true revelation comes from personal change and growth. Although the novel deals with a particular political time period, implications of moral responsibility, love, and sacrifice transcend the specific, making *Meridian* a novel of timely worth.

THE COLOR PURPLE

First published: 1982
Type of work: Novel

Celie's letters to God and to her sister Nettie illustrate her metamorphosis from oppression to confidence; Nettie's letters from Africa record her experience as a missionary.

Walker's third novel, *The Color Purple*, made her famous, winning both the Pulitzer Prize and the American Book Award. The novel takes the form of letters: from Celie to God and Nettie, from Nettie in Africa to Celie. The letters afford the characters the opportunity to speak in their own voices, their own unique language. Not only does the language enhance the storytelling qualities of the novel, but the changes in Celie's language also particularly illustrate her emotional growth.

Warned by her father to tell "nobody but God" about his sexual abuse of her, Celie writes letters to God that tell of repeated rape resulting in the births of two babies, of the babies' removal by her father, and of being married off to Mr. _____, a man whose name Celie will not speak. Woven into the letters as well are details of a day-to-day farming life in the South that involves racism and economic hardship.

Celie's life of mistreatment and drudgery continues unabated until Shug Avery, blues singer and Mr. _____'s former lover, appears. Shug is beautiful, stubborn, and independent—traits that Celie has never seen in a woman. Their unlikely friendship changes Celie's life. Shug convinces Mr. _____ to stop beating Celie and encourages her to see herself as a worthwhile person. The feeling between them intensifies and they become lovers for a time.

It is Shug who discovers and procures the years of letters from Nettie hidden in Mr. _____'s trunk. From Nettie's letters, written in a language illustrating her education, Celie learns that the man who raped her was not her biological father and that her two children were adopted by the same missionaries with whom Nettie lived and traveled to Africa. Although it intensifies her hate for Mr. _____, the culmination of this knowledge, coupled with loving Shug, frees Celie from the guilt and poor self-image she had developed at the hands of men.

Exemplifying Walker's theme of self-determinism, Celie, at Shug's urging, exhibits a "womanist," entrepreneurial streak and begins to create and sell pants for men and women. The pants allow her a creative expression and suggest Celie's liberation from men on an economic as well as a physical level. Through Shug's belief of God's existence in everything, Celie reclaims her spirituality as she reclaims her body and soul by becoming comfortable with herself, a transformation that occurs in her language as well. This new Celie eventually makes peace with Mr. _____, whom she comes to call Albert. Albert's maturation and Celie's forgiveness reflect Walker's recurrent theme of the possibility of change—that there can be respectful relationships between black men and women.

Nettie, her husband Samuel, and Celie's children return from Africa to reunite the family, their missionary work having proved futile. Much as Celie's was, Nettie's God has been transformed to an immediate, internal spirituality. Nettie's faith in Celie, shown through years of unanswered letters, coupled with Celie's reciprocal faith, even after Nettie's supposed drowning on the return ship, underscores the kindred spirit of the long-separated sisters.

For all the praise it received, *The Color Purple* also received much criticism for its negative portrayals of black men. The optimism of the novel outweighs its negativity, however, and Celie's triumphant embrace of a vital existence reflects Walker's hope for humanity.

1955

First published: 1981
Type of work: Short story

A white rock-and-roll singer becomes famous by singing a song purchased from a black woman blues singer, but never understands the song's meaning.

The story "1955" appears in Walker's collection of stories *You Can't Keep a Good Woman Down*; it is a creative depiction of one incident of black musicians' exploitation by the white-dominated entertainment industry. Elvis Presley made Mama Thornton's "Hound Dog" a hit; similarly, in "1955," Traynor sings Gracie Mae Still's song into stardom.

The story clearly addresss a political issue, but Walker's approach transcends the political theme by creating multidimensional characters, drawn together by what separates them. Traynor becomes a pitiable character, as victimized by the entertainment industry as Gracie Mae—more so, in that he lacks her sense of self-worth. The greatest irony involves Traynor's lack of understanding of the song; never being in emotional possession of the song brings Traynor repeatedly to Gracie Mae, who cannot explain what lies beyond his understanding.

Over the years, Traynor gives Gracie Mae a car, a farm, a house, and countless other presents in an attempt to return some of the wealth her talent helped him attain. Traynor's success debilitates him spiritually, while Gracie Mae maintains a wisdom and integrity that Traynor cannot attain. Walker's "womanist" message is clear in Gracie Mae's inner strength and compassion that is great enough to embrace the man she so easily could have hated.

A SUDDEN TRIP HOME IN THE SPRING

First published: 1981
Type of work: Short story

A black student returns South from her Northern college for her father's funeral and sees new worth in what she left behind.

"A Sudden Trip Home in the Spring" appears in Walker's collection of stories *You Can't Keep a Good Woman Down*. The story examines a turning point in the psychological development of a black college student who has left Georgia for an exclusive Northern college, a scenario reminiscent of Walker's personal experience, and employs recurring themes of family dynamics, racism, and feminism.

Sarah Davis feels better suited to her Northern home and is not pleased with the idea of going South for her father's funeral. Her opinion of the South and of her father in particular has inhibited her growth as an artist; she cannot render black men on paper at all, not having the strength to draw what she sees as complete defeat. While she is home, however, interactions with her brother and grandfather, made more meaningful by her recent distance from them, open her eyes to her grandfather's innate dignity and her brother's youthful promise. Free from a single, oppressed image of all black men, Sarah feels she may now portray her grandfather in stone.

Mirroring Walker's own diverse experiences, the story underscores the significance of recognizing the worth in one's diversity. As Walker's writing is influenced by everything from her sharecropper beginning to the Civil Rights movement, so Sarah's work is broadened by reopening a door she thought closed. Sarah's pivotal trip home allows her to see the narrowness of the Northern college as well. Choosing not to allow one environment to define her gives her the freedom to define herself.

Summary

Alice Walker's recurrent, controversial themes—violence in the black family, racism, and "womanism" among them—will always draw her mixed attention. The broad social scope of her work, from Georgia to Africa, from folklore to civil rights philosophy, will continue to influence the way readers perceive black women. Her bold literary experimentation and clarity of vision have earned acclaim for her work in spite of controversy. Above all else, Walker strives for honest portrayals in her work, believing that truth makes even the painful tellable, and curable in the telling.

Bibliography

Banks, Erma Davis, and Keith Byerman. *Alice Walker: An Annotated Bibliography, 1968-1986.* New York: Garland, 1989.

Christian, Barbara. "Novel for Everyday Use: The Novels of Alice Walker." In *Black Women Novelists: The Development of a Tradition, 1892-1976.* Westport, Conn.: Greenwood Press, 1980.

O'Brien, John. *Interviews with Black Writers.* New York: Liveright, 1973.

Parker-Smith, Bettye J. "Alice Walker's Women: In Search of Some Peace of Mind." In *Black Women Writers (1950-1980): A Critical Evaluation,* edited by Mari Evans. Garden City, N.Y.: Anchor, 1984.

Tate, Claudia. *Black Women Writers at Work.* New York: Continuum, 1983.

Willis, Susan. "Black Woman Writers: Taking a Critical Perspective." In *Making a Difference: Feminist Literary Criticism,* edited by Gayle Greene and Coppelia Kahn. London: Methuen, 1985.

Claudia Emerson Andrews

ROBERT PENN WARREN

Born: Guthrie, Kentucky
April 24, 1905
Died: Stratton, Vermont
September 15, 1989

Principal Literary Achievement

Warren, the first American poet laureate, is known primarily as a prolific poet and novelist; with Cleanth Brooks, Jr., he significantly influenced the teaching of literature.

Biography

Robert Penn Warren was born to Anne Ruth Penn Warren on April 24, 1905, in Guthrie, a tiny community of twelve hundred persons in southwestern Kentucky. His father, Robert Franklin Warren, was a banker—according to Warren, a "misplaced" person who gave up early aspirations of a literary nature for more practical aims of making money. Warren's relationship to his father was a subtle and important one for its impact on his fiction and poetry, which often dramatized father-son relationships. He had a deep admiration for his father's rectitude, especially his humane resolution of the conflicts between personal desires and family duty. This admiration was coupled with a curious feeling of guilt because he, Robert Penn Warren, lived the literary aspirations that his father had abandoned.

Warren's summers were spent on his maternal grandfather's tobacco farm, an environment supporting his deep love of nature. His grandfather's personality, however, was fully as important as the rural setting for Warren's development. Gabriel Thomas Penn had been a Confederate cavalryman, as well as an ardent reader of military history and poetry. He could and did quote poetry vigorously and told exciting stories of the Civil War. The young Warren considered the Civil War the great American epic, analogous to the Trojan War for the Greeks. This gift of spontaneous storytelling had a profound effect upon Warren's writing style in both prose and poetry. Though Warren had no literary aspirations at all when he was growing up, he was absorbing the traditional tales of the South, the characters, and the dialects, which would emerge years later in fiction and poetry.

In his early years, Warren wanted to be an outdoorsman or an adventurer on the high seas. He might have done so, for his father was getting him an appointment at Annapolis—the first step, Warren hoped, to being an admiral of the Pacific Fleet.

Unfortunately, a childhood accident when he was fifteen years old destroyed one of his eyes. Although it was tragic at the time and contributed to feelings of depression for several years, it may have been crucial to America's gaining a great literary artist instead of a naval officer.

Warren enrolled instead in Vanderbilt University, where he became friends with Allen Tate, another gifted young man who would become a writer, and the well-known poet and teacher John Crowe Ransom, who perceived Warren's talent with words and encouraged him to write poetry. Warren became the youngest recruit to a literary group called "the Fugitives," who published some of his first verse. The Fugitives had some notion of creating a new Southern literary tradition, in opposition to the stereotyped, romantic "magnolia image" of the South found in popular, cheap fiction.

After being graduated from Vanderbilt in 1925, Warren earned an M.A. from the University of California at Berkeley and started postgraduate work on a scholarship at Yale University. That program was interrupted, however, by his being chosen to be a Rhodes scholar. He earned a bachelor of letters degree at the University of Oxford in 1930. Meanwhile, he had published his first book, a historical study, *John Brown: The Making of a Martyr* (1929), and his first short story, "Prime Leaf," which he would expand into his first novel, *Night Rider* (1939). During his training at Oxford, Warren also contributed to the Southern Agrarian writers' manifesto, *I'll Take My Stand: The South and the Agrarian Tradition, by Twelve Southerners* (1930).

Warren started his teaching career as assistant professor of English at Southwestern College in Memphis. The next year, he returned to his alma mater, Vanderbilt, and taught there for three years. In 1934, he moved on to Louisiana State University, where he taught until 1942. There Warren watched at first hand the political demagogue Huey Long, who provided the germ of the character Willie Stark in *All the King's Men* (1946). When Warren was actually writing the novel several years later (first as verse drama), he was living in Italy on a Guggenheim Fellowship, watching another popular people's choice, Benito Mussolini, the Fascist dictator, rise to power.

At Louisiana State, Warren began one of the most genial and fruitful partnerships in American letters—his professional relationship with Cleanth Brooks, Jr. He and Brooks cooperated first to create and edit the literary magazine *Southern Review*. Their most lasting contributions to the profession of teaching, however, were the textbooks *An Approach to Literature* (with John Thibaut Purser, 1936), *Understanding Poetry: An Anthology for College Students* (1938), and *Understanding Fiction* (1943). These did more than anything else to propagate the New Criticism, which emphasized a close examination of works of literary art to see what makes them effective.

Warren taught at the University of Minnesota between 1942 and 1950, with one year out to occupy the chair for poetry at the Library of Congress in Washington, D.C. Warren's friend, the novelist Katherine Anne Porter, who occupied the chair for fiction at the Library of Congress at that time, brought his attention to a peculiar document she had found in the archives. It was the confession of Jeremiah Beauchamp, who had been hanged for murder in Kentucky in 1826. This was the genesis of Warren's longest and most complex novel, *World Enough and Time: A Romantic Novel* (1950). Warren's last academic appointment was as professor of play writing at Yale University.

Warren was married twice, first in 1930 to Emma Brescia; they were divorced twenty years later. In 1952, he married the writer Eleanor Clark, with whom he had two children. His enchantment with his new family reawakened his poetic abilities, which had been seriously blocked for ten years. In 1953, he published his unique *Brother to Dragons: A Tale in Verse and Voices*, then, in 1957, *Promises: Poems 1954-1956*, inspired by his children. His poetic output, winning numerous literary honors and awards, continued into the 1980's.

Analysis

Warren's poetry and fiction often meditate on the twin mysteries of time and identity. Childhood is half remembered and half mythologized as a time of ignorance and innocence, sometimes expressed in terms borrowed from religion. It is a remembered paradise from which one inevitably falls from grace through original sin—that is, some malicious act or an insight into the moral ambiguity of oneself and others.

Original sin, as Warren uses the term, is not traceable to evil inherited from Adam's initial disobedience, as Christian myth describes it, but is a normal development in the process of growing up. In that sense, guilt is inevitable, and the need for redemption is a psychological state peculiar to the human psyche. There is some element of inheritance in the nature of one's individual burden of guilt, however, since the time and place of one's birth help determine the kind of illusion, sin, or temptation one encounters. Like many Southern writers of Warren's generation, his being engrossed in the history of the South, with its double jeopardy of inherited racial conflicts and defeat in the Civil War, adds a special depth to more personal family and individual problems. In this affinity for regional sorrows and predicaments, he is akin to his contemporary William Faulkner.

In some cases, the problem of identity and its moral implications are dramatized as a quest involving fathers and sons. The protagonist is often a young man in search of his father—that is, the source of his being. He may reject his biological father and choose a surrogate father whom he admires more. The ambitious protagonist of *At Heaven's Gate* (1943) despises his lowborn parent and idealizes a successful but unscrupulous business tycoon. The romantically deluded young man in *World Enough and Time* kills the surrogate father who has been his friend and benefactor. The protagonist of *A Place to Come To* (1977, a title suggesting a spiritual home) has both envied and despised his father, but, in retirement, becomes reconciled to his childhood roots in the South and befriends the foster father that he had never acknowledged. In *All the King's Men*, Jack Burden, whose very name may suggest unresolved guilt, does not even know who his father is. Moreover, Willie Stark in that novel is at least partially responsible for the death of his son.

In some poems using a very young persona, such as "Court Martial," the child gains a forboding insight into the darker side of an idealized older man—in this case, Warren's beloved grandfather. The episode is both historical and autobiographical, as well as a striking symbolic image of the frightening shadow-self that lurks in the unconscious mind. The moment when the child first glimpses the dark side of a loved person may pave the way for an understanding of his own capacity for evil. That self-recognition is necessary for emotional and moral maturity.

Trained as he was in the classical tradition of Greek, Shakespearean, and Jacobean drama, which he often taught, Warren was very conscious of the tragic sense of life. While human destiny may seem fated or inevitable, it is nevertheless self-chosen and rooted in individual character. One learns through error and suffering. The self-knowledge gained in this process may end in disaster or, in more fortunate circumstances, may result in a reconciliation and renewed love for life. Warren has noted how, in his classes at Louisiana State, which was Huey Long's alma mater, the students' attention sharpened as he discussed the political background of William Shakespeare's *Julius Caesar*. Tragedy came alive when Huey Long was assassinated almost on the steps of the state capitol in a seeming replay of historical drama.

Warren often used local legends or adapted historical events for literary purposes. He made no claims for literal accuracy. He disclaimed any actual knowledge of Huey Long, for example, but he listened to the endless legends that circulated among the common people who thought they had found a champion at last against the aristocratic, wealthy families who controlled Southern politics.

Physical deformity was sometimes used by Warren to suggest or symbolize the human character flaw that afflicts all men. Such flawed characters are not necessarily bad persons; in fact, in some cases, such a visible sign of imperfection seems to help the sufferer to avoid inordinate pride and attain a measure of redemption. In the poem "Original Sin," the defect is first associated with an old man's disfiguring wen, later with some foolish monster, and still later rather fondly with an old dog, scratching at the door, or a tired horse put out to pasture. Warren has even used a glass eye, which he himself wore, as indicative of some secret flaw. Sometimes the sign is more obvious, such as the clubfoot of the idealistic young immigrant who comes to America to help free the slaves in the Civil War novel *Wilderness: A Tale of the Civil War* (1961).

In his long career, Warren sought to reconcile some of the most contradictory elements of American intellectual life, particularly the inheritance of eighteenth century optimism about man's essential goodness and social progress with the darker, romantic consciousness of good and evil advanced by such American writers as Nathaniel Hawthorne and Herman Melville. Although he may lean heavily on the symbolism and imagery of romanticism, he does so with an irony that recognizes illusion and myth as necessary parts of human consciousness. Warren believed that the self is not synonymous with the ego alone but must include irrational elements of the subconscious, through which the individual is bound to all humanity and to nature.

ALL THE KING'S MEN

First published: 1946
Type of work: Novel

Jack Burden, former newspaperman and former graduate student of history, gains self-knowledge through his association with a charismatic politician.

All the King's Men, which won the Pulitzer Prize in Fiction, has sometimes been called the best political novel written in the United States. Nevertheless, its emphasis is on the private psychological roots of action that is played out on a public political stage. The social milieu is authentically drawn, with redneck farmers pitted against entrenched aristocratic families.

Jack Burden is in between the political forces, initially simply a spectator and a reporter from an upper-middle-class background, watching with curiosity and a certain fascination as a man from the farm becomes a self-taught lawyer and moves into politics. Plain-speaking Willie Stark, who hardly looks like a hero, learns to capture an audience of poor dirt farmers and small-town businessmen, in whom he inspires almost fanatical devotion. He is a cunning, hardworking, expedient politician, promising to build roads and bridges in the isolated rural areas and hospitals for the common people.

It is a story of several men who do not know themselves: Willie Stark, who thinks he can use evil means to achieve good ends; Jack Burden, who tries to avoid guilt by running away from it or simply not seeing it, and who does not recognize his own father and inadvertently kills him; Judge Irwin, representative of the old genteel tradition, who literally forgets his original sin; Adam Stanton, the puritan idealist, who suddenly casts off all restraints to kill Willie Stark.

Stark attains power partly by understanding and controlling other men. He recruits Jack for his personal staff, partly for his skill in research. Jack's first task at the outset of their relationship is to "find something" on an old friend of his father's, Judge Irwin, who had been like a father to Jack in his younger days. The reason for the investigation is that Judge Irwin has come out for Stark's opponent in the upcoming election.

Jack pursues this inquiry into Judge Irwin's background with a curious objectivity, convinced, on the one hand, that there can be no hint of wrongdoing in what he calls "the case of the upright judge" and, on the other hand, wondering whether Stark's assessment of human nature may, after all, be accurate. Stark's answer to Jack's assurances that there could be nothing dishonorable in the background of Judge Irwin is reiterated three times in the novel: "Man is conceived in sin and born in corruption and he passeth from the stink of the didie to the stench of the grave. There is always something." Burden does, in fact, find "something" in the forgotten past. Not only did the upright judge once accept a bribe, but he was also protected by the equally immaculate Governor Stanton, father of Adam and Anne, Jack's dearest childhood friends. Anne had been Jack's first love.

The career of Willie Stark quickly becomes, to Jack, more than an interesting spectator sport, and his employment becomes more than a convenient job serving a dynamic personality. Burden becomes enmeshed in a complex web of relationships and circumstances that involve his own past, as well as the uneasy present and the dubious future. Burden holds on to his knowledge about the judge until Anne herself asks him to convince her brother Adam, now a celebrated surgeon, that he should accept the directorship of the new medical center that Willie wants to build.

Jack understands that the only way to influence Adam in this respect is to change his mind about the moral nature of the world—to break his conviction that good and evil can be kept separate. How better to achieve this than to reveal that the idealized father and the irreproachable judge were themselves guilty of political crimes?

The bitter knowledge of his father's expedient compromise with honor has the desired effect on the puritanical Adam. He makes an uneasy alliance with Stark (whom he despises) for the sake of doing good. Stark seems to have made his point—good must be made out of evil, because, he says, that is all there is from which to make it. Even Stark, expedient and pragmatic as he is, has a vision of the hospital, which is to be free to anyone who needs medical service, as an unsullied oasis in a grimy world, a monument of his own submerged idealism. This tension between persons who seem unalterably opposed, yet are drawn to a common purpose, is one of Warren's favorite devices for revealing the moral ambiguity of human motivations.

Burden, still withholding from Stark the information about Irwin, suffers a profound shock when he learns from Stark's secretary and sometime mistress that Stark has become Anne Stanton's lover. Burden precipitously drives out West until he is stopped by the Pacific Ocean. There he drops into what he calls the "Great Sleep," a neurotic reaction which has afflicted him before—once when he walked out on his Ph.D. studies in history and once when he walked out on his wife.

From the Great Sleep, Jack is born again into a bleak but emotionally insulating belief in the "Great Twitch"—an understanding of the world as completely amoral and mechanistic, wherein nobody has any responsibility for what happens. He returns to his job as if nothing had happened. He hardly hesitates at all when Stark wants to use the evidence against Judge Irwin. Burden's education in hard reality has only begun, however, and the shell of indifference is irrevocably broken with even more unexpected revelations. It is a lesson in tragedy that involves several families, with Jack Burden, Anne Stanton, and Willie Stark's faithful wife as survivors.

Quite aside from the dramatic elements of political chicanery, adultery, suicide, and murder that make this an exciting story, the novel suggests a more subtle observation about a symbiotic psychological dependency between people. No one is complete and self-sufficient—not even Anne, though the narrator, Jack, early in the book assumes that she is peculiarly integrated and whole. Anne actually shares with Jack an essential passivity that makes them both feed emotionally on the dynamic energy of Willie Stark. The gravitation of the passive personality to the active man also has its political expression, accounting for the success of the demagogue with his constituency, who feel themselves to be socially and politically helpless.

THE BALLAD OF BILLIE POTTS

First published: 1944
Type of work: Poem

A rascally innkeeper fails to recognize his own son, who is returning home from the Western frontier, and murders him for his gold.

"The Ballad of Billie Potts" is perhaps the most striking of Warren's early poems. In a little over thirteen pages, it brings together several of the themes that would concern him for a lifetime: the passage from childhood innocence into guilt, the journey that ends with a return to the father or to the place of origin, the undiscovered self, and a certain mysticism that unites each person with mankind and with nature.

Warren prefaced the poem with this note: "When I was a child I heard this story from an old lady who was a relative of mine. The scene, according to her version, was in the section of Western Kentucky known as 'Between the Rivers,' the region between the Cumberland and the Tennessee." According to legend, Billie Potts kept an inn on one of the popular frontier routes along which early travelers passed traveling to the West. He communicated regularly with bands of cutthroats, notifying them of the route his guests were taking into the wilderness. The robbers shared with him any booty that they could acquire from ambushing the travelers.

Billie Potts and his wife have a son whom they both adore. The son, thinking he will prove his worth to his father, attempts to kill and rob a stranger by himself instead of conveying the information to more experienced killers, as he was told to do. He botches the job and returns home in humiliation. His father, in anger, turns him out to make his fortune as best he can.

Years later, the son, having prospered out West, returns in triumph, sporting a heavy beard, a handsome coat, and a bag of gold. He conceals his identity for a while, hoping to tease his parents, but they, thinking he is only another traveler, murder him for his money. The parents learn too late, through an identifying birthmark, that they have killed the only person they ever loved. Warren captures the rhyming, lilting, occasionally uneven rhythm of folk ballad, its colloquial language combined with an occasionally oracular tone.

The comment upon the action, which universalizes the legend, appears in parentheses. Warren uses the second person, as he does in a number of poems, to indicate the conscious self, which does not recognize the unconscious shadow-self. What at first seems a simple device to show what it was like in those days—a guided tour of the past, so to speak—becomes a way of involving the reader, as conscious ego, in a somber psychodrama. The final meditation is almost a benediction, likening the wanderer's return (not only Billie's now, but also the reader's own) to the mysterious natural forces which direct the salmon's return to the "high pool" of his birth, with its ambiguous implications of both innocence and death.

> The salmon heaves at the fall, and wanderer, you
> Heave at the great fall of Time, and gorgeous, gleam
> In the powerful arc, and anger and outrage like dew,
> In your plunge, fling, and plunge to the thunderous stream:
> Back to the silence, back to the pool, back
> To the high pool, motionless, and the unmurmuring dream.
>
> .   .   .   .
>
> And the father waits for the son.

BROTHER TO DRAGONS

First published: 1953
Type of work: Poem

Characters from the past and present, including Thomas Jefferson and RPW (Warren), comment upon the brutal murder of a slave.

After a ten-year period of writing prose, during which he found poems impossible to finish, Warren emerged as a poet of peculiar power and originality with the publication in 1953 of *Brother to Dragons: A Tale in Verse and Voices*, a book-length poem unlike any in American literature. The subject was a shocking real-life murder perpetrated by Lilburne Lewis, a nephew of Thomas Jefferson (primary author of the Declaration of Independence and the third president of the United States).

Warren invented a unique mode of presentation for this work—neither narrative poem nor play, but a discussion by characters long dead (except for one, the poet himself, designated as RPW), who try to understand the grisly event that occurred in the meat house when Lilburne Lewis hacked to pieces with an axe a teenaged slave because he broke a pitcher belonging to Lucy Jefferson Lewis, Lilburne's deceased mother. The other slaves were forced to witness this performance. As Warren explains in a brief preface: "We may take them to appear and disappear as their urgencies of argument swell and subside. The place of this meeting is, we may say, 'no place,' and the time is 'any time.'" Besides the victim, the main characters include Lilburne, the killer; Isham Lewis, who watched his older brother commit the murder; their mother, Lucy; her brother, Thomas Jefferson; Letitia, Lilburne's wife; Aunt Cat, Lilburne's Negro mammy; Meriwether Lewis, Lilburne's cousin, who went West on the Lewis and Clark expedition; and RPW.

The central character, if the poem can be said to have one, is not the hapless victim, who has only one brief speech in the first edition (three in the 1979 revision). It is not even Lilburne, the moral monster, but Thomas Jefferson, inheritor of the eighteenth century optimism about the perfectibility of man. The poem examines the hideous event and ponders why it occurred, but it is Jefferson who develops and changes in the poem. There is no evidence that the historical Thomas Jefferson ever discussed or even acknowledged the murder, a fact which suggested to Warren that he could not face the thought of such barbarity in one of his own blood.

Actually, the stance of Jefferson in the poem is initially quite grim and cynical. He has already recognized that he had been overly optimistic in his view of human nature. The moral project of the poem is not to convince Jefferson of the reality of evil, which he affirms from the first, but to convince him that he himself shares that burden of human evil. This humbling of Jefferson is achieved primarily by burdening him with some guilt for the fate of Meriwether Lewis, who had once been his secretary; this part of the poem is not completely convincing. The real Meriwether Lewis committed suicide when he was governor of the Louisiana Territory, but the reader does not know, from the poem itself, what happened or why Jefferson should share any guilt in the matter. Jefferson ultimately achieves some kind of universalized feeling for his fellows that includes even the despised Lilburne.

The discussion and the narrative action of the first hundred pages is gripping both mentally and emotionally. At the psychological level, Warren suggests that the act of murder was a ritualized attempt to purge Lilburne's own evil. The slave is Lilburne's shadow-self, the scapegoat whose elimination will bring order in a chaotic world or in Lilburne's chaotic psyche. The butcher block, on which the boy lies curled in the fetal position with eyes tightly closed, suggests an altar to some savage god. The death of Lilburne repeats the psychological ritual, with Lilburne playing victim, the dark shadow of his brother Isham. Lilburne forces Isham into a suicide pact, whereby they will shoot each other at the count of ten over their mother's grave. He counts to ten very slowly, knowing full well that Isham will panic and shoot first, then try to escape. During this melodramatic scene, there is a great earthquake. This event may seem like a piece of Gothic fiction, but, in fact, there was such an earthquake at about that time—one of the biggest ever recorded in that area.

Jefferson observes in the poem that slain monsters and dragons are innocent. All heroes, whether Hercules, David with his sling, or Jack of the beanstalk, are playing "the old charade" in which man dreams that he can destroy the objectified bad and then feel good: "While in the deep/ Hovel of the heart the Thing lies/ That will never unkennel himself to the contemptible steel."

TO A LITTLE GIRL, ONE YEAR OLD, IN A RUINED FORTRESS

First published: 1957
Type of work: Poetry

His child's innocent delight in natural beauty helps a father to accept the suffering that life brings.

Warren broke away from his somewhat morose obsession with evil with his spar-
kling *Promises*, winner of his first Pulitzer Prize in Poetry. The first five poems of
Promises are dedicated to Warren's daughter Rosanna under the general title "To a
Little Girl, One Year Old, in a Ruined Fortress." The setting is the imposing ruin
overlooking the Mediterranean where Warren and his second wife, Eleanor, lived in
Italy—Cesare Borgia's hunting ground, said Warren, who always knows his history—"those blood-soaked stones." The first poem of the series, "Sirocca", speaks
of Philip of Spain, "the black-browed, the anguished,/ For whom nothing prospered, though he loved God." His arms, carved in stone, which once stood over the
drawbridge, have long since fallen into the moat buried in garbage. Yet the blue
blooms of rosemary and the gold bloom of thistle flourish there, bringing gay laughter to the golden-haired child.

The poem establishes a contrast of perception, maintained through the five poems,
between the innocence and delight of the child's view of the world and the darker
awareness of the father, who knows the evil and suffering enacted here—which still
goes on in the world. Nevertheless, because he participates in and marvels at the
child's innocent joy in nature, the speaker becomes reconciled to the world, believing, or at least praying, that all can be redeemed.

The second and third poems introduce some of the human misery existing in this
beautiful setting. The pathetic, defective child next door has cried all night; she is
the result of an unsuccessful attempt at abortion. The "monster's" twelve-year-old
sister, who is "beautiful like a saint," has taught the defective child to make the
Italian sign for *ciao*. The speaker, galled at the assumption that suffering and tragedy
have any such simplistic solution as a catchword for "okay," is moved to metaphysical rebellion, like Russian novelist Fyodor Dostoevski's Ivan Karamazov, who refused salvation at the price of the suffering of children.

The fourth poem, "The Flower," is the climax, where the little daughter's joy in a
natural ritual dispels the speaker's rebellion against the world's injustice and pain.
He is carrying the child up the cliff from the beach, where in the past she has been
given a white flower to hold and a blue one for her hair. Since it is now fall, the
parents are hard-put to find a white bloom not sadly browned and drooping, but the
child accepts gladly the best one they can find, "as though human need/ Were not for
perfection." The lyrical joy of this hour seems to transfigure time itself. The parents
look back and see a single gull hovering on a saffron sunset. They note that the
white gull looks black, but it swings effortlessly as it descends, changing from black
to white and back, according to its background and the direction of light, suggesting
to the poet that at least some aspects of reality are matters of human perception.
Context determines meaning.

The final poem in this sequence, "Colder Fire," is less serene than "The Flower,"
with its sense of exaltation. It begins humbly, re-admitting, so to speak, the persistent negative. Though the speaker knows that "the heart should be steadfast," he
is often helpless to command his own moods. The speaker sits in the sun with his
child on his lap, watching the white butterflies, soon to die, in their "ritual carouse,"

nature's assurance of an immortality of the flesh; the butterflies reflect the father's sense of immortality in his child. Warren achieves a remarkable fusion of thought, passion, and concrete imagery in this to form a vision of spiritual transcendence without violating or misrepresenting actual human experience, with its reality of pain and death.

Summary

Robert Penn Warren, the first poet laureate of the United States, produced ten novels and eighteen books of poetry, as well as short stories, plays, biography, social commentary, and literary criticism. His best novels are probably *All the King's Men* and *World Enough and Time*; his best-known short story is "Blackberry Winter." He won his third Pulitzer Prize when he was seventy-three years old for *Now and Then: Poems 1976-1978*. At age seventy-eight, he produced his last book-length poem, *Chief Joseph of the Nez Perce* (1983). A colleague at Yale University once called Warren the "most complete man of letters we've ever had in this country."

Bibliography

Beebe, Maurice, and I. A. Field, eds. *Robert Penn Warren's "All the King's Men" : A Critical Handbook.* Belmont, Calif.: Wadsworth, 1966.

Bohner, Charles H. *Robert Penn Warren.* New York: Twayne, 1964.

Casper, Leonard. *Robert Penn Warren: The Dark and Bloody Ground.* Seattle: University of Washington Press, 1960.

Guttenberg, Burnett. *Web of Being.* Nashville, Tenn.: Vanderbilt University Press, 1975.

Huff, Mary Nance. *Robert Penn Warren: A Bibliography.* New York: David Lewis, 1968.

Justus, James H. *The Achievement of Robert Penn Warren.* Baton Rouge: Louisiana State University Press, 1975.

Longley, John Lewis, Jr., ed. *Robert Penn Warren: Collection of Critical Essays.* New York: New York University Press, 1965.

Snipes, Katherine. *Robert Penn Warren.* New York: Frederick Ungar, 1983.

Stranberg, Victor. *The Poetic Vision of Robert Penn Warren.* Lexington: University Press of Kentucky, 1977.

Walker, Marshall. *Robert Penn Warren: A Vision Earned.* New York: Barnes & Noble, 1979.

Katherine Snipes

EUDORA WELTY

Born: Jackson, Mississippi
April 13, 1909

Principal Literary Achievement

Welty is ranked high among Southern fiction writers because of her unique kind of realism, which is detached but compassionate and always holds out hope that the conflicting claims of society and of the individual can be resolved for the benefit of both.

Biography

Eudora Welty was born in Jackson, Mississippi, on April 13, 1909. Her father, Christian Webb Welty, was originally from rural Ohio; he had met Mary Chestina ("Chessie") Andrews when he was working in West Virginia, where she was a teacher in the mountain schools near her home. To the dismay of her five adoring brothers, the new bride and her husband decided to move to Jackson, Mississippi. There Christian became a successful businessman. Eudora was their second child. As she recalls in *One Writer's Beginnings* (1984), her parents did not speak freely of the baby boy who had died at birth, but Eudora was aware of being cherished and even sheltered.

Eudora Welty was an observant child. Sounds and sights, musical harmonies and the cadences of human voices, the coming and the fading of the seasons, the subtle changes in human beings—all were fascinating to her. With her two younger brothers, Eudora could disappear into the world of the imagination. There were also trips north and east to visit both of her parents' families. Eudora's world was filled with stimuli, yet it was safe; the serenity that is evident in her fiction began with a happy childhood in a family filled with love.

Encouraged by her mother, Welty read a wide variety of books. Soon she was also writing. Her gifts were not only literary however; in high school and later in college, she took lessons in drawing and painting. This visual gift was to be utilized in her photographs as well as in the memorable descriptive passages in her fiction.

After she was graduated in 1925 from Central High School in Jackson, Welty spent two years at Mississippi State College for Women. In 1927, she transferred to the University of Wisconsin, where she majored in English. In *One Writer's Beginnings*, she recalls the moment when she knew that literature must be her life; as she explains it, a poem by William Butler Yeats so imbued her with passion that she believed she could live within it, possessing it and possessed by it.

After Welty was graduated from college in 1929, however, she followed her father's advice: She went to New York City and entered the School of Business at Columbia University, studying advertising, so that she would be able to get a job. Unfortunately, when the Depression hit, there were no jobs in New York. In 1931, Welty returned to Jackson. That year, she suffered a great loss in the death of her father, who called himself the family optimist.

During the next several years, Welty worked for a radio station, several newspapers, and, perhaps most important, as a junior publicity agent for the Works Progress Administration. This job took her all over Mississippi; she interviewed ordinary people, wrote articles, and took photographs. Although she was writing regularly, it was her photographs that Welty first tried to sell. In 1936, she had a one-woman show of them in New York; that same year marked the appearance of her first published story, "Death of a Traveling Salesman." It was not the work of an apprentice, but of a polished, mature writer whose vision and approach were uniquely her own.

After "Death of a Traveling Salesman," Welty's stories began appearing regularly in *The Southern Review* and in mass-circulation magazines such as *The Atlantic.* In 1941, her first book-length collection, *A Curtain of Green and Other Stories* was published. It was followed by a novel, *The Robber Bridegroom* (1942), the story of a magical romance, which ends when the lovers see each other as the ordinary people they really are.

Now a full-time writer, Welty entered her most productive period, with a collection of short stories, *The Wide Net and Other Stories* (1943); a novel, *Delta Wedding* (1946); another short story collection, *The Golden Apples* (1949); the novella *The Ponder Heart* (1954); and a collection of stories, *The Bride of the Innisfallen and Other Stories* (1955). A number of the works produced during this time were singled out for literary honors. For example, in 1942, "The Wide Net" won an O. Henry Award, and "Livvie Is Back" won the same prize in 1943. *The Ponder Heart* won the William Dean Howells medal; it was dramatized and became a Broadway hit in 1956.

During the next three decades, Welty published less frequently. She spent much time working on what was to be her most complex novel, *Losing Battles* (1970). Furthermore, she had family problems—her mother's long illness and death and the death of a brother—which are reflected in her Pulitzer Prize-winning novel, *The Optimist's Daughter* (1972). *The Eye of the Story* (1978) is a collection of essays and reviews that reveals much about Welty's views of art. It was followed by *The Collected Stories of Eudora Welty* (1980).

Eudora Welty's standing among scholars and critics is evidenced by the many awards she has received and by the long list of articles and books written about her and her work. The pride of her native state in her accomplishments has been shown in celebrations such as one held on May 2, 1973, which was Eudora Welty Day by proclamation of the governor of Mississippi, and one held on April 13, 1984, on the writer's seventy-fifth birthday. In 1985, New Yorkers flocked to an Off-Broadway one-woman show, *Sister and Miss Lexie*, which dramatized Welty's hilarious story

"Why I Live at the P.O." and a section from *Losing Battles*. Perhaps most telling is the fact that Welty's autobiography, *One Writer's Beginnings*, stayed on the best-seller list for many months. This writer, who has lived a quiet life in her native Mississippi, observing ordinary people and writing about ordinary events, has captured the imaginations of millions of people throughout the world.

Analysis

In *The Eye of the Story*, there is an essay called "Reality in Chekhov's Stories," which explains as much about Eudora Welty as it does about Anton Chekhov. Welty comments that one of Chekhov's most important contributions to fiction was his redefining of reality. Before Chekhov, there was one viewpoint in fiction, directly or obliquely the author's; after Chekhov, the writer felt free and even compelled to present various viewpoints as versions of reality. This approach necessitates a determined detachment on the part of the fiction writer. As Welty has frequently explained, she does not consciously manipulate her characters; instead, she creates them and lets them speak for themselves. As a result, her short stories and novels often have the quality of a stage play.

In "A Visit of Charity," for example, Welty begins with a brief mention of the time of day; she proceeds to describe the appearance of a young girl and to give the directions for her coming onstage—in this case, into the Old Ladies' Home. Although the point of view of this story is that of fourteen-year-old Marian, who notices everything, even the smell of the room that she has chosen to enter, the minute that the two old women begin to talk, there are two additional versions of reality. The old women do not agree about anything. One says that another girl has visited them, and the other says she did not; one says that her roommate is sick, and the roommate denies it; one begins to speak of her school days, and the other interrupts with a tirade to the effect that the first speaker had no life whatsoever before she came to the home to torture her roommate.

With all the controversy going on, it is no wonder that the girl herself feels as if she is in a dream; in other words, her own view of reality becomes shaky. In the final scene, after escaping from the Old Ladies' Home, Marian bites into an apple. The implication is clear: She is returning to the single and simple reality of her own appetite.

Welty's dramatic structure, then, is her way of stressing a major theme: that each character is living in a unique world. Furthermore, although when Marian focuses on her apple, she can shut out the past and the future, most characters live in memory and in anticipation as well as in observation of the present. In *One Writer's Beginnings*, Welty explains her idea of the basic pattern of life. Everyone is involved, she says, in a continual process, moving from memories of the past to discoveries about the present and then again back to memories. There are, however, occasions when the memories and discoveries converge in a single moment, annihilating the conventional divisions between past and present, the living and the dead. Welty calls these times "confluences." In Welty's fiction, the confluences are usually both heal-

ing and strengthening, at least for the characters who pay attention to them, such as
the naturalist James Audubon in "A Still Moment" and Phoebe in "Asphodel," who
finds in the retelling of an old love story, an appearance of a naked hermit, and an
attack by hungry goats the occasion for joy. The theme of confluence is reflected in
the final sentence of the story, as Phoebe's reaction is described:

> She seemed to be still in a tender dream and an unconscious celebration—as though
> the picnic were not already set rudely in the past, but were the enduring and intoxicat-
> ing present, still the phenomenon, the golden day.

Even though Welty emphasizes the uniqueness of each individual's perception,
she does not therefore assume that there can be no connection between people.
Indeed, most of her stories and all of her novels stress the need for acceptance, for
tolerance, for a sustaining community. Welty often chooses a ceremonial gathering
as the setting for a story or a novel. The title of *Delta Wedding* suggests that occasion; *Losing Battles* takes place at a birthday celebration; *The Optimist's Daughter*
involves a deathbed vigil and a funeral. Even the student recital in the short story
entitled "June Recital" and the weekly meeting in the beauty shop described in
"Petrified Man" are times when human beings come together to deal with their
uncertainties and to resolve their conflicts.

As a writer, Welty is conscious of the joys of solitude; however, as a human being,
she believes that there is also strength in community. The revelation that comes too
late to the protagonist of "Death of a Traveling Salesman" is that his life was a waste
because he never chose to become involved with other people. Although Welty never
minimizes the difficulties that arise from being subject to the rules and customs of
any group, she chooses to have her characters work out their own independence
without rejecting their ancestors, their extended family, their neighbors, and their
community.

DELTA WEDDING

First published: 1946
Type of work: Novel

A young girl, visiting relatives who are preparing for a wedding on their
Mississippi plantation, finds her own identity as part of the family.

Delta Wedding is a study of the relationships among the individual members of
the Fairchild family and between that family and the rest of the world. The setting
for the story is Shellmound, the Mississippi plantation that is the home of Battle
Fairchild, his wife Ellen Fairchild, and their eight children, as well as of various
female relatives and black servants. Shellmound is not merely a backdrop; it is the
center of family life. The sound of Shellmound is the sound of conversation; this is a

place where people gather to talk. The conversations at Shellmound may appear to be superficial, examples of the Southerners' need to fill every silence, yet they serve important purposes. They enable family members to explore their own feelings and to understand those of others, to connect living people with those who are dead, and to comprehend the events taking place in the present by recalling similar occasions in the past.

It is therefore not mere provinciality or possessiveness that causes the Fairchilds to consider it a tragedy when one of them moves away from that sustaining influence. They mention the girl who married a Northerner and moved far away from them; obviously, she understood what she had left behind, because she returns to her parents' home to have her babies.

To its credit, the Fairchild family is willing to change, to open its ranks to those who would once have been considered outsiders. The wedding for which they are gathering is an example of the family's flexibility, for they will be celebrating the marriage of Battle's daughter, seventeen-year-old Dabney Fairchild, to the plantation overseer, Troy Flavin, an outsider from the hill country. If the Virginian Ellen Fairchild is still somewhat ill at ease in the family, Troy, who is socially and culturally inferior to the Fairchilds, should feel totally rejected; however, he does not. The Fairchilds have come to appreciate his virtues, his diligence, his love of the land, and his own understanding of Dabney's need to remain near her roots.

In contrast, Robbie Reid Fairchild is jealous of the family into which she has married. Early in the novel, Robbie's husband, George Fairchild, who is Battle's brother, arrives from Memphis with a fine little filly for Dabney's wedding present, but without his wife. Robbie has left George. The cause of the breach was an action that the family sees as heroism, but that Robbie sees as George's desertion of her. Two weeks before, the family had gone fishing. As they crossed a railroad trestle on the way back, George's mentally handicapped niece, Maureen, got her foot caught. Even though a train was coming, George stayed with her, working to free her. The train stopped in time; however, Robbie interpreted the incident as George's choosing his family instead of his wife, and therefore she has left him. If one movement of the novel is toward the family's complete acceptance of Troy, another is toward Robbie's acceptance of her husband and of his needs for his family. Halfway through the book, Robbie arrives, still furious; by the end of the novel, however, she has realized that George's love for her is not diminished by his sense of duty toward the Fairchilds, and she can agree to move back home with George.

Most of the events in *Delta Wedding* are reflected through the eyes of another outsider, nine-year-old Laura McRaven, who has come from Jackson to visit the relatives of her dead mother. Laura is fascinated by Shellmound—the constant motion, the talk, the exclamations, the laughter, the embraces. She desperately needs the security that Shellmound offers her, desperately needs to replace the love of her dead mother with the love of her mother's family. On the other hand, she notices that Shellmound can be restrictive; it is a difficult place to read, she observes, and in some ways it is a difficult place to find oneself. Laura manages to achieve a balance between her conflicting needs. When the assigned flower girl gets chickenpox, Laura takes her place, thus becoming part of the wedding and, she believes, of the family. George, whom she adores, assures her that she is truly a Fairchild. When Laura returns to Jackson, she can take with her all that is best at Shellmound. She will always be a part of it, yet she will always have her own secrets and her own identity.

LOSING BATTLES

First published: 1970
Type of work: Novel

A clan gathers to celebrate the ninetieth birthday of a matriarch and to avenge the imprisonment of one of their finest young men.

Losing Battles is a book-length illustration of Welty's theory of confluence. When the Beechams, the Renfros, and the Vaughns gather to celebrate Granny Vaughn's ninetieth birthday, they all talk. In the Southern social tradition, this talk involves a great deal of storytelling and reminiscence. In this way, people long dead appear among the living, and past events are revived to determine present actions.

As the title implies, there are many conflicts in the novel. Many involve an outsider's attempt to deal with a highly structured society—in this case, the large, extended family present at the reunion. Aunt Cleo Webster is one of the characters who has a problem with the family, into which she has recently married. Early in the novel, it is clear that her questions show her ignorance of the family heritage and, worse, her slightly different perspective. Since she is from southern Mississippi and the reunion takes place in the hill country of northern Mississippi, there is a geographical explanation; however, when the family discovers that she was previously married to a member of the Stovall clan, the hereditary enemies of the Beechams and the Renfros, Aunt Cleo becomes, to a degree, the object of suspicion. Fortunately, by the end of the novel, Aunt Cleo has been taught much about family history and, by learning the correct responses in the never-ending conversations, has become a part of the family into which she has married.

Another outsider is Gloria Renfro, who is waiting for the return of her husband, Jack Renfro, from the penitentiary, where he had been sent because of an altercation involving a Stovall snatching a family ring from Jack's young sister. After Jack—the family hero and Granny's favorite—returns, Gloria has a difficult time even getting him alone. The family demands that he avenge himself on the judge who sent him to the penitentiary. Desperately, Gloria plays every card she holds in order to keep Jack from getting in trouble and being sent away again. She tries to focus his attention on the baby he has never met, on her own physical charms, and on their life together. Yet the family does not want to let go of the past; they would rather have another mythic character to tell stories about than have a real Jack Renfro, happy at home. It is chance, Gloria, and the Renfro sense of honor that unite to keep Jack at home. When Judge Moody, who had sentenced Jack, sacrifices his wife's beloved car in order to keep from hitting the baby and Gloria, Jack cannot harm him; instead, he invites him and his wife to the reunion.

During the celebration, Gloria undergoes a kind of initiation into Jack's family. At one point, several of the women hold her down and force watermelon into her mouth; at another, they criticize her wedding dress, which she has worn to welcome back her husband, and end by cutting it up because they say it has far too much material in it. For a time, Gloria feels that Jack must choose between his family and her; eventually, however, she realizes that the love between them is so strong that she can afford to share him with his family.

These main plot lines indicate the importance of the theme of reconciliation in *Losing Battles*. In all these cases, individuals become accepted by a society that had initially viewed them as outsiders. Yet there is another character in the novel who has chosen to remain an outsider—Miss Julia Mortimer, the influential school-teacher, who has just died. Her presence at the reunion is entirely through anecdote, but she is a very real presence. Early in the novel, Gloria has to choose whether to go to the funeral of Miss Julia, her friend and mentor, or to stay and wait for Jack. She chooses Jack, as she had chosen him when she left teaching to marry him. In her battle for Gloria, Miss Julia loses, as she had lost most of the battles that she had waged against ignorance. At the end of her life, she was still fighting, but she had come to the conclusion that if her students did learn anything, it would be more or less a miracle rather than anything she had consciously done.

Despite its length, its structural complexity, and the innumerable characters, living and dead, that crowd its pages, *Losing Battles* is considered one of Welty's most interesting novels. Superficially, it appears to be little more than a record of conversations, yet it is a superb exploration of the subjects and themes that dominate Welty's works.

THE OPTIMIST'S DAUGHTER

First published: 1972
Type of work: Novel

A young woman must face the death of her beloved father and her conflicts with his vulgar, greedy second wife.

The Optimist's Daughter deals with family relationships, as do the earlier novels *Delta Wedding* and *Losing Battles* and many of Welty's short stories. *The Optimist's Daughter*, however, focuses on a family of only three people: Laurel McKelva Hand, a widow, the protagonist; her ill father, Judge Clinton McKelva; and his second wife, Fay Chisom McKelva, who is even younger than Laurel. It is not the difference between generations that causes conflict in this novel, however; as in "Moon Lake" and "A Memory," it is the difference in attitude and in conduct between two social classes, a difference that cannot easily be reconciled.

The old, educated Southern aristocracy, connected by common memories and by generations of intermarriage and marked by the restraint which they show in times of crisis, is represented by Judge McKelva, his dead wife Becky McKelva, and their daughter Laurel. Fay comes from a lower social level, one which people such as the McKelvas generally view with embarrassment and distaste. People of Fay's class, whatever their income, can be counted on to be loud, aggressive, and insensitive to social nuances.

Although it would seem that the hospital room in New Orleans where the story begins would be a neutral ground in the class conflict, it is not. The Judge's doctor is at ease with the Judge and Laurel; a native of Mount Salus, Mississippi, where the McKelvas live, he behaves as the Judge and Laurel do—they become more and more controlled as the Judge's health declines. It is not surprising that the doctor is appalled by Fay's behavior. Evidently she is convinced that if she pouts and complains enough about how bored she is, the Judge will rise from his bed and take her around New Orleans. Laurel, remembering her own refined, dead mother, loathes Fay. The family of the Judge's roommate, however, whose background is the same as Fay's, understands that her temper tantrums are simply the appropriate way for people of her class to respond to stress. It is to these people that Fay turns for understanding and comfort when the Judge dies.

In Mount Salus, as in New Orleans, there are two distinct groups of people. The friends of the McKelvas have one code; Fay's relatives, who come to attend the funeral, have another. From the vantage point of Laurel, with whom Welty clearly sympathizes, Fay is an intruder who intends to take the Judge's effects and, more important, to destroy the memories that are still present for Laurel in her childhood home.

For Laurel, the turning point of the story comes after the funeral when Fay tries to appropriate a breadboard that Laurel's dead husband had made for her mother. In a moment of fury, Laurel very nearly hits Fay over the head with the breadboard; however, Laurel realizes that such an action would be like Fay, not like the McKelvas. She also realizes that whatever material things Fay may claim, she cannot take either Laurel's sense of the family past or her memories of her husband, her mother, and her father.

At the end of the story, although she may not realize it, Fay has been defeated. She will always be an outsider in the society which she had hoped to enter by marrying the Judge. However much she mocks and attacks the aristocrats, she has a deep sense of inferiority when she is around them, based, Laurel sees, on Fay's very real defects, not simply on Laurel's distaste for her. Fay does not have enough imagination to understand a person of intelligence and of sensitivity. Therefore, she can neither love nor defeat such a person.

The Optimist's Daughter is different from Welty's other novels in that Fay comes close to being a real villain, rather than simply a person whose perceptions are different from those of others. Unlike the other novels, it ends without a reconciliation between characters in conflict, without the family incorporating unlike people into their society. Instead, there is a personal victory for Laurel: After her experience of confluence, her assurance of the presence of the dead she mourns, she knows that Fay and her like can never defeat her.

A MEMORY

First published: 1937
Type of work: Short story

A young girl at the beach finds her proper, orderly world threatened by the antics of a vulgar family.

In "A Memory," her second story to be published, Welty shows how difficult life with others can be, as in her earlier story, "Death of a Traveling Salesman," she had emphasized the appeal of human contact. In both stories, the family that the solitary protagonist encounters is a very ordinary one. In "Death of a Traveling Salesman," the salesman perceived a natural mannerliness in the young couple who offered him their hospitality. In "A Memory," however, the girl who is telling the story perceives only ugliness in the people who come to disturb her daydreams.

One reason for her reaction, she admits, is the fact that she is suffering from first love, cherishing the memory of an accidental touch by a boy whom she does not even know. The result of this condition, she says, is that she lives a life of heightened observation at the same time that she is creating a world of dreams. This is essentially the pattern Welty later described in *One Writer's Beginnings*; certainly the symptoms are those of the creative artist. What this protagonist wishes to do, however, is to select only the most beautiful memories and observations for her private world. When the boy she loves gets a nosebleed at school, she faints. Fearing another shock, she takes care not to find out where he lives or who his parents are. The world that she has created will not admit the world that, in the course of human life, she is bound to encounter.

It is this rejection of the whole of life that makes the protagonist's encounter with the vulgar family such a shock to her. The strangers on the beach do not even speak to her, yet she is offended by their ugliness, their noisiness, even their energy. When they leave, she is overcome by pity not for them, but for the little pavilion that had to endure them. At the end of the story, she recognizes how difficult it is to fit anything distasteful into an ideal world that one has invented and in which one wishes to dwell.

THE WIDE NET

First published: 1943
Type of work: Short story

A young husband spends a long day looking for his pregnant wife, who supposedly had run away to drown herself.

"The Wide Net" is a story about the conflict between the needs of the individual and the claims of the community. Young, pregnant Hazel Jamieson feels that the primary allegiance of her husband, William Wallace Jamieson, should be to her. When he stays out all night drinking with his friends, Hazel interprets his action as a rejection of her and of their marriage. She decides to take action.

When he arrives home, William Wallace finds a note from Hazel indicating that she has gone to drown herself. He is shocked. All he can think of is to turn once again to his friends, to the very friends who got him into difficulty in the first place. Since they are used to the unfathomable ways of women, they have a remedy for every kind of trouble that women can cause men, even the threat of suicide. Although they cannot prevent Hazel from killing herself, the men can provide the necessary procedure for recovering the body. They must gather by the river and drag it with a wide net until Hazel is found.

At first, the mood is suitably gloomy; however, as the day progresses, the atmosphere becomes festive. Other people join them. With the net, they bring up a baby alligator and an eel. They swim. They feast. At times, even William Wallace forgets the occasion of the gathering in the general excitement.

At the end of the day, the gathering disperses and William Wallace must go home. He has cut his foot, and he needs someone to take care of it for him. When Hazel comes out of hiding, the couple are reconciled. Even though she pretends submission, what Hazel now knows is that she can always find a way to throw William Wallace off balance. The day he has spent searching for her is proof of his love.

What she does not realize is that the strength of the male community was demonstrated when he turned to his friends for help, and that even before she came forward to relieve his apprehensions, William Wallace had undergone a healing ceremony in the company of those friends. There need not be a conflict, however; as long as William Wallace comes home early enough to convince Hazel that he loves her, she will not object to the rituals which involve his male friends. The story is resolved in Welty's usual pattern: Her characters settle their differences without withdrawing from the community which, though flawed, is needed to sustain its members.

MOON LAKE

First published: 1949
Type of work: Short story

During a week at summer camp, upper-class girls try to understand what it would be like to be people other than themselves.

"Moon Lake" illustrates how complex the relationships within a group can be and how subtly the distinctions between insider and outsider can be drawn. The story begins by pointing out that the girls at summer camp on Moon Lake are very much aware of lifeguard Loch Morrison's deliberate dissociation from them. Although Loch must work as their lifeguard, he does not intend to become a member of their group. The group of girls is split into two segments: the regular, paying campers from Morgana, Mississippi, three miles away, and the charity campers, who are orphans from the county home. The two groups dress differently and behave differently. The Morgana girls swim confidently, while the orphans, who cannot swim, simply stand nervously in the water until they are allowed to come out.

As the story progresses, Welty makes it clear that different people have different perceptions of social acceptance. For example, from Loch's lonely eminence as the only male in camp, all the girls are beyond the pale; he is secure in his society of one. To the leaders of the Morgana group, Nina Carmichael and Jinny Love Stark, it is the orphans who are outsiders. The Morgana girls automatically stick out their tongues at the orphans, only occasionally shifting from contempt into condescending pity. Easter, however, the leader of the orphans, scorns the soft girls from town, who do not even own jackknives, must less know how to throw them.

One example of the difference in viewpoint is the lengthy discussion among Nina, Jinny Love, and Easter about their names. Because no one around Morgana is named Easter, Jinny says, Easter's name is not a real name. Troubled, Nina tries to convince Easter that her name is merely misspelled; if it is in fact Esther, she says, it could be a real name, because there are other people around Morgana who are named Esther. Nevertheless, Easter will not be renamed. While the girls from Morgana derive their sense of identity from their sense of family and community, Easter is proud of being her own creation. She has no father; her mother has abandoned her. She was free to name herself, and now she is free to choose her own future, in a way that Nina and Jinny Love cannot be. If Easter goes off to become a singer, as she plans, no one will argue with her.

The girls from Morgana are always alert for outward signs of social deficiency— for example, the dirt ring at the back of Easter's neck or the mispronunciations of the Yankee counselor, Mrs. Gruenwald. They already know that Loch is different, because he is a boy; when at the end of the story, they see him silhouetted in his tent, stark naked, they speculate as to whether he has been beating his chest, Tarzan-like. Nina is fascinated enough by the outsiders to wish that she could slip into their skins, if only briefly, in order to know how they really feel. One night in the tent, Nina touches Easter's hand and almost makes contact; again, when Easter is unconscious, Nina comes so close to her that she faints. Ironically, it is the outsiders Loch and Easter who are symbolically united when he resuscitates her, while Nina and Jinny Love once more become simply Morgana girls.

Summary

In Eudora Welty's fiction, there is great variety as to point of view, structure, and the degree of complexity. In some works, the focus is on the experience of one person, who, though an accepted member of society, has retreated enough from it to view the world with a certain detachment. In others, Welty presents a number of different perceptions, maintaining a dramatic detachment and refusing to take sides in the conflicts she presents.

Sometimes the individual comes to terms with a sense of alienation; more often, the resolution involves an individual learning to preserve some independence while being incorporated into a society which at first had been intolerant, a society that should be valued for its preservation of the rich past.

Bibliography

Devlin, Albert J. *Eudora Welty's Chronicle: A Story of Mississippi Life.* Jackson: University Press of Mississippi, 1983.

_____, ed. *Welty: A Life in Literature.* Jackson: University Press of Mississippi, 1987.

Dollarhide, Louis, and Ann J. Abadie, eds. *Eudora Welty: A Form of Thanks.* Jackson: University Press of Mississippi, 1979.

Kreyling, Michael. *Eudora Welty's Achievement of Order.* Baton Rouge: Louisiana State University Press, 1980.

Prenshaw, Peggy Whitman, ed. *Eudora Welty: Critical Essays.* Jackson: University Press of Mississippi, 1979.

Vande Kieft, Ruth M. *Eudora Welty.* Boston: Twayne, 1987.

Welty, Eudora. *The Eye of the Story.* New York: Random House, 1978.

_____. *One Writer's Beginnings.* Cambridge, Mass.: Harvard University Press, 1984.

Rosemary M. Canfield Reisman

NATHANAEL WEST

Born: New York, New York
October 17, 1903
Died: El Centro, California
December 22, 1940

Principal Literary Achievement

West's fiction depicts the loneliness and frustration of urban life and reflects the destructiveness of lives based on empty illusions; his work prefigured the existentialism and black humor of works of the 1960's.

Biography

Nathanael West was born Nathan Weinstein in New York City on October 17, 1903, the only son of Russian Jewish immigrants. His father, Max Weinstein, was a prosperous building contractor and his mother, née Anna Wallenstein, was from a cultivated family. West was devoted to his father and to the younger of his two sisters, Lorraine.

An ungainly boy, West attended public schools in Manhattan, where he showed no academic distinction. According to his sisters' reports, he spent much of his time reading. He irregularly attended DeWitt Clinton High School, where he was a weak student and left without being graduated. His summers were spent in a camp in the Adirondacks, where he liked baseball but proved more talented as arts editor of the camp newspaper, printing his own cartoons satirizing his fellow campers.

In 1921, West entered Tufts University on the strength of an apparently forged high school transcript and flunked out during his first term. The following year he was admitted to Brown University as a transfer student from Tufts, probably on the basis of someone else's advanced grade record. There West became a serious student and was graduated in two and a half years with a bachelor's degree in English.

At Brown, West revealed a sociable nature. He dressed fashionably, engaged in campus social life despite non-acceptance by Gentile-only fraternities, and enjoyed a circle of friends including S. J. Perelman (the future humorist and columnist for *The New Yorker* who later married West's sister Lorraine). Having great college success as an aesthete, West studied medieval Catholicism and the lives of saints, and he avidly read the works of Irish writer James Joyce, the French Symbolist poets, and Euripides. As the editor of the Brown literary magazine, he designed its first cover and contributed a poem and an article.

After graduation, West legally changed his name to Nathanael West and intermittently worked for his father, who, then suffering setbacks in his business, eventually accepted his son's rejection of a commercial career and was persuaded to secure funds to send West to Paris in 1925 for a short stay. Once there, he affected the look of the expatriate bohemian writer and became intrigued by dadaism, with its foundation of cynicism and despair, and surrealism, with its Freudian connections.

Returning to New York, West (through a family connection) secured a job as night manager at a hotel in 1927 and later moved on to a fancier one. During his stint as a night clerk from 1927 to 1930, he put up indigent writers at reduced rates, including Dashiell Hammett, who finished *The Maltese Falcon* (1930) as West's bootleg guest. West wrote not-to-be published short stories and revised his first novella, begun in college. The latter, a surrealist fantasy about a young man's abortive search for life's meaning, was published in 1931 as *The Dream Life of Balso Snell* in a limited edition by a small press. The short novel, drawing only one journal review, caused no stir. In that same year, West became coeditor of a little magazine called *Contact* and published articles and chapters of the then-unpublished but completed *Miss Lonelyhearts* (1933) in it. He also became associate editor of the magazine *Americana*, which published a West short story about Hollywood entitled "Business Deal."

Miss Lonelyhearts was published in 1933 and received largely positive reviews, but only two hundred copies of the edition appeared, since the publisher went bankrupt. By the time West got the work republished, the reviews were forgotten; fewer than eight hundred copies were sold. Shortly after, however, the novel was purchased by a Hollywood studio, and an offer to write an original screenplay followed from Columbia Pictures. West accepted and worked in Hollywood for $350 a week on two projects, which did not materialize into films, before his contract was terminated.

After seeing *Miss Lonelyhearts* twisted into a murder thriller entitled *Advice to the Lovelorn* (1933) starring Lee Tracy, a disillusioned West returned to New York impressed with the idea that both Hollywood and life generated the lie of false dreams. He enlarged this notion in two still unpublished short stories: "Mr. Potts of Pottstown" and "The Sun, the Lady, and the Gas Station." In 1934, West published his third short novel, *A Cool Million: Or, The Dismantling of Lemuel Pitkin*, a black comedy satirizing the Horatio Alger myth and the American dream. The book was unfavorably reviewed and sold poorly.

Returning to Hollywood in 1936, West was first hired as a writer for Republic Productions and later worked through 1940 for other studios, turning out a number of undistinguished screenplays, alone or in collaboration. Because of his facile scriptwriting ability, West was able to make a securely comfortable living for the first time since 1929. With many of his fellow artists of the 1930's, West assumed a leftist outlook, becoming active in social causes and joining the embryonic Screen Writers Guild, then considered leftist by Hollywood executives. As early as 1935, West had espoused liberal views by signing the manifesto of the 1935 American Writers Congress, which had advocated a proleterian revolution.

Continuing to be well paid as a screenwriter, West completed his fourth novel:

The Day of the Locust (1939). It was based on West's perceptions of Hollywood and was published in 1939. Despite some good reviews, it was a commercial failure, selling fewer than fifteen hundred copies. The author's disappointment was forgotten when, in 1940, he fell in love with and married Eileen McKenney, celebrated as the protaganist of Ruth McKenney's *My Sister Eileen* (1938). This happy period in West's life was brief. On December 22, 1940, the Wests, returning from a hunting trip in Mexico, were both killed in an automobile accident in El Centro, California. He was thirty-seven. He was buried in a Jewish cemetery in New York City.

West's posthumous reputation has expanded considerably. His two major novels, when reprinted, sold thousands of copies. Scholarly articles about West multiplied. *The Day of the Locust* was made into a successful 1974 film. In 1957, the collected four novels were published to favorable reviews and critical recognition of West as an important 1930's writer. The black-comedy tone of his work had a demonstrable influence on many writers that succeeded him.

Analysis

Nathanael West shared with his fellow writers of the 1930's a disillusionment with the American Dream in the wake of the upheaval of World War I and the worldwide Great Depression. While most expressed their protest in realistic form, West developed an oblique vision of reality less overtly concerned with sociopolitical causes than with aesthetic and psychological ones. It tended toward bleakness and surrealism. For West, life presents a masquerade of false dreams concealing a reality that grotesquely contradicts the expectation; in each of his four novels, this pattern emerges. In *The Dream Life of Balso Snell*, the dream of art is exploded. In *A Cool Million*, the Horatio Alger myth that good intentions and virtuous hard effort will win the day is proved ineffective. *Miss Lonelyhearts* exposes a reality that will not permit living by the Golden Rule and Christ-like behavior. *The Day of the Locust* unmasks the deceptiveness of Hollywood. In the latter two major novels, the protagonist of each embarks on a quest for self-fulfillment, lured initially by a dream that ultimately turns to dust; the effort leads to grotesque revelation.

In addition to the myth pattern of the quest (for Holy Grail or golden fleece), other classical motifs found in myth and literature appear in West's work. Most evident are the scapegoat, who takes on the community's sins and becomes a sacrificial victim; the holy fool, a lowly person raised to an elevated state and allowed to partake of saturnalian pleasures for a limited time and then symbolically or literally killed in a rite of purgation; and the medieval concept of the Dance of Death, which allegorically represents the triumph of Death reminding people of their mortality and the need for repentance. Such motifs are found in the action and climax of both major novels.

Painter-protagonist Tod Hackett in *The Day of the Locust* provides a thematic statement when he observes that the need for beauty and romance, however "tasteless, even horrible" the result, cannot easily be laughed at; it is "easy to sigh. Few things are sadder than the truly monstrous." West's ability is to delineate the monstrous in a grotesque world that hangs ambiguously between the laughably ridiculous and the heartbreakingly sad. Not unlike poet T. S. Eliot's *The Waste Land* (1922), which presents a world of disassociated fragments suggesting the broken pieces of the past, West's work is hallucinatory, but it is more pessimistic and more comic. It is indebted to the techniques of surrealism, with its focus on dreams, and to psychoanalysis, which West especially develops in *Miss Lonelyhearts*. Also in his work is a moral irritation possibly stemming from his experience as an assimilated American Jew who discovered at college the uncomfortable ambiguity of that status.

In both *Miss Lonelyhearts* and *The Day of the Locust*, West cultivates a compact, cinematic style, advancing his narrative in a sequence of intense and fragmented scenes. West's skills and discipline as a Hollywood screenwriter in the last years of his life were compatible with his inclination for constructing stories out of dominantly visual images. Like a film script, which often contains less dialogue than directions regarding visualization, West's short fiction is terse and usually describes character and action in terms of movement, activity, and visual impressions.

To portray his landscapes of a desolate American wasteland of decay and pain, West employs images of the grotesque. Such images encompass violence, animalistic sexuality, the mechanical, and death. Among the inhabitants of these landscapes are the malformed—a cripple, a dwarf in a Tyrolean hat, a young girl without a nose— and the victimized—women who have suffered rape or domestic sexual brutality or loveless marriages. The spiritually dead are described in mechanical terms such as "a poorly made automaton," "a phallic Jack-in-the-box," "a wound-up cowboy toy," "a mechanical woman self-created from bits of vanished film heroines," or a face like a frozen and cubistic clown mask. An uncontrolled mob, first peaceably gathered to ogle celebrities at a film premiere, becomes a nightmarish group of figures akin to those in a Hieronymous Bosch (a fifteenth century Dutch painter) painting of hell. A character subconsciously retreating from reality experiences distorted perceptions, seeing a man's cheeks as rolls of toilet paper or a woman's buttocks as enormous grindstones. Such images are stylistically influenced by the nihilistic side of surrealism, destroying the world of rationalism with the surrealistic world of individual perceptions.

Evident in West's work is the influence of dadaism and surrealism, cubism, the French Symbolists, Freudian psychoanalysis, the lives of saints, and of such individual writers as James Joyce, Fyodor Dostoevski, and Euripides. Such influences can be seen in the structure, character delineation, depiction of events, overall images, tone, and thematic outlook of West's fiction.

The world of West's novels is a pessimistic one exuding a pervasive atmosphere of failure and defeat and peopled by the lost and the victimized. Yet West describes this world with a darkly comic vision which recognizes that it holds humor if little real joy. His fiction not only foreshadowed the existentialism of 1960's writers such as Samuel Beckett but also introduced "black humor" as an influence over a number of American writers when, after World War II, his works were republished. In that sense, West was a most modern American writer.

MISS LONELYHEARTS

First published: 1933
Type of work: Novel

A columnist advising the lovelorn finds that Christ-like behavior will neither assuage their misery nor effect his salvation in a callous and spiritually bankrupt world.

Miss Lonelyhearts, the author's first major novel, stands as West's most critically successful, influential, and representative work. The short novel clearly reflects West's pessimistic view of the world and his characteristic narrative technique, employing graphic and often surreal visual images in describing characters and events. The work's expressionistic approach, coupled with its nihilistic outlook and sardonic tone, foretold the existentialism of 1960's writers and became recognized as an early example of black comedy, serving as a model of stimulation to such American writers as Carson McCullers, James Purdy, Flannery O'Connor, and John Hawkes.

Miss Lonelyhearts is the pseudonym of a bachelor newspaper columnist assigned to advise the lovelorn, whose desperation he first finds amusing. His initial attitude fades as he becomes obsessed with his correspondents' misery, cynically illuminated by the city editor, and sees his own helpless condition in that of his supplicants. He embarks on a self-perceived Christ-like pilgrimage to attain salvation for himself by helping the hopeless. His messianic quest only serves to exacerbate the impotence of his own relationships and alienates him from those around him who view such a search as insanely futile. When his perceptions of reality become increasingly surreal, he meets a ludicrously ironic death as he intervenes in the life of one lovelorn supplicant whom he thinks he has redeemed, only to be shot by her confused husband. His death becomes a futile sacrifice added to the novel's world of unhelped humanity.

The single work most representative of West's style, *Miss Lonelyhearts* shares common features with his other novels. Like his immediately preceding first novella, *The Dream Life of Balso Snell*, it introduces a lost protagonist set on an abortive quest to find meaning in an American wasteland masked by false dreams and devoid of beauty, charity, and love. The novel's metaphor for that wasteland is New York City's seedy apartments, bars, and newspaper offices (in West's second major novel, it is Hollywood). While the overall tone of West's novels is a sardonic one, here the fevered messianic religiosity of the nameless Miss Lonelyhearts lends the story distinctiveness and intensity, as that central figure pursues a once-powerful dream now rendered puerile and powerless in a modern America. No longer operative in West's world, the Christ dream will betray and ultimately destroy the dreamer.

Similar to his first novel, *Miss Lonelyhearts* follows an episodic narrative pattern. Yet here the work refines an abbreviated cinematic style that spills the story out in an expressionistic sequence of fragmented scenes, described in terms of visual images somewhat like a cartoon strip or the storyboards used in preparing a screenplay for filming. The scenes externalize the inner state of the protagonist's mind—an expressionistic technique—as he progresses from reality, often perceiving people and events in surrealistically grotesque images that mirror the ugliness and loveless-ness of West's world. It is a surrealist world, as seen through the eyes of the protago-nist, governed by individual perceptions that contradict the world of rationalism; a woman is seen as a tent, veined and covered with hair, and a man as a skeleton in a closet. West offers objective correlatives for human fears, perverted love, ambivalent sexuality, ineffective concern for suffering, and other problems of modern conscious-ness. Apparent in *Miss Lonelyhearts* is the theme that the quest for either personal salvation or Christ-like ministration to others is impossible in a morally and spir-itually decaying world in which the dreams that people employ to contend with misery have become false and powerless.

THE DAY OF THE LOCUST

First published: 1939
Type of work: Novel

In the dream factory of Hollywood, a young studio designer finds neither beauty nor romance but only falsity, desperation, and the emptiness of the Amer-ican Dream.

The Day of the Locust (originally entitled *The Cheated*) is the last, the longest, and the most realistic of West's novels. Set in 1930's Hollywood, the novel, drawing on West's experiences as a studio screenwriter, won critical recognition and, upon its republication in the 1950's, popular success that was capped by a 1974 motion pic-ture that was faithful to the original. Less surreal in style and slightly more comic in tone than *Miss Lonelyhearts*, the story depicts a similarly bleak world. Hollywood, with its masquerade of beauty and romance, contains neither but conceals frustrated hopes and false dreams of success. Unlike other Hollywood novels (commonly fo-cusing on the successful and the powerful), *The Day of the Locust* chiefly concentrates on the unsuccessful, the untalented, and the impotent: the bit players, the hangers-on, the displaced persons from mid-America, all of whom represent disillusioned or lost searcners cheated of their romantic expectations and fantasies stimulated by films.

Observing those lives is the novel's protagonist, a college-educated painter named Tod Hackett. He finds success as a studio designer but comes to realize the frustra-tion and the spiritual and moral emptiness of Hollywood, where the natural is the artificial. Hackett, himself cheated in the pursuit of romance with an artificial and ungifted bit player incapable of returning his love, ultimately leaves the dream capi-tal. The characters are seen by the painter-protagonist's eyes as often-grotesque im-ages that parallel their needs for meaningful emotional lives. Their unfulfilled needs lead to actual and vicarious violence and lust and to an ultimate feeling of spiritual and emotional death with the realization of betrayal. Their lives are ones of desperation, boredom, and frustrated search.

Stressing the failure of dreams, the novel culminates in the violent, orgiastic riot of frenzied movie fans at a Hollywood premiere. The riot embodies Hackett's progressive panoramic painting of the city depicting an apocalyptic vision of terrified citizens facing fiery destruction. It epitomizes the novel's indictment of the destructiveness of false dreams in modern America.

The novel's principal themes are the tension between disillusion and romance and the impact of the realization of betrayal. *The Day of the Locust* is a trenchant exposure of the decay and violence arising from the betrayal of dreams. Life as an illusion, implies West, masks a discontent capable of explosion. Conveying the dilemma of the modern American psyche, the work is a savage satire on America and its dreams.

Summary

In his two major novels, Nathanael West created a sardonic vision of a moral and spiritual American wasteland disguising its emptiness with romance and dreams. Sadly, the seekers after such dreams are doomed to frustration. West's early existential vision foreshadowed the mood of the 1960's as well as subsequent literary views of life.

Miss Lonelyhearts represents the best expression of West's vision. Yet both of West's major novels together constitute a distinctive and powerful body of work marking their author as an American writer ahead of his time.

Bibliography

Bloom, Harold, ed. *Modern Critical Views: Nathanael West*. New York: Chelsea House, 1986.

Comerchero, Victor. *Nathanael West: The Ironic Prophet*. Syracuse, N.Y.: Syracuse University Press, 1964.

Hyman, Stanley Edgar. *Nathanael West*. Minneapolis: University of Minnesota Press, 1962.

Light, James F. *Nathanael West: An Interpretative Study*. 2d ed. Evanston, Ill.: Northwestern University Press, 1971.

Martin, Jay. *Nathanael West: The Art of His Life*. New York: Farrar, Straus & Giroux, 1970.

Reid, Randall. *The Fiction of Nathanael West: No Redeemer, No Promised Land*. Chicago: University of Chicago Press, 1967.

Vannatta, Dennis P. *Nathanael West: An Annotated Bibliography of the Scholarship and Works*. New York: Garland, 1976.

Widmer, Kenneth. *Nathanael West*. Boston: Twayne, 1982.

Christian H. Moe

EDITH WHARTON

Born: New York, New York
January 24, 1862
Died: St. Brice sous Forêt, France
August 11, 1937

Principal Literary Achievement

Best known for her realistic novels of manners depicting the lives of the upper classes in late nineteenth and early twentieth century New York society, Wharton is one of America's most distinguished women writers.

Biography

Edith Wharton was born Edith Newbold Jones on January 24, 1862, into the wealthy "aristocracy" of the old New York society which would become the focus of much of her fiction. Her mother and father, George F. and Lucretia Stevens Rhinelander Jones, both traced their family lines back three hundred years; their ancestors were mentioned in Washington Irving's history of the Hudson River.

Wharton spent most of her childhood in Europe, where her family fled to avoid post-Civil War inflation. Returning to the United States in 1872, the Whartons followed the pattern common to their social set, wintering in New York City and summering in Newport, Rhode Island. As was the practice for a girl of her social status, she was educated primarily by governesses and tutors, made her debut to society at eighteen, and then traveled abroad.

In 1882, Wharton's father died, and she lived in New York City with her mother. During this period, she met Walter Berry, a wealthy lawyer, and began one of the most important relationships of her life—it was to last more than thirty years. Berry acted as Wharton's unofficial editor and literary adviser, beginning with her first book, *The Decoration of Houses* (1897), a volume on interior decoration inspired by her reaction against the ornate fashions then popular in America, and continuing throughout her career until his death in 1927. Although controversy exists as to both the quality and extent of Berry's effect on her work, it remains clear that his influence was strong.

In 1885, Wharton married Edward R. "Teddy" Wharton, a member of socially well-connected families from Boston and Philadelphia. Although Teddy loved to travel as much as his wife did, the two had little else in common; he shared none of her love of the arts or the life of the mind. They spent the early years of their

marriage traveling abroad, but in the early 1890's Wharton suffered from a depressive illness which lasted until 1902, at which time Teddy began to show signs of the mental disorder that would plague him for the rest of his life. Because of his unstable condition and the financial difficulties which ensued, the couple curtailed their travels and settled into a pattern of wintering in Paris or New York and summering at The Mount, a home in Lenox, Massachusetts, designed by Wharton. Here she found the solitude necessary to pursue her writing. Teddy's mental condition was diagnosed as incurable in 1910, and in 1913 Wharton divorced him.

Wharton began to pursue a writing career seriously, partly as a cure for the depressive illness she suffered; she first gained recognition for short stories such as "The Greater Inclination" (1899), "Crucial Instances" (1902), and "The Descent of Man" (1904). Also during this period she followed her popular first book with *Italian Villas and Their Gardens* (1904). She experimented with novellas early in her career, producing *The Touchstone* (1900) and *Sanctuary* (1903), but her greatest success with that form would come later with the publication of *Ethan Frome* (1911). Her first novel, *The Valley of Decision* (1902), a historical romance set in eighteenth century Italy, received mixed reviews, but her second novel, *The House of Mirth* (1905), was a critical and commercial success. It marked the beginning of her career as a prominent literary figure.

The publication of *The House of Mirth* began a very productive period in Wharton's career, during which she wrote the novellas *Madame de Treymes* (1907) and *Ethan Frome* and the novels *The Reef* (1912) and *The Custom of the Country* (1913). During this period, Wharton developed a long-standing friendship with American author Henry James, with whom she has often been compared. James's influence on Wharton is especially evident in *The Reef* but is present throughout her work.

Wharton was extremely active during World War I, living in Paris and performing extensive volunteer work for the Red Cross, serving as the head of the American Committee of the Acueil Franco-Americain, which by 1918 was caring for five thousand refugees settled in Paris. Wharton also founded the Children of Flanders Rescue Committee to send 650 orphans and children displaced by the war to families who lived away from the battle zones. She cared for six children in her own apartment, finding permanent homes for them after the war. Wharton was decorated with the Cross of the Legion of Honor in 1917 for these activities. Her war experiences produced *Fighting France, from Dunkerque to Belfort* (1915), which describes her inspection tour of hospitals in the battle zone, and a novel, *A Son at the Front* (1923).

Following the war she continued to reside permanently in France, making only one trip to America, in 1923, to receive an honorary doctorate from Yale University. In 1920, she moved from Paris to the eighteenth century Pavillon Calombe outside of Paris; she also restored an ancient monastery on the French Riviera, in which she spent her ensuing summers. During this period she produced *The Age of Innocence* (1920), generally considered her best work, for which she received a Pulitzer Prize in 1921. She also became the first woman gold medalist of the American Society of Arts and Letters in 1924.

Her work after *The Age of Innocence* did not achieve the critical or popular success of her earlier books, although she remained prolific. Two novels, *The Glimpses of the Moon* (1922) and *The Mother's Recompense* (1925), were not up to her usual standards and did not enhance her reputation, but with *Old New York* (1924), a collection of novellas, she regained her form. She published five more novels before her death in 1937, including *Hudson River Bracketed* (1929), her autobiography, *A Backward Glance* (1934), and the promising but unfinished *Buccaneers* (1938). Wharton died of a stroke at the age of seventy-five and was buried next to the ashes of Walter Berry in the Cimetière des Gonards at Versailles.

Analysis

Too often known only as "that society lady author," a writer of irrelevant and obsolete books, Edith Wharton cannot be dismissed so easily. Although primarily dealing with a narrow social range and short historical span—the upper echelons of New York society from the 1870's to the 1920's—she mines verities about the whole of human nature from these small, seemingly unrepresentative samples of humanity. Far from being anachronistic or irrelevant, Wharton's novels go deeper than their surface manners and mores to reveal universal truths about individuals in relation to their society, and she explores themes relevant to any era.

Regarded as one of America's finest realists, along with her friend and literary inspiration Henry James, Wharton emphasized verisimilitude, character development, and the psychological dimensions of experience, all of which placed her in this tradition, although with some significant variations. Some of her fiction, such as *Ethan Frome*, owes a greater debt to romantics such as Nathaniel Hawthorne than to the realists, and most of her work deals with the upper rather than the middle classes more common to realist fiction; critic Blake Nevius remarks:

> [S]he was destined from the beginning to be a realist. As a child in Paris, she used to . . . make up stories about the only people who were real to her imagination—the grownups with whom she was surrounded. . . . Mother Goose and Hans Christian Andersen bored her.

The United States' premiere novelist of manners, Wharton employs intricately detailed descriptions of outward form, including manners, customs, fashion, and decor, to reveal the inner passions and ideals of her characters. Using manners to register internal events as well as external circumstances allows her to indicate deeper emotions indirectly. The constricting effect of an elaborate and confining set of behavioral guidelines on the human psyche and the human spirit's survival within these narrow boundaries provide one of the overriding themes of her fiction.

This emphasis on the power of environment over the individual sets her apart from the writer to whom she is most often compared, Henry James. Frequently mentioned in the same breath, the two indeed have many similarities. They traveled in the same social circles, wrote about similar kinds of people, held the same values, and dealt with many of the same themes, particularly innocence versus experience. James, however, placed more emphasis upon the individual within the society than on the society itself. Perhaps the strongest bond between these two writers lies in their mutual devotion to the art of fiction, their continual study of the novel's form, and their interest in the technique and processes of art.

As a realist, Wharton describes the houses, fashion, and social rituals of "Old New York" in minute detail, studying this small stratum of society as an anthropologist might study a South Sea island. *The Age of Innocence*, for example, abounds in anthropological terminology, as the protagonist, Newland Archer, reveals when reflecting that "there was a time when . . . everything concerning the manners and customs of his little tribe had seemed to him fraught with world-wide significance"; he describes his own wedding as "a rite that seemed to belong to the dawn of history." Archer's use of this anthropological jargon reveals Wharton's almost scientific fascination with the social milieu.

Similarly, in *The House of Mirth*, structured as a series of scenes that reflect the social status of its heroine, Lily Bart, Wharton meticulously records even the finest lines between classes, noting that "the difference [between them] lay in a hundred shades of aspect and manner, from the pattern of the men's waistcoats to the inflexion of the women's voices." Although no such subtlety of detail exists in the very different world of *Ethan Frome*, a nevertheless fixed and immovable social structure offers the novel's protagonist no avenue of escape from his equally barren business and marriage. In all these novels, the elaborate rituals that sustain a culture protect tradition and stabilize the society, but they also constrict the freedom of the individual within that society.

Often victims of society's narrow definition of acceptable behavior, Wharton's multifaceted, psychologically complex characters are also victimized by their own weaknesses. Lily Bart, one of Wharton's most fully realized characters, suffers under the limitations placed on women in her circumstances, but she falls equally victim to her own selfishness and snobbery. Similarly, Newland Archer, imprisoned within the narrow behavioral confines of old New York, is also imprisoned by prejudices and lassitude. The eponymous character of *Ethan Frome*, as a result of his own and society's limitations, also fails to escape a suffocating town, business, and marriage to find intellectual and emotional fulfillment.

Although not involved in the feminist movement of her day, Wharton's preoccupation with the limiting effects of societal restrictions on the human soul necessarily invokes feminist issues, for women especially were the victims of this society's narrow boundaries. Lily Bart, for example, finds her options severely limited because of her sex; even taking tea alone with a man in his apartment results in social condemnation. Newland Archer often muses on the peculiar demands and expectations placed on women; when he declares, "Women ought to be free—as free as we are," Wharton notes that he is "making a discovery of which he was too irritated to measure the terrific consequences." May Welland Archer is yet another victim—in this case, of her husband's narrow definition of her character, and Ellen

Olenska is the victim of society's preconceptions of a woman's behavior.

The principal theme of Wharton's fiction involves the individual in society: how personal relationships are distorted by societal conventions, the clash between changing characters and fixed society, and the conflict between nature and culture. Wharton therefore stands a bridge between an older, more established nineteenth century world and the world of the twentieth century, which placed increasing emphasis on individual experience.

THE HOUSE OF MIRTH

First published: 1905
Type of work: Novel

A young woman falls from the heights of New York society to the depths of poverty and despair when she fails to conform to society's expectations.

The House of Mirth, Wharton's second full-length novel, not only guaranteed her literary reputation but also established the setting and themes she would explore throughout her career. Set in the early twentieth century New York society with which she was so intimately familiar, the novel offers an angrier and more bitter condemnation of this social milieu than Wharton's later work, which mellowed with the passage of time. Both a meticulously thorough examination of a complex social structure and a brilliant character study, it offers a compelling exploration of the effects of social conformity upon the individual.

As the novel opens, its heroine, twenty-nine-year-old Lily Bart, has achieved the height of her powers: Beautiful, intelligent, charming, and sought after, she has nevertheless reached a turning point, knowing too well that society has no place for an unmarried woman past her prime. Her parents having left her no legacy but an appreciation for the finer things in life, Lily occupies a precarious social position under the protection of her dreary, socially prominent Aunt Peniston, and she must rely on the favors of the wealthy ladies and gentlemen who find her company amusing. Lily's craving for the secure foothold that only marriage can provide cannot entirely overcome her distaste for the hypocrisy and insensitivity of her class. Hardly lacking for opportunities to marry well, Lily nevertheless manages to sabotage her best chances, as she does in bungling her courtship with Percy Gryce, an eminently eligible but overwhelmingly boring pillar of the community.

Lily's unique place in New York society—simultaneously insider and outsider—makes her one of Wharton's most fascinating creations and offers the reader a privileged perspective on this world. A product of her society, "at once vigorous and exquisite, at once strong and fine. . . . [who] must have cost a great deal to make," Lily is also "so evidently the victim of the civilization which had produced her that the links of her bracelet seemed like manacles chaining her to her fate." Lily's need to be surrounded by the beautiful things that only immense sums of money can buy and her distaste for the common and ugly enslave her to those she might otherwise find at best ridiculous and at worst repellent; they cause her to reject the only person for whom she feels genuine emotion, Lawrence Selden, a cultivated lawyer of modest means. As Lily can neither totally accept her society's values nor be hypocritical enough to survive without doing so, she finally must perish.

Lily's fall from social grace is incremental rather than precipitous, occurring gradually as she makes small compromises in order to survive. The novel opens with one of many small lapses in judgment, as she accepts Lawrence Selden's impromptu invitation to take tea alone at his apartment. An ill-advised financial arrangement with Gus Trenor, the husband of her friend and social arbiter, Judy Trenor, leaves her further compromised, as does her well-intentioned effort to keep socially powerful Bertha Dorset's husband occupied while Bertha conducts an affair. Ostracized by the aristocracy and the nouveau riche, she then fails to succeed as a milliner's apprentice and finally finds herself alone and nearly penniless.

Paradoxically, as Lily descends through these various layers of society, her strength of character grows, as evidenced by her determination to use the entirety of her meager inheritance to repay her debt to Gus Trenor and by her unwillingness to accept a handout from rich industrialist Simon Rosedale. Yet her fragile new sense of self cannot survive unsupported. She has "the feeling of being something rootless and ephemeral, mere spindrift of the whirling surface of existence, without anything to which the poor little tentacles of self could cling before the awful flood submerged them," before succumbing to an overdose of sleeping pills.

Far from creating a clear-cut good versus evil or spirit versus materialism dialectic, Wharton establishes a more subtle and interesting conflict. Many of the novel's characters embody such antithetical attributes, as, for example, the social worker Gerty Farish, who reveals more "good" attributes than Lily, including honesty, generosity, and devotion to good works. Nevertheless, she is not a particularly attractive or sympathetic figure, lacking Lily's charm, perceptions, and sensitivity to beauty. Simon Rosedale, on the other hand, a ruthless businessman and ambitious social climber, is one of the rare characters who shows genuine sympathy for Lily when she descends to the bottom of the social heap. Lawrence Selden, although largely sympathetic, exhibits a weakness of character that proves fatal for Lily; he is unwilling to relinquish his safe niche in the social order for her sake until too late. Like Lily, he senses that life holds more than exists in his narrow social milieu, but also like Lily he is loathe to give up his social acceptance to explore the possibilities. Lily, while too self-centered and elitist to be a conventional heroine, still possesses many qualities that attract the reader.

More naturalistic than her other novels, *The House of Mirth* contains too many coincidental plot twists to make Lily's fall entirely believable, and Wharton's portrayal of the lower classes, as illustrated by her portrait of Nettie Struthers, the poor shop girl, possesses none of the subtlety or believability of her presentation of the upper classes; it often descends to melodrama. Despite these minor flaws, however, *The House of Mirth* portrays a small strata of society and one character within that society to perfection, brilliantly illustrating the power of social conformity over individuality.

ETHAN FROME

First published: 1911
Type of work: Novella

In the bleak landscape of New England, an outsider pieces together the tragic history of the town's most striking character.

Ethan Frome, neither a commercial nor a critical success when first published, actually offended many of Wharton's contemporaries by its harsh portrayal of New England life and its characters' failure to triumph over adversity. Nevertheless, its popularity gradually increased until, by 1920, it had become the best-known and most widely read of Wharton's works. Wharton herself believed that too much attention was paid to *Ethan Frome* at the expense of her other novels. Indeed, to judge her career solely by this single novella would prove misleading, because it is very unlike her other major novels in setting, tone, and characterization. Like much of her other work, however, it deals with the relationship between an individual and his or her society.

Structured as a frame tale, the story unfolds from the point of view of Lockwood, a young engineer on assignment in the isolated New England village of Starkfield. His curiosity about one of the town's characters, the physically deformed but striking Ethan Frome, drives him to construct a "vision" of Ethan's history, assembled from information gathered in conversation with various townspeople and from his own observations of the fifty-two-year-old farmer. The significance of this structure cannot be overestimated; Wharton even adds an uncharacteristic introduction to explain her decision to employ this literary device, which achieves perspective by creating an educated, observant narrator to intercede between the simple characters and the more sophisticated reader. Wharton also adds poignancy by setting the novella twenty-four years after the main action occurs.

Lockwood relates the simple but compelling story of twenty-eight-year-old Ethan Frome, a farmer and mill owner left nearly destitute after the death of his parents, both of whom suffered mental disorders. After enduring lonely years of silence with his mother, who was too busy listening for imagined "voices" to converse with him, Frome marries Zenobia Pierce, seven years his senior, who had nursed Mrs. Frome in her dying days. The sound of Zeena's voice in his house is music to Ethan's starved ears, and by marrying her he hopes to escape further loneliness. Soon after their marriage, however, Zeena becomes obsessed with her various aches and pains, and she concerns herself solely with doctors, illnesses, and cures, falling as silent as his mother.

At her doctor's advice, Zeena takes in her homeless young cousin, Mattie Silver, to help with the housework. Although a hapless housekeeper, Mattie brings a vitality to the Frome house that has been absent for years, and she and Ethan fall in love. Trapped by circumstances, as well as by Ethan's strong sense of responsibility toward Zeena, the two foresee no future together. On the evening that Zeena sends her away for good, Mattie persuades Ethan to aim their sled straight for a giant elm so that they might find mutual solace in death. Both, however, survive the plunge, which paralyzes Mattie and disfigures Ethan. Zeena takes responsibility for caring for Mattie and Ethan, and the three live on in the Frome house, as Mattie becomes as querulous and unpleasant as Zeena and Ethan attempts to scratch out a living from his failing farm and mill.

In Ethan, "the most striking figure in Starkfield, though he was but the ruin of a man," Wharton fashions a character of heroic proportions. He is a country man who would have preferred the intellectual stimulation of the city, a sociable man doomed to silent suffering, a man whose misshapen body mirrors his thwarted intellectual and emotional life. Like Lily Bart in *The House of Mirth*, he is "more sensitive than the people about him to the appeal of natural beauty" but finds little of it in his own life. Like Lily, he feels trapped by society's demands on him: "The inexorable facts closed in on him like prison-warders handcuffing a convict. There was no way out— none. He was a prisoner for life."

As always in Wharton's work, setting figures prominently, but in *Ethan Frome* the stark landscape of New England, rather than the elegant brownstones of New York City, provides the background. Wharton draws a close parallel between the action and the emotions of the characters and the bleak landscape; the two are inextricably intertwined. Ethan "seemed a part of the mute melancholy landscape, an incarnation of its frozen woe, with all that was warm and sentient in him fast bound below the surface." Even Frome's house, lacking the "L" wing common to New England farm structures, reflects the emotionally stunted life existing inside, and the withering orchard of starving apple trees and crazily slanting gravestones in the family plot also mirror Frome's blighted life.

Wharton uses irony, as well as landscape and imagery, to great effect in this work, often juxtaposing scenes for ironic effect. When Zeena greets Ethan at the kitchen door in the evening, "The light . . . drew out of the darkness her puckered throat and the projecting wrist of the hand that clutched the quilt, and deepened fantastically the hollows and prominences of her high-boned face under its ring of crimping-pins." Later, however, when Mattie stands "just as Zeena had stood, a lifted lamp in her hand, against the black background of the kitchen. . . . [I]t drew out with the same distinctness her slim young throat and the brown wrist no bigger than a child's." *Ethan Frome*'s ultimate irony lies in the suicide pact which ends not in the mutual release of death but in endless years of pain and suffering and in the transformation of the vibrant young Mattie into a mirror image of the whining Zenobia.

THE AGE OF INNOCENCE

First published: 1920
Type of work: Novel

In "old New York" society, a young man must choose between his innocent young fiancée and her more worldly, sophisticated cousin.

The Age of Innocence, often considered Wharton's masterpiece, takes a nostalgic look at the New York society of her childhood, which had undergone enormous changes by 1920. In a mood tempered from that expressed in the 1905 *The House of Mirth*, Wharton criticizes many aspects of this society, especially its hypocrisy and tendency to stifle creativity and genuine emotion, but in this retrospective she also finds value in its stability and traditions. At the height of her powers in this novel, Wharton brilliantly uses plot, character, dialogue, point of view and irony to express her themes, including the needs of the individual versus the claims of the society, and the tenuous balance between the values of innocence and experience and between tradition and change.

The novel's plot revolves around the choice the protagonist, Newland Archer, must make between two women—his fiancée, May Welland, the flower of New York society, and her cousin, Countess Ellen Olenska, recently separated from her abusive husband and settled in New York. The Welland family enlists Archer to talk the countess out of seeking a divorce in order to avoid scandal and pain to her family. Archer soon falls in love with Ellen and, reversing his position, asks her to divorce her husband to marry him. Ironically, Ellen refuses, persuaded too well by Archer's arguments against divorce, and Archer marries May. Ellen eventually returns to Europe, May announces her pregnancy, and Newland Archer's fate is sealed. Twenty-five years later, after May's death, Archer passes up an opportunity to see Ellen in Paris, realizing that his dreams have become more important to him than reality.

The society Wharton describes in *The Age of Innocence* values conformity over originality, superficial pleasantness over reality, and respectability over individual freedom. Archer understands that "they all lived in a kind of hieroglyphic world, where the real thing was never said or done or even thought, but only represented by a set of arbitrary signs," but he does not disapprove. Smugly self-satisfied, he feels intellectually and culturally superior to his social set but nevertheless embraces most of its moral doctrines and values, never fully realizing the extent of his own conformity.

In fact, Newland's attraction to May is indicative of his acceptance of the establishment's values. Initially, "[n]othing about his betrothed pleased him more than her resolute determination to carry to its utmost limit that ritual of ignoring the 'unpleasant' in which they had both been brought up." May's innocence, which Archer initially finds appealing, becomes oppressive, however, and Newland feels trapped by this creature he helped to create. Ironically, although May does represent the weaknesses of the old guard—innocence, hypocrisy, and stifling propriety—she also embodies its strength: stability and respect for tradition. Yet for twenty-five years, Archer failed to look beyond his own preconceptions of his wife to appreciate these qualities.

Ellen Olenska, on the other hand, embodies experience, intellect, freedom, and individuality. Separated from her husband, a stranger in her own country, and largely ignorant of the strict codes of the society she was born into, she symbolizes disintegration of tradition and lack of stability. At the same time, she offers honesty and genuine emotion to a culture sorely lacking these qualities.

Wharton invests the novel's minor characters with symbolic weight as well. The van der Luydens, the social establishment's judges of morals and taste, appear in terms of death and dying; Mrs. van der Luyden "struck Newland Archer as having been rather gruesomely preserved in the airless atmosphere of a perfectly irreproachable existence, as bodies caught in glaciers keep for years a rosy life-in-death." At the other end of the social spectrum, the immensely wealthy Julius Beaufort represents the threat of the new materialism. Tolerated only because he married into the aristocracy, his open philandering and questionable business dealings typify the crass vulgarities of those breaking down society's barriers. Mrs. Manson Mingott, combining both the old and new, stands for the stability of class combined with the vigor and independence of the nouveau riche, and Archer's two companions, the gossiping Sillerton Jackson and womanizing Lawrence Lefferts, symbolize the establishment's most hypocritical aspects.

Wharton also employs irony and symbolism to great effect in *The Age of Innocence*, particularly to describe the romance of Ellen Olenska and Archer Newland. Although their passion for each other is evident and genuine, Wharton never allows the romance to descend into the tragic or melodramatic. Each of the couple's interludes is somehow ironically undercut: Archer tenderly kisses what he believes to be Ellen's pink parasol, only to discover it is not hers at all; the couple boards a ferry for a romantic tête-à-tête only to be surrounded by a gaggle of schoolteachers on holiday, and, finally achieving solitude, they cannot forget that they are alone together in May's wedding carriage.

Rich in characterization, symbolism, and irony, the novel deals with several powerful themes, including the balance between innocence and experience, tradition and change, and individual and society. It also addresses the repression of women, the role of marriage and family, and the conflict between sexual passion and moral obligation. In *The Age of Innocence*, Edith Wharton perceives the repression of the self in the old ways and fragmentation of the self in the new. Wharton's alter ego, Newland Archer, feels comfortable with neither the old nor the new order; he inhabits a lonely middle ground, searching for a workable compromise between individual freedom and the claims of society.

Summary

No other writer of her time knew the upper classes of the United States more intimately or detailed their lives more movingly or convincingly than did Edith Wharton. Her attitude toward "old New York" was one of both anger and nostalgia—anger at its stifling hypocrisies and moral passivity and nostalgia for the stability and sense of tradition which were being assaulted by the rise of the new industrial classes at the beginning of the twentieth century. The tension between these two conflicting emotions provides the subject matter for most of Wharton's work. Torn between scorn and admiration for the old ways and fear of the chaos she saw accompanying the new, her fiction stands at the threshold of the twentieth century, a harbinger of the changes to come in American life.

Bibliography

Auchincloss, Louis. *Edith Wharton*. Minneapolis: University of Minnesota Press, 1961.

Bell, Millicent. *Edith Wharton and Henry James: The Story of Their Friendship*. New York: George Braziller, 1965.

Lewis, R. W. B. *Edith Wharton*. New York: Harper & Row, 1975.

Lindberg, Gary H. *Edith Wharton and the Novel of Manners*. Charlottesville: University Press of Virginia, 1975.

Lubbock, Percy. *Portrait of Edith Wharton*. New York: Appleton-Century-Crofts, 1947.

McDowell, Margaret B. *Edith Wharton*. Minneapolis: University of Minnesota Press, 1976.

Nevius, Blake. *Edith Wharton: A Study of Her Fiction*. Berkeley: University of California Press, 1953.

Walton, Geoffrey. *Edith Wharton: A Critical Interpretation*. Rutherford, N.J.: Fairleigh Dickinson University Press, 1971.

Wolff, Cynthia Griffin. *A Feast of Words: The Triumph of Edith Wharton*. New York: Oxford University Press, 1977.

Mary Virginia Davis

WALT WHITMAN

Born: West Hills, Long Island, New York
May 31, 1819
Died: Camden, New Jersey
March 26, 1892

Principal Literary Achievement

Regarded by many as America's greatest poet, Whitman employed an innovative verse form in visionary celebrations of personal liberation and American democracy.

Biography

Walt Whitman was born on May 31, 1819, in West Hills, near Huntington, Long Island, New York, the second child of Louisa and Walter Whitman. His father was a carpenter, who later speculated unsuccessfully in real estate. The family moved to Brooklyn in 1823, and Whitman attended school until the age of eleven, after which he worked as an office boy in a law firm. The owner of the firm enrolled him in a library, and Whitman was soon engrossed in reading, particularly the novels of Scottish writer Sir Walter Scott. The following year, he worked in the printing office of a newspaper, and by 1835 he had found work as a typesetter in New York. He was also contributing conventional poems to an established Manhattan newspaper.

The poor economic situation in New York compelled Whitman to seek work elsewhere, and in 1836 he began teaching at a school on Long Island. This was the first of several poorly paid, short-term teaching positions that Whitman held on and off for four years. His interest in journalism continued, and in 1838, with financial support from his family, he founded, published, and edited a newspaper, *The Long Islander*, which continued under his stewardship for a year. Whitman had also developed an interest in politics; in 1840, he campaigned for President Martin Van Buren, and the following year he addressed a Democratic political rally in New York. In 1841, he published eight short stories in the Democratic party paper, the *Democratic Review*.

Over the next decade, Whitman remained active in politics and continued his journalistic career, editing the *Brooklyn Daily Eagle* from 1846 to 1848. Fired from the *Eagle* for being a Free-Soiler (the Free-Soilers opposed slavery in newly annexed territories), he edited the *Brooklyn Freeman*, a Free-Soil journal, until September, 1849. From 1850 to 1854, Whitman operated a printing shop and worked as a part-

time journalist and building contractor. He followed an irregular routine, spending much time walking and reading. His family was puzzled by his apparently aimless life, not realizing that Whitman was developing the knowledge and aesthetic vision that would shortly burst forth in spectacular fashion.

In July, 1855, the first edition of *Leaves of Grass*, containing twelve untitled poems and a preface, was printed in Brooklyn at Whitman's own expense. Ralph Waldo Emerson, one of the most eminent men of letters in America, received it with enthusiasm, but others were shocked by Whitman's bold celebration of the pleasures of the senses and his sometimes coarse language. The following year, Emerson and Henry David Thoreau, the author of *Walden* (1854), visited Whitman at his home, and a second edition of *Leaves of Grass* appeared. Twenty new poems were added, as was Whitman's poetic manifesto, under the guise of a letter to Emerson.

From 1857 to mid-1859 Whitman was editor of the *Brooklyn Daily Times*. After leaving this post he continued to write; he also became a member of a bohemian circle that met at Pfaff's Restaurant in New York City. In 1860, Whitman traveled to Boston to oversee the printing of the third edition of *Leaves of Grass*, containing sixty-eight new poems, by the young firm of Theyer & Eldridge, Whitman's first commercial publishers. During Whitman's visit, Emerson advised him not to include the sexually oriented "Children of Adam" poems, but Whitman would not be persuaded. In 1861 the Civil War broke out, and in December, 1862, Whitman traveled to Falmouth, Virginia, to seek out his brother George, who had been slightly wounded at the battle of Fredericksburg. He returned to Washington, D.C., and worked part-time as a copyist in the paymaster's office. He also served for several years as a visitor and volunteer nurse to soldiers in hospitals. His tender, fatherly concern and unselfish dedication to his task made a profound impression on the soldiers.

In January, 1865, Whitman became a clerk in the Department of the Interior, and in March he attended the second inauguration of President Abraham Lincoln. A month after Lincoln's assassination in April, 1865, Whitman's poems of the war, *Drum Taps*, were printed at his own expense. A sequel to *Drum Taps*, containing the great elegy to Lincoln, "When Lilacs Last in the Dooryard Bloom'd," followed in September. In the meantime, however, Whitman had been fired from his job on the grounds that *Leaves of Grass* was indecent. After a friend intervened, however, Whitman was reemployed the next day in the attorney general's office.

In 1867, Whitman's reputation began to develop internationally, stimulated by the interest of William Michael Rossetti in England, who published an expurgated edition of the fourth edition of *Leaves of Grass* (which Whitman had printed in 1867). In 1871, *Democratic Vistas*, consisting of essays on democracy, social philosophy, and literature, was published.

In January, 1873, Whitman became partially paralyzed after a stroke, and in the summer he moved into the house of his brother George, in Camden, New Jersey. With financial support from distinguished writers in England, a centennial edition of *Leaves of Grass* and the volume *Two Rivulets*, appeared in 1876. Whitman could now count Alfred, Lord Tennyson, the Poet Laureate of England, as an admirer, but he was still under-appreciated in his own country. His publishing difficulties reappeared in 1882, when the district attorney threatened to prosecute the Boston firm of James R. Osgood for its publication of the seventh edition of *Leaves of Grass*. In the same year, Whitman published *Specimen Days and Collect*, much of which consists of diary notes of his experiences during the Civil War.

In 1884, Whitman bought a small house on Mickle Street in Camden, New Jersey, where he lived for the remainder of his life. After years of declining health, he died on March 26, 1892.

Analysis

When Walt Whitman first thrust *Leaves of Grass* on an unsuspecting and unresponsive American public, it was clear that he viewed himself as a national bard who would inject something "transcendent and new" into the poetic veins of his country. In the preface, which was strongly influenced by Emerson's essay *The Poet*, Whitman discussed the kind of American bard he envisioned and the kind of poetry that such a bard would write. Believing that "Americans of all nations . . . have probably the fullest poetical nature" and that "the United States themselves are essentially the greatest poem," Whitman's ideal was a poet whose "spirit responds to his country's spirit. . . . [H]e incarnates its geography and natural life and rivers and lakes." The truly American poet, like the American people, must embrace both the old and the new, but he must not be bound by conventional poetic forms, whether of rhyme and meter or subject matter. (Whitman had in mind both the didactic verse of American poet Henry Wadsworth Longfellow and the work of the "graveyard school.") Rather, the poet must seek to incarnate that which lies deeper than form and which reflects the laws and realities that are implanted in the human soul. Advocating a poetry of simplicity and genuineness, Whitman's advice to his reader was to "dismiss whatever insults your own soul."

In successive editions of *Leaves of Grass*, Whitman undoubtedly succeeded in his attempt to articulate an authentic American poetic voice, one which was not dependent on models derived from English literature. Further, by applying the central premises of Romanticism and Transcendentalism in a wider and more daring form than any American poet had done, he created a visionary and prophetic book which ranks as one of the great achievements of nineteenth century literature.

Perhaps the most startling aspect of Whitman's poetry for the modern reader is not its free-verse form, to which readers have become accustomed, but the extraordinary metaphysical thought that underlies so much of it. Whitman is the supreme poet of the expanded self. His poetic persona continually celebrates, as a fait accompli, the achievement of the goal to which Romanticism and Transcendentalism aspired: a state of being in which humankind's sense of separateness and isolation in the universe is overcome, a state in which subject and object are unified and the perceiving self feels deeply connected, emotionally and spiritually, with the rest of creation. The "I" in Whitman's poems, like the figure of Albion in English Romantic poet William Blake's epic poem *Jerusalem* (1804-1820), merges with all things and contains all things. Whitman expressed this succinctly in his poem "There Was a Child Went Forth":

> There was a child went forth every day,
> And the first object he look'd upon, that object he became,
> And that object became part of him for the day or a certain part of the day,
> Or for many years or stretching cycles of years.

Whitman's poetry thus abolishes "otherness." Although English novelist D. H. Lawrence complained that Whitman had accomplished this only by suppressing his own individuality, this was not Whitman's intention.

Thoreau was more appreciative, stating that Whitman's philosophic vision was "Wonderfully like the Orientals," and several modern scholars have analyzed Whitman's poetry in the light of the Vedic literature of India. According to this analysis, Whitman's understanding of the self can best be understood by reference to doctrine found in the *Upanishads* and *Bhagavad Gita*, that the "atman," the essence of the individual self, is identical to Brahman, the universal self. It is not known for certain how well Whitman was acquainted with Eastern thought, and it may be that his philosophy was based as much on personal experience as on the reading of books. "Song of Myself" is notable for its denigration of book learning in favor of the direct intercourse of the self with the natural world.

The doctrine of the self sheds light on another leading theme in *Leaves of Grass*, Whitman's celebration of American democracy. He admired democracy because it combined individualism with the needs of the whole society, and he believed unreservedly in the wisdom of the common man and woman. The "I" of Whitman's poetry sees in all people the same divine status that he experiences within himself. Whitman's poetic program was essentially a democratic one, as is clear from the following passage from the preface to the first edition of *Leaves of Grass*: "The messages of great poets to each man and woman are, Come to us on equal terms, Only then can you understand us, We are not better than you, What we enclose you enclose, What we enjoy you may enjoy."

Equally important for a full picture of Whitman's poetry is his attitude toward sex, which shocked his early readers. Whitman did not regard sex as an inappropriate subject for poetry, and he insisted that it was central to the design of *Leaves of Grass*. He rejected a dualistic view of human life that would relegate the body to an inferior place; on the contrary, he honored sexual desire as a pure expression of the life force that flows through all things. The act of procreation, Whitman believed, furthered the evolution of the human race, and he looked forward to the emergence in America of a race of sturdy, physically healthy human beings who would build a civilization free of the disease and degeneration that in this view afflicted the old civilizations of Europe.

As a complement to the love between men and women, Whitman also celebrated, in the "Calamus" poems, comradely love between men, which he called "adhesiveness." Many readers have taken these poems to be expressions of homosexual feelings, although in *Democratic Vistas* Whitman insisted that such love would help to spiritualize the nation and offset the vulgar aspects of American democracy. The Calamus poems therefore take their place in the grand vision that Whitman held of *Leaves of Grass* as a new bible, with every leaf contributing to a new heaven and a new earth.

SONG OF MYSELF

First published: 1855
Type of work: Poem

A celebration of the human self and all that it can see, hear, touch, taste, smell, intuit, and contemplate in the human and natural world.

"Song of Myself," the longest poem in *Leaves of Grass*, is a joyous celebration of the human self in its most expanded, spontaneous, self-sufficient, and all-embracing state as it observes and interacts with everything in creation and ranges freely over time and space. The bard of the poem, speaking in the oracular tones of the prophet, affirms the divinity and sacredness of the entire universe, including the human body, and he asserts that no part of the universe is separate from himself—he flows into all things and is all things.

The "I" of the poem is quite clearly, then, not the everyday self, the small, personal ego that is unique and different from all other selves. Rather, the persona who speaks out in such bold terms is the human self experiencing its own transcendental nature, silently witnessing all the turbulent activity of the world while itself remaining detached: "Apart from the pulling and hauling stands what I am, . . . Both in and out of the game and watching and wondering at it." This "I" is immortal and persists through numberless human generations and through all the changing cycles of creation and destruction in the universe. It cannot be measured or circumscribed; it is blissful, serenely content with itself, and needs nothing beyond or outside itself for its own fulfillment. In "Song of Myself," this large self continually floods into and interpenetrates the small, personal self, including the physical body, and becomes one with it. It is this union of the absolute self with the relative self that allows the persona of the poem to express such spontaneous delight in the simple experience of being alive in the flesh. "I loafe and invite my soul,/ I lean and loafe at my ease observing a spear of summer grass," announces the persona in the very first section of the poem. This is a state of being that does not have to perform any actions to experience fulfillment; it simply enjoys being what it is: "I exist as I am, that is enough,/ If no other in the world be aware I sit content,/ And if each and all be aware I sit content."

It is in this context that the persona's celebration of the pleasures of the body should be understood. Lines such as "Walt Whitman, a kosmos, of Manhattan the son,/ Turbulent, fleshy, sensual, eating, drinking and breeding," do not signify mere sensual indulgence. The human body is a microcosm of its divine source, in which there is always perfection, fullness, and bliss. There is no dualism of soul and body, because, as William Blake put it in *The Marriage of Heaven and Hell* (1790), a prophetic work which bears a strong resemblance to "Song of Myself," "that call'd Body is a portion of Soul discern'd by the five senses." Hence the Whitman persona can declare that "I am the poet of the Body and I am the poet of the Soul"; he will not downgrade one in order to promote the other. The senses themselves are "miracles," no part of the body is to be rejected or scorned, and sexual desire should not be something that cannot be spoken of: "I do not press my fingers across my mouth,/ I keep as delicate around the bowels as around the head and heart,/ Copulation is no more rank to me than death is."

This perception of the divine essence in the physical form extends to everything in the created world, however humble its station:

> I believe a leaf of grass is no less than the journey-work of the stars,
> And the pismire is equally perfect, and a grain of sand, and the egg of the wren,
> And the tree-toad is a chef-d'œuvre for the highest,
> And the running blackberry would adorn the parlors of heaven.

Heightened perception such as this also extends to other human beings, all of whom are viewed as equally divine by the persona. It is this conviction of the shared divinity of the self that enables the persona repeatedly to identify and empathize with other human beings, as in section 33: "I do not ask the wounded person how he feels, I myself become the wounded person."

In the worldview of the persona, man and nature interpenetrate each other in the most intimate way. The cycle of death, rebirth, and transformation is endless and unfathomable. The grass may, the persona muses, be made from the breasts of young men or from the hair of old people; he bequeaths himself to the earth and counsels the curious reader to look for him "under the boot-soles." This points to a paradox, one of many in the poem. The self is immortal, yet it will also go through many transformations ("No doubt I have died myself ten thousand times before"); similarly, the universe is complete and perfect at every moment, yet it is also perpetually flowing onward in dynamic transformation and evolution. Finally, the self merges with everything in the world, yet also stands aloof and apart from the world. Paradoxes such as this cannot be rationally explained, but they can, the persona would argue, be spontaneously lived through.

Scholars have discussed whether "Song of Myself" has its origins in Whitman's own mystical experiences or whether the persona is solely a literary invention designed to embody the kind of universal, all-seeing American bard that Whitman believed was appropriate for a vast and still expanding land. Such questions are impossible to answer with any certainty; however, it might be noted that in section 5, the Whitman persona records a significant moment when the transcendent soul seemed to descend and envelop him in an intense, almost sexual embrace, as a result of which "Swiftly arose and spread around me the peace and knowledge that pass all the argument of the earth." He then knows, as an immediate fact of awareness, that his own spirit is a brother of the spirit of God, that all humankind are his brothers and sisters, and that the whole universe is bound together by love.

Attempts have also been made to discern a structure to the poem, but these have not in general proved satisfactory. Rather than trying to find a linear progression of themes, it is perhaps more useful to think of each of the fifty-two sections as spokes of a wheel, each expressing the same theme or similar themes in diverse ways, from diverse angles. As the persona states, "All truths wait in all things."

THE SLEEPERS

First published: 1855
Type of work: Poem

In a dream vision, the persona moves among a varied group of people as they sleep, sympathetically identifying with their inner lives.

"The Sleepers" has been called a surrealistic poem. Although it certainly possesses the disconnected incidents and imagery characteristic of dreams, however, it also has a discernible, tripartite structure that suggests a myth of initiation, death, and rebirth. In the first part, which consists of the first two sections, the persona wanders freely at night and sympathetically identifies with a wide variety of sleeping people; in part 2 (sections 3-6) the persona experiences vicariously the destructive and painful aspects of human experience; part 3 (sections 7-9) celebrates the night world of restoration, rebirth, and cosmic unity.

In section 1, as the persona overlooks the sleepers—drunkards, idiots, the insane, a married couple, a mother and child, a prisoner, and others—the night in which they sleep is presented almost as a mystic presence which "pervades them and infolds them," rather like the Oversoul in the thought of Emerson. The speaker then undergoes some kind of initiation: He pierces the darkness, new beings appear, and he dances and laughs in a bacchanalian whirl, accompanied by divine spirits. The result is that he is able to become the people he is observing and dream their dreams with them. This mystic expansion of the self into all things is similar to the central idea in "Song of Myself."

Part 2 consists of three unconnected visions. First, a beautiful, nude, male swimmer is caught in a tide which draws him to death; there is also a shipwreck, and the persona desperately tries to effect a rescue, but no one survives. Second, the persona goes back in time to the defeat of General George Washington at Brooklyn Heights in August, 1776. He pictures Washington on two occasions: weeping in defeat with a group of officers around him, and embracing his officers in a tavern when peace was declared. The third vision is a memory from the persona's early life, when a beautiful Indian woman came to the family homestead one breakfast time. She was received with warmth by the persona's mother, even though she had no work to give her. The squaw left in the afternoon, never to return, much to the mother's regret. Perhaps this incident was meant to symbolize the loss of an old way of life, in which pure and generous social intercourse was the norm.

In the first version of the poem, it is clear that at this point in his experience, the persona is in a state of psychic disintegration. Three verse paragraphs followed, including the line "Now Lucifer was not dead . . . or if he was I am his sorrowful heir." All three paragraphs were omitted in the version of the poem published in *Leaves of Grass* in 1871.

Part 3 marks a change of atmosphere, beginning with images of sunlight, air, summer, and the burgeoning fullness of nature. Travelers of all nations are returning to their homelands, including the lost swimmer, the Indian squaw, and others with whom the persona has earlier identified. Sleep and the night have restored them and made them all equal, peaceful, and beautiful. The speaker realizes that this is the true state of things.

Section 9 presents a fine vision of the night as an experience of transcendental unity. As the sleepers lie at rest, people of all nations "flow hand in hand over the whole earth from east to west as they lie unclothed": The chain of unity includes the learned and the unlearned, father and son, mother and daughter, scholar and teacher. All those who were diseased have been cured. The poem concludes with the serene thoughts of the persona, who is happy to take part in the the day world of conscious activity but feels no fear at the thought of returning to the secret regenerative powers of the night, now suggestive of a nourishing earth mother.

CROSSING BROOKLYN FERRY

First published: 1856 (as "Sun-Down Poem")
Type of work: Poem

Observing the sights and sounds of a mass of people crossing from Brooklyn by ferry, the poet contemplates the link between past and future.

"Crossing Brooklyn Ferry" is a subtle, oblique attempt to transcend time and persuade the reader of the simultaneity of past, present, and future. Whitman shed light on the poem in the preface to the 1855 edition of *Leaves of Grass*: "Past and present are not disjoin'd but joined. The greatest poet forms the consistence of what is to be from what has been and is. . . . He . . . places himself where the future becomes present." The poem is also rich in imagery which suggests the coexistence of opposite values, such as fixity and motion, rest and activity, time and eternity.

"Crossing Brooklyn Ferry" is divided into nine sections. In the first section, the poet observes the crowds of people crossing the East River to Manhattan by ferry and thinks of those who will be making the crossing in years to come. He develops this thought in section 2, as he contemplates the ties that bind him to the people of the future. In a hundred years time, others will be seeing the same landmarks, the same sunset, the same ebb and flow of the tides. The speaker also hints that the scene he contemplates forms part of a grand, spiritual "scheme" of life, in which everything possesses its own individuality yet is part of the whole; that sense of wholeness has power to impart glory to all the poet's daily activities and sense perceptions. The poet makes this hint explicit at the end of the poem.

Having evoked the passage of time and underscored it with images of flux—the tide, the sunset—the poet in section 3 does everything he can to negate it: "It avails not, time nor place—distance avails not,/ I am with you, you men and women of a generation, or ever so many generations hence." Whatever future generations might see, the poet has also seen. He recalls the many times he has crossed the river by ferry, and he catalogs the sights that met his gaze: steamboats and schooners, sloops and barges, circling seagulls, sailors at work, the flags of many nations, the fires from the foundry chimneys on the shore. Most notable in this section are the images that combine motion and stasis and that reinforce the theme of time which is no-time. The poet pictures the people who stand still on the rail of the ferry "yet hurry with the swift current," and he observes the seagulls "with motionless wings, oscillating their bodies." Underlying the whole section (indeed, the whole poem) is the great central symbol of the river, forever flowing, yet forever appearing the same.

After the recapitulation which makes up the fourth section, sections 5 and 6 take the theme to a more intimate level. The poet again asserts that time and place do not separate. Now, however, instead of evoking sense perceptions only, he asserts that the thoughts and feelings experienced by future generations have been his too. His soul knew periods of darkness and aridity; he, too, experienced self-doubt, and he committed most of the sins of which humanity is capable. In this respect he was one with everyone else, whether present or future.

Section 7 is a direct address to the reader of the future. The poet's tone becomes increasingly intimate and personal as he suggests that he is drawing ever closer to the reader. Three rhetorical questions follow, the last of which suggests a linking of past and future that is at once mysterious and mystical: "Who knows, for all the distance, but I am as good as looking at you now, for all you cannot see me?" This implies that the fullest human self is part of a larger entity which is not subject to the limitations of time or space and which endures through all things. Because of this, the awakened consciousness of the poet (or of any man or woman) may perceive past, present, and future fused into a single enlightened moment.

The rhetorical questions continue in section 8, at the end of which the poet hints cryptically and conspiratorially that his purpose has been accomplished obliquely: The reader has accepted what the poet promised, without him even mentioning what it was. Poet and reader have accomplished what could not be accomplished by study or preaching.

The final section begins with an apostrophe to the river—which also symbolizes the world of time and change—urging it to continue its eternal ebb and flow. More apostrophes follow, in excited and exclamatory vein, to the clouds at sunset, to Manhattan and Brooklyn, to life itself. This section is both a recapitulation and a renewed celebration of what the poet has earlier described—the everyday sights and sounds encountered while crossing the river—but now with the separation between past and future irrevocably broken (or so the poet would believe) in the reader's mind.

In the final lines of the poem, the poet reveals the deepest reasons for his wish that the myriad phenomena of the natural and human world should continue to flourish, with even greater intensity, in the vast sea of time. They are all "dumb, beautiful ministers": Through the material forms of temporal life, the poet and the reader (now no longer referred to as "I" and "you" but as "we"), having engaged in the process of revelation which is the poem, are able to perceive the eternal, spiritual dimensions of existence. This conclusion has already been suggested by a marvelous image in section 3, when the poet, looking into the sunlit water, sees "fine centrifugal spokes of light round the shape of my head." In section 9 the image is repeated and universalized: anyone who gazes deeply into the flux will also see his own head aureoled in splendid, radiating light.

OUT OF THE CRADLE ENDLESSLY ROCKING

First published: 1859 (as "A Child's Reminiscence")
Type of work: Poem

The poet describes an incident from his childhood in which he first realized that his destiny was to become a poet.

"Out of the Cradle Endlessly Rocking" is a poem of reminiscence, in which the poet, at a crisis in his adult life, looks back to an incident in his childhood when he first became aware of his vocation as a poet. The structure of the poem owes a great deal to music, particularly grand opera, which Whitman loved. He once said that without opera he could not have written *Leaves of Grass*, and an anonymous review in the *Saturday Press* in 1860 (which was actually written by Whitman himself) commented, "Walt Whitman's method in the construction of his songs is strictly the method of Italian opera."

The musical quality of the poem can be seen in the opening section of twenty-two lines, with its incantatory rhythms and wave-like quality, the latter suggesting the restless motion of a turbulent sea. This is most notable in the buildup of pressure in lines 8 to 15, each of which begins with the word "from"; the effect is like the inexorable rising of a powerful wave before it crests, breaks, and laps quietly onto the shore in the final half-line ("A reminiscence sing"). The meaning of the opening section is simple: Under moonlight on an Autumn evening, the poet, caught in a moment of personal despair, has returned to a place on the seashore that he had known as a young boy. The scene reminds him of a moment of great significance in his life.

The next nine lines are the equivalent of the recitative (or narrative portion) in opera. The poet recalls that as a boy he spent many days one spring on Paumanok (the Indian name for Long Island), closely observing the nest of two mockingbirds. Recitative now alternates with the arias of the mockingbirds, who at first sing of their togetherness. One day the she-bird disappears, and all summer long the boy listens to the solitary song of the remaining bird.

The boy interprets the song as the bird calling for his absent mate, and now as a man he claims that he, a poet and a "chanter of pains and joys," understands the meaning of the lonely song better than other men. Lines 71 to 129 are a long, unashamedly sentimental lament by the mockingbird; the natural world seems to be rejoicing in love, but he cannot do so. He convinces himself that every vague shape in the distance must be his mate, and then he persuades himself that he has heard her responding to his song. Finally, however, he realizes that his quest is useless, and he ends sorrowfully.

The boy listens to the aria in ecstasy and in tears because he feels that its meaning has penetrated to his soul. From that moment, he is awakened; he knows his purpose and his destiny, and a thousand songs—poems—begin to stir within him. He, too, will sing of unsatisfied love and explore "the sweet hell within,/ The unknown want."

Then a new revelation comes as the boy learns to listen to the sea. All night long the sea whispers to him only one word, "the low and delicious word death," and this has a profound effect on him (which is emphasized in the poem by the repetition of the word nine times). The knowledge of the universality and inevitability of death—that all of nature is a field of death—comes upon him not with anguish, but like a gentle, loving caress. The final immensely evocative image is of the sea "like some old crone rocking the cradle." The image is striking because it suggests both age and infancy; it makes clear that the first stirrings of life are also a movement toward death. The sea, although it perpetually whispers "death," is a mother nevertheless (elsewhere in the poem, the sea is referred to as a "fierce" and "savage" "old mother"), and the rocking of a cradle is a soothing and comforting motion.

Whitman has been called the poet of death—although such a description hardly does justice to the massive life-affirming vision of his greatest poems—and sometimes this poem has been interpreted psychoanalytically as a regressive wish to return to the unconscious, to the undifferentiated security of the womb. Yet it might also be argued that such a conclusion runs contrary to the poem's main theme, which in the terms used by psychologist Carl Jung, records an important moment in the process of the individuation of the self: The poet discovers his personal destiny.

WHEN LILACS LAST IN THE DOORYARD BLOOM'D

First published: 1865
Type of work: Poem

An elegy in memory of President Abraham Lincoln.

Whitman wrote "When Lilacs Last in the Dooryard Bloom'd" in the months following the assassination of President Lincoln on April 14, 1865. Whitman felt the loss of Lincoln personally. He had observed the president on a number of occasions in Washington, D.C. Once he saw him chatting with a friend at the White House and commented, "His face & manner . . . are inexpressibly sweet. . . . I love the President personally." The elegy contains many of the elements that make up the traditional pastoral elegy, including the expression of grief and bewilderment by the poet, the sympathetic mourning of nature for the dead man (expressed by means of the pathetic fallacy), the rebirth of nature, a funeral procession, the placing of flowers on the bier, and finally, reconciliation and consolation. Whitman's elegy is also about how the poet transmutes his sorrow, which at the outset is so great that it prevents him from writing, to the point where he can once more create poetry.

The elegy centers around four symbols: the lilac, the evening star, spring, and the hermit thrush, a bird that sings in seclusion. These symbols recur in varied forms throughout the poem, like musical motifs. The poet first declares his grief and invokes Venus, the evening star, which has now fallen below the horizon and left him in darkness and sorrow. He then develops the lilac symbol: In the dooryard of an old farmhouse, a lilac bush blossoms. Each heart-shaped leaf (a symbol of love) he regards as a miracle, and he breaks off a sprig. The fourth symbol, the thrush that sings a solitary song, is introduced in section 4.

Section 5 describes the coffin of Lincoln journeying night and day across the country (as it did in reality on its journey from Washington to Springfield, Illinois), as spring bursts through everywhere. Church bells toll, and as the coffin moves slowly past the poet, he throws his sprig of lilac onto it, although he makes it clear that this act is not for Lincoln alone (who is never mentioned by name in the poem) but for all who have died.

After an apostrophe to the evening star, which, in sympathy with the poet's own state of mind, is sinking in woe, the poet returns to the song of the hermit thrush. Although he hears and understands the call, he cannot yet sing with the thrush, because the star (now clearly associated, as "my departing comrade," with Lincoln himself) still holds him. Eventually, as he looks out one spring evening on a serene landscape, an understanding of the true nature of death comes upon him like a mystical revelation. He personifies the knowledge of death, and his own thoughts about death, as two figures walking alongside him. Now he is able to interpret the song of the bird as a "carol of death." A long aria, reminiscent of the song of the bird in "Out of the Cradle Endlessly Rocking," follows. Death is described as soft, welcome, delicate, blissful, and as a "strong deliveress."

In section 15, the poet sees a surrealistic vision of a battlefield, on which lie myriad corpses and whitened skeletons. Yet the poet sees that the dead are at rest and do not suffer; it is only those left behind—families and comrades—who suffer.

He leaves the vision behind and is also able to leave behind the birdsong, the lilac, and the evening star. The meaning of all these symbols now remains a permanent part of his awareness, however, so the elegy can move to its stately and moving close: "For the sweetest, wisest soul of all my days and lands—and this for his dear sake,/ Lilac and star and bird twined with the chant of my soul,/ There in the fragrant pines and the cedars dusk and dim."

PASSAGE TO INDIA

First published: 1871
Type of work: Poem

A celebration of the progress of human civilization and the spiritual evolution of the human race.

"Passage to India" is a salute to the idea of the evolutionary progress of the human race; it celebrates the scientific achievements of the age, looks forward to the imminent dawning of an era in which all divisions and separations between man and man, and man and nature, will be eliminated, and it heralds the spiritual voyage of every human soul into the depths of the inner universe. Whitman himself described the meaning of his poem, saying "that the divine efforts of heroes, and their ideas . . . will finally prevail, and be accomplished, however long deferred."

The poem begins by celebrating three achievements of contemporary technology: the opening of the Suez Canal in 1869, the laying of the trans-Atlantic cable, and the growth of the American transcontinental railroad. These achievements outshine the seven wonders of the ancient world; however, the poet still hears the call of the ancient past, embodied in the myths and fables of Asia, with their daring reach toward an unfathomable spiritual truth. The refrain "Passage to India" therefore suggests the theme of inner as well as outer exploration.

Section 3 elaborates on two of the new wonders, picturing the opening ceremony of the Suez Canal and the grand landscapes through which the American railroad passes. The poet has been careful to establish that the great works of the present should be celebrated not merely for the human skill and knowledge to which they testify, but also because they mark an important stage in the fulfillment of the divine plan: The human race coming together in unity. The section ends by flashing back to the past and invoking the name of Christopher Columbus. Whitman liked to present himself as a Columbus figure, exploring new literary and psychic worlds, yet rejected by his countrymen. Perhaps he had in mind Thoreau's injunction in the conclusion to *Walden*: "[B]e Columbus to whole new continents and worlds within you, opening new channels, not of trade, but of thought."

Section 5 is central to the poem because it conveys Whitman's vision of the role of the poet in human evolution. Whitman first stretches the reader's awareness by evoking the vast earth "swimming in space/ Cover'd all over with visible power and beauty." He then describes the troubled history of the human race; the myriad restless, dissatisfied, questing lives. He alludes to the Transcendentalist idea that man and nature have become separated. No connection is perceived between the human, feeling subject and the apparently unresponsive external world: "What is this earth to our affections? (unloving earth, without a throb to answer ours . . .)." Yet the divine plan remains and shall be achieved, with the help of the poet, who is the "true son of God."

Coming after the inventors and the scientists, the poet will justify them (a deliberate echo of seventeenth century English poet John Milton, who wrote that he sought to justify the ways of God to man) by fully humanizing a mechanized world: He will soothe hearts, open all secrets, and join nature and man in unity. Whitman thus reiterates the poetic manifesto contained in the preface to the 1855 edition of *Leaves of Grass*: "folks expect of the poet more than the beauty and dignity which always attach to dumb real objects . . . they expect him to indicate the path between reality and their souls."

After section 6 has presented a panorama of some of the great events in human history and again invoked the hero Columbus—the poet argues that all neglected heroes will have their reward in God's good time—section 7 develops the theme implicit earlier in the poem, of the poet as spiritual explorer. This theme carries the poem through to its conclusion. The poet must journey, in partnership with his soul, to "primal thought," beyond all limitations of the physical body, to the infinite regions of the cosmic mind. The restless desire to expand, to voyage on the ocean of Being, becomes more and more urgent in the final section of the poem. The poet and his soul have lingered long enough. Now is the time to be bold and reckless, for the cosmic seas are safe: "[A]re they not all the seas of God?"

SONG OF THE REDWOOD TREE

First published: 1876
Type of work: Poem

A dying redwood tree sings of the might and virtue of the coming human civilization.

In "Song of the Redwood Tree," the poet injects himself into the consciousness of a century-old Californian redwood tree as it is being felled. In a musical structure that Whitman often used, the song of the tree is presented as a grand operatic aria, and it alternates with passages of recitative in which the poet repeats and expands upon the message that the great tree imparts. The poem testifies to Whitman's belief in the evolutionary growth of the universe towards perfection, culminating in the new land and peoples of America. These themes are particularly evident in Whitman's poems written after 1865, such as "Song of the Universal," "Pioneers, O Pioneers," and "Passage to India."

In Whitman's universe, consciousness pervades everything, even vegetable and mineral forms, and the sensitive soul of the poet can tap into the consciousness of the nonhuman world and interpret its meanings. Thus the death chant of the tree, which is accompanied by wood spirits who have dwelt in the woods of Mendocino for a thousand years, is unheard by the workmen who are felling the tree, but the poet hears it.

The tree chants not only of the past but also of the future. It sings of the joy it has known throughout all the changing seasons in its long life—it has delighted in sun, wind, rain, and snow. It confirms that it, too, has consciousness and a sense of selfhood, as do rocks and mountains. The tree declares that it and its companions are content to abdicate their position to make room for the arrival of a "superber race," for which they have been long preparing.

The tree then gives expression to Whitman's belief in the special destiny of the American people. The new race has emerged peacefully to inherit a new empire. It has not come from the old cultures of Asia and Europe—the latter, stained with the blood of innumerable wars, is particularly unfit to give birth to a new kind of men and women. The building of America is the fruition of a long process of hidden growth. Deep within the continent has lain a secret, national will, working below the turbulence of surface events in order to manifest itself. Here in California, sings the tree, may the new man grow and flourish in freedom, "proportionate to Nature," acting on his own inner promptings, not bowing to the moral formulas and creeds of others. A new woman will emerge also, and she will be the nourishing source of life and love.

Listening in the woods, the poet catches the message of the "ecstatic, ancient and rustling" voices of the tree and its accompanying dryads, and in sections 2 and 3 he takes up and amplifies their themes. He celebrates America, with its fields and mountains bathed in healthier air, from Puget Sound to Colorado. He praises the new race that arrived after "slow and steady ages" in which the earth was preparing itself for them. He lauds American civilization but states that the achievements of American technology are useful only because they help to push the race on to a state of perfection in which the ideal (the spiritual level of life) is lived in the midst of the real (the material world).

Summary

"The proof of a poet is that his country absorbs him as affectionately as he has absorbed it," wrote Whitman in his letter to Emerson that prefaced the second edition of *Leaves of Grass*. According to this criterion, Walt Whitman has indeed proved himself many times over, since it is hard to imagine twentieth century American poetry without him. His influence has extended to poets such as William Carlos Williams, Hart Crane, Robinson Jeffers, Carl Sandburg, and Allen Ginsberg. Their admiration for Whitman is a tribute to the universal appeal of his long song of himself: his transcendental metaphysics, his emotional honesty and complexity, his lyric skill, and his faith in the future of his country.

Bibliography

Allen, Gay Wilson. *A Reader's Guide to Walt Whitman*. New York: Farrar, Straus & Giroux, 1970.

Aspiz, Harold. *Walt Whitman and the Body Beautiful*. Urbana: University of Illinois Press, 1980.

Bloom, Harold, ed. *Walt Whitman*. New York: Chelsea House, 1985.

Chari, V. K. *Whitman in the Light of Vedantic Mysticism*. Lincoln: University of Nebraska Press, 1964.

Kaplan, Justin. *Walt Whitman: A Life*. New York: Bantam Books, 1982.

Miller, Edwin H. *Walt Whitman's Poetry: A Psychological Journey*. New York: New York University Press, 1968.

Miller, James E., Jr. *Walt Whitman*. New York: Twayne, 1962.

Pearce, Roy Harvey, ed. *Whitman: A Collection of Critical Essays*. Englewood Cliffs, N.J.: Prentice-Hall, 1962.

Bryan Aubrey

JOHN EDGAR WIDEMAN

Born: Washington, D.C.
June 14, 1941

Principal Literary Achievement

A major literary voice since the mid-1960's, Wideman's writings combine modernist and postmodernist metafictional techniques with African-American themes concerning social injustice and the violence it generates.

Biography

The oldest of five children born to Bette French and Edgar Wideman, John Edgar Wideman grew up in Homewood, a black community in Pittsburgh, Pennsylvania, whose history roughly parallels Wideman's familial ancestry in the North. As a youth, Wideman sought to distance himself from the perceived constrictions of his African-American identity, experiencing the doubleness and alienation he later recognized as a condition of growing up black in the United States; Wideman has made that odyssey away from and back to his roots a central theme of his fiction. After attending the racially integrated Peabody High School, where he excelled in sports and academics and was graduated as valedictorian, he was awarded the Benjamin Franklin scholarship to the University of Pennsylvania. He was recruited for its basketball team in 1959, and his youthful goal was to play in the National Basketball Association.

Despite the pronounced strain of being one of only a handful of black students at the University of Pennsylvania, he earned a place in the Philadelphia Big Five Basketball Hall of Fame, was elected to Phi Beta Kappa, and won a Rhodes Scholarship as evidence of his twin accomplishments as an athlete and scholar. Upon receiving a B.A. in 1963, he went on to earn a B. Phil. in 1966 from the University of Oxford, where he was a Thouron Fellow. Wideman has candidly acknowledged that these achievements came at the price of his own psychological health, however, and his later career has been dedicated to professional and artistic endeavors that allow him to recuperate the identity as an African American that he had sacrificed to attain the mainstream cultural definitions of the "intellectual." In England, Wideman had concentrated his studies on the eighteenth century origins of the novel, a field far removed from the cultural environment from which he had sprung—and which ill-prepared him for requests from African-American students at the University of Pennsylvania that he teach courses in black literature. It was through his efforts to ac-

commodate them that he began to investigate the rich tradition of black American literary expression that has since energized and directed his own creative and scholarly activities. Besides adapting black American and African mythologies, folk arts, and storytelling methods to create his distinctive narrative technique, he frequently reviews black literature and criticism for *The New York Book Review* and has written academic essays on such literary forebears as Charles Chesnutt and W. E. B. DuBois.

Having distinguished himself as a writer even as an undergraduate English major, Wideman was accorded a Kent Fellowship to attend the University of Iowa Writers Workshop in 1966 and, at age twenty-six, published his first novel, *A Glance Away*, in 1967. Hired at the University of Pennsylvania in 1966, he headed its Afro-American Studies program from 1971 to 1973 and rose to the rank of professor of English; he also served as assistant basketball coach from 1968 to 1972. Other academic appointments have included posts at Howard University; the University of Wyoming, Laramie; and the University of Massachusetts, Amherst. Named as Young Humanist Fellow by the National Endowment for the Humanities in 1975, in 1976 he conducted a State Department lecture tour of Europe and the Near East as well as holding a Phi Beta Kappa lectureship. Married in 1965 to Judith Ann Goldman, Wideman has three children: Daniel, Jacob, and Jamila.

From the start of his publishing career, critics have remarked on the striking juxtaposition of Wideman's sophisticated literary style, characterized by modernist and postmodernist complexities of voice, metaphor, and structure, with his graphically realistic subject matter, often drawn from the streets of the inner city. *A Glance Away* deals with the world of a drug addict; *Hurry Home* (1970) depicts the deeply divided sensibility of an upwardly mobile young man whose efforts to escape the ghetto through education give way to the pursuit of lost connections with his African-American heritage; *The Lynchers* (1973) examines American racial terrorism; *The Homewood Trilogy* (1985) explores the origins and decay of a black urban community; *Reuben* (1987) interweaves the stories of a self-proclaimed attorney and two of his clients—a prostitute trying to secure custody of her child and a directionless former athlete implicated in a bribery scandal. While his early work heavily reflects the influence of Anglo-American modernism, *The Homewood Trilogy* (which comprises *Damballah*, 1981; *Hiding Place*, 1981; and *Sent for You Yesterday*, 1983) demonstrates his increasing preoccupation with African-American literary forms, an aesthetic consequence of his personal rediscovery at his grandmother's funeral in 1973 of his childhood community's richly evocative history. Accordingly, he chose to issue the volumes as Avon paperbacks rather than in hardcover to improve their accessibility to the black reading public he most sought to reach. The third volume in that series earned the prestigious PEN/Faulkner Award for Fiction.

Wideman's creative indebtedness to his familial past was rendered baldly evident in a memoir published in 1984 as *Brothers and Keepers* and nominated for the National Book Critics Circle Award. In it, Wideman examines his youngest brother Robby's descent into crime and his life sentence for murder in Pennsylvania's Western Penitentiary. In the process, Wideman exposed his continued racial ambivalence as a self-made success compromised by the haunting mirror image that Rob presents. The family nightmare embodied in Robby's drug addiction, criminality, and incarceration was brutally reiterated more recently with the 1988 conviction of Wideman's second son, Jacob, then eighteen, for the 1986 murder in Arizona of a teenage traveling companion.

Analysis

Over the course of his writing career, John Edgar Wideman has composed fiction that synthesizes twentieth century aesthetic concerns with the thematic emphases of the African-American literary tradition. His early works, stylistically indebted to T. S. Eliot, James Joyce, and William Faulkner, demonstrate modernist preoccupations with myth and ritual, fractured narrative, surreality, and polyphonic voicings. Wideman also possesses a postmodernist affinity for fantasy and the use of deconstructive self-reflexiveness to probe the convoluted reality of the psyche as it processes the incoherencies of daily life, particularly those generated by the jarring and irreconcilable paradoxes of racism. It is his preoccupation with the consequences of racism that prevents Wideman's wholesale adoption of postmodernist sleight of hand, however; while he continually documents the mind's entrapment within its own subjective fabrications, his fiction does not withdraw into apolitical minimalism or self-enclosed fabulation isolated from the social matrix in which his characters exist. Moving beyond the realist or naturalistic mode of previous generations of black writers, Wideman's postmodernism identifies concepts of racial difference themselves as divisive and deluding cultural fictions, and it dramatizes the equally powerful role of the imagination in dismantling such fallacies.

Wideman's literary techniques also express his belief in the accessibility of a collective African-American racial memory kept alive through the networks of family, community, and culture. Thus his fictional plotting often juxtaposes quite disparate time frames to emphasize the organic and multifaceted relationship between past and present—particularly as it is embodied in the unfolding of generations within the same family, as is the case with *The Homewood Trilogy* and *Brothers and Keepers*. By collapsing traditional distinctions between narration and dialogue, he creates a fluid linguistic matrix that does not try to approximate the "reality" of the psyche so much as suggest an extended imaginative meditation on the power of language to fuse different modes of experience. Similarly, Wideman elides the voices and thoughts of different characters with abandon, making the resultant narrative a continually shifting kaleidoscope of perspectives devoted to creating the dense interiority of his subjects. Among those voices is often that of the writer himself, who steps from behind the mask of narrator to discuss quite self-consciously the challenges posed by a subject, character, or plot.

Wideman is at home in both the short story and the novel: The former allows him to pursue discrete character analyses that, when connected, comment upon one another thematically, and the latter, while following the same polyphonic construction, enables him to integrate narrative strands into tighter unified patterns. In both forms he explores the thesis that from fragmentation the imagination can generate potentially healing linkages and echoes—an activity always complicated, however, by the suspicion that human vision is so clouded as to make real communion among individuals inescapably flawed if not impossible.

THE HOMEWOOD TRILOGY

First published: *Damballah*, 1981; *Hiding Place*, 1981; *Sent for You Yesterday*, 1983; as a trilogy, 1985
Type of work: Short story collection and two novels

Three separate works united under this title record the human history of a black neighborhood in Pittsburgh through several generations of the Hollinger/French family.

The Homewood Trilogy collects in a single volume works previously published individually but conceptualized and written as interdependent fictional treatments of the African-American community in which Wideman was reared. The texts evolve from the family lore surrounding John French, Wideman's grandfather, and his descendants, including two brothers whose current circumstances mirror those of the author and his youngest brother Rob. The trilogy resulted from Wideman's discovery that in the stories of Homewood's inhabitants (which he had been hearing all of his life) lay an untapped reservoir of creative inspiration that he had undervalued as the legitimate raw material of literary art. By recovering those stories, he sought to demonstrate "that Black life for all its material impoverishment continues to produce the full range of human personalities, emotions, aspirations." Finally, Wideman's aim is to use racial experience to challenge delimiting racial categories:

Homewood is an idea, a reflection of how and what its inhabitants do and think. . . . [It] mirror[s] the characters' inner lives, their sense of themselves as spiritual beings in a realm that rises above racial stereotypes and socioeconomic statistics.

Recalling Faulkner's Yoknapatawpha County, the trilogy opens with an elaborate family tree delineating the kinship ties that provide the work's imaginative spine. The texts born of this network become metafictions, not only absorbing into themselves the many oral forms whereby the past has been kept alive but also drawing attention to the writer's self-conscious act of creative synthesis and the obstacles that keep him from achieving an aesthetically "finished" design.

Damballah includes twelve short stories that demonstrate Wideman's approach to the human diversity of Homewood's landscape. The book's title derives from African myth: Damballah is the "good serpent of the sky," a benevolent paternal deity whose detachment and wisdom integrate the cosmos into a transcendent family. The title story of the volume involves an African-born slave named Orion whose spiritual strength rests upon native religious beliefs which he communicates to a slave boy through the repetition of Damballah's name; not long after, Orion, falsely accused of sexual misconduct, is brutally executed, and the child returns his severed head to the natural world he had so revered. In the final story of the work, "The Beginning of Homewood," Wideman expands the historical context of the present by tracing his maternal ancestry to an escaped slave, Sybela Owens, and her master/lover, whose flight North brought them to Bruston Hill, the symbolic umbilicus of Homewood. Juxtaposed time frames abound in the volume, and Sybela's tale appears within a contemporary meditation written to "Tommy," the narrator's brother, now in prison for murder; his situation raises the same issues of freedom, escape, and spiritual survival addressed in the slave's story and allows Wideman to construct metafictional layerings as he muses on the act of writing and its relationship to lived events.

Between those two framing tales unfold stories of black men and women struggling to maintain or recover an authentic existence in the face of unrelenting danger or disappointment. Among them are John French, the hard-drinking, tough-minded patriarch whose emotional presence dominates the twentieth century history of the French/Lawson clan; Freeda Hollinger French, his wife, whose violent act to save John's life resonates through the text and expresses the complex emotional dynamic that Wideman maps between black men and women; Lizabeth French Lawson, the narrator's mother and another heroic embodiment of the integrity and strength of black women under crushing familial pressures; Reba Love Jackson, a Gospel singer whose faith and artistry combine to create the song of a people; and Tommy Lawson, French's grandson, whose reliance on drugs and crime dramatizes Homewood's collapse beneath the mounting hopelessness of its citizens and the cynical indifference of the larger society. Based on Wideman's brother Rob, to whom *Damballah* is dedicated, Tommy is an early fictional examination of the family crisis that recurs in Wideman's writings.

Hiding Place, a novel and the second volume in the trilogy, is one such reiteration of Rob's story. Wideman expands his characterization of the aged "Mother" Bess Simkins, introduced in "The Beginning of Homewood," and elaborates on the links between the old woman and young man that had been sketched in that story. The granddaughter of Sybela Owens, Bess still lives on Bruston Hill as the novel opens, but while she signifies Tommy's family heritage, she herself has retreated from any real intercourse with the community since the loss of her only child and later the death of her husband. She is joined in her decrepit shack by a more literal fugitive in the person of Tommy, who is fleeing capture following an abortive robbery that has led to murder. Tommy is also hiding metaphorically, evading an honest assessment of his own responsibility for his circumstances. In Bess he encounters a hostile commentator on the situation he faces, and his consistent response is to withdraw into sleep. Yet sleep can also regenerate, and in their series of confrontational exchanges, both come to recognize their shared need to re-enter life, with all its attendant grief and outrage.

Among the alternating voices that structure the text is that of a third character, a youth named Clement, whose simple-mindedness offers another version of the self-involved, solipsistic dreaminess into which each of the protagonists retreat. Yet he is also Bess's errand boy and not only links her to the outside world she has shunned but also expands the human geography of the novel. Clement intuits realities that are obscured or falsified by the defensive façades constructed by other individuals in the novel, and he thereby offers an implicit critique of the ruses that thwart authenticity in the ghetto.

Wideman's sword cuts two ways in his examination of Homewood: Intensely aware of the role played by racism in the deterioration of his old neighborhood and the loss of spiritual purpose among its inhabitants, he is just as sharply insistent on the need for black men and women to attend to their own souls by rejecting the duplicities by which they distort the truth and cheapen their lives. Bess and Tommy both undergo this kind of soul-searching in *Hiding Place*, a process that leads them to turn away from the "deadness" of their lives. Tommy chooses to return to town and confront whatever awaits him, and Bess, seeing the police corner him on the water tower outside her home, decides to leave Bruston Hill to testify on his behalf. The closing scene is apocalyptic; searchlights cut the darkness and bullets fly as the police pursue Tommy, and Bess's shack bursts into flames while she plans her departure. Violence is thus the companion and catalyst to their respective existential reckonings.

Sent For You Yesterday, a novel accorded the PEN/Faulkner Award, opens with an epigraph announcing that "[p]ast lives live in us, through us." As in the preceding texts in the trilogy, Wideman intertwines narratives belonging to different generations and spun out of individual memories. This time he solidifies the imaginative sensibility that unites them into a character nicknamed "Doot." Doot is actively engaged not only in collecting the stories of his familial past but also in clarifying his own temporal and emotional relationship to them as a means of reversing his estrangement from Homewood. If Tommy's crisis becomes one axis of the trilogy, then his older brother's penetrating self-scrutiny as a differently motivated but equally remorseful prodigal son seeking return offers another axis—each revolves around the imaginative model of black manhood represented by John French.

At the heart of the novel is Albert Wilkes, a legendary Homewood musician and friend of French whose affair with a white woman leads to the killing of her policeman husband (Wilkes's own guilt is still highly contested in the community); seven years later, he returns to Homewood and is gunned down by white lawmen in the house where he was reared, sitting at the piano he had always instinctively known how to play. Among those who embody Wilkes's legacy is Brother Tate, an orphan adopted by the same couple who reared Wilkes and who, as a young man, spontaneously demonstrates the same musical genius. Its title taken from a blues song, this novel is deeply involved with the music of African Americans, which has so effectively documented and interpreted their experience. Because Brother is an albino, his incongruous "white blackness" provides a telling metaphor for a society fixated on racial categorizations; when his young son Junebug is victimized and finally killed by his half-siblings because he, like his father, is so markedly different, Brother confronts the fratricidal character of all racism and its violent dislocation of the human family.

Brother's story intersects with that of his adoptive sister Lucy and his closest friend Carl French, Doot's uncle. It is through Lucy and Carl, lifelong lovers whose failure to marry seems the natural consequence of their intimate knowledge of one another, that Doot untangles the narrative skeins that make up the novel's fabric, on which he embroiders his own imaginative designs. Carl's history painfully brings to the surface elements reiterated in the experiences of the next generation: A war veteran, Carl returns to a country which short circuits the ambitions of eager young black men and women; his art school lessons are abandoned when a "helpful" instructor warns that there are no jobs for him, and his best friend withdraws into silence and then apparent suicide following Junebug's racist persecution. All three—Carl, Lucy, and Brother—descend temporarily into drug addiction, with Carl's cure still incomplete as in late middle age he continues to be dependent on methadone. Yet what Doot takes away from his conversations with Carl and Lucy is a keen respect for their resiliency and spirit. Wideman subtly balances his determination to validate the lives and sufferings of such individuals with the need to show them wrestling with their own weaknesses and failures in a struggle to maintain their dignity. *The Homewood Trilogy* poignantly evokes the deeply felt humanity of a community, which is too often reduced in fiction to mechanical naturalistic formulae.

BROTHERS AND KEEPERS

First published: 1984
Type of work: Memoir

Writing about his youngest brother's crime and punishment, Wideman investigates many interrelated personal and social issues.

Brothers and Keepers demonstrates once again Wideman's complex imaginative response to his brother Rob's life sentence for murder in 1978 and its illustration of the pathological interplay of white exploitation, racist neglect, and internal despair that have intensified rather than lessened since the 1960's. Family historiography again allows Wideman to meditate on the converging lines of human activity that brought him into existence. Like the narrator of *The Homewood Trilogy*, Wideman presents himself with a bittersweet awareness that his lifelong efforts to straddle black and white cultural expectations have made him an incongruous figure in both. The book opens in 1976 with the writer in the doubly white world of a snowy late winter in Laramie, Wyoming, where he teaches at the university, waiting for the word from his fugitive brother, which he intuitively knows will come.

In facing Rob when he does arrive, and in their subsequent meetings in jail over the years, Wideman recognizes that their polarized circumstances provocatively express the duality that is the African American's psychological legacy in the United States. Moreover, each has pursued a path he has equated with the American Dream of material success and personal self-definition: John Wideman in the "safe" and deracinated terms of career and family championed by white society, Rob along more dangerous lines that challenge the racist obstacles in his way through illegal channels promising victors the celebrity and glamor of the outlaw. That both men, despite their very different choices, now find themselves fumbling to recover what they sacrificed in pursuit of America's elusive seduction of "making it" is one of the deeply felt ironies of the text. Wideman also contextualizes his personal and familial anguish within a layered analysis of the American penal system that renders imprisonment a political, cultural, and existential condition.

Yet Wideman is also keenly suspicious of his own motives in making Rob's experience the focus of his writing and understands the exploitative potential of his endeavors. As much as it is the study of two brothers caught in a tragedy that brings them back into meaningful communication with each other and with the family from which they have both wandered, *Brothers and Keepers* documents its author's complex struggle to subordinate his voracious fictionalizing imagination and colonizing ego to the primacy of his brother's emergent voice articulating his own story. As a result, the narrative texture of the memoir boasts myriad linguistic styles as Wideman searches for a language that will reconnect him to Rob. Not only does John himself speak in differing voices, sometimes using the formal constructions of standard English and other times employing the black spoken vernacular, but he also allows Rob to enter the text from equally various directions. Wideman freely admits to adopting fictional strategies in re-creating conversations held with Rob at the prison, but he does include letters and poems written by Rob as well as a speech he had given upon receiving an associate's degree through a prison education program. Moreover, he confesses that Rob's critique led him to reject an earlier version as a usurpation of the other's story. Wideman tries to shake off the writer's tricks with which he typically makes a subject his own, all the while relying on them to construct a powerful narrative that possesses the power to move and elucidate; at the same time, they inevitably must obscure and misrepresent Rob's heroic efforts to come to terms with the life he has led and the future he now faces. Rob's story becomes that of the individual who, in losing his life, finds it: His is an existential odyssey that Wideman doubts he himself could complete. While the book initially seems to speculate on the more obvious question as to why one brother has "gone bad" when another has "made good," it finally asserts Wideman's conclusion that Rob is the better man, possessing far greater spiritual courage and stamina than his publicly accomplished sibling.

Wideman cannot manipulate the facts to construct a satisfactory resolution to Rob's tale—no amount of authorial skill can overturn Rob's sentence or the governor's refusal of a pardon, and John's published testament to Rob's strength cannot ensure that he will escape the ravages of encroaching despair or the very real threats posed by hostile guards and other inmates. The book's abrupt ending dramatizes the limits of the writer's imagination to effect real change in his brother's life, a realization bleakly consonant with Wideman's postmodernist skepticism in those very constructions of the imagination on which his own activity rests.

FEVER

First published: 1989
Type of work: Short story

A minister struggles to transcend racist injustices while providing care for victims of Philadelphia's 1793 yellow fever epidemic.

"Fever," the title story in Wideman's 1989 collection of short fiction, provides an illuminating metaphor for the various episodes of racial antagonism depicted in the volume. As one of the story's narrative voices explains, "Fever grows in the secret places of our hearts, planted there when one of us decided to sell one of us to another. The drum must pound ten thousand thousand years to drive that evil away."

The narrative focus of the tale reflects Wideman's desire to correct the inaccurate historical record about the role of African Americans during the 1793 yellow fever epidemic that devastated Philadelphia; he dedicates the story to the author of one such fraudulent account and relies instead upon the eyewitness record left by black commentators. Among the chorus of voices in the text are those of two black men, one of them the historical Richard Allen and the other his fictionalized brother Thomas, whose differing perspectives on the disaster and its resultant hypocrisies work in counterpoint. Allen, a former slave, minister, and the founder of the African Methodist Episcopal Church, is a deeply spiritual man who identifies his vision of the mass emancipation of slaves with the promise of Christianity. Allen has been ordered to serve a Dr. Rush in his ministrations to and autopsies of plague victims. After performing exhausting labor among the whites, he turns to the destitute habitations of poor blacks whom the disease ravages with equal savagery and devotes himself to their spiritual and physical health despite their contempt.

Like many other elements of the narrative, Thomas' story further documents the presence of blacks in the public sphere of American history: Thomas fought with the rebels in the American Revolution and, as a prisoner of the British, recognized the degree to which he had been denied participation in the society whose ideals he championed. His embittered outlook on the situation now facing blacks in the plague-ridden city stems from the opportunistic shifts of white opinion regarding blacks during the epidemic; while slaves were initially blamed for importing the disease following a bloody revolt in the Caribbean, blacks were later declared immune from its ravages and coerced to serve sick and dying whites. Each of these civic fictions exposes the denial of humanity underlying racism and responsible for the cultural pathology which is Wideman's principal target.

Philadelphia operates as symbolic setting for this story on religious as well as political grounds: Its Quaker egalitarianism does not preclude Allen's being refused a place at the communion table with white Christians, nor does the city's birthing of the young republic ensure that its African-American citizens will be accorded the same possibilities for prosperity available to the unending waves of European-born newcomers. Rather than boasting a vigorous democratic climate, Wideman's Philadelphia festers in a stagnant environment whose waters breed contagion both literally and metaphorically. Nor is water the only sinister natural element pervading the landscape; apocalyptic fire fills the streets of the city as a grim purgative for its soul-sickness.

The story evolves through a polyphonic orchestration of voices combining the points of view of slave and freedman, black and white, Christian and Jew, historian and eyewitness.

Wideman's characteristically fractured narrative jarringly shifts perspective to suggest that no one interpretation or "story" exists independent of the wider human drama playing itself out across time. Within his textual montage, Wideman melds such disparate elements as a newly enslaved African making the middle passage; a series of scientific descriptions of the fever and its assumed insect carriers; and a report of autopsy results documenting the common physical devastation visited upon Black and white plague victims alike.

Added to the individualized voices of Richard and Thomas Allen is the combative monologue of a dying Jewish merchant who describes his own experiences with bigotry and aggressively challenges Allen's continued attentions to the white populace. This character, Abraham, alludes to the Lamed-Vov, or "Thirty Just Men" of Judaic tradition, designated by God "to suffer the reality humankind cannot bear" and bear witness to the bottomless misery and depravity of existence. Richard Allen is one such figure among many in these stories whose compassion in the face of unbearable injustice and grief offers the only hope for salvation that Wideman can envision.

To underline the timeliness of this meditation on so seemingly remote a historical episode, Wideman introduces toward the end of the story the voice of a contemporary black health-care worker contemptuous of his elderly white charges and the society that has discarded them. Finally, within a single paragraph, Wideman links the disease wasting Philadelphia's citizens in the late eighteenth century to the factual 1985 bombing of a black neighborhood ordered by the city's first black mayor, Wilson Goode, to eradicate the black radical group MOVE. Wideman claims that in "Fever" he "was teaching myself different ways of telling history"; with the publication of *Philadelphia Fire* in 1990, a novel that extends his analysis of the MOVE bombing, he returned to this later historical incident as evidence of the paradoxes of the United States' continuing racial self-destructiveness.

Summary

John Edgar Wideman's writing, from fiction to memoir to literary criticism, testifies to his deeply felt commitment to document the African-American experience by subjecting it to the illuminating lens of art. His work combines a personal journey to recover a cultural tradition he had once shunned with postmodernist literary methods.

Wideman dramatizes the challenges facing black men in a racist society that continually compromises their masculinity and demands ingenious strategies for reinventing male integrity. Family and community provide the bedrock of that integrity, and history is the fluid medium through which it must travel.

Bibliography

Bell, Bernard W. *The Afro-American Novel and Its Tradition*. Amherst: University of Massachusetts Press, 1987.

Bennion, John. "The Shape of Memory in John Edgar Wideman's *Sent for You Yesterday*." *Black American Literature Forum* 20 (1985): 143-150.

Coleman, James W. *Blackness and Modernism: The Literary Career of John Edgar Wideman*. Jackson: University Press of Mississippi, 1990.

O'Brien, John, ed. *Interviews with Black Writers*. New York: Liveright, 1973.

Samuels, Wilfred D. "Going Home: A Conversation with John Edgar Wideman." *Callaloo* 6 (1983): 40-59.

Barbara Kitt Seidman

RICHARD WILBUR

Born: New York, New York
March 1, 1921

Principal Literary Achievement

Wilbur has published some of the finest poetry of the mid-twentieth century; he was appointed poet laureate of the United States by the Library of Congress in 1987.

Biography

Richard Wilbur was born in New York City on March 1, 1921, the son of Lawrence L. Wilbur, a portrait painter, and Helen R. (Purdy) Wilbur, a daughter of an editor of the Baltimore Sun. He attended public schools in Essex Falls, New Jersey, and North Caldwell, New Jersey, and attended Montclair High School, where he was editor of the school paper.

In 1938, he matriculated at Amherst College; there he wrote editorials for and was chairman of the student newspaper, *The Student*, and was a contributor to *The Touchstone*, the student magazine. He once said that there he submitted an awful poem about a nightingale, a bird that he had never seen. He received a dollar for it. He received his A.B. at Amherst College in 1942, but before he could continue his studies, he was drafted into the Army; he served until 1945, when he was discharged with the rank of technician third class. He then went on to get his A.M. in Religion at Harvard University in 1947. He had married Charlotte Ward in 1942; they had four children, Ellen, Christopher, Nathan, and Aaron.

After he received his master's degree at Harvard, he was elected junior fellow there from 1947 to 1950. In 1950, he became an assistant professor of English at Harvard, where he remained until 1954. In that year he became associate professor of English at Wellesley College, where he was promoted to professor in 1957; he taught there until 1977. Unlike many other poets of his generation, he did not look down on teaching as a job that spoiled his writing. Indeed, he pointed out in an interview given to Peter Stitt that the constant reading and the necessity of understanding one's reading very clearly were good exercises for the mind. In 1977, he was appointed writer-in-residence at Smith College, a position he held until 1986.

In 1947, while he was at Harvard's graduate school, a friend sent a sheaf of his poetry to Reynal & Hitchcock, who liked it so much they published it under the title *The Beautiful Changes and Other Poems* (1947). Other books of original poetry

followed: *Ceremony and Other Poems* in 1950, *Things of This World* in 1956, and *Advice to a Prophet and Other Poems* in 1961. A paperback collection, *The Poems of Richard Wilbur*, put out by Harvest Books, came out in 1963. *Walking to Sleep: New Poems and Translations* was published in 1969, *The Mind-Reader: New Poems* in 1976, and *New Poems* in 1987. In 1988, a collection of poems from all of his books was published under the title *New and Collected Poems.*

His original poetry is augmented by his many translations from the French. In 1955, he translated *The Misanthrope* by Molière, the seventeenth century French comic dramatist. This version is now standard for performance. It was first played by the Poet's Theater in Cambridge, Massachusetts, in 1955 and was performed Off-Broadway at Theater East in 1956-1957. He translated Molière's *Tartuffe* in 1963, for which he was the corecipient of the Bollingen Prize, and published *The School for Wives* in 1971 and *The Learned Ladies* in 1978, finishing his Molière translations. He also translated *Phaedra* (1986) and *Andromache* (1982) by Jean Racine, the seventeenth century classic French tragedian.

Other works include two juvenile books, *Loudmouse* (1963) and *Opposites* (1973), and an edition of Edgar Allan Poe's poetry for Dell in 1959. He wrote or rewrote most of the lyrics for *Candide* by Leonard Bernstein, the famous modern American composer, which was published by Random House in 1957, and he coauthored a cantata, *On Freedom's Ground*, with William Schumann, a prominent modern musician and educator. He edited the *Selected Poems* of Witter Bynner in 1978 and *Shakespeare: Poems* in 1966. He also published a book of literary criticism, *Responses: Prose Pieces, 1953-1976* in 1976.

He is the winner of many awards, the chief of which are the National Book Award and the Pulitzer Prize (both for his book of poems *Things of This World*), the Bollingen award for his translation of *Tartuffe* in 1971, and his appointment as poet laureate of the United States in 1987.

Analysis

Summing up the poetic achievement of Richard Wilbur seems at first too easy. After all, he began his career writing beautiful short poems about the surrounding natural world. A close look at some poems of his throughout his career and a glance at his translations and other interests will find a writer more important than a painter of pretty pictures. He does, certainly, enjoy the world of living creatures: The very first poem in his first volume is called "Cicadas." Yet one must read carefully before judging it to be about cicadas. A close reading proves it to be about nature: These insects fill the world with song but are themselves deaf.

Animal titles are sprinkled throughout his work: There is "Still, Citizen Sparrow," "The Death of a Toad," "All These Birds," "The Pelican," and the delightful "A Prayer to Go to Paradise with the Donkeys," translated from the French of Francis Jammes, a modern French poet. A closer look at these poems, however, will reveal that these animals are chosen because they are a key to the surrounding world. "Still, Citizen Sparrow" is really about how the vulture (and all he stands for) is needed in the world; "The Death of a Toad" shows how all death is tragic, and the "Grasshopper" helps to distinguish the peace that is death from that which is contentment in activity.

Many critics think of Wilbur as a poet uniting flesh and spirit, discerning both, glorifying both. In "Running," he describes a day when his body as a boy was in perfect shape and the run he had was a glory of perfect control. "Thinking of happiness," he says, "I think of that." In "The Juggler," after lamenting the pull of gravity on a rubber ball, he praises the juggler for keeping the balls, brooms, and plates whirling in air. He discovers how people resent the weight that holds them to the earth, both physically and spiritually; he thereby discovers the reason for juggling, for dreams of flying, and perhaps for all the earth's restless desires.

Perhaps the characteristic that can be most commonly illustrated in Wilbur is his uncanny ability to pinpoint the essential interplay between man and nature. In a poem called "On the Marginal Way," he begins, in a sedate six-line stanza ending with a final couplet, to describe a beach littered with boulders; they remind him first of naked women, but then of a beach full of dead people, whose story he begins to imagine. He pulls himself short by exclaiming: "[It is] the times's fright within me which distrusts/ least fancies into violence." He reminds himself that though it was "violent" volcanic action that created these boulders, it is a beautiful day, and joy comes with the faith, however, momentary, that "all things shall be brought/ to the full state and stature of their kind." In the short poem "Seed Loves," Wilbur patiently describes the phenomenon that every gardener knows: The first two leaves of every plant are always the same. The plant is in a state of pure potency, and it both wishes and fears to grow. Then the third and fourth leaves come out, and the plant resigns itself to be itself. A simple botanical fact echoes deep inside the human spirit.

There are more direct approaches, as in "Advice to a Prophet," which counsels the doomsayer not to predict a nuclear holocaust or the end of mankind on earth: "How should we dream of this place without us?" Tell us instead, he says, how all the beautiful things in nature will disappear. In "A Summer Morning," he tells how the cook and the gardener, because their rich young employers got in late, enjoy the beautiful big gardens and house on a sunny morning, "Possessing what the owners can but own," bringing a moral insight to a small incident that would make Saint Francis proud.

The critics insist that Wilbur is a classic rather than a Romantic poet. The words "classic" and "Romantic" are hopelessly vague, but if one allows them to indicate general tendencies, "classic" pointing toward public themes, wit, and an intellectual acceptance of the human condition, and "Romantic" meaning personal, emotional, and the tendency to yearn after transcendent goals, then Wilbur can be said generally to be on the classic side. His choice of poetry to be translated is headed by the French classics—works by Molière, Racine, and Voltaire, the eighteenth century satirist and political commentator. Perhaps a single Wilbur poem will illustrate. In "A Wood," a parable emerges from Wilbur's observation of the forest. It is an oak forest, an impressive place, but someone looking carefully, he points out, would notice dogwood and witch hazel fighting to keep their places in the forest. Classically enough, he provides a moral—"no one style, I think, is recommended"—but the true meaning in the poem is the feeling of sympathy for the underdog trees trying to survive in a forest of important oaks.

Finally, at least occasionally, Wilbur is a Christian poet. Biographers list his religion as Episcopalian, but his few religious poems are very generic. His "A Christmas Hymn," for example, presents a brief history of salvation, with the refrain "And every stone shall cry" leading the reader from the stable through Palm Sunday and the crucifixion to His presence in glory. The whole of Wilbur's poetry can be called, at least in a transferred sense, sacramental. Like a medieval poet, he reads the Book of the World, and all of its aspects—vegetable, mineral, animal, and human—are rife with meaning, which he, as a patient anatomist, discovers with care and love.

A WORLD WITHOUT OBJECTS IS A SENSIBLE EMPTINESS

First published: 1950
Type of work: Poem

The poet tries to discern which is the true spiritual goal, spirit or flesh.

The title of the poem is a quote from Thomas Traherne, a seventeenth century mystic and poet. The poem is written in a stanza form which would certainly feel at home in the seventeenth century, with four-line stanzas rhyming abab, though some of the rhymes are slant rhymes. Line one is trimeter; line two, pentameter; line three, hexameter; and line four, trimeter.

The central metaphor of conceit of the poem is that the search for Traherne's "sensible emptiness" is a camel caravan, leaving the security of the oasis for a "desert experience." It "move[s] with a stilted stride/ to the land of sheer horizon." The camels search for a place where there is nothing but sand and sky. This central metaphor uses the ambiguous connotations of desert and oasis to structure the poem into a basic statement on the search for spiritual perfection. The desert is traditionally a place where the ascetic goes to find God; on the other hand, it is the very image of hell, the dry place without rejuvenating water. Similarly, the oasis is the place of refreshment, the goal of the desert traveler, while at the same time it is the place of temptation for the desert saint, a return to the "Fleshpots of Egypt." In fact, the central archetype here is the exodus, the stately camels leaving the oasis to find God in the desert.

The speaker plays on the ambiguity of the imagery, however; the camels are "Beasts of my soul," they are "slow and proud" and "move with a stilted pride." He suggests that the camels are not ascetics but aesthetes, calling them "connoisseurs of thirst," and says that what they thirst for is "pure mirage." The goal of their quest seems to be an illusion.

The poet in stanza four refuses this goal of mirage and nothingness. He insists that "all shinings need to be shaped," and he appeals to "painted saints" and "merry-go-round rings." He exhorts these camels to turn away from the sand and the desert to (in stanza six) "trees arrayed/ in bursts of glare," and then names other green and substantial things—country creeks and hilltops illuminated by the sun. Stanza seven advises the searcher/camels to watch "the supernova burgeoning over the barn" and then pronounces the true goal "the spirit's right oasis, light incarnate."

The poem, then, interprets the ambiguous associations in its own way. It takes the quote of the title as a mere description, which the "camels of the spirit" have mistaken for a spiritual goal. It rejects the desert as an ascetic goal, because to conquer it as the camels seek to do is not a human act but an example of pride, an attempt to overrun the limits of human nature; a human cannot pursue a goal where there are no objects. The last line hints at the incarnational theology of a spirituality that pursues both body and spirit. Each object to be sought at the end of the poem is bathed in the "spiritual" light of the sun.

LOVE CALLS US TO THE THINGS OF THIS WORLD

First published: 1956
Type of work: Poem

The poet tries to describe and then deal with the moment between sleeping and waking when life seems glorious and beautiful.

"Love Calls Us to the Things of This World" is one of a precious few in the English language that operates as a perfectly delightful rendering of an experience that rides joyfully just outside the rational world. It can be seen as a companion piece to some of the poems of Wallace Stevens, the great modern American poet, such as "The Emperor of Ice-Cream" or "That November off Tehuantepec."

The stanza is of five lines of alternating trochaic and iambic patterns, with the second and fourth lines tending toward rhyme. The poem opens with a reference to a "cry of pulleys" as an unseen neighbor puts laundry out on the line; the pulleys may also be an allusion to the poem "The Pulley" by George Herbert, the seventeenth century English religious poet. In that poem, the pulley is an emblem of the means by which God draws humankind to Himself—in that case, by making humans dissatisfied with life here on earth. In Wilbur's poem, the moment being described is the moment between sleeping and waking when the world is in a state of perfect delight. Fitting in with the slightly nonrational tinge of the poem, the central conceit used here is that the moment is like laundry.

Strange are the characteristics of this moment, described in terms of the laundry hanging on the line outside the window. "Angels" in sheets, blouses, and smocks abound; they rise "together in calm swells/ Of halcyon feelings." In stanza three, they perform the astounding feat of flying at top speed while not moving—"staying like white water"—and then become so quiet that "nobody seems to be there." The soul begins to be aware of its situation, however, and in stanza four it looks forward with fear to the prospect of waking up to "the punctual rape of every blessèd day" and cries out irrationally, "Oh, let there be nothing on earth but laundry."

As stanza five acknowledges, the day must come, the sleeper must fully awake, and the soul must "in bitter love/ . . . accept the waking body." What, then, can be gained from this prewaking experience? The last stanza is a prayer—an eloquent one—asking that the laundry that bundles the angels in the vision become part of everyday life: "clean linen for the backs of thieves," new clothes for lovers so that they may "go fresh and sweet to be undone," and "dark habits" for "the heaviest nuns," who are "keeping their difficult balance." Significantly, it is love that ends the dream of the angels and forces one to wake up from the insubstantial dream world. One is called now, to the things of this world, not to dreams of the next.

IN THE FIELD

First published: 1969
Type of work: Poem

This poem compares the feelings aroused by looking at the stars with those caused by a field of flowers.

The title, "In the Field," is an ambiguous reference to the two halves of the poem: The poem chronicles two walks in the same field, the first set at night (the speaker looks at the stars), and the second one on a sunny day (the speaker looks at the flowers of the field). The poem has both a speaker and someone spoken to, who is probably a wife or lover, and the poem is a looking back at the events delineated there.

The stanza form is simple—four lines each of trimeter, pentameter, tetrameter, and trimeter, rhyming abab. The poem has a classical feel with a personal twist. It may be said to have as its subject the fear of Blaise Pascal, the seventeenth century French philosopher and mathematician, of the immensity of the universe, but it relates this topic not as an abstract concept but as resulting from a personal discovery of the poet and his beloved.

The poem opens as the two are walking through the field on a moonless night looking at the stars. The imagery of stanzas 1 and 2, however, suggest that they are wading in the sea, their "throw-back heads aswim." The meditation begins with discussions of anciently named constellations, pointing out that Andromeda no longer fears the sea even though she moves "through a diamond froth of stars." Nor does she need Perseus, her godlike savior in the myth, or even Euripides, the famous ancient Greek tragedian, to preserve her memory. The dolphin of Arion, the legendary Greek bard, is still there as flawless as he was in ancient times.

Stanza 5, however, turns the poem in a new direction. The speaker, as if discovering what he had forgotten, says that none of the legends written in the stars "are true." He explains by noting that the stars have moved slightly since ancient times: The pictures visible to the ancients are "askew" and, therefore, meaningless. The heavens have burst "the cincture of the Zodiac" and "shot flares" (meteors), and they no longer have anything to say.

So the two talk of them in modern astronomical terms—star magnitude, nebulae, and star clusters—which is fine until the imagination gets into the act with a "nip of fear" and it fakes "a scan of space/ Blown black and hollow"; perhaps the imagination thinks of a time ahead when the stars go out, an intimation of apocalypse. The air becomes chill, and the two go home to bed.

The second half of the poem describes the field in sunlight. The stars are gone; the "holes in heaven have been sealed." The only galaxies they see are "galaxies/ Of flowers," images that populate stanzas 16 and 17. Yet what do they mean? Do they refute the fear felt in the night walk? No, that would be a mistake. In a complicated answer, the poet discovers the "heart's wish for life." He opines that this wish "pounds beyond the sun" and "is the one/ Unbounded thing we know."

When one has finished analyzing the poem, one finds that the ambiguous title "In the Field" now has a third meaning. Besides indicating the dark field of the stars and the bright sunny field of flowers, it indicates that the speaker has taken a "field trip": an experience that backs up an abstract idea, Pascal's fear, which his mind had already grasped. The stars are frightening and the flowers comforting, but the infinite wishes of the human heart are the only "unbounded thing" humankind has from experience.

THE MIND-READER

First published: 1976
Type of work: Poem

A dramatic monologue in which the speaker tells the poet how he became a mind reader and what are his thoughts on the human mind.

"The Mind-Reader" is a dramatic monologue in the tradition of Robert Browning, the nineteenth century British poet, written in blank verse. It is the statement of a mind reader, one perpetually ensconced in a café somewhere in Italy. He talks to the poet about how he came to be a mind reader, how he practices his "craft," and how he feels about what he does.

The poem begins with nineteen lines of a discussion of what it means that something is really lost. Not till the end of the poem does the reader really find out why he speaks of these things. He begins with an image of a young lady's hat being blown off a parapet and sailing endlessly down into a vast ravine with a river at the bottom. He tells of a pipe wrench falling out of a pick-up truck into a brook or culvert, then of a book slipping out of the hand of a reader on a cruise ship and into the sea. These things are "truly lost." Four mysterious lines follow which declare that it is another thing to be caught inside the prison of someone's head. (Was he so imprisoned? Was it traumatic?)

He explains in the next twenty-one lines that he, as a child, had a gift of finding things that others had lost. He tries to describe how it felt to be able to do this. He uses a metaphor of a moon bumping through a deep forest through

> paths which turned
> to dried-up stream-beds, hemlocks which invited
> Through shiny clearings.

All of a sudden the lost object would be there, shining.

Perhaps he feels that this metaphor does not quite make the process clear, for he tries again. He says that it is like a train with fogged windows coming into a station where a young woman is waiting for you (his listener) to come, though she does not know what you look like. He alludes to the saying "out of sight, out of mind" and seems to imply that it is not precisely true. "What can be wiped from memory?" Nothing, he answers no matter how mean or terrible the event. That is presumably why he, with his gift, can always find the thing that was misplaced. Everything is still there.

This arcane skill leads him to become the mind reader at the corner table of the café. He describes the credulous people who come to have their futures predicted, even though he cannot predict the future, and the skeptics who are afraid that if he can read minds, all the old superstitions will come rushing back. They are his "fellow-drunkards."

He describes his method: They write a question on a piece of paper, and he lays his hand on theirs and goes into a frenzy; he describes his act (for so it is) in terms that resemble the routine of the Delphic Oracle, the smoke from his cigarette substituting for the incense in the oracle's tripod. It is easy, he says, to know what they are thinking—everyone is the same. Sometimes he cheats, but remember, he says, every other skilled worker (a tailor, for example) can make a mistake and still be trusted. If he makes one, he is a fraud. Then he concludes with images of squalor: His mind is filled with anger, insomnia, mutterings, complaints, and "flushings of the race."

His gift is to find in others' minds their own misplaced questions, but, as he admits, he has no answers. He gives them answers that are the stock-in-trade of palm readers and astrologers everywhere, each bit of advice prefaced with a commonsense "if," each prediction based on a commonsense understanding of how life is led. He describes his stock answers as lies and evasions, although he believes that his clients are happy that he read their desire. These people are filled with "selfish hopes/ And small anxieties." True virtue and heroism are rare indeed. Maybe, he says, he simply cannot hear that part of them; maybe there is "some huge attention" which "suffers us and is inviolate," which "remarks/ The sparrow's weighty fall." The speaker seems oblivious to the reference to Christ's sermon on the mount, and he declares that he would be glad to know this if it were so.

The poem concludes with his own desire "for that place beyond the sparrow" and to find those things that are truly lost, which were mentioned in the opening of the poem—the falling hat, the wrench in the ditch, and the book in the sea. The listener apparently offers to buy him a drink, and he replies, perhaps smiling, "You have read my mind." Perhaps Wilbur, in this poem, wishes to illustrate what the human mind and its desires are like, apparently trivial and squalid like those the mind reader finds in his clients, yet perhaps containing way down the true desires, the infinite desires, symbolized by the lost hat, wrench, and book.

TROLLING FOR BLUES

First published: 1987
Type of work: Poem

The act of fishing inspires a wry meditation on the pitfalls of metaphor and humanizing the nonhuman.

"Trolling for Blues" could be styled a work whose metaphor took over the poem and changed it into something other than it started out to be. It is written in a five-line stanza of loose pentameters without rhyme. It begins with the poet talking to himself about metaphors: The "dapper terns" and the cloud that "moils in the sky" like an embryo are seen in human terms—humanity is projected upon them. (Only a person could be "dapper.") Wilbur then analyzes his fish-is-like-man metaphor. Humans make the fish, he points out, a "mirror of our kind."

Immediately he begins to mock the poet in everyone: Only if, he says, one sets aside the fish's "unreflectiveness," his habit of leaping up out of the water, and his strange practice of swimming a hundred miles out to sea to spawn is he just like humans.

One conceives of the fish, the poet says, as blue, "which is the shade / Of thought." He becomes at this point a symbol of the intellect "on edge/ To lunge and seize with sure incisiveness." The fish, however, does not cooperate with the poet; suddenly he strikes the lure and dives into the deep, "Yanking imagination back and down/ Past recognition" to the dark places at the bottom of the water. There the fish becomes a symbol of the unconscious, of the place where there is no intellect. He is also a symbol of the evolutionary past—the dark, mindless Devonian age where there was no man. This is where humanity began, coming up from the depths to find the cool blue intellect.

This poem, then, by a whimsical, circuitous route, mocking the poetic power that created it, sets up an allegory of human psychology. This fact begins to explain the title—as usual in Wilbur, a play on words. If one thinks of the fish as "blue," one is trolling for "blues," but if one thinks of the fish as intellect, one is trolling for a kind of melancholy reflection; the reader catches the idea that humankind's "roots" are far from intellectual, that its beginnings are at the bottom of the sea in "the unlit deep/ Of the glass sponges, of chiasmodon." The poem also reveals the dangerous human habit of projecting humanity onto things which only remotely resemble humans: In humanizing everything, it may be that one begins to fail to understand one's own humanity.

Summary

Richard Wilbur began his poetic career when a friend submitted some poems to a publisher. He continues, modestly writing poem after poem showing profound insights into how the human imagination delves into man's relationship with nature and civilization. To this can be added his skill in translation, especially in the area of French classical drama, an effort which has humanized these remote masters for an American audience. Wilbur has probed the world with a keen, calm voice filled with wisdom and insight.

Bibliography

Faverty, Frederick. "The Poetry of Richard Wilbur." In *Modern American Poetry*, edited by Greg Owen. Deland, Fla.: Everett/Edwards, 1972.

Reibetang, John. "What Love Sees: Poetry and Vision in Richard Wilbur." *Modern Poetry Studies* 11 (1982): 60-85.

Salinger, Wendy, ed. *Richard Wilbur's Creation*. Ann Arbor: University of Michigan Press, 1983.

Stitt, Peter. *The World's Hieroglyphic Beauty: Five American Poets*. Athens: University of Georgia Press, 1985.

Waggoner, Hyatt. *American Poets from the Puritans to the Present*. Boston: Houghton Mifflin, 1968.

Robert W. Peckham

THORNTON WILDER

Born: Madison, Wisconsin
April 17, 1897
Died: Hamden, Connecticut
December 7, 1975

Principal Literary Achievement

Considered one of America's most important, versatile, and innovative writers, Wilder wrote plays that rank him as one of America's top dramatists.

Biography

Thornton Niven Wilder was born in Madison, Wisconsin, on April 17, 1897. He was a surviving twin, and all of his life he searched for the alter ego lost at birth. He had an older brother by two years, Amos Niven, a well-known theologian, professor, and writer. He also had three sisters: Charlotte, born in 1898; Isabel, born in 1900, a writer herself who devoted her life as confidante and secretary to Thornton; and Janet, born in 1910.

Thornton was named for his mother, the talented Isabella Thornton Niven, daughter of a Presbyterian minister; his brother Amos was named for their father, Amos Parker Wilder. Their father, a handsome, robust individual, held a doctorate in political science and was editor of the *Wisconsin State Journal*. He was a strict Congregationalist whose moral rectitude and constant career moves placed hardships on his wife and family. These served as important influences on Wilder, infusing him with a sense of unworthiness that haunted him all his life.

Amos Parker Wilder was an uncompromising individual whose strong editorial opinions clashed with those of Wisconsin's powerful senator, Robert M. La Follette. By 1906, Amos believed it was time to leave the state and accepted the appointment of American consul in Hong Kong. Within six months, Isabella and Amos agreed to a temporary separation. She returned to the states with the children to live in Berkeley, California. Over the next eight years, Thornton attended various schools as he moved back and forth across the Pacific Ocean, finally completing his high school education at Berkeley High School in 1915. Amos forced Thornton to attend Oberlin College for two years and then transferred him to Yale University, his own alma mater.

Wilder began his writing career in college. Several of his pieces appeared in the *Oberlin Literary Magazine* and the *Yale Literary Magazine*. After he was graduated

from Yale in 1920, he traveled to Rome and attended the American Academy, where he worked on his first novel, "The Memoirs of a Roman Student." Thornton returned to the states to teach French at Lawrenceville Academy during the early 1920's. He also attended Princeton University; he was graduated with an M.A. degree in 1926. The same year, Thornton saw the publication of his novel, now retitled *The Cabala*. In 1927, his first play, *The Trumpet Shall Sound*, was produced. Both creative efforts met with an indifferent reception. Not so his second novel, *The Bridge of San Luis Rey* (1927), which was an immediate success and won for him his first Pulitzer Prize. A number of one-act plays, written over a twelve-year period, were published in 1928 under the title *The Angel That Troubled the Waters and Other Plays*. The sixteen brief plays offer a fascinating glimpse into Wilder's outlook on philosophy, literature, and history, and into his concept of theatricality that found mature expression in his later works.

The 1930's was a very busy decade for Wilder. In 1930, he wrote a novel, *The Woman of Andros*, based on Roman playwright Terence's *Andria*; in 1931 he published *The Long Christmas Dinner and Other Plays in One Act*, continuing his experiments in nontraditional theater. He adapted two works for the stage—André Obey's *Le Viol de Lucrèce* (called *Lucrece*) in 1932 and Henrik Ibsen's *A Doll's House* in 1937—as showcases for actresses Katherine and Ruth Gordon, respectively. He also found time to teach one semester each year from 1930 to 1936 at the University of Chicago and to publish the novel *Heaven's My Destination* in late 1934, a work hailed by Gertrude Stein as the quintessential American novel. Stein's praise of Wilder initiated a correspondence between them that ripened into friendship. Her positive influence on Wilder's further writings is inestimable. Wilder tired of his teaching responsibilities and in 1936 resigned his position at the University of Chicago. He was then free to concentrate on writing, traveling, and visiting with friends. Two years later, he wrote the Pulitzer Prize-winning *Our Town*, arguably the United States' favorite, most-produced, and most-read play. The production opened to indifferent reviews but soon won over the public. In 1938, Wilder opened another Broadway production, entitled *The Merchant of Yonkers*, based on Johann Nestroy's *Einen Jux will er sich machen* (1842). Not an immediate hit, it was revised and retitled *The Matchmaker* in 1954. The play enjoyed successful revivals in London, Edinburgh, and New York. Later, the work was revised again and became the hit musical comedy *Hello Dolly!* The original Broadway production ran for only thirty-nine performances, compared with 486 for the 1955 New York production of *The Matchmaker* and almost three thousand for *Hello, Dolly!*

During World War II, Captain Wilder (later Lieutenant Colonel Wilder) of the Intelligence Corps of the United States Army Air Corps opened his play *The Skin of Our Teeth* in 1942, despite misgivings by some of the people involved in the production because of the play's surreal structure. The public loved it, however, and the comedy earned for Wilder his third and final Pulitzer Prize. In 1947, he wrote a short dramatic burlesque called *Our Century*, which had limited distribution, followed by a novel based on the last days of Julius Caesar entitled *The Ides of March*

(1948), widely praised abroad, but not in the United States.

During the last years of his life, Wilder received numerous awards, including the 1963 United States Presidential Medal of Freedom and the 1965 National Medal of Literature. He wrote two more novels, *The Eighth Day* (1967), a much praised work that he believed was a disappointment, even though it earned the National Book Award, and his final fiction, *Theophilis North*, published in 1973, a novel more admired by his devoted readers than by critics. Two years later, on December 7, 1975, he died, suffering from the ravages of old age and a debilitating stroke that had partially blinded him.

Analysis

Thornton Wilder achieved a successful career as a writer of both fiction and drama. His success is especially remarkable given his small literary output over the five decades that he wrote. In theater, for example, he is considered one of America's best playwrights, yet his fame rests squarely on three full-length plays and a handful of shorter ones. He wrote seven novels and received numerous awards including a Pulitzer Prize. Wilder achieved national success and celebrity status with his second novel, at age thirty, *The Bridge of San Luis Rey*; he remained in the public eye during the rest of his literary career, although he wrote only four more novels during the last forty years of his life.

Wilder was heavily influenced at the beginning of his career by the nonrealistic movement of the 1920's that was quite popular abroad. Unlike the American writers Theodore Dreiser, Sinclair Lewis, and Eugene O'Neill, who were championed by such influential critics as H. L. Mencken and Edmund Wilson, Wilder found himself alone in his search for a new humanism that affirmed the dignity of humankind. In his first novel, *The Cabala*, published in 1926, Wilder introduced a theme that recurred in his later work: the possibility that an American could travel abroad, partake of the cultural experiences that Europe had to offer, and return enriched but not overwhelmed. Wilder believed that America could benefit from the Old World but was still the land of golden opportunity. This concept ran counter to the thinking of the "lost generation" of writers, who could not reconcile themselves to their homeland. Wilder was able to fuse the humanistic spirit of the past with the temper of the present.

In his work, Wilder explored moral and religious themes and tried to capture the complex chemistry of human life. He believed in the absolute mystery of life, the workings of which defy rational explanations. Wilder also believed in a higher power of love that did not simply spring from sexual desire. For Wilder, love was an indispensable part of life and a moral responsibility. One of the characters in *The Bridge of San Luis Rey*, who could be commenting on Wilder's work, observes:

> But soon we shall die . . . and we ourselves shall be loved for a while and forgotten. But the love will have been enough; all those impulses of love return to the love that made them. Even memory is not necessary for love. There is a land of the living and a land of the dead and the bridge of love, the only survival, the only meaning.

The eternal optimist, Wilder firmly believed that the human race, despite its ignorance, cruelty, self-destructive nature, and subjection to natural disasters, will always manage to survive.

Wilder's deep philosophical beliefs, along with the quiet encouragement of his friend Gertrude Stein, propelled him on a quest for the universal and the eternal. Perhaps that is why he often turned to the theater. In his preface to a collection of plays published in 1957, he wrote: "The novel is pre-eminently the vehicle of the unique occasion, the theater of the generalized one." His convictions found their deepest expression in the theater, where he could stretch the boundaries of convention. He made it clear that the small, ordinary events of daily life can take on a great significance. This concept runs through most of his early plays, but *Our Town* elevates it to the highest level. Wilder stresses that humans fail to understand and appreciate the priceless value of everyday events, wasting their lives by not valuing every moment of them.

What is remarkable about Wilder's work is the innovative spirit that animates it. From the first, Wilder tried to explore unique ways of presenting his ideas. In his early collection, *The Angel That Troubled the Waters and Other Plays*, and in his 1931 *The Long Christmas Dinner and Other Plays in One Act*, for example, Wilder was already experimenting with the conventions of theatricality, experimentation that found its artistic fulfillment in the Pulitzer Prize winners *Our Town* and *The Skin of Our Teeth*. Both acclaimed and condemned for his nonrealistic approach, Wilder remained absolutely unapologetic. He stated, "I became dissatisfied with the theater because I was unable to lend credence to such childish attempts to be 'real.'"

Wilder's literary life was fairly serene. He cultivated a large and adoring public but on two occasions came under vicious attack. He was accused in 1942 of plagiarizing *The Skin of Our Teeth* from Irish writer James Joyce's *Finnegan's Wake* (1939); it became an unpleasant affair that lasted for months. The first and perhaps the most damaging incident, however, temporarily dimming his national reputation, occurred in 1930 when Michael Gold, a Communist journalist and writer, excoriated the rising young writer. In an article in *The New Republic* entitled "Wilder: Prophet of the Genteel Christ," he attacked Wilder for his "new humanism" principles (emphasizing classical restraint associated with the ancient Greek tradition) at a time when the United States had plunged into the Depression. Examining Wilder's work to date, Gold criticized *The Bridge of San Luis Rey* as a "daydream of homosexual figures in graceful gowns moving archaically among the lilies." (Wilder was a confirmed homosexual, although he never had a long-term sexual relationship in his life.) Gold then switched his attack to Wilder himself, derisively calling him "this Emily Post of culture. . . . always in perfect taste." Gold taunted Wilder about writing a book to "reveal all his fundamental silliness and superficiality." Angered and hurt by the criticism, Wilder rose to the challenge, and his reputation and credibility returned slowly.

Wilder remains eminently readable today. He enjoyed writing novels and plays and always cherished a deep love of humanity. Perhaps Chrysis, one of the characters in his novel *The Woman of Andros*, said it best: "Remember some day, remember me as one who loved all things and accepted from the gods all things, the bright and the dark. And do you likewise. Farewell."

THE BRIDGE OF SAN LUIS REY

First published: 1927
Type of work: Novel

Five strangers plunge to their deaths on a rope bridge near Lima, Peru, and their lives are reexamined by a Catholic priest who witnessed the tragedy.

Wilder's second novel, *The Bridge of San Luis Rey*, published in November, 1927, rocketed the modest author to celebrity status. Its extraordinary public reception and favorable reviews caught Wilder by surprise. Critics hailed it as a "work of genius," a "little masterpiece" with a "deceptive clarity of style that marks pellucid depths." The novel was viewed as a breath of fresh air as opposed to the downbeat realistic works of Upton Sinclair and Theodore Dreiser. Wilder was awarded the Pulitzer Prize on May 7, 1928. In 1929, and again in 1944, the novel was adapted into a film, but both were disappointing ventures.

Wilder's writing was influenced by two important factors. First was the historical figure of Camila Perichole. A famous actress in late eighteenth century Lima, Peru, she had played the central character in Prosper Merimee's play *La Carosse du Saint-Sacrament* (1829), dazzling audiences with her performances. She became the mistress of the viceroy and donated his gifts to the church to help the poor and dying. In *The Bridge of San Luis Rey*, Camila is a pivotal character who appears in all three main stories, coming in contact with every important character. The second historical event concerned a real rope bridge that had been built in Peru in A.D. 1350, which collapsed centuries later, plunging people to their death.

The Bridge of San Luis Rey is set in early eighteenth century Peru. The novel opens simply: "On Friday noon, July the twentieth, 1714, the finest bridge in all Peru broke and precipitated five travellers into the gulf below." The tragic accident is witnessed by Brother Juniper, a rational theologian, who attempts to piece together the story of the victims—why they were at the bridge at the same time and whether it was an accident or God's will. The victims included a young boy, an adolescent, a young man, a middle-aged man, and an old noblewoman.

The Bridge of San Luis Rey is divided into five sections, with the shorter opening and closing chapters serving as a framing device. The first major story involves the old, ugly Marquesa de Montemayor, her grief-ridden relationship with her unloving daughter, and the devoted servant Pepita. The middle tale concerns two inseparable twins, named Manuel and Esteban, who share a telepathic closeness. They suffer an estrangement when Manuel falls in love with the actress Camila; he later dies from blood poisoning. The final story is the love-hate relationship of Uncle Pio and Camila, his protégé, whom he has tutored to be Peru's finest actress. Wilder shows that all five sufferers were victimized in life not only by the falling bridge, but also by loving someone who could not or would not love them in return. All five realize their folly at the end and set out to start their lives in new directions.

After telling his tale of the five doomed travelers, Wilder focuses on the survivors, those whose unrequited loves are not destroyed by falling bridges. He makes the final point that they have lost individuals very precious to them and yet have gained something in return, the bridge of love drawing together the living and the dead.

Wilder raises many questions about why these people were killed, including whether it was simply an accident, whether they were responsible for their own lives, or whether they were part of some divine plan and were doomed to die together. He does not answer any one question but suggests that it may have been a combination of all four, reaffirming his central belief that life's mysteries cannot be divined. Wilder ends the book with Brother Juniper, after years of research, attempting to publish his findings; the work, however, is declared heretical, and he and his research are burned by the Inquisition.

Wilder's Christian humanism is clearly evident in *The Bridge of San Luis Rey*. The concepts of wastefulness, sinfulness, and the failure to appreciate one's life— recurring themes in later works, particularly *Our Town*—are presented here forcefully and without sentimentality. The author's straightforward prose style, combined with an intriguing plot structure and compelling central characters, make it Wilder's most successful fiction and his most widely read novel.

OUR TOWN

First produced: 1938 (first published, 1938)
Type of work: Play

Life, love, and death are seen through the lives of residents of a small New Hampshire town in early twentieth century America.

In the drama *Our Town*, Thornton Wilder would find the fullest expression of his humanistic convictions, pouring all of his genius into it. The play, which opened on Broadway on February 4, 1938, reaffirmed his deep-seated belief that eternal human truths can be observed in American life. Today, the play is regarded as an American classic. It was a different matter, however, in the beginning. The play had a rocky out-of-town reception by the critics before opening in New York City, but thanks to the strong support of doyen Brooks Atkinson, it caught on with the public and ran for 336 performances. It was turned into a film in 1940, which, despite a serious change in plot structure, was almost as popular as the stage presentation. Even though denied the prestigious New York Drama Critics Circle Award, the play did garner a second Pulitzer Prize for Wilder.

Wilder believed that he could achieve in drama what he failed to do in the novel.

He opens *Our Town* simply: "No curtain. No scenery." He soon introduces the people of Grover's Corner, New Hampshire, on specific days during the period from 1901 to 1913. The almost nonexistent plot revolves around two neighboring households—the Webbs and the Gibbs. Both families, eventually united by marriage, are unremarkable, and nothing very special happens to them or the other characters.

What makes *Our Town* unique is the character of the Stage Manager, who narrates the play, a technique Wilder had previously used in his one-act play *The Happy Journey to Trenton and Camden* (1931). Wilder's innovative use of this device sets him apart from other contemporary dramatists; the device draws its strength and roots from the Chorus concept employed by William Shakespeare and earlier by the Greeks. The character is not only a stage manager and narrator, but also a philosopher, druggist, Congregational minister, and wise seer. He represents a distillation of all of Wilder's wisdom, a fact not lost on the playwright, as he often played the role himself in various stage productions.

The Stage Manager embodies the spirit of the town by introducing a large number of characters and presenting the scenes chronologically to demonstrate his basic themes. Act 1 is called "Daily Life" and gives a glimpse of the people living in Grover's Corner and the two families. In act 2, three years later, entitled "Love and Marriage," the eldest child of each household—Emily Webb and George Gibbs—are married, and the events leading to that happy occasion, including their first date and declaration of love, are dramatized. The act concludes with the wedding ceremony.

Act 3 occurs nine years later and is called "Death." It is set in the town's cemetery, with dead townspeople sitting in chairs. Emily Webb Gibbs has died in childbirth, and she soon joins the others. Here Wilder cleverly brings past and present together by having Emily go back to Grover's Corner one more time to relive her twelfth birthday with her family. She quickly realizes that it is a mistake to be back among the living and cries out: "It goes so fast. We don't have time to look at one another." Wilder presses the point by having her also ask, "Do any human beings ever realize life while they live it?" The Stage Manager replies: "No. The saints and poets, maybe—they do some."

In *Our Town*, Wilder points out the precious gift of life and the value of even the most common and everyday events. Unaware of this, the people of Grover's Corner seldom scratch beyond the surface of their lives, the banal and the beautiful. Artistically, Wilder manages to make his point by taking the ordinary events and making them priceless. By focusing on growing up, love, marriage, and death and providing a running commentary via the Stage Manager on each phase, Wilder portrays life as trivial and absurd as well as significant and noble.

With *Our Town*, Wilder taps into a mythic vision of America and presents his characters, foibles and all, with love. He presents an ideal America that believes in the dignity of the human spirit. The playwright captures the essence of human nature, dramatizing the spirit of the eternal residing in the collective human psyche.

THE SKIN OF OUR TEETH

First produced: 1942 (first published, 1942)
Type of work: Play

A humorous and allegorical look at the survival of the family unit as it evolved during the prehistoric, biblical, and modern era.

Thornton Wilder's last great play was *The Skin of Our Teeth*, which opened on Broadway on November 18, 1942. The play, with its allegorical mixture of contemporary and biblical events, confused some of the critics but proved delightful to audiences and ran for 355 performances. The play has been revived frequently and in 1961 was given an international tour by the State Department with Helen Hayes and Mary Martin in the leading roles.

What Wilder dramatizes in *The Skin of Our Teeth* is the struggle of humankind to survive, a conceit much appreciated by wartime audiences. Again the author focuses on the family unit to make his point—in this case, the Antrobus (*anthropos* meaning story of humans) family living in Excelsior, New Jersey. The play does not have a continuous action. Although the settings are contemporary, each act is structured around a historic catastrophe: the Ice Age, the Flood, and modern war. Respectively, humans must pit themselves against nature, the moral order, and, finally, against themselves. Wilder's play can also be seen as units of time: geologic, biblical, and recorded.

Wilder's characters in *The Skin of Our Teeth* are all allegorical figures and exist on three planes: American, biblical, and universal. Mr. and Mrs. Antrobus are the simultaneous embodiment of Adam and Eve, Everyman and Everywoman, and an average American couple. Mr. Antrobus has created the wheel, the alphabet, and the lever; his spouse has contributed the apron. They keep as pets a dinosaur and mammoth. Their motto is "Save the Family." Daughter Gladys becomes increasingly sluttish and by play's end has an illegitimate baby. Son Henry (his name had been Cain but it was changed) accidentally kills his brother and now combs his hair to hide the mark on his forehead. In opposition to the Antrobus family is Lily Sabina (combination of Lilith and the Sabine women), who moves in and out of their lives in a variety of roles including that of a servant, a beauty contestant, and a Jezebel out to snare Mr. Antrobus.

As he did in *Our Town*, Wilder is able to employ in *The Skin of Our Teeth* a nontraditional, theatrical approach. By this device, the playwright draws the audience directly to the characters as individuals, at the same time making them function as representatives of the human race. To achieve this effect, Wilder has the characters drop their characterizations from time to time and reveal the performers hired to play the roles. He is thus able to present various personalities within each character.

The Skin of Our Teeth generally received favorable reviews, particularly for the acting of Tallulah Bankhead, who played Sabina. Unfortunately, the play also plunged Wilder into an unpleasant controversy. Three months after the play opened, Joseph Campbell and Henry M. Robinson wrote "The Skin of Whose Teeth?" in *The Saturday Review of Literature*, charging in the article that Wilder had borrowed the theme and technique of his play from James Joyce's *Finnegans Wake*, thus accusing him of plagiarism. Many writers and critics came to Wilder's defense and *Time* magazine, while not liking the play, asserted the attackers were "trying to make headlines out of what should have been footnotes." Wilder said nothing at the time, but in the 1957 edition of *Three Plays*, he admitted in the preface that he owed a debt to Joyce and slyly noted that he hoped "some author should feel similarly indebted to any work of mine."

As in other works, Wilder demonstrates an appreciative view of life in *The Skin of Our Teeth*. He shows how the human race can survive disasters, both natural and human-made. It is Wilder's humanity ending in faith that suffuses the entire play. Again, Wilder concentrates on the family, an emphasis technique found in his plays but not his other work. He skillfully juggles the serious and comic elements, telescopes time, and conveys his philosophic and poetic ideas. Wilder presents truth through the use of artifice and theatricality.

THEOPHILIS NORTH

First published: 1973
Type of work: Novel

A meddling, good-hearted stranger comes to Newport, Rhode Island, in the 1920's and proceeds to change the lives of all the people he meets.

Theophilis North, which was published in October, 1973, turned out to be Wilder's last novel published while he was still alive. Wilder's publishers, knowing their market, took out a full-page ad promoting the novel in *The New York Times*, an honor most authors never realize. The publicity worked and the novel received very favorable comments from the critics. *Theophilis North* was a huge success with Wilder's adoring public. The book remained on the best-seller list for twenty-one weeks. It is a nostalgic piece with many autobiographical elements. Wilder's own brother, Amos, in his critical study, *Thornton Wilder and His Public*, believed that the author was haunted throughout his life by his missing twin, his alter ego. Amos suggested that "North" represented an anagram for Thornton, and "in this way he was able to tease both himself and the reader as to the borderlands between autobiography and fable." *Theophilis North* is labeled a novel but is really a collection of short stories held together by a narrator who willingly participates in all the events he describes. Wilder labeled the book fictionalized memoirs, an autobiography, and a novel. The central character did indeed have similar experiences to those of Wilder, but the author reshaped the material so much that the work should be viewed as a series of tales in the tradition of works by Lucius Apuleius, Geoffrey Chaucer, or Giovanni Boccaccio.

Early in the book, the reader is told by Theophilis North that he had many ambitions in life. He proceeds to enumerate them in the following order: saint, anthropologist, archaeologist, detective, actor, magician, lover, and a free man. The narrator is quick to point out that he never wanted to be in business or politics. A few pages later, North describes Newport, Rhode Island, as if he were the archaeologist Heinrich Schliemann commenting on the fabled Troy's nine cities piled on top of one another. Each of North's "cities," beginning with the first seventeenth century village, becomes increasingly complex until he reaches the eighth level, full "of campfollowers and parasites—prying journalists, detectives, fortune-hunters . . . wonderful material for my Journal."

The narrator's series of adventures varies according to his involvements. He comes to Newport in 1926 to teach tennis to children, give language instruction, and read classical literature to older people. North is quickly drawn into the social life of the very rich because he is a Yale University man and a Christian. In short order, he thwarts an elopement between an heiress and a divorced athletic instructor, removes the taint of ghosts from a beautiful haunted mansion, brings back to health a retired diplomat being manipulated by his children, shrewdly exposes a gang of counterfeiters, and fathers a child for a married woman whose husband is sterile. Both praised and despised, North becomes a manipulator for good in people's lives. Wilder makes it clear that Theophilis North is a liberating influence who can mend broken marriages and inspire men and women to achieve their most secret desires. North never changes despite his myriad experiences, the numerous people he has helped, and the beautiful woman with whom he is intimate. He is a superior creature with no apparent flaws. He remains to the end an idealized boy scout who proves that good can overcome evil.

Theophilis North would be Wilder's last happy affirmation of life. He created a character who enjoyed life to the fullest and, in some ways, honestly reflected the author's own views of life. To the end of his literary career, Wilder was still concerned about injustice, the achievement of the human spirit, and the positive values of humanistic belief in individual responsibility.

Summary

Thornton Wilder remains one of America's most beloved novelists, dramatists, and persons of letters. His books and plays are widely read and staged, continuing to give enjoyment and intellectual stimulation. Wilder was the first author to win Pulitzer Prizes in both fiction and drama. His work includes both a large dose of human suffering and the belief that life is a miraculous gift to be cherished. Wilder was a mature humanist who reaffirmed the dignity of the individual and the uniqueness of American democracy. His classic work, *Our Town*, has been performed many thousands of times since its premiere in 1938.

Bibliography

Goldstein, Malcolm. *The Art of Thornton Wilder.* Lincoln: University of Nebraska Press, 1965.

Goldstone, Richard H. *Thornton Wilder: An Intimate Portrait.* New York: Saturday Review Press, 1975.

Grebanier, Bernard. *Thornton Wilder.* Minneapolis: University of Minnesota Press, 1964.

Haberman, Donald. *The Plays of Thornton Wilder: A Critical Study.* Middletown, Conn.: Wesleyan University Press, 1967.

Harrison, Gilbert A. *The Enthusiast: A Life of Thornton Wilder.* New York: Ticknor & Fields, 1983.

Papajewski, Helmut. *Thornton Wilder.* New York: Frederick Ungar, 1965.

Simon, Linda. *Thornton Wilder: His World.* Garden City, N.Y.: Doubleday, 1979.

Stresau, Herman. *Thornton Wilder.* New York: Frederick Ungar, 1971.

Wilder, Amos Niven. *Thornton Wilder and His Public.* Philadelphia: Fortress Press, 1980.

Terry Theodore

TENNESSEE WILLIAMS

Born: Columbus, Mississippi
March 26, 1911
Died: New York, New York
February 25, 1983

Principal Literary Achievement

One of America's major dramatists, Williams, also a poet and writer of short stories, is considered the poet of the American theater; he is to drama what William Faulkner is to the American novel.

Biography

Thomas Lanier Williams, known as Tom during his boyhood and later as Tennessee, was born in his maternal grandparents' home, an Episcopalian rectory in Columbus, Mississippi, on March 26, 1911, to Edwina Dakin and Cornelius Coffin Williams. His mother came from a prominent old Mississippi family with a liberal tradition, and his father from an equally prominent old Tennessee family, but with a proud military and patriotic background. Williams was immediately thrust into a conflict between the genteel Puritanism of his mother and the cavalier life-style of his father. From his father's origins, he was given his nickname, and he chose to stay with it for the rest of his life. Because of his father's continual absence from home during Williams' boyhood, he developed an unusual closeness to both mother and sister and a distance from, and sometimes hostility toward, his father. His escape from his family was, ironically, similar to that of his father, even though it was a result of the classical conflict between the restrictions of the conventionally polite Southern upbringing and the necessary freedom of the artistic life.

His boyhood experiences included many happy hours of reading spent in the library of his maternal grandfather, with whom Williams maintained a close relationship until his grandfather's death in his nineties. Williams had strong support, as well, from his maternal grandmother, who would send him money from time to time.

Few dramatists write so autobiographically as did Williams in *The Glass Menagerie* (1944). Williams based the character of Amanda Wingfield on his mother. Her husband, a shadowy but important character who does not appear in the play (except for his picture hanging on the wall), is referred to as having run away as a result of a love affair with long-distance telephone wires. Williams' own father once worked

2135

briefly for a telephone company before becoming a traveling salesman for the International Shoe Company. The fragile, introverted character of Laura Wingfield is drawn from his sister Rose, the victim of a cruel prefrontal lobotomy, an event that left its psychological mark on her brother. Tom Wingfield, like the real-life Tom, leaves home, but wherever he travels for the rest of his life, he is haunted by the memory of Laura. Finally, there is the shabby St. Louis apartment in which the Wingfields live, like the progressively downscaled residences of the Williams family as their financial condition declined. Considered by many Williams' best play, *The Glass Menagerie* is one of the three most famous plays about the American family. The other two are Eugene O'Neill's *Long Day's Journey into Night* (1956) and Arthur Miller's *Death of a Salesman* (1949), the Catholic and Jewish versions, respectively, of Williams' Protestant family. Williams' other plays, although not so closely autobiographical, also draw on Williams' own experiences and, for all their theatricality, have the ring of authenticity.

Williams' nomadic life began during his university years. Having won literary prizes at the University of Missouri and then having been withdrawn from the university by his father for failing a Reserve Officers' Training Corps course, he worked as a shoe company stock clerk for three years. Finding the work intolerably boring, he returned to university, this time enrolling at Washington University in St. Louis, where he soon found congeniality with a theater group, The Mummers. In still another move, he transferred to the famous writers' school at the University of Iowa, from which he graduated in 1937.

After his first produced play (in Memphis, 1935), a farce entitled *Cairo, Shanghai, Bombay!*, Williams had two plays produced by the Mummers in St. Louis in 1936. Soon, grant money began coming in from the Group Theater, the Rockefeller Foundation, the American Academy of Arts and Letters; Williams also received money from Hollywood in the form of a six-month contract with Metro-Goldwyn-Mayer. Among the many ironies of his life, one of the earliest is MGM's turning down of his writing, including *The Glass Menagerie*, in 1943. He continued, however, to be paid for the six months of his contract.

There is hardly a year after 1944 (when *The Glass Menagerie* opened in Chicago) in which a new play, a revised play, a play adapted from a short story, a film, or a collection of poems or short stories was not produced or published. In New York, *The Glass Menagerie, A Streetcar Named Desire* (1947), and *Cat on a Hot Tin Roof* (1955) won prizes such as the Drama Critics Circle Award, the Pulitzer Prize, and the Sidney Howard Memorial Award. With the influx of success and money, Williams' nomadic life included trips to Paris and Italy and various residences in New York, Nantucket, Key West, and New Orleans. Like his boyhood, his adult life included bouts with illnesses, some of them nervous breakdowns. These were complicated by drink, barbiturates, and his rebelliously bohemian life-style as a homosexual in a puritanically repressed society. Late in life, Williams converted to Roman Catholicism.

In his *Memoirs* (1975), Williams reveals with graphic detail his intimate personal and professional experiences. His most enduring and serious relationship was with Frank Merlo, whose death from cancer in the 1960's devastated Williams. Among his long-standing theater friends were his New York agent, Audrey Wood, and actresses Maureen Stapleton and Anna Magnani. His plays and films attracted the major acting talents of his time, among them Margaret Leighton, Vivien Leigh, Vanessa Redgrave, Geraldine Page, Katharine Hepburn, Elizabeth Ashley, Paul Newman, and Jason Robards. On stage, Laurette Taylor in *The Glass Menagerie* and the duo of Marlon Brando and Jessica Tandy in *A Streetcar Named Desire* became legends in their own time. An important part of those legends was director and personal friend Elia Kazan, who was involved in the direction of a number of Williams' plays.

The awards heaped on his three most successful dramas, however, avoided many of Williams' other plays. Consequently, disappointment and bitterness with critics took their toll on him physically and psychologically. In *Small Craft Warnings* (1972), Williams even acted in a small role, hoping thereby to prolong the play's run.

The circumstance of Williams' death is ironically trivial. On February 25, 1983, he was found in his New York apartment, choked by a plastic bottle cap, evidently in an attempt to ingest barbiturates. Despite his nomadic life-style, Williams had a constant need for some permanent human attachment—provided early by his maternal grandparents, his mother, and sister, and later by Merlo. All but Rose were gone at the time of his death. One is reminded of the loneliness of many of his characters and of what is one of the most famous lines in his plays, pronounced by Blanche DuBois in *A Streetcar Named Desire*, a line referring to her constant dependence on the kindness of strangers.

Analysis

Among the four generally acknowledged major American dramatists—Eugene O'Neill, Tennessee Williams, Arthur Miller, and Edward Albee—Williams holds the distinction of being the poet in the theater. The same year, 1944, that *The Glass Menagerie* opened in Chicago, some of his poems were published in *Five American Poets*. Revised, some of these poems reappeared in a later volume, *In the Winter of Cities* (1956). Williams' poems contain many of the themes, images, and musical qualities that dominate the style of his plays. One of his most famous characters, Tom Wingfield, was nicknamed Shakespeare by his fellow workers in a shoe factory because, as a loner, he wrote poems rather than join in their social amenities.

Williams' most prominent and all-inclusive theme is the effect of an aggressively competitive society on sensitive characters such as Laura and Tom Wingfield (*The Glass Menagerie*), Blanche DuBois (*A Streetcar Named Desire*), Brick and Maggie Pollitt (*Cat on a Hot Tin Roof*), Alma Winemiller (*Summer and Smoke*, 1947), Catharine Holly and Sebastian Venable (*Suddenly Last Summer*, 1958), and The Rev. Shannon and Hannah Jelkes (*The Night of the Iguana*, 1961)—all social outcasts in that society.

Related to the theme of the outcast is that of the poet-artist. Laura has her collection of glass animals, Tom his poetry, Blanche and Alma that extraordinary delicacy of Williams' heroines which made irreconcilable the conflict between mind and body, Sebastian his poetry, and Hannah (the daughter of a ninety-seven-year-old poet) her portrait painting. Basic to the artistic nature is the insistence on, indeed passion for, truth and an equally persistent hatred of hypocrisy. The consequence of this love-hate duality is the doomed fate of the artist, who is therefore frequently depicted in Darwinian images of fragile creatures devoured by monstrous animals in the fight for survival of the fittest.

The dominance of the strong over the weak and of the "normal" over the poetic finds its most recurrent expression in Williams in repressed, perverse, or abnormal sexual experiences, demonstrated most delicately in the life of Laura and most violently in that of Sebastian. Between these extremes are found Blanche, Brick and Maggie, Alma (a "white-blooded spinster"), and Shannon and Hannah (a strong and practical support of her nonagenarian poet-father).

The landscapes of the plays are as important as are the characters and the themes; all are inextricably bound up in one another. The world of Laura and Tom is that of the 1930's, in which the atrocities of the Spanish Civil War, suggested in a reference to what is generally regarded as the single most famous painting of the twentieth century, Picasso's "Guernica," are ignored by a United States described as a school for the matriculation of the blind. More immediately, the Wingfield family is imprisoned in a shabby apartment described as resembling a cage (a symbol that evokes the same situation in O'Neill's 1922 play *The Hairy Ape*). Blanche's New Orleans is dominated by the images of two streetcars, one named Desire and the other Cemeteria, with Blanche's stop on that famous streetcar ride being the Elysian Fields. The landscape inhabited by Alma Winemiller includes a statue of Eternity in a public square—wings outstretched—and the office of a doctor: the eternal pitted against the ephemeral, the idealistic or spiritual against the physical. In their separate battles for survival, Brick and Maggie, a childless couple, find themselves in a Southern mansion, opposing the insensitivities of a normal family with the famous "no-neck monsters." The most exotic of Williams' landscapes, perhaps, is the veritable hothouse of *Suddenly Last Summer*—a luxuriant, junglelike profusion of an Henri Rousseau painting, again in New Orleans—created by Sebastian's mother in order to provide her son with the necessary seclusion and atmosphere for his poetry writing. Like Blanche, Sebastian and his mother travel, but their journey takes them to the Galápagos Islands (or the Encantades, the "enchanted isles"), where Galápagos sea turtles flee from flesh-eating birds, and then to Italy, where the symbolic eating of human flesh occurs.

Williams' themes are dramatized in three major styles in *The Glass Menagerie*, *A Streetcar Named Desire*, and *Suddenly Last Summer*. These styles—poetry, theatricality, and lush symbolism—at their strongest, are found, respectively, in the realistic expressionism of *The Glass Menagerie*, the naturalistic theatricality of *A Streetcar Named Desire*, and the exotic surrealism of *Suddenly Last Summer*. Perhaps the least successful of the styles he employed is illustrated in *Small Craft Warnings*, written in the mode of Maxim Gorky's *Na dne* (1902; *The Lower Depths*, 1912) and O'Neill's

The Iceman Cometh (1946). A gathering of a variety of social outcasts in a California oceanside bar, a means to examining a cross-section of society, becomes a pale reincarnation of characters in his earlier plays.

Attacked in the 1950's by *Time* magazine and by some critics, such as George Jean Nathan and Mary McCarthy, for his increasing violence, depravity, and vulgarity, Williams found his critical stature bolstered not only by prestigious awards but also by other critics and by scholars whose analyses have offset what seem, in retrospect, like incredibly puritanical earlier views. In 1971, Ruby Cohn wrote that although she regards Williams' plays as narrow in range and his heavy reliance on symbols as weakening the drive of some plays, in his best work "Williams expands American stage dialogue in vocabulary, image, rhythm, and range." It is the impact of Williams' poetic language and imagery on the American stage that remains his distinctive contribution to American drama, even though they are extravagantly overdone in his lesser plays.

C. W. E. Bigsby, a British scholar of American drama, contends that with the single exception of the plays of O'Neill, those of Williams, Miller, and Albee are undoubtedly "the outstanding achievement of the American theatre." In his obituary on Williams, Frank Rich, a critic for *The New York Times*, places Williams second only to O'Neill.

THE GLASS MENAGERIE

First produced: 1944 (first published, 1945)
Type of work: Play

In the Depression era of the 1930's, an unhappy St. Louis family of three—mother, son, and daughter—is caught in a struggle between economic survival and keeping some semblance of beauty in their lives.

Tennessee Williams begins *The Glass Menagerie* with a comment by Tom Wingfield, who serves as both narrator of and character within the play: "Yes, I have tricks in my pocket, I have things up my sleeve. But I am the opposite of a stage magician. He gives you illusion that has the appearance of truth. I give you truth in the pleasant disguise of illusion." In one sentence, Williams has summarized the essence of all drama. To the very end of the play, he maintains a precarious balance between truth and illusion, creating in the process what he contends is the "essential ambiguity of man that I think needs to be stated."

Williams suspends the audience of his interplay between reality and illusion by having Tom, who has run away from home, serve as a storyteller. As he remembers bits of his past, he fades from the role of narrator into the role of character and then back again, providing a realistic objectivity to a highly subjective experience. The transitions between past and present are accomplished by the use of lighting, legends (signs), and mood-creating music. Both outsider and insider, Tom cannot escape from the memories that haunt him; traveling in some foreign country, he sees or hears something that reminds him of his past. In writing a memory play, Williams successfully balances past with present, illusion with reality, fragility with brutality, mind with body, freedom of the imagination with imprisonment of the real world, and other unresolvable paradoxes of life. The combining of narrator and character in one person is itself a paradox, as Tom tells his story both from the outside looking in and vice versa.

Tom Wingfield's story is about himself, a young man who finds himself working as a stock clerk in a shoe factory to provide a living for his mother, Amanda, and his sister, Laura. The father has long since deserted the family. Only his larger-than-life photograph hangs on a wall to remind Tom of a father "who left us a long time ago" because, as a telephone man, he had "fallen in love with long distances . . . and skipped the light fantastic out of town."

Both the photograph and the family's economic plight serve to remind Amanda of the many "gentleman callers" she might have married instead of her ne'er-do-well husband. She escapes into the past even as she attempts to make things happen in the present, supplementing Tom's income by selling women's magazines over the telephone. She also attempts to provide Laura with some means of earning a living by sending her to a business school to learn typing. Rather than having Laura become a barely tolerated spinster among her relatives, Amanda wishes to see her able to support herself. Amanda's instinct for the preservation of the family (reality) and her memories of her girlhood and the many gentleman callers (illusion) give her life a balance in a world that otherwise would be overwhelming in its dreariness.

Laura, a victim of her family situation, is painfully conscious of her "crippled" condition, one leg being shorter than the other. She throws up from nervous indigestion in her early days at Rubicam's Business College and, after that experience, spends her time walking in the park and visiting the art museum, the zoo, and the "big glass house where they raise the tropical flowers." She herself is a hothouse flower, needing special care. In the family apartment, she has still another escape, her collection of glass animals, the most singular of which is a unicorn, a nonexistent animal. In a Darwinian world, her survivability, like the unicorn's, is questionable.

Like his mother and sister, Tom, suffocated by the mindlessness of his job, has created his own world, writing poetry at work and earning the nickname "Shakespeare" from his fellow workers. He spends his evenings attending motion pictures, which in the 1930's also included live acts, frequently those of a magician.

All three family members hold in precarious balance their respective worlds of reality and illusion. In an ironic sense, all three are like the husband and father who sought escape. The catalyst for a change in the family situation is Laura's inability to continue in business college and Amanda's decision that a gentleman caller be found for Laura. Much against his better judgment, and after many emotional arguments with Amanda, Tom gives in to her repeated requests that he invite a fellow worker, Jim, to dinner. On that fateful day, a rather ordinary one which Williams succeeds in making extraordinary, Jim arrives.

Predictably, Amanda has bought new furnishings—a floor lamp and rug—and new clothes for Laura. Appearances, so important to Amanda, have improved, but ironically Laura is seized with a nervous attack. To make matters worse, the electricity goes off during the dinner, Tom having failed to pay the electric bill. Candles, however, save the day. Laura recovers a bit, and in one of the most touching scenes in American drama, she enjoys a brief romantic moment with Jim—a dance and kiss. In that dance, however, the unicorn, swept off its shelf, is broken, a symbol of Laura's shattered dream when she is told by Jim that he is already engaged to someone else.

Following one final, desperate argument with the bitterly disappointed Amanda, who shouts to him to "go to the moon," Tom runs away, not to the moon, as he says, but "much further—for time is the longest distance between two places." He attempts "to find in motion what was lost in space."

Williams' techniques, in addition to the use of a narrator, are those made famous by Bertolt Brecht, a German dramatist whose expressionism influenced many modern dramatists. Among the Brechtian techniques found in *The Glass Menagerie* are its use of lighting, the signs (legends) that provide the audience with information, and music that enhances either the romance or the harshness of the mood of the moment. Brechtian techniques make for a loosely told story in episodic scenes rather than a tightly knit sequence of actions that produce high drama.

A STREETCAR NAMED DESIRE

First produced: 1947 (first published, 1947)
Type of work: Play

In a run-down 1940's New Orleans French Quarter setting, Blanche DuBois, Williams' most famous Southern belle, finally resolves a lifetime of psychological and cultural conflicts.

On a streetcar named Desire, Blanche DuBois travels from the railroad station in New Orleans to a street named Elysian Fields, where her sister, Stella, married to Stanley Kowalski and pregnant, lives in a run-down apartment building in the old French Quarter. Having lost her husband, parents, teaching position, and the old family home—Belle Reve in Laurel, Mississippi—Blanche has nowhere to turn but to her one remaining close relative. Thirty years old, Blanche is emotionally and economically destitute. The most traumatic experience in her life was the discovery that her husband—a poet whom she had married at the tender age of sixteen—was a homosexual. Soon after she had taunted him for his sexual impotence, he committed suicide. Their confrontation had occurred in Moon Lake Casino, ubiquitous in Williams' plays as a house of illusions. In her subsequent guilt over his death, she found temporary release in a series of sexual affairs, the latest having involved one of her young students and having resulted in her dismissal.

She is horrified at the circumstances in which her sister Stella lives and at the man to whom she is married. Polish, uneducated, inarticulate, and working-class, but sexually attractive, he has won Stella by his sheer masculinity. Stella, according to production notes by director Elia Kazan, has been narcotized by his sexual superiority. A fourth important character, Stanley's poker-playing companion Mitch, is attracted to Blanche. She is attracted to his kindness to her, for he is gentle in his manner, as Stanley is not. She refers at one point to having found God in Mitch's arms, a religious reference frequently made by Williams' characters at important moments in their lives.

The action of the play, then, as in Greek tragedy, consists of the final events in Blanche's life. Tensions grow between her and Stanley, even as her physical attraction to him becomes palpable. She expresses her contempt for his coarseness and animality. In scene after scene, she reminds him constantly of their cultural differences. Their hostilities develop into a Strindbergian battle of the sexes for the affection of Stella. Blanche eventually loses not only Stella but also Mitch, a possible husband.

The theatrically ironic climax occurs on Blanche's birthday while Stella is in the hospital giving birth to her baby. Blanche has prettied up the apartment for her birthday. Drunk and inflamed by Blanche's taunts into proving his superiority, Stanley rapes her in what is Williams' most famous and most highly theatrical scene. Simultaneously repulsed and attracted by his sheer rawness, Blanche acts out her final rebellion against her genteel but sexually repressive background, as though to punish herself for violating her "soul." Her struggle with Stanley is the last in a series of losses in Blanche's life. Her delicate sensibility already strained to the breaking point when she had first arrived, she breaks down and at the end is led away to a mental institution.

As in *The Glass Menagerie*, there are candles, these on her birthday cake. Like the lights that go out in Laura's life and that forever after haunt Tom, Blanche's are symbolically extinguished. In the red pajamas that Stanley wears for the occasion, the blue candles on the cake, the extravagantly old-fashioned dresses that Blanche wears, the festive decorations, and Williams' use of music and lights, the illusions of Blanche's world are highlighted. In contrast, the repulsive vulgarity and the attractive animality of Stanley's world are symbolized in details such as the opening scene in which Stanley throws Stella a package of raw meat and the famous beer-bottle-opening scene at the birthday party. Such violently opposing images are the hallmarks of Williams' highly theatrical poetry.

Even more than in *The Glass Menagerie* when Tom descends the staircase of the Wingfield's St. Louis apartment for the last time, Blanche's arrival at the Kowalski's home suggests a descent into the lower regions. It is her final descent into a mythical underworld, in which, like Orpheus, she is psychologically mutilated and eaten. In this modern American variation of the Greek myth, which Williams dramatizes more directly in *Orpheus Descending* (1957) and more violently in *Suddenly Last Sum-*

mer, one of the stops the streetcar makes is Cemetery; the Elysian Fields, ironically, is Blanche's last stop before her insanity and death.

The play's strongest effects can be found in Williams' use of language and in the many symbols. The lines remaining in the memories of those who have seen *A Streetcar Named Desire* epitomize the strong contrasts which lie at the center of the play: Stanley's bullish bellowing of "Stella, Stella" and Blanche's confession, "I have always been dependent on the kindness of strangers." Brutishness and reason, body and soul, mastery and dependency vie for survival in Stanley and Blanche. As the full embodiment of the Williams heroine, Blanche evokes the character of Margaret Mitchell's Scarlett O'Hara in *Gone with the Wind* (1936). Stanley is one of a long line of American anti-heroes—inarticulate, alienated, and sexually powerful, similar to popular film heroes of the 1950's such as Marlon Brando and James Dean.

In the loss of Belle Reve and the acceptance by Stella of a new life—the world of Stanley and of the kind but inarticulate Mitch—Williams, like Anton Chekhov in *Vishnyovy sad* (1904; *The Cherry Orchard*, 1908), dramatizes the replacing of one era by another. Like August Strindberg in *Fröken Julie* (1888; *Miss Julie*, 1912), Williams sees the social aristocracy being replaced by a coarser but more vital one. Social Darwinism is the basis for the change. As Stella rejects the old values and asserts dominance, audience sympathy for Blanche's vulnerability grows measurably. Regarded generally as Williams' most compactly constructed play, *A Streetcar Named Desire* is a dramatization of a heroine with few, if any, peers in her impact on the consciousness of the American theatrical tradition.

SUMMER AND SMOKE

First produced: 1947 (first published, 1948)
Type of work: Play

Alma Winemiller finds the irreconcilability of the conflict between body and soul impossible and eventually gives up one for the other.

Stylistically, *Summer and Smoke* is Williams' realistic compromise between the poetic expressionism of *The Glass Menagerie* and the violent theatricality of *A Streetcar Named Desire*. Although this play is more conventionally realistic than the other two, it is also his most allegorical statement on the conflict between the soul and the body, between innocence and experience, and between eternity and life—themes taking various forms in all of Williams' plays. The play is also one of Williams' three treatments of a character named Alma, the other being an earlier short story, "The Yellow Bird," and a later play, *The Eccentricities of a Nightingale* (1964).

Its allegorical realism consists of Williams' apparently simple and clear portraits of three women, the most important of whom is Alma (her name means "soul") the daughter of a minister and his increasingly senile wife. Like Laura Wingfield, Alma has a deformity, but hers is of the soul rather than of the body: a chastity of mind that in the early years of her life repressed her sexuality and slowly developed into a revulsion against the physicality of sex and then, later in the play, into an unconventional (for her) appetite for the physical aspects of sex. Rosa Gonzales, on the other hand, the daughter of the owner of Moon Lake Casino (a recurrent symbol of the pleasures of the body in Williams' plays), is the embodiment of physical (sexual) attraction, the allegorical opposite of Alma's chastity-dominated soul. A third character, Nellie Ewell, a former piano pupil of Alma's, represents a balance between the extremities represented by Alma and Rosa. Eventually, she marries Dr. John Buchanan, the young doctor who has been at various times attracted to Alma and Rosa. As a character, Nellie is even less developed than is Stella in *A Streetcar Named Desire* and is much less interesting dramatically. Even their names suggest their respective fates: Alma, purity; Rosa, the glow of life; and John and Nellie, normality.

Alma, the minister's daughter who has grown up next door to John, and John, the son of a doctor, are representative small-town American characters. John had his taste of an exciting life away in medical school, but Alma retained her small-town interests. Still in love with John, she has remained the product of the polite and conventional Southern white, Protestant ethic. Her life consists of participation in the usual local events, such as the town picnics at which she sings. John, just graduated from medical school, returns home, still sowing his wild oats. He is attracted sexually to Rosa and, in one brief and unsuccessful encounter, to Alma. Characters change, as John slowly settles into the domestic and professional routines of a doctor's life, and Alma, like Blanche DuBois, reverses dramatically, giving herself up to the claims of the body. She is seen at the end leaving for Moon Lake Casino with Archie Kramer, a traveling salesman. Roger Boxhill, in his 1985 study of Williams' plays, sees John's change as developmental and Alma's as fundamental.

The mixture of the realism of small-town life with allegorical symbolism contrasts with the artistry of *The Glass Menagerie* and *A Streetcar Named Desire*. Symbols and their meanings tend to have a one-to-one ratio, a characteristic of the allegorical style. There is, for example, the opening scene at the fountain square, with the statue of an Angel of Eternity, her wings outspread and her hands cupped as through ready to drink. Lights flash on and off the statue at various points in the play, indicating the change that is happening to Alma. At the end, as she walks away with the salesman, she waves her hand in what seems like a goodbye, first to the angel and then to her house. Seen by some as an allegorical treatment of the conflict between body and soul, the play is seen by others as a painfully sensitive farewell by Alma to the values of her Southern small-town legacy. The world to which she bids farewell is a variation of that of Amanda and Laura Wingfield, Blanche DuBois, and women in later plays.

The young Dr. Buchanan is one of Williams' rare healthy survivors in the conflicts generated between body and soul. Like Stella, Nellie married, but unlike Stella, her marriage represents an ascent, rather than a descent. As decent and "normal" human beings, they are juxtaposed against the pathetic Alma. With its theatricality and poetry muted by the allegorical style, *Summer and Smoke* is less forceful than *The Glass Menagerie* and *A Streetcar Named Desire*, but it is nevertheless a moving drama.

CAT ON A HOT TIN ROOF

First produced: 1955 (first published, 1955)
Type of work: Play

In a wealthy Southern ancestral home, a family celebration becomes the scene of major confrontations.

In *Cat on a Hot Tin Roof*, the cat is Maggie Pollitt, married to Brick, the favorite son of a wealthy plantation owner, Big Daddy, and the hot tin roof is the desperate measures she takes to regain her husband's sexual interest and to lay claim to her husband's family fortune. Opposing her are the family members of Gooper Pollitt, Brick's brother. Gooper's family consists of his pregnant wife and their five children (Williams' famous "no-neck monsters"). Finally there is Big Mama, whose current status with her own husband is much like Maggie's with Brick.

The estrangement between the silently suffering Brick and his loquacious father is the result of Brick's dropping out of professional football and sportscasting and his turning to alcohol. Pained by the suicide of his best friend, Skipper, he says he must drink until he hears a click in his head, a guarantor of relief from his pain. Big Daddy's inability to understand Brick is fueled by rumors that Brick's and Skipper's closeness was homosexual in nature. The strain between Maggie and Brick is caused by Maggie's having gone to Skipper to confront him with his possible homosexuality. Shortly thereafter, Skipper committed suicide. Brick's loss of Skipper is intensified by Maggie's having made something dirty of what he said was a pure love.

Contrasting strongly with Brick, Gooper is successful both as a lawyer and as a prolific breeder of children. Gooper's family, particularly his wife, resents Big Daddy's favoritism regarding Brick and take advantage of every opportunity to change the situation. Thus the battle lines are drawn on what was to be a festive occasion, a celebration of Big Daddy's sixty-fifth birthday. Maggie, playing on his favoritism, lies about being pregnant and then attempts to seduce Brick into making her pregnant. In a climactic scene between Big Daddy and Brick, the latter drops a bombshell: the truth regarding his father's cancerous condition.

The play exists in several versions, the original having been altered by Elia Kazan for the premiere in New York in 1955. The original version was partly restored in 1974 and completely performed in 1990. In the three major productions, Barbara

Bel Geddes, Elizabeth Ashley, and Kathleen Turner, respectively, played Maggie, the different verions allowing each to play distinctively different Maggies. In the original version, Brick does not support Maggie in her lie to Big Daddy, and it is uncertain whether Maggie has wooed Brick from his alcoholism and whether in his own mind Brick was convinced that his feeling for Skipper was Platonic. Also, Big Daddy does not reappear on stage after his big scene with Brick.

The play's structure is unwieldy and irregular, in contrast with the rhythmically expressionistic structure of *The Glass Menagerie* or the rapidly developing tensions in *A Streetcar Named Desire*. Maggie's long speeches are like operatic arias, accompanied by the equally long silences of Brick. Similarly, the towering role of Big Daddy seems at times to vie with Maggie's. Both have the same purpose: to rescue Brick and to rehabilitate him. Despite Maggie's titular role, her sexual attractiveness, and her sympathy-evoking if "mendacious" attempts to triumph over Gooper's family, it is the strong emotional honesty between Big Daddy and Brick for which Williams writes his most compelling moment in the play. Big Daddy's sudden and unexpected confrontation with the imminence of his death (at a time when he was looking forward once more to testing his sexual prowess) and Brick's silent suffering of pain and guilt over Skipper's death brilliantly counterpoint Maggie's attempt to create life, even when that attempt involves a distant husband and a lie that she hopes to turn into a truth.

The big scene between Big Daddy and Brick is magisterial in the former's disclosure of all the lies he has put up with all of his married life and his true feelings toward Big Mama, Gooper, Mae, and their five noisy children. Torn between his hatred of them and his reluctance to make Brick, an alcoholic, the legatee of his will, he insists on honesty from Brick regarding his drinking and his relationship with Skipper. It is Big Daddy's reference to homosexual innuendoes regarding Skipper that causes Brick to disclose Maggie's jealousy of his clean friendship with Skipper during their road trips as professional football players. He accuses Maggie of destroying Skipper by suggesting to him a "dirty" relationship. Big Daddy, however, refuses to allow Brick to "pass the buck," whereupon Brick, inflamed, taunts Big Daddy with the irony of the requisite happy returns of his sixty-fifth birthday "when ev'rybody but you knows there won't be any." One truth after another tumbles from the opera-like duet between father and son, replacing the lies with which both have lived. Big Daddy's anger is that of a man betrayed, as he leaves the stage howling with rage. Although he does not appear in act 3, he is heard offstage crying out in pain. The scene between Big Daddy and Brick is one of two legendary father-son confrontations in American drama, the other being that between Biff and Willy Loman in Arthur Miller's *Death of a Salesman*.

With much of the humor and theatricality of *A Streetcar Named Desire*, but without its compact structure, *Cat on a Hot Tin Roof* remains a compelling play. The names of Big Daddy, Maggie, and Brick have been imprinted permanently on the American stage along with those of Amanda, Laura, and Tom Wingfield, Blanche DuBois, and Stanley Kowalski.

SUDDENLY LAST SUMMER

First produced: 1958 (first published, 1958)
Type of Work: Play

Catharine Holly, despite the threat of a lobotomy, finds peace when she is finally able to tell the truth of the fate of her cousin, Sebastian Venable.

"Suddenly last summer" is a refrain that runs through the many interrupted attempts of Catharine Holly to tell a psychologist the truth about what happened to Sebastian Venable along the harbor of an Italian resort, Cabeza de Lobo. He had been protected all of his life by his mother, and he had used her the last few years of his life to procure partners for his sexual appetite. On her part, Mrs. Venable will go to any length to preserve the reputation of her son as a poet, for to her "the work of a poet is the life of the poet" and vice versa. Together, she and Sebastian traveled widely and luxuriously for twenty years. During each summer, he composed a poem, which Mrs. Venable had compiled into a gilt-edged volume. Then one summer he suddenly stopped writing. It is what happened this summer, the final one in Sebastian's rapidly deteriorating life, that Catharine, like Samuel Taylor Coleridge's ancient mariner, must tell.

When Mrs. Venable had a stroke one summer, Sebastian asked Catharine Holly, his cousin, to travel with him in his mother's place. Loving her cousin, even when she realized that she was being used as a lure to attract homosexual partners for him, she subsequently witnessed his physical mutilation by a mob of hungry young Italians who tore at his flesh, stuffing their mouths as they did so.

The play is set in the Garden District of New Orleans, a contrast with the old French Quarter setting of *A Streetcar Named Desire*. The setting includes the surrealistically lush fantastic garden "which is more like a tropical jungle." Everything about the garden is violent—its colors, its harsh and sibilant noises that resemble "beasts, serpents and birds, all of a savage nature." Throughout the play, harsh noises as background underscore the harshness of the action.

In this setting, one year after her son's death, 1936, Mrs. Venable, in an attempt to preserve her son's memory, threatens to contest her son's will, which leaves a substantial amount of money to Catharine. Suffering from the trauma of witnessing the death of Sebastian and from her inability to stop his mutilation, she has been under intense psychological stress. The plot of the play involves the arrival of Catharine, her mother, her brother, a doctor, and a Catholic sister at the Venable residence; the psychologist has come to discover the truth and Mrs. Venable to preserve her illusion about Sebastian. When Catharine finally reveals all, with the help of a drug, her revelation includes an even more lurid detail: Mrs. Venable herself had, like Catharine later, been a procuress for her son's sexual habits. The play concludes with Mrs. Venable's attempt to strike Catharine upon the latter's concluding her story with the graphic details of Sebastian's mutilation.

At one point, Catharine's necessity to tell the truth, a truth so horrible that even God could not change it, is a contrapuntal theme to Mrs. Venable's talk about Sebastian's search for God, whom Sebastian had once tried to find in a Buddhist monastery. That search is linked with another trip on which she had taken Sebastian—to the Galápagos Islands, where they witnessed giant sea turtles (after being hatched) fleeing from flesh-eating vultures. Most turtles did not survive. In that experience, she says, Sebastian had seen God. Ironically, that Galápagos image, Mrs. Venable's legacy to her son, became a self-fulfilling prophecy.

The action of the play, consisting of Catharine's many attempts to tell the truth, ends with that truth finally being told and with her finally finding some respite from the mental torture of living with her story for the past year, unable to utter its horror.

THE NIGHT OF THE IGUANA

First produced: 1961 (first published, 1961)
Type of work: Play

In a seedy Mexican tourist hotel during the off-season, three expatriate Americans are caught up in a private war among themselves and with a group of tourists.

In *The Night of the Iguana*, two main characters—Shannon, a defrocked minister and recovering alcoholic, now a tour guide for a cheap Texas-based travel agency, and Hannah Jelkes—meet at a shabbily run Mexican tourist hotel that is run by an oversexed American expatriate, Maxine. As one of Williams' survivors, Maxine supports herself, hoping some day to return to the United States to manage a motel.

Shannon's battles are internal, involving dismissal from the church for reasons of alcoholism and sexual promiscuities. Throughout the play, he attempts to write a letter to his superior for reinstatement in the church. His failure even as a tour guide only emphasizes the illusionary nature of his attempt at reinstatement. The play opens with a conflict between him and his tour group—ladies from a Baptist college in Texas—regarding their hotel for the night. Shannon insists that they stay at Maxine's rather than, as the tour brochure states, in the town below. Their arguments are protracted through the length of the play.

Arriving penniless at the hotel at the same time as Shannon are Hannah Jelkes and her nonagenarian grandfather, Nonno, who make their living in their travels, she by drawing portraits of tourists and he by reciting poems that he writes in his memory. Hannah has a purity and strength of character which is not of the world she inhabits. In her behavior and her many conversations with Shannon, she is a painful reminder to him of lost ideals. Her honesty and courage contrast with the conventional hypocrisy of the American women and the smug complacency of the Germans, one of

Fluvanna County High Library
Rt. 1, Box 41
Palmyra, VA 22963

whom constantly listens to his radio for reports on Adolf Hitler's success in bombing England (the play is set during World War II). Hannah, a sharp contrast to the Americans and Germans, cannot endure seeing a creature, human or otherwise, suffering.

At the end, she convinces Shannon to untie a captive iguana, which has been kept tied for the next meal at the hotel. Against Maxine's wishes, Shannon frees the iguana, just as he had earlier freed himself in his rebellion against his tour group. His act is a triumphant assertion of Hannah's religion of kindness to all living things and of his own former beliefs. Nonno dies shortly, having composed his last poem, which, for once, he had Hannah write down.

With their dependencies gone—Hannah's grandfather and Shannon's illusions as tour guide and minister—they are free, yet they are also alone. For Shannon, there is only one possibility: to stay with Maxine and help her manage the hotel. For Hannah, there is a return to her nomadic existence. Even the nymphomaniacal Maxine, to Shannon's surprise, becomes poetical as she invites him down for a swim in the "liquid moonlight." When Hannah lights her cigarette, Shannon stares at her, wanting to remember her face, which he knows he will not see again.

Each of the three main characters has her or his "spooks" (Shannon's word). His are professional failure and alcoholism; Maxine's are loneliness and the Mexican "beach boys" she employs for business and personal reasons; Hannah's are her spinsterish life-style, which she endures in crucial moments by stopping to inhale deeply. All three have met life on their terms and all three have survived. Shannon's freeing of the iguana is a metaphor for the resolutions of the private wars of the three main characters.

Structurally, the play's actions are loosely plotted, consisting mostly of episodic conversations between two of the three main characters. The moral landscape is that of World War II and of the petty lives of the German and American tourists, insulated from the cruelties of the public and private battles being waged around them.

Summary

A few other plays that are important to the Williams canon must be mentioned: *Camino Real* (1953), *The Rose Tattoo* (1951), *Orpheus Descending* (1957), *Sweet Bird of Youth* (1959), *The Milk Train Doesn't Stop Here Anymore* (1963), and *Small Craft Warnings* (1972). Tennessee Williams' stylistic distinction consists of his theatrically poetic language. His main thematic concerns are sympathetic portraits of women (sometimes a disguise for himself), his creation of what Ruby Cohn calls "garrulous grotesques," who have left an indelible impression on the American consciousness, his rebellion against the repressiveness of puritanical attitudes, and his use of Darwinism's "nature red in tooth and claw" as a metaphor for the cruelty of repressive, conventional attitudes.

Bibliography

Bigsby, C. W. E. *A Critical Introduction to Twentieth Century American Drama.* Vol. 2. Cambridge, England: Cambridge University Press, 1984.

Bloom, Harold, ed. *Tennessee Williams.* New York: Chelsea House, 1987.

Boxill, Roger. *Tennessee Williams.* New York: St. Martin's Press, 1987.

Falk, Signi. *Tennessee Williams.* 2d ed. Boston: Twayne, 1961.

Jackson, Esther Merle. *The Broken World of Tennessee Williams.* Madison: University of Wisconsin Press, 1965.

Stanton, Stephen S., ed. *Tennessee Williams: A Collection of Critical Essays.* Englewood Cliffs, N.J.: Prentice-Hall, 1977.

Tischler, Nancy. *Tennessee Williams: Rebellious Puritan.* New York: Citadel Press, 1961.

Williams, Tennessee. *Memoirs.* Garden City, N.Y.: Doubleday, 1975.

Susan Rusinko

WILLIAM CARLOS WILLIAMS

Born: Rutherford, New Jersey
September 17, 1883
Died: Rutherford, New Jersey
March 4, 1963

Principal Literary Achievement

One of the most accomplished and influential American writers of the twentieth century, Williams developed distinctly modern poetic forms through which he expressed the American idiom and landscape.

Biography

A first-generation American, William Carlos Williams was born in Rutherford, New Jersey, on September 17, 1883. His father, William George Williams, of English ancestry, had been born in England and reared in the West Indies. His mother, Raquel Hélène Rose Hoheb Williams, whose ancestry contained elements of French, Spanish, and Jewish cultures, had been born in Puerto Rico.

With his younger brother, Edward, Williams went to public schools in his hometown. When he was fourteen, he went with his family to Europe for two years, where he attended school first near Geneva, Switzerland, and later in Paris. When his family returned to the United States, he was sent to Horace Mann High School in New York City. He commuted daily from Rutherford by streetcar and Hudson River ferryboat. Williams entered medical school at the University of Pennsylvania in 1902. While there, because of his interest in poetry, he met the poets Ezra Pound and H. D. (Hilda Doolittle) and the painter Charles Demuth, all of whom became his lifelong friends.

After his graduation from medical school in 1906, Williams interned at the old French Hospital and the Nursery and Child's Hospital in New York City. His first volume of poetry, *Poems*, published at his own expense, appeared in 1909. That same year he went to Europe again, where he did postgraduate work in pediatrics in Leipzig, Germany. While in Europe he renewed his friendship with Ezra Pound and through him was introduced to many writers and artists of prewar London.

After brief trips to Italy and Spain, he returned to Rutherford in 1910 to begin the practice of medicine. In 1911, he married Florence Herman, the "Flossie" of his

poems. During the next few years, Williams became the father of two boys, William and Paul. In 1913 he bought the house at 9 Ridge Road in Rutherford which would be his residence for the rest of his life; his second volume of verse, *The Tempers*, was published in England that same year. Williams was a very active pediatrician with a wide practice among the industrial workers of northeastern New Jersey. Nevertheless, he continued to be a deeply committed poet and literary man eagerly involved in the artistic life, publishing ventures, and general creative climate of Greenwich Village in the years of World War I and after.

During this decade, Williams contributed to numerous magazines, including *The Glebe, Poetry, Others* (of which he was associate editor for a time), *The Little Review, The Dial*, and *Broom*. He became acquainted with Walter Arensberg, Kenneth Burke, Marsden Hartley, Alfred Kreymborg, Marianne Moore, Charles Sheeler, and other poets and painters. Williams published his third collection of poems, *Al Que Quiere!*, in 1917 and *Kora in Hell: Improvisations*, an experimental collection of poetry and prose, in 1920. From 1920 until 1923, Williams edited *Contact* with the publisher Robert McAlmon and during these years published three daring experiments in prose and poetry: *Sour Grapes* (1921), *Spring and All* (1923), and *The Great American Novel* (1923).

In 1924 he went to Europe with his wife for six months and savored the expatriate life of the most important members of the American "lost generation" and their French counterparts. He was guided again by Ezra Pound, along with Robert McAlmon, and through them Williams associated with such writers and artists as George Antheil, Sylvia Beach, Kay Boyle, Ford Madox Ford, Ernest Hemingway, James Joyce, Man Ray, Gertrude Stein, and such French men of letters as Valery Larbaud and Philippe Soupault.

Williams published one of his most influential prose works, *In the American Grain*, in 1925; it is a collection of essays on American history, and during the following decade contributed to *transition, The Exile, Blues, Front, Pagany, Alcestis*, and other magazines. In 1926 he received the Dial Award for Services to American Literature. Still a full-time pediatrician with a large private practice among the working class of Rutherford, he joined the staff of the Passaic General Hospital, while maintaining his general practice.

In 1927 he made another European visit when he and his wife escorted their two sons to school in Switzerland. While his wife remained with their sons in Switzerland for a year, Williams returned to his medical practice and to writing in New Jersey. During that time, he wrote a novel, *A Voyage to Pagany* (1928), based on the family's visit to Europe.

Williams continued in the following years to write prose (short stories, essays, novels, and an autobiography), poetry, and plays; despite the pressures of constant professional demands and intrusions in those years, he published more than twenty volumes. Collected editions of his poems were published in 1934 and 1938. In 1941 and ensuing years, as his literary reputation grew, Williams lectured at the University of Puerto Rico, Harvard University, Dartmouth College, and elsewhere. In 1946

Williams began publication of *Paterson*, his long verse masterpiece. Individual books of the poem were published in 1946, 1948, 1949, 1951, and 1958. Notes for a sixth book were published posthumously.

Williams received the first National Book Award for Poetry (for *Paterson*, Book III and the 1949 collection *Selected Poems*) in 1950. His autobiography, published in 1951, shows the extent of his association with the avant-garde of American letters, especially during the important twenty years between 1910 and 1930. In 1952, Williams was appointed Consultant in Poetry to the Library of Congress, a position roughly equivalent to poet laureate. The appointment was withdrawn before he could take office, however, partly because of accusations about his supposed leftist sympathies, owing much to his long friendship with Ezra Pound, who had been accused of being a traitor to the United States during World War II. Williams was subsequently reinstated to this position, but because of ill health he was never able to take it up.

A series of strokes that eventually made him a semi-invalid forced Williams to turn over his medical practice to his son William in the 1950's. He continued to devote himself to writing, however, and made frequent appearances at colleges and universities to lecture and to read his poems. In spite of periods of difficulty with his vision and his speech, he continued to live a vigorous creative life and to travel in the United States and, on two occasions, to the Caribbean.

During the forty years he practiced medicine in Rutherford, Williams wrote in his autobiography, he saw a million and a half patients and delivered two thousand babies. Meanwhile, scribbling or typing rapidly between patients, jotting down images and ideas on prescription blanks between house calls, and typing late into the night after his work day as a pediatrician was over, he laid the foundation of the most extensive one-man body of literature in American history: a total of forty-nine books in every possible literary form. He wrote about six hundred poems, four full-length plays, an opera libretto, fifty-two short stories, four novels, a book of essays and criticism, his autobiography, a biography of his mother, an American history, and a book of letters.

When William Carlos Williams died, at the age of seventy-nine, on March 4, 1963, in Rutherford, New Jersey, his reputation as a major poet was firmly established. He had won numerous awards during his lifetime, and two months after his death, he was posthumously awarded the Pulitzer Prize in Poetry for *Pictures from Brueghel* (1962) and the Gold Medal for Poetry of the National Institute of Arts and Letters.

Analysis

The writing of William Carlos Williams is one of the major achievements in twentieth century American literature. As a significant representation of the modern American consciousness, it must be placed with that of four other poets born between 1874 and 1888: Robert Frost, Wallace Stevens, Ezra Pound, and T. S. Eliot. Williams' work complements theirs in important ways. He was less ready than they to maintain traditional techniques or assimilate the discoveries made in other literatures, but he was more genuinely open and responsive to both the fullness and the emptiness of contemporary life in the United States. He listened more keenly to the dance rhythms and the flat cadences of American speech, observed more accurately the degradation and the unexpected beauties of its cities and countrysides, and explored more intensely the immediate historical ground on which Americans stand. He did all this, moreover, without slighting the spiritual emptiness that has haunted twentieth century writing. Williams may well be, of those five poets, the most important influence on the development of the American idiom in poetry during the last years of the twentieth century. His work in both poetry and prose combines great technical ability with a passionate humanity. The major beauty of Williams' art is perhaps that of a hard-won honesty, achieved through his attempt to isolate individual experience, to make the distinctions necessary to its proper perception, yet to acknowledge at the same time the continuity of all experience.

The content of Williams' writing tends toward "pure poetry." He seldom moralizes or indulges in philosophical or religious sermonizing. Criticism of capitalism is sometimes found in his fiction (for example, in the story "Jean Beicke") and other prose (as in parts of *In the American Grain*), but almost never in his poetry ("The Yachts" is one notable exception). The same thing is true of his medical background. He uses his scientific training and his experience as a doctor frequently in his fiction (as in his fine 1932 short story collection, *The Knife of the Times and Other Stories*), but it seldom appears in his poetry except in an occasional term or phrase borrowed from medicine. As a writer of fiction—he published four novels and a number of first-rate short stories—Williams' style is more conventional than in his poetry, but it is often ironic, sometimes even apparently callous, in attitude. His medical stories contain some of the most powerful descriptions of disease and suffering in modern fiction. In his fiction as in his poetry, however, Williams is objective rather than indifferent. He shows the sympathetic detachment of a man who combined the writing of literature with a full-time career as a practicing physician.

William Carlos Williams united a lifelong dedication to writing with a medical practice in New Jersey by writing emphatically about the life around him—the ordinary, and even apparently uninteresting, people, events, and landscapes that he encountered during his daily routine. His writing embodies two major tendencies. The first is vigorous formal experimentation in poetry and prose, frequently in the direction of abandoning traditional forms and, in his poetry, of mastering the possibilities of free verse, of which he remains the most influential practitioner. The second is a plain-speaking directness of manner well suited to his native subjects and settings—for example, city streets, vacant lots, workers and their tools, a retarded servant girl, a wheelbarrow, scraps of conversation, a sheet of paper rolling along in the wind, pieces of broken glass behind a hospital, the number five on a speeding fire engine. Nature, especially as represented by flowers and trees, is also an active presence in his poems, and it is celebrated without ever being idealized; it is puddles rather than lakes, sparrows rather than nightingales, weeds rather than roses. Everything is presented tautly, with a minimum of comment or judgment, in the simplest language and according to a lifelong preference for the concrete as expressed in his famous motto: "No ideas but in things."

Early in his career, Williams rejected the literary heritage of the Victorian era, particularly its trite diction and stultified verse forms. He strove constantly to achieve the brusque nervous tension, the vigor and rhetoric, of American speech. Although he avoids slang, his language is thoroughly idiomatic. He seldom uses a word that is beyond the vocabulary of the ordinary reader, and the rhythm and intonation of his language are those of common speech. A careful study of his typography and punctuation shows that they, too, are intended to reproduce the rhythm—the pauses and emphases—of ordinary speech.

Williams' poetry may be the most accessible and humane in modern American literature. He had a special knack for using natural speech poetically and an unusual appreciation of how other people feel and think. Virtually all of Williams' lyrics illustrate his determination to develop in poetry the rhythm, diction, and syntax of the language actually spoken in Rutherford, New Jersey. Many of his lyrics are about poetry—what it is, how to write it—but a poem about poetry is also, for Williams, about how to live, for poetry is essentially the direct "contact"—the fresh perceiving and feeling by which life becomes worth living.

The music of Williams' poems seems at first to be a deliberate absence of music, and it takes some time to perceive the finely controlled dance that the hesitations and abruptnesses of the free-verse line accomplish. Reading them aloud should include experimentation with the pauses to be found on the page and listening for the plain, emerging music. The recognition of this unlikely lyricism involves the same kind of delighted surprise that can be experienced from Williams' ways of finding beauty in unexpected places. Subject and style have the same aims, and an aesthetic of discovery through reduction and directness lies behind everything Williams did. To put it in terms of the visual analogies that very much interested him, his poems combine the freshness and daring of cubist painting and the candor and unmediated confrontations of photography.

Williams' revolutionary ideas led him to write poetry that was simple, direct, and apparently formless. He seemed to be a "nonliterary" writer, yet his poetry, for all its freshness and seeming spontaneity, was the result of constant rewriting and refinement. Like nineteenth century American poet Walt Whitman, he used commonplace American scenes and speech to portray contemporary urban America. Like Whitman, he was a significant force in the freeing of poetry from the restraints and predictive regularity of traditional rhythms and meters. Williams was a prime literary innovator in prose and poetry, and he was the poet of the twentieth century most sensitive to the teeming squalor of modern America.

In all of his work, Williams carried forward a revolutionary heritage that was welcomed by younger writers responsive to his example and influence. While steadfastly supporting the principle of free organic form, he also helped refresh and renew the language of poetry by freeing it from stereotyped associations. In his passionate equalitarianism, he has been more attractive to younger generations of poets than the more aristocratic Ezra Pound and T. S. Eliot. His writing reveals an openness to experience of all kinds and a refusal to accept doctrinaire theories and solutions. While insisting upon the authenticity of his own vision, he has at the same time insisted upon the relativity of all knowledge and the inadequacy of dogma. To this extent at least, despite his distance from the confident rationalism of the Enlightenment (which he also distrusted), his work as a whole supports the Jeffersonian principle of "eternal hostility to every form of tyranny over the mind of man."

TRACT

First published: 1917
Type of work: Poem

   While describing how to conduct a funeral, Williams' speaker gives advice that applies to many communal activities.

"Tract," from *Al Que Quiere*, Williams' second book of poetry, appears at first to be a frankly didactic poem in which the speaker attempts to teach the proper way "to perform a funeral." The speaker gives advice in four areas: hearse, flowers, driver, and bereaved. In stanzas 1-3, objecting to the usual funeral, with its standardized conventions which insulate mourners from the meaning of death, the speaker would substitute for the polished black hearse a "rough dray" to be dragged over the ground, with no decoration other than perhaps gilt paint applied to the wheels for the occasion. In stanza 4, in place of the usual wreaths or hothouse flowers, the speaker recommends "Some common memento . . . / something he prized and is known by:/ his old clothes—a few books perhaps—/God knows what!" In stanza 5, he would have the driver pulled down from his seat to "walk at the side/ and inconspicuously too!" His final admonition, in stanza 6, is to the mourners:

> Walk behind—as they do in France,
> seventh class, or if you ride
> Hell take curtains! Go with some show
> of inconvenience; sit openly—
> to the weather as to grief.
> Or do you think you can shut grief in?
> What—from us? We who have perhaps
> nothing to lose? Share with us
> share with us—it will be money
> in your pockets.
>   Go now
> I think you are ready.

By such simplicity and show of inconvenience, the poem holds, the townspeople "are ready" to conduct a funeral properly.

At first glance, "Tract" seems to be a poem of direct statement: The speaker attempts to reform his neighbors' ideas about the proper conduct of a familiar ritual by setting forth specific precepts. The speaker's impulse to reform, however, reveals a preoccupation with the idea of form that goes beyond the subject of funerals. The fact that the funeral is a common ritual is a reminder that any such group activity is inevitably symbolic and, in Williams' view, a kind of art. From this perspective, the speaker's injunctions apply not only to one rite but also to a whole range of symbolic activity in which members of a community may be involved. Metaphorically, the "tract" becomes a statement of an aesthetic as the poet asserts his commitment to certain principles of form which he urges upon his unenlightened townspeople. These are, not surprisingly, the familiar tenets of an organic theory in which rigid, predetermined conventions are rejected in favor of forms which are free and functional and adapted to the circumstances from which they arise. The separate assertions of what had seemed a poetry of statement are revealed to be integral parts of a more comprehensive, dramatically unified symbolic art.

THE RED WHEELBARROW

First published: 1923
Type of work: Poem

Williams discovers an aesthetic pattern and sensory pleasure in an ordinary wheelbarrow and a few chickens.

"The Red Wheelbarrow" is perhaps one of the shortest serious poems ever published by an American poet. The structure is rigidly formal. The poem consists of four miniature stanzas of four words each. Three images are involved: the wheelbarrow, described simply as "red," the qualifying adjectival phrase "glazed with rain/water," which relieves the excessive severity of the second stanza, and the contrasting white chickens of the final stanza. The first line is colloquial and open in its invitation; the second line, the preposition "upon," then prepares the reader for the specifics to follow. Each two-line stanza has two stressed syllables in the first line and one in the second, and yet there is lively variation in where the stresses fall.

In "The Red Wheelbarrow," Williams discovers an aesthetic pattern and sensory pleasure in an ordinary sight. The poem—or the moment of perception it reports—evokes no cultural traditions or literary associations. The absence of these is strongly noticed, however, for if the poem is an immediate experience, it is also a demonstration and argument. "So much depends," it says, on the object being there, but it also means that so much depends on the reader's response to what is seen. If one's response is dull, the world takes on this quality, and the converse is also true. Thus, although Williams believed that the American environment offered a new challenge and possibility to poetry, his deeper meaning was that anything, however familiar or even drab, would become significant and moving when met with a full response.

SPRING AND ALL

First published: 1923
Type of work: Poem

Williams celebrates the struggle of all new life to assert itself and discover its innate form.

"Spring and All" is a poem of only twenty-seven lines, yet it echoes some of the imagery as well as the concepts of T. S. Eliot's *The Waste Land* (1922) and is filled with Williams' desire to break with poetic tradition. The poem reveals this in the second and third words of the title. Spring is one of the most traditional themes of poetry; "and All" deflates it. The poem corrects poetic notions of spring—those one finds, for example, in Geoffrey Chaucer's famous opening of *The Canterbury Tales* (1387-1400), in which he describes the "sweet" season of flowers, bird songs, and balmy winds. Beginning with a description of a bleak winter scene on a road through muddy fields, the poem turns (in stanza five) to the tentative awakening of spring and the "naked,/ cold, uncertain" leaves of grass which are the first evidence of the return of life to the world. At first unconscious, the spring plants gradually acquire awareness as they come to life: "rooted, they/ grip down and begin to awaken."

Thus the poem depicts the cyclical rebirth of life, which is here, through the allusion to the "awakening" and awareness of plants, connected to intelligence and thus to humanity. A deft touch is the transition from winter images to images of spring, achieved in only seven words in the fifth stanza; the two lines of the stanza are connected organically to the preceding passage by one word, "lifeless," which echoes "leafless" in the fourth stanza. The poem's simple and understated ending is typical of Williams' pared-down style. Through Williams' sensitive concentration on the new life of trees and shrubs struggling into being in the cold spring wind, "Spring and All" celebrates the struggle of all new life to assert itself.

THE YACHTS

First published: 1935
Type of work: Poem

Despite its beauty, a yacht race during the Depression reminds Williams' speaker of social inequality and injustice.

In "The Yachts," Williams' more typical penchant for imagistic presentation coexists with a tendency toward symbolism. Halfway through the poem, there is an interesting and unusual shift from an imagistic to a symbolic mode. The occasion is a yacht race in a bay protected from the "too-heavy blows/ of an ungoverned ocean."

During the preparations for the race, the speaker is impressed by the physical beauty of the graceful craft, "Mothlike in mists, scintillant in the minute/ brilliance of cloudless days, with broad bellying sails." Although the appeal is primarily imagistic, there is a metaphoric suggestion in the observation that the yachts, surrounded by more clumsy "sycophant" craft,

> appear youthful, rare
>
> as the light of a happy eye, live with the grace
> of all that in the mind is feckless, free and
> naturally to be desired.

As the race begins, however, after a delaying lull, the scene changes ominously. The waves of the roughening water now seem to be human bodies overridden and cut down by the sharp bows of the yachts: "It is a sea of faces about them in agony, in despair/ until the horror of the race dawns staggering the mind." The original appeal of the beautiful spectacle of pleasure boats is broken and then displaced by the revelation of deeper meaning. The race is finally shown to be a symbol of human struggle, in which the mass of men are cut down and destroyed.

There remains a question as to the nature of the struggle. Is it to be understood simply as a common battle for survival in nature, in Darwinist terms, or does it have more specific social implications? The yachts inevitably suggest a privileged life. As the fruits of surplus wealth acquired within a protected socio-economic preserve (like an enclosed bay), the leisure and beauty of the life they represent exists at the expense of an exploited class. For all its seductive appeal, supported by long custom and tradition, the spectacle of the yacht race in a poem of the Depression period (the poem was written in 1935) must be a reminder of social inequality and injustice.

The movement of the poem from imagistic charm to symbolic horror is in accord with the shift in the poet's perception from a preoccupation with sensuous phenomena to an awareness of human meaning and value—the necessary movement, in short, from image to metaphor, without which the poetic presentation of such an event would remain an innocuous imagistic diversion.

PATERSON

First published: 1946-1958
Type of work: Long poem

Paterson envisions the epic development of that New Jersey town and its inhabitants as representative of modern urban America.

Paterson is a long poem originally in four parts, or books, published separately in 1946, 1948, 1949, and 1951 (although sections of them had existed in various forms in earlier works). Williams added a fifth part in 1958, and fragments of the incomplete Book VI were published posthumously (1963) as an appendix to the collection of the first five parts. According to most critics, *Paterson* is one of Williams' greatest works and one of the finest long poems by an American.

Like most long modern poems that abandon traditional narrative forms, *Paterson* is not easy to follow. One must first understand its basic and arbitrary symbols. The protagonist, Paterson, is a city, man, doctor, and poet. The land (sometimes personified as a woman) is not only that waiting to be civilized but also the poet's raw material. The river is both language and the natural movement of historical life. Thus, before the poem begins, the author's note declares, "A man in himself is a city, beginning, seeking, achieving and concluding his life in ways which the various aspects of a city may embody—if imaginatively conceived—any city, all the details of which may be made to voice his most intimate convictions."

Although primarily a book-length poem, the work also incorporates prose passages from historical documents, newspaper accounts, geological surveys, literary texts, and personal letters. As subject, Williams uses the city of Paterson on the Passaic River near his hometown of Rutherford, New Jersey, so as to bring forth the universal from a local setting (there are "no ideas but in things"). The poem presents local history and the natural scene (particularly Passaic Falls and Garrett Mountain) as well as the consciousness of a gigantic, mythic man (Paterson) and of the author— poet and doctor. Paterson's struggle to interpret the language of the falls, his search for an expressive American language, is the major motif of the poem. *Paterson* swarms with characters, incidents, impressions, and dramatic passages, bound together by the work's wide-ranging introspective and associative process and its quest: "Rigor of beauty is the quest. But how will you find beauty when it is locked in the mind past all remonstrance?" Williams dissociated and consciously recombined these narrative, descriptive, and lyric elements in the manner of a montage or cubist painting. The jagged, juxtaposed collage effects are one way Williams hopes to break through contaminated words to reality.

Although there are echoes of both Pound and Eliot, the poem's basic technique is that of Irish novelist James Joyce's *Finnegans Wake* (1939). Williams took certain historical places and events (the town of Paterson, the Passaic River, and events recorded in local histories and newspapers) and forged them into a myth. The poem's general theme is the decay of life in a small Eastern town meant to mirror American society. The falls above the town suggest both the possibility of good and healthy life and the correlative health of native speech. True to both history and myth, however, the river below the falls becomes polluted by industry, and the people's language and the people themselves take on a parallel dirtiness, loss of purpose, and inability to communicate. The process of decay, however, is not irreversible, as Williams indicates late in Book IV of the poem, when he insists that the sea (into which the river issues) is not man's true home.

Book I, "The Delineaments of the Giants," mythologizes the early history of Paterson in an effort to define the "elemental character of the place" and introduces the city (a masculine force), the landscape (a feminine principle), and the vital, unifying river. In this book, the city is linked with the as-yet-undiscovered identity of the poet. The river, which "comes pouring in above the city," is the stream of history and of life, as well as the stream of language from which the poet must derive his speech:

> (What common language to unravel?
> .   . combed into straight lines
> from that rafter of a rock's
> lip.)

Book II, "Sunday in the Park," concerned with "modern replicas" of the life of the past, meditates on failures in communication through language, religion, economics, and sex. The park, "female to the city," brings the poet into contact with the immediate physical world, the sensual life that he must transform. Here the Sunday crowd, the "great beast" (as Alexander Hamilton had called the people), takes its pleasure, pursues its desires among the "churring loves" of nature and within the sound of the voice of an evangelist, who vainly tries to bring them into the truth through the language of traditional religion, which Williams regards as outworn and simply another block to expression. Williams suggests, however, that redemption is possible through art, imagination, and memory.

In Book III, "The Library," the poet turns in his search for a common language from his immediate world to the literature (broadly interpreted) of the past. He moves from the previous section's "confused uproar" of the falls to find that "books will give rest sometimes"; they provide a sanctuary for "dead men's dreams." The past, however, represents only desolation, destruction, and death. Paterson's quest for beauty must continue. He says, "I must/ find my meaning and lay it, white,/ beside the sliding water: myself—/ comb out the language—or succumb."

Book IV, "The Run to the Sea," treats the polluted water below Passaic Falls in terms of corruption by modern civilization, while recognizing innovations in science, economics, and language. Finally, however, the identity of the river is lost in the sea, although the individual man (Paterson) survives and strides inland to begin again.

Book V, published seven years after Book IV, reveals a substantial continuity of image, theme, and metrical form, but there are significant differences in Williams' attitudes and in the treatment of certain themes carried over from the earlier books. Untitled, but dedicated to the French Impressionist artist Henri Toulouse-Lautrec, Book V is like a separate work, an oblique commentary on the poem by an aged poet from a point of view more international and universal than local. As for the poem's quest for beauty, this book shows that the only beauty that persists is art. Of the various Patersons (Paterson the Sleeping Giant; Paterson, New Jersey; Paterson-Williams), *Paterson*, Book V is most intimately concerned with Paterson as Williams himself. The first four books found the place; it is himself the poet must now find—or rather, find again.

Paterson is a complex and difficult poem, yet it is honest and uncompromising. Williams lives in a world in which wholeness is intellectually indefensible; thus he makes no suggestion of the possibility of a wholeness representative of a systemized worldview. In this respect, *Paterson* is more modern and representative of its science-minded, skeptical age than myth-oriented poems such as *The Waste Land* of Eliot and *The Bridge* (1930) of Hart Crane, which depend for their basic organization upon the pattern of the rebirth archetype. On a much larger scale than in Williams' other poetic works, *Paterson* is a vigorous effort to discover the "common language" shared by the poet and the American people.

THE CLOUDS

First published: 1948
Type of work: Poem

Clouds take on many meanings in this poem about individual expression and the life of the imagination.

Williams' insistence upon the freedom of the mind and hatred of conventional restraints is powerfully expressed in "The Clouds," a four-part poem in which the central image is the march of the ever-changing clouds across the sky. As natural phenomena, the stuff on which the mind and imagination feed, they symbolize the shifting flux of experience in which man must find human significance if he is to be more than a turtle in a swamp. They also represent the "unshorn" minds of free spirits such as François Villon, Desiderius, Erasmus, and William Shakespeare, who "wrote so that/ no school man or churchman could sanction him without/ revealing his own imbecility." These minds, like the skeptical Socrates, "Plato's better self," accepted the fact of man's mortality and devoted themselves to the life of the mind and imagination—a life to which Williams gives precedence: "The intellect leads, leads still! Beyond the clouds."

In a brief and lively "Scherzo" (part 3 of the poem), Williams remembers coming as a tourist upon a priest in St. Andrew's in Amalfi, "riding/ the clouds of his belief," as he performed a Mass, "jiggling upon his buttocks to the litany":

> I was amazed and stared in such manner
>
> that he, caught half off the earth
> in his ecstasy—though without losing a beat—
> turned and grinned at me from his cloud.

Although he recognizes the ritual to be an act of the imagination, to Williams, the priest's cloud is not enough. In its regularity and neat order, reassuring though these may be to believers, it stands in contrast to "the disordered heavens, ragged, ripped by winds," which the poet, who accepts a naturalistic outlook, must confront in his search for form and meaning. The "soul" is the precious burden of the life of the imagination that each individual has a share in carrying forward, humanistically, from generation to generation: "It is that which is the brotherhood:/ the old life, treasured."

IN THE AMERICAN GRAIN

First published: 1925
Type of work: Essays

Williams attempts to discover the essential qualities of the American character by focusing on the lives and words of major and minor figures in American history.

Williams' collection of essays *In the American Grain*, first conceived in the early 1920's, was undertaken, Williams said, "to try to find out for myself what the land of my more or less accidental birth might signify" by direct examination of the original records of American founders. His hope was to rediscover the unmediated truth about the founders, the makers, and the discoverers of America. "In letters, in journals, reports of happenings," he says, "I have recognized new contours suggested by old words so that new names were constituted."

Williams divided *In the American Grain* into twenty chapters ranging in time and place from the settlement of Greenland, through the voyages of Christopher Columbus, to the exploration of Kentucky and the Civil War. In form the essays include dramatic narratives, lyric interludes, brief character sketches, whole sections of Columbus' journals, Cotton Mather's *The Wonders of the Invisible World* (1693), Daniel Boone's autobiography, and excerpts from John Paul Jones's letters and log entries. Taking his subjects in chronological order, Williams begins with the exploration and settlement of Greenland by Eric the Red and his son, Lief Erickson; he ends with a prose poem on Abraham Lincoln during the Civil War. The collection includes sketches of such major or representative historical figures as Columbus, Hernán Cortés, Sir Walter Raleigh, Cotton Mather, Daniel Boone, Benjamin Franklin, George Washington, John Paul Jones, Edgar Allan Poe, and Abraham Lincoln. In addition, Williams wrote essays on minor figures, such as Ponce de León, Hernando de Soto, Père Sebastian Rasles, Aaron Burr, and Sam Houston. Most of these apparently minor figures, especially Père Sebastian Rasles, assume heroic proportions after Williams' assessment of their encounters with the New World. Williams' meditations on America's discoverers also include consideration of attitudes toward violence, sports, and commerce in the United States of the 1920's, as well as such blights on the American conscience as the slaves ("Poised against the *Mayflower* is the slave ship . . . bringing another race to try upon the New World") and the suppression of women ("So Jacataqua gave to womanhood in her time, the form which bitterness of pioneer character had denied it").

Williams' hope in these essays is to restore the readers' awareness of the past.

Even the original records distort the truth about the past, Williams claims, so that it must be searched out and reconstituted in new writing in order to be understood. In his attempt to get back to "the strange phosphorus of the life" that precedes every effort that has been made to record it, he therefore metaphorically repeats or imitates the action of his subjects, who essentially abandoned the advanced culture of Europe in order to go back to the beginning again, back to the forces and conditions that precede culture.

In order to restore a past lost through use of the wrong words to describe it, Williams often employs the words of his subjects so as to convey their ways of vision and expression. He attempted to compose each chapter in a style suited to its subject, copying and using what the subject himself had recorded. In "The Discovery of the Indies," for example, Williams makes extensive use of Columbus' journals. In some chapters Williams allows his subjects to speak for themselves, verbatim. "Cotton Mather's *Wonders of the Invisible World*" consists entirely of excerpts from that book. A major theme of *In the American Grain* results from Williams' strategy of exploring, through myriad voices, ways in which his subjects viewed new worlds. Williams contends that history is as much a matter of language and imagination as of data; the past may be falsified by a misuse of language, failure to recognize its nuances, failure to perceive "new contours" in "old words." His use of sources is somewhat like his friend Ezra Pound's approach to translation. Williams is not afraid to compress, adapt, or modify in order to express more strongly and succinctly the spirit of his subjects; he does not feel it necessary to provide scholarly footnotes explaining his method.

To Williams, then, American history is not a result but a process. Because history is what is alive or dead in a present mind, any fixed idea of the past that one might hold is a fixation in oneself. That is why Williams urges, "History must stay open, it is all humanity." In order to keep history open, Williams orchestrated a conversation of many voices, dramatizing the continuing discovery (of the past and of oneself) that may occur as a man pays attention to his historical ground.

From the beginning of his series of essays, Williams is sensible of a dichotomy, of two types of people. On the one hand were those, the Indians and some explorers, travelers and settlers, whose contact with the new continents of North and South America was positive. On the other were those who voyaged to the new land to prey upon it and either to return to the Old World with their plunder or, somewhat later, to settle on the land, as the Puritans did, and yet reject contact with it and inhibit the contact of others. Another keen observer of the American spirit, D. H. Lawrence, expressing what he had learned from Williams' books, identified two major ways that Americans react to their continent. The first, and most common, is to recoil into individual smallness and insentience, and then to gut the great continent in mean fear. It is the Puritan way. The second way is to touch America as she is; to dare to touch her. This is the heroic way. Thus Williams' true heroes are those, like Columbus, Pere Rasles, Daniel Boone, and the American Indian, who had embraced the gritty, fearful truth of America and had loved it.

In the American Grain is not a history book, but an act of discovery, in which Williams attempted to "find out for myself what the land of my more or less accidental birth might signify." In its treatment of the makers of American history, ranging from Lief Erickson to Lincoln, *In the American Grain* has impressed many as Williams' most succinct definition of America and its people. The collection of essays is an exhilarating effort to re-examine the key figures, historical events, and documents that reveal the essence of America's myth about itself and its underlying psychological pressures. With D. H. Lawrence's *Studies in Classic American Literature* (1923), it stands as a pioneering effort in critical thinking.

Summary

For most of his life, William Carlos Williams waged war against reductiveness—the tendency of human beings to mistake the part for the whole or the explanation for the reality. He wrote lyric poems, an epic, short stories, novels, essays, a remarkable volume of American history, and an autobiography, consciously reshaping these literary forms in the hope of engaging readers more directly and fully with experience. The cultural impact of Williams' achievements was registered slowly, but his influence on major poets of the succeeding generation has been pivotal, and a sense of the importance of his example continues to increase.

Bibliography

Coles, Robert. *William Carlos Williams: The Knack of Survival in America*. New Brunswick, N.J.: Rutgers University Press, 1975.

Doyle, Charles. *William Carlos Williams and the American Poem*. New York: St. Martin's Press, 1982.

Guimond, James. *The Art of William Carlos Williams: A Discovery and Possession of America*. Urbana: University of Illinois Press, 1968.

Mariani, Paul. *William Carlos Williams: A New World Naked*. New York: McGraw-Hill, 1981.

Miller, J. Hillis, ed. *William Carlos Wiliams: A Collection of Critical Essays*. Englewood Cliffs, N.J.: Prentice-Hall, 1966.

Simpson, Louis. *Three on the Tower: The Lives and Works of Ezra Pound, T. S. Eliot, and William Carlos Williams*. New York: William Morrow, 1975.

Wagner, Linda W. *The Poems of William Carlos Williams: A Critical Study*. Middletown, Conn.: Wesleyan University Press, 1964.

——————. *The Prose of William Carlos Williams*. Middletown, Conn.: Wesleyan University Press, 1970.

Whitaker, Thomas R. *William Carlos Williams*. New York: Twayne, 1968.

Whittemore, Reed. *William Carlos Williams: Poet from New Jersey*. Boston: Houghton-Mifflin, 1975.

James W. Robinson, Jr.

LARRY WOIWODE

Born: Carrington, North Dakota
October 30, 1941

Principal Literary Achievement

Novelist, short story writer, and poet, Woiwode is credited with reviving the genre of the family chronicle in postwar American letters.

Biography

Larry Alfred Woiwode was born in Carrington, North Dakota, October 30, 1941, and spent his early years in nearby Sykeston, a predominantly German settlement amid the rugged, often forbidding north-Midwestern terrain. No doubt the beauty as well as the stark loneliness of this landscape heightened the author's appreciation for the effect of nature upon individual character. At the age of ten, he moved with his family to Manito, Illinois, another evocatively Midwestern environment capable of nurturing the descriptive powers of a budding fiction writer.

He attended the University of Illinois for five years but failed to complete a bachelor's degree, leaving the university in 1964 with an associate of arts degree in rhetoric. He met his future wife, Carol Ann Patterson, during this period and married her on May 21, 1965. After leaving Illinois, Woiwode moved to New York City and supported his family with free-lance writing, publishing in *The New Yorker* and other prestigious periodicals while working on two novels.

During his career, Woiwode has been known primarily for his longer fiction, but he has frequently published short stories in such prominent literary periodicals as *The Atlantic* and *The New Yorker*, and he published a well-received collection of poems, *Even Tide*, in 1977. Several of his short stories have been chosen for anthologies of the year's best. Woiwode's first novel, *What I'm Going to Do, I Think*, won for him the prestigious William Faulkner Foundation Award for the "most notable first novel" of 1969 and brought him immediate critical attention. It reached the best-seller list and has been translated into several foreign languages.

His second novel, *Beyond the Bedroom Wall: A Family Album* (1975), actually begun before *What I'm Going to Do, I Think*, was nominated for both the National Book Award and the National Book Critics Circle Award. It became an even bigger commercial and critical success than his first novel. Woiwode's third novel, *Poppa John* (1981), however, was much less successful commercially and critically; it departed from his signature, the Midwestern prairie setting, and located its protago-

nist, an aging soap opera actor, in New York City. *Born Brothers* (1988), the long-awaited sequel to *Beyond the Bedroom Wall*, returned readers to the unfolding lives of a quintessential Midwestern family, chronicling the tensions of two Neumiller brothers, Charles and Jerome. *The Neumiller Stories* (1989), a collection of reworked short stories about the Neumiller clan, expanded the "snapshot album" of narratives about this family and continued Woiwode's refinement of the psychic landscape first begun as episodes in his novel *Beyond the Bedroom Wall*.

In 1977, Woiwode was awarded an honorary doctor of letters degree from North Dakota State University. In academic life, Woiwode has served as a writer-in-residence at the University of Wisconsin, Madison, and has had extended teaching posts at Wheaton College (Illinois) and at the State University of New York at Binghamton, where he has served as a faculty member intermittently since 1983.

Analysis

Larry Woiwode's quirky, family-centered narratives signal the rehabilitation of the venerable genre of the family chronicle, a kind of fiction once pervasive in American novel writing but regarded by many critics as defunct. In the family chronicle, a writer basically builds a narrative around the history of one family, often an immigrant family whose daughters and sons fight to establish their own identity in the "new world" to which their parents or grandparents have brought them. Authentic and engaging family chronicles normally depend upon adherence to a meticulous realism that requires careful attention to the nuances of family life and conversation. Woiwode is equal to this task, and he unabashedly admires the traditional nuclear family. Consequently, his fiction underscores the value of finding one's way in the modern world by retracing one's steps in his or her family legacy.

Woiwode refuses to drown his characters in the angst-ridden excesses that have become so conventional in the modern American novel. Even to readers accustomed to cynical and world-weary protagonists preoccupied with discovering the mysteries of life in the squalor of the city while involved in some illicit relationship, Woiwode can make such old-fashioned values as family loyalty seem startlingly fresh and appealing. His characters are not helpless victims of their times but participants in them; they are accountable not so much for what has happened to them but for what they do in response to their circumstances. This is a world which registers as authentic to the reader precisely because of Woiwode's gift for psychological realism made more engaging because of his command of the role of human memory in shaping one's perception of one's relationships.

Woiwode's characters eventually recognize that the answer to their dilemmas is only partly in themselves. In the reestablishment of personal trust in friendships and the nostalgia of forgotten familial relationships, they recover a sense of balance and worth in themselves. However obliquely, each major Woiwode character finds himself in a quest for a transcendent moral order, a renewed trust in God and man that would give him a reference point for his life. This quest animates their rejection of narcissism and a search for a love and security that only marital and familial relationships can foster.

Woiwode's willingness to affirm that these relationships are central to self-fulfillment and to the stability of true American culture makes him unique among a generation of writers whose thematic concerns tend to focus on their characters' dehumanization in society, their alienation from family life, and their eschewing of marital fidelity. Woiwode thus belongs in the company of self-consciously moralistic writers such as Walker Percy and Saul Bellow, writers more interested in the ways human beings survive and thrive in a fallen world than in the ways they capitulate to it. His characters' conflicts, from Chris Van Eenanam's enigmatic search for manhood in *What I'm Going to Do, I Think* to Poppa John's drive to recover his self-identity, are not merely contrived psychological dramas played out inside their own consciousness; they are compelling confrontations with the very concrete world of everyday life.

Despite his solid reputation in modern letters, Woiwode's career, especially when compared with other writers of his calibre, does not represent the work of a particularly prolific author. In the two decades after he ended his abortive college career to pursue free-lance writing, he produced few major works: one long, rather complex family chronicle, one medium-length novel, one short novel, a short story collection, and a book of poems. Yet two of his three novels were critically acclaimed, national best-sellers and are arguably among the best American novels written since 1960.

A highly acclaimed first novel can often prove to be a mixed blessing, as it can overshadow a writer's subsequent efforts. *Poppa John*, Woiwode's third novel, was greeted with some disappointment; that reaction, coupled with a long period in which Woiwode published nothing, led some critics to wonder about his commitment to his vision. After the period of relative inactivity following the success of his first two novels nearly twenty-five years earlier, Woiwode returned to the family chronicle in *Born Brothers* and *The Neumiller Stories*. Their appearance seems to have effectively answered the concerns of his critics.

WHAT I'M GOING TO DO, I THINK

First published: 1969
Type of work: Novel

A newlywed couple search together for meaning and purpose against the bleak, faithless landscape of the late 1960's.

Woiwode's first novel, *What I'm Going to Do, I Think*, is an absorbing character study of two newlyweds, each of whom is originally drawn to the other as opposites proverbially attract. Chris Van Eenanam, the protagonist, is a listless mathematics graduate student, an unhappy agnostic preoccupied with his unsure footing in life; put simply, he lacks vocation or a consuming vision of what he should do with his life. The novel's title thus accentuates his self-doubt and indecision, echoing something Chris's father once said in observing his accident-prone son: "What I'm going to do, I think, is get a new kid." Ellen Strohe, his pregnant bride, is a tortured young woman, dominated by overbearing grandparents who reared her after her parents' accidental death. Neither she nor Chris can abide her grandparents' interference and meddling.

Little action takes place "live" before the reader, as Woiwode's psychological realism deploys compacted action and flashbacks and the patterned repetition of certain incidents to carry the reader along as effortlessly as might a conventionally chronological narrative. The reader learns "what happens" primarily as events filter through the conversations and consciousness of Chris and Ellen Van Eenanam during their extended honeymoon at her grandparents' cabin near the northwestern shore of Lake Michigan. This tantalizing use of personal perception and vaguely unreliable memory has become a trademark of Woiwode's characterization. It permits him wide latitude in choosing when and how to reveal his characters' motivations and responses to the events that shape their lives.

In their retreat from the decisions that Chris elects not to face, the couple, now intimate, now isolated, confront a grim modern world that has lost its faith in a supreme being who is fully in control of his created universe. This loss is exemplified most dramatically in the lives of Chris and Ellen as they try to sort out the meaning of affection and fidelity in their new relationship as husband and wife and as potential parents. Ellen's pregnancy is at first a sign of a beneficent nature's approval of their union, but later, as each has a premonition of their unborn child's stillborn delivery, it becomes a symbol of an ambivalent world's indifference to their marriage and its apparent fruitlessness.

In the absence of a compensatory faith even in mankind itself (a secondary faith arguably derived from faith in God), Chris and Ellen come to realize that they have lost their ability to navigate a hostile world with a lasting, meaningful relationship. The "student revolutions" of the 1960's had promised social enlightenment and unadorned love, a secure replacement for the tottering scaffold of religious faith and civic duty that undergirded their parents' generation. They discover, however, that neither science, as represented in Chris's mathematics pursuits, nor nature, as a metaphor for the modern world's hostility to metaphysical certainty, can fill the vacuum left by a waning faith in God or man. Such a committed faith, whose incessant call is to fidelity and perseverance, cannot survive without passion or understanding in the perplexity of the young married couple's inexperience in living.

In a suspenseful epilogue that closes the novel with an explanation of what has happened to them in the seven years following their marriage, Chris and Ellen return to their honeymoon cabin. Chris retrieves the rifle that he has not touched in many years, and, as the action builds toward what will apparently be his suicide, he repeats to himself the beginning of a letter (perhaps a suicide note) that he could not complete. *"Dear El, my wife. You're the only person I've ever been able to talk to and this is something I can't say. . . . "*

As he makes his way to the lake, he fires a round of ammunition into a plastic bleach container half-buried in the sand. In the novel's enigmatic final lines, Chris fires "the last round from his waist, sending the bullet out over the open lake." This curious ending seems intended by Woiwode to announce Chris's end of indecision— a recognition that his life can have transcendent meaning only in embracing fully his marriage commitment to Ellen.

BEYOND THE BEDROOM WALL

First published: 1975
Type of work: Novel

A sprawling chronicle of an immigrant family's vitality and enduring faith despite the obstacles to its survival in the modern world.

The expansiveness and comic twists of Woiwode's second novel, *Beyond the Bedroom Wall: A Family Album*, offer a marked contrast to *What I'm Going to Do, I Think*. In *Beyond the Bedroom Wall*, Woiwode parades sixty-three characters before the reader by the beginning of chapter 3. True to its subtitle, "A Family Album," *Beyond the Bedroom Wall* is a rather impish and gangly work of loosely connected snapshots of three generations of the German Catholic immigrant Neumiller family. Woiwode straightforwardly invites the reader to leaf through this "album" not as a rigorously chronological narrative but as a curiosity piece, pausing at particular episodes and events.

From sentimental scenes of a father telling his children stories, and the poignancy of a child fighting a nearly fatal illness, to the agonizing grief of losing one's spouse, *Beyond the Bedroom Wall* is an engaging homage to the seemingly evaporating family unit at the end of the twentieth century. Nevertheless, the novel's "plot" is nearly impossible to paraphrase, consisting as it does of some narrative, some diary entries, and even its protagonist Martin Neumiller's job application for a teaching position. Woiwode had published nearly a third of the forty-four chapters of *Beyond the Bedroom Wall* as self-contained short stories in *The New Yorker*; thus it is no surprise that the book reads as a discontinuous montage of events, images, and personalities. Woiwode reworked many of these episodes, foregrounding other characters and character traits, for his collection *The Neumiller Stories* (1989).

Part 1 of the novel opens with the funeral of Otto Neumiller, a German immigrant farmer who had brought his family to the United States before the war, and it continues, to part 5, with stories of the third generation of Neumillers, concluding in 1970, thus bringing members of the Neumiller family full circle from birth to life to death. Otto Neumiller had emigrated to America in 1881, relocating in the plains of North Dakota. As the reader meets him at the end of his life, he stands poised between two worlds, knowing neither the love nor the admiration of his neighbors, but seeking to bequeath something of value to his son, Charles. The farm he tended and leaves behind becomes emblematic, not of his success as a man of the soil, but of his life as a devoted father who has sown and reaped a loyal and steadfast family, one whose strength is not in great friendships or possessions but in mutual love.

After setting this context, Woiwode moves the narrative forward quickly, introducing the family of Charles's son, Martin, who is the "family album's" true focal point. Martin Neumiller, like his father and grandfather, is a God-fearing, devoutly Catholic man and proud son of North Dakota whose ordinary adventures and gentle misadventures give the novel any formal unity it possesses. "My life is like a book," he says at one point, "There is one chapter, there is one story after another." To see his life as a story, written by God in the gives and takes of everyday life, Martin must accustom himself to finding profundity and sustenance in the painfully ordinary patterns and repetitions of life and not in the frantic and guilt-ridden excesses of sophisticated city life or Hollywood romanticism. To accentuate this resolution, Woiwode peoples the novel with odd folks who serve as Martin's extended family, a naturally burlesque troupe of characters who boisterously sample both the joys and the sorrows of life on Earth within the confines of small-town America.

The Neumiller family over which Martin presides is hardworking, intelligent, and generally steady; they are manifestly not extraordinary when measured against the typical families of traditional, rural, Midwestern life. Martin, like Woiwode, revels in their normality. Driven to resign as an underpaid and underappreciated small-town teacher and principal, Martin takes on odd jobs as a plumber and insurance salesman to provide an income while waiting for another opening. Hearing of a principalship in the small Illinois town where his parents live encourages him to move there from North Dakota. Completely loyal to his wife, Alpha, Martin clearly treasures her and the six children she bears for him. They have committed themselves to each other "till death parts them."

The move to Illinois is disastrous, however, as anti-Catholic bigotry denies Martin the job he sought and Alpha subsequently dies abruptly. The reader discerns, with Martin, that it was his break from "ordinariness," from typical family patterns of mutual decision-making—found in his uncharacteristically sudden decision to move his family east—that has animated most of the tension and diversion within the novel and which ultimately delivers its theme. Left to serve as "father, mother, nurse, teacher, arbiter, guardian, judge," Martin appears to shrivel up inside. Outwardly stoic about his life's ups and downs, he continues to be resolute about how to face disappointments and discouragements: "A man should be grateful for what he gets and not expect to get one thing more."

Using this "family album" approach, Woiwode lends concreteness to his notion that reality is a fragile construction, one that sometimes cannot bear scrutiny "beyond the bedroom wall"—that is, beyond the dreamy world of sleep, of its visions of what might be. Woiwode intimates that whatever hope there may be for fulfilling one's dreams, it is anchored in "walking by faith, and not by sight," by trusting in and actively nurturing family intimacy. The rather sentimental, "old-fashioned" quality Woiwode achieves in this family chronicle, his evocation of once-embraced and now-lamented values, prompted critic and novelist John Gardner to place Woiwode in the company of literature's greatest epic novelists: "When self-doubt, alienation, and fashionable pessimism become a bore and, what's worse, a patent delusion, how does one get back to the big emotions, the large and fairly confident life affirmations of an Arnold Bennet, a Dickens, a Dostoevsky? *Beyond the Bedroom Wall* is a brilliant solution."

Woiwode's eye for the rich details of daily life enables him to move through vast stretches of time and space in executing the episodic structure in this novel. His appreciation for the cadences of Midwestern speech and his understanding of the distinctiveness of prairie life and landscape and its impact on the worldviews of its inhabitants recalls other regional writers such as Rudy Wiebe and Garrison Keillor at their best.

POPPA JOHN

First published: 1981
Type of work: Novel

An aging actor fights to regain his self-respect and recover his own identity after his soap opera character dies.

When compared with the massive *Beyond the Bedroom Wall*, *Poppa John* is shockingly short and is more a finely wrought character study than a novel. Consequently, Woiwode relies on subtle symbolism and poignant imagery to convey the story's essentially religious themes. The book takes its title from the character that aging actor Ned Daley has played for many years on a popular television soap opera. With his character's immense personal popularity beginning to overshadow the show itself, he is eventually written out of the show in a dramatic "death." Now close to seventy, outspoken, and Falstaffian in appearance and behavior, he seeks to recover his identity as "Ned," which has been sublimated during his twelve years as the imperious Poppa John.

Poppa John's compressed action takes place on two days in the Christmas season, a Friday and a Sunday—nakedly separated by a vacant and voiceless Saturday— and the novella is thus divided into two parts, decisively marked by the calendar: Friday, December 23, and Sunday, December 25. As in his other fiction, Woiwode is concerned that the reader discover the nature of his characters' predicaments by "listening" to their own thoughts and memories as they recall them, rather than by intrusive exposition by an omniscient narrator. Progressively but achronologically, one learns the relevant facts of Ned's past; recollection, in fact, dominates present action in the evolving narrative.

Therefore, in responding to the novella, it is important to recognize the character traits that Ned has sought to embody in Poppa John for twelve television seasons. Part King Lear, part Santa Claus, Poppa John evinces a kind a tragic benevolence, resolving contrived soap opera dilemmas with well-chosen biblical verses. Though easily spouting scripture while in character, Ned rarely discerned its significance for himself, nor has the sage presence of Poppa John transferred any benefits to his own relationships. In this portrayal, Ned found inspiration in his own grandfather, a fiery evangelical preacher scandalized when his daughter, Ned's mother, married a Catholic and converted to this alien faith. His father, a vaguely corrupt policeman, had died a violent death that Ned himself overheard taking place while hiding in a warehouse—a signal event that drove him into an adult acting career that has prevented him from becoming the unique individual he was born to be.

Consequently, Ned has a complex and paradoxical relationship to religious faith. It at once circumscribes his life and distances it from its reality. The "Scriptures," Woiwode's narrator opines, "had given him slivered glimpses into the realm of time, from the vantage of his years, where a central pureness . . . held the continual revolving of days into weeks—into months, into ages—in balance with the compiled weight of the ages revolving beneath the particular minute of each day." When Poppa John dies, Ned's own life begins to unravel, and he is increasingly forced to face his own inconsistencies, his doubts, and even his sins.

The novel opens as Ned and his devout and devoted wife, Celia, dress for a day of Christmas Eve shopping. Ned has been out of work for more than a year and the couple must withdraw money from savings to fund any gift buying for each other. "Ned" only to his wife (he is "Poppa John" to everyone else), he is lost in the malevolent nostalgia of growing old without a true self or true self-respect. Ned is tentative about this trip uptown; he has been in analysis, seeking to exorcise the ghost of Poppa John from his psyche. He no longer knows how to "be himself." As he strolls the streets of New York, he moves intermittently in and out of his Poppa John identity, conversing amiably with strangers who recognize him, all the while employing the gestures and intonations his adoring fans have come to expect. He is simultaneously a captive of the public who gave him his livelihood and the victim of a medium that rewards popularity by "killing" its source.

The more his casual acquaintances offer their condolences for his fictional death, the more self-pitying he becomes. After he and his wife agree to split up so each can shop for the other, Ned succumbs to an old temptation, alcohol. In a neighborhood bar, he allows himself to be "picked up" by an admiring fan and would-be dancer who takes him to her apartment. When her roommate returns to find the drunken and blubbering old man, she persuades the dancer to return him to the bar from whence they came, and eventually they send him on his way in a cab. Exiting at the next block, Ned wanders the streets and eventually collapses in a street mission, which he mistakes for the homely Catholic cathedral of his youth. The next face he sees, now on Christmas morning, is that of his wife. Confined to a hospital psychiatric ward, Ned is "coming to himself," realizing that he, after all these years, does believe in God and therefore can come to believe in himself.

In minimizing the action of the novella and compressing it into only two days, Woiwode places special weight on two different and compelling Christian images he seeks to juxtapose: the joyful incarnation of the baby Jesus, foregrounded in the Christmastime setting; and Christ's crucifixion and resurrection, a dark Friday and a buoyant Easter Sunday separated by a bleak, lost Saturday. As Christ is in the grave, his fate unknown, Ned/Poppa John is also buried and left for "dead" in his drunken stupor. When he awakens to receive his wife's Christmas gift of a briefcase bearing his initials N. E. D., his life as Ned Daley is restored and he is thereby enabled to embrace a future he despaired of finding again. What Woiwode offers in *Poppa John* is a modern parable of life, death, and rebirth.

BORN BROTHERS

First published: 1988
Type of work: Novel

The continuing saga of the Neumiller family, whose characters were introduced first in *Beyond the Bedroom Wall.*

Woiwode calls this novel a "companion volume" to *Beyond the Bedroom Door,* and it returns to the characters and setting of that work. Beginning in the middle of the twentieth century, *Born Brothers* is filtered through the perceptions of Charles Neumiller; through his memories, he is seeking a meaning and purpose for his life. As elsewhere, Woiwode eschews chronological narrative, and the present is submerged deeply into the past; the novel progresses through various memories of Charles. To speak of a plot or setting is unhelpful; to force Woiwode's uniquely fashioned version of family chronicle into such misleading categories is to misconstrue Woiwode's vision—that lives do not neatly fit into prescribed, sequential patterns. Family members appear in a seemingly random way that shows Charles's quest for an answer to the plaintive cry of his heart: Is there life after childhood?

A gifted raconteur and orator, Charles has followed his voice into a New York career as a "voiceover" in commercials and as a "radio personality" focused on small-town life. He is thus accustomed to creating illusions and re-creating forgotten, homely images in the minds of his listeners. In fact, he is incapable of conceiving of a meaningful world outside the psychic landscape of his own family structure. Having endured assaults on his marriage and having struggled with alcohol, Charles leaves New York behind for his beloved North Dakota. A suitable anthem for Charles Neumiller's life can be drawn from his own musings: "Imagination is, indeed, memory—that is more profound than any fantasy." The events and relationships of the past are as concrete as any the contemporary present can offer him.

His childhood and his own fatherhood have profoundly shaped his life in ways that preclude other influences and forces from engaging his life. The minutest detail of a past experience is recalled and rehearsed in Charles's mind as the reader is invited to share vicariously in its warmth and vitality. Errant smoke from a father's cigar, a mother's bedtime stories, a life-threatening fall—each of these recollected events breathes life into Woiwode's protagonist as he searches for an anchor to hold onto in the storms of modern life.

The thematic key to the novel may be found in a recognition that Charles longs for a restored bond of brotherhood he once shared with elder brother, Jerome—drawn from a childhood which the adult Charles visits frequently, once again inhabiting what now seems an idyllic Garden of Eden in North Dakota, free from the cares and motivations of prurient, polluted, industrial life. That Charles's radio job comprised the roles of both the interviewer and the interviewee encapsulates his need for conversion, of freedom from self. He needs an outside, a reference point, which, implicitly, he seeks in his older brother Jerome—an affirmation he anticipates but does not truly realize in a New York reunion in a dingy hotel room. If their memories are not "mutual," he fears, "I might have invented our love." Ultimately, Woiwode hints, Charles will find "a place to stand" only through a renewed faith in the transcendent, and eventually Charles concedes that the only proof of God's existence "is God's existence in you for eternity."

At times, the tedious details of Charles's recollections are dizzying, even unedifying. Yet it is the totalizing effect, the sheer volume of Charles's "unedited" introspections, that gives the novel its weight and its merit. In part, it is Woiwode's intent to lay the blame for American society's apparent moral disintegration—rampant promiscuity, unwanted pregnancy, and divorce—to the absence of strong family ties, but he leaves open the question of whether Charles's captivity to the past is the solution or part of the problem. In the end, *Born Brothers* can perhaps be received as fiction's most ambitious, if not most successful, attempt since the work of French novelist François Mauriac to capture the vagaries of the active conscious mind and tortured spirit within the linearity of print.

Summary

While believing that the most important human questions are, in fact, religious ones, Larry Woiwode rejects the notion that there can be legitimate, compelling "novels of ideas." Woiwode handles such questions by creating authentically ordinary characters and settling them into the concrete and mundane world of daily life as filtered through human imagination and memory.

Woiwode's prose is consistently active, alive, and unassuming, with a finely tuned lyricism. His keen eye for the extraordinary ordinariness of life makes his narrative vision compelling and believable. Woiwode thus stands out as a moderating influence among contemporary novelists, an advocate for restoring a moral, even religious voice to modern letters.

Bibliography

Connaughton, Michael E. "Larry Woiwode." In *American Novelists Since World War II*, edited by James E. Kibler, Jr. Detroit: Gale Research, 1980.
Dickson, Morris. "Flight into Symbolism." *The New Republic* 160 (May 3, 1969): 28.

Gardner, John. Review of *Beyond the Bedroom Wall. The New York Times Book Review* 125 (September 28, 1975): 1-2.

Marx, Paul. "Larry (Alfred) Woiwode." In *Contemporary Novelists*, edited by James Vinson. 3d ed. New York: St. Martin's Press, 1982.

Pesetsky, Bette. Review of *Born Brothers. The New York Times Book Review* 93 (August 4, 1988): 13-14.

Prescott, Peter S. "Home Truths." *Newsweek* 86 (September 29, 1975): 85-86.

Woiwode, Larry. "An Interview with Larry Woiwode." *Christianity and Literature* 29 (1979): 11-18.

Bruce L. Edwards

THOMAS WOLFE

Born: Asheville, North Carolina
October 3, 1900
Died: Baltimore, Maryland
September 15, 1938

Principal Literary Achievement

By recasting in a fictional guise characters and events from his own life, Wolfe created situations that evoked the underlying, quintessential ethos of Southern and American ways of life during the period of his youth and early manhood.

Biography

Because so much of his writing was based upon his own background and upbringing, critics and biographers have often interpreted the novels of Thomas Wolfe by reference to the author's personal life. Although occasionally his fictional vision diverged from the realities of Wolfe's life, often the correspondence between literary narration and actual events was so close that the sources of his works could easily be traced to his own experiences. The last of eight children, Thomas Clayton Wolfe was born in Asheville, North Carolina, on October 3, 1900. His parents, Julia Elizabeth Westall Wolfe and William Oliver Wolfe, were of widely contrasting temperaments. While his father, a stonecutter, was an ingratiating sort who nevertheless was prone to angry outbursts and wild drinking sprees, his mother was of a practical turn; she was somewhat avaricious, and she became involved in local real estate ventures. She doted on her youngest son, however, and it would seem that Thomas Wolfe's attachment to his mother was part of the basis for that element of fondness with which he later recalled the years of his childhood. A family business, a boarding house called the Old Kentucky Home, was opened in 1906; it was managed by Julia Wolfe. From relatively early, Thomas Wolfe acquired some notions about the sorts of people who had settled in the area or who stayed there during their travels in the region.

In 1905, Wolfe entered the Orange Street Public School in Asheville; in 1912, he was enrolled in the private North State Fitting School. He was an avid, incessantly curious boy who combed the shelves of the local public library for reading material. Because of his aptitude for academic work, it was decided (after he himself had set his hopes on out-of-state schools) that he should attend the University of North Carolina in Chapel Hill. Although he experienced some difficulties in adjustment

when he entered as a freshman in 1916, Wolfe later became well known at the university for his involvement with campus organizations and literary projects. For a time he edited the school's newspaper. In 1919, *The Return of Buck Gavin*, a play he had written for one of his courses, was staged by the local Carolina Playmakers; Wolfe himself performed in it and delighted many with his extravagant portrayal of the title character. As a college student, his consuming determination to read as widely as possible continued unabated. In many courses he did well. Wolfe was often regarded as showing particular promise; by 1920, when he began graduate studies at Harvard University, he seems to have become settled in his ambition ultimately to be a writer. In addition to studies which brought him into contact with leading specialists on English literature, such as John Livingston Lowes, he was associated with a well-known theater workshop group. He received a master's degree in 1922, and in 1923 his play *Welcome to Our City* was performed. During this period, however, he was deeply saddened by the loss of family members; in 1918 his brother Ben died of tuberculosis, and after a prolonged struggle with cancer his father died in 1922.

In February, 1924, Thomas Wolfe accepted a position as an instructor in English at New York University, and he taught there intermittently for about six years. In October, 1924, he set off on the first of seven journeys to Europe. On his return, in August, 1925, he met a wealthy married woman, Aline Bernstein, who was about nineteen years older than he; a strange and turbulent love affair followed, which lasted until 1932, a year after his wife apparently tried to resolve matters by threatening suicide. All along, Wolfe worked steadily at composing prose fiction. After three years of work, the manuscript of his first novel had been prepared; it was partly because of the extraordinary efforts of Maxwell Perkins, the editor for the publisher Charles Scribner's Sons in New York, that *Look Homeward, Angel* could be published in October, 1929. The success of this work, and the award to Wolfe of a Guggenheim fellowship in 1930, which supported further travel overseas, instilled in him added confidence to continue writing.

Important works of short fiction were published during the early 1930's, and beginning in 1933, Wolfe was also assisted by Elizabeth Nowell, who served as his literary agent and found journals that would publish his stories. With the invaluable aid of Maxwell Perkins, during some protracted and arduous editing sessions, Wolfe's second novel, *Of Time and the River*, appeared in 1935. Wolfe traveled widely during this time, both in the United States and abroad. While on a visit to Germany during the Berlin Olympic Games of 1936, he developed a deeply felt antipathy to Nazi ideology, and he subsequently presented this theme with great effect in his fiction. Back in New York, complications about his dealings with his publisher broke into the open; in particular, there were quarrels over the handling of legal matters, and there were some recriminations about a royalty agreement which he considered unsatisfactory. In 1937, he signed a contract with Harper and Brothers and entrusted further manuscripts to Edward C. Aswell, the editor for that firm. The following year he traveled extensively in America, and he delivered an important lecture, which was later published, at Purdue University. He visited Western states, and in Seattle he came down with pneumonia. A latent tubercular lesion had been opened, and miliary tuberculosis of the brain set in. Although he was taken finally to The Johns Hopkins Hospital in Baltimore, doctors found his condition beyond hope of treatment, and he died on September 15, 1938. His last two novels, *The Web and the Rock* (1939) and *You Can't Go Home Again* (1940), were published posthumously, as was some of his other prose fiction. Over a period of several decades, the publication of personal letters, collected interviews, plays, and other literary fragments he had left cast further light on his outlook and interests.

Analysis

Typically, Thomas Wolfe composed his novels as vast sprawling narratives that, beginning with the origins, early childhood, or youth of his protagonists, would recount in abundant detail memorable impressions and episodes from his past. Those who knew Wolfe personally and who had heard him speak described him as capable of extraordinary, vivid, and tumultuous outpourings of words that could be prompted spontaneously by suitable occasions; this quality may be seen in much of his writing. Many of the particularly evocative passages in his novels display descriptive powers that he developed at some length, and which in turn were related to the thematic currents underlying his works. His writings were particularly effective in conveying sights and sounds of locales that were familiar to him; inner reactions and the subjective life of his fictional alter egos were also depicted in depth. Resonant and seemingly universal in their appeal were Wolfe's evocations of the timeless joys and travails of childhood and youth and the many-faceted manifestations of the American spirit. He also had a definite sense for the specific characteristics of certain regions and groups; in some passages he would contrast Southern ways with those that prevailed in other parts of the country. Often he would indulge in written mimicry of dialects, whether Southern or Northeastern, and sometimes he attempted to reproduce the intonations of English spoken with an Italian, French, or German accent. He also had a satirical bent and was wont to portray those who seemed typecast in somewhat overblown guises.

Some parts of his works have been taken as suggesting tolerance of racial prejudices, and it would appear that he also had ambivalent—and at times not necessarily sympathetic—feelings about Jews, but as such matters are handled in his novels, attitudes of this sort could also be regarded as to some extent characteristic of the times during which he lived. Otherwise, however, in many respects Wolfe's protagonists could be considered as expressing, in a somewhat larger-than-life form, the yearnings and ambitions of many who might feel that in America a quest for learning, love, or fulfillment might be realized.

It would appear that, among the numerous authors, classical and modern, with whom Wolfe was familiar, he was probably influenced as much by the works of James Joyce and by any other writer. Wolfe's writings were known to most of his contemporaries, as well as to the wider reading public; in particular, Sinclair Lewis

esteemed his work highly—in the speech he delivered when he won the Nobel
Prize, Lewis took particular note of Wolfe's attainments. In a somewhat cryptic vein,
William Faulkner pointed to Wolfe as a failure, but a failure on a magnificent scale
which others of their generation had not reached. Readers and reviewers of Wolfe's
own time, and later, often enough were prone to complain of the extreme wordiness
that burdened all of his major works. It has also been maintained that because of the
all but limitless concern Wolfe had for his protagonists, his writing bordered on the
overwritten, the puerile, and the mawkish. His defenders, both during his lifetime
and subsequently, have contended, however, that even where his efforts were flawed
and overly effusive, the scale and depth of his achievements still could not be denied.

LOOK HOMEWARD, ANGEL

First published: 1929
Type of work: Novel

Family life and self-discovery show the way for the development of a young
Southern man during the first twenty years of his life.

As childhood may be composed in part of the recollections and impressions passed
along by parents, so it may seem not to have a precisely fixed beginning or end.
Look Homeward, Angel: A Story of the Buried Life, the story of Eugene Gant, com-
mences not with the boy's first conscious sensations but with the origins of his father
and mother. William Oliver Gant, whose ancestors had settled in Pennsylvania, had
been apprenticed to the stonecutter's trade; he moved eventually to the South and,
after two marriages, he came to the rural mountain city of Altamont, the fictional
equivalent of the author's native Asheville. There he met Eliza Pentland, who came
from an established, if somewhat eccentric, family of that region, and after some
courtship he married her. Even then, Gant was a wild and exuberant sort, who was
capable of epic drinking bouts; he also possessed a certain untamed vitality, and by
the end of the nineteenth century, when he was nearly fifty years old, his wife had
conceived their last child.

By way of this oddly retrospective narrative introduction, the circumstances of
Eugene Gant's early years are set forth, and events from his life even as a small child
are then recorded at some length. For example, from the age of six he could recall
the many colors of bright autumn days, and he was aware of the many smells of food
in all its varieties, and of wood and leather; he was alive to the crisply etched sights
of furniture, hardware, trees, and gardens that were to be found around his home
and in the city. Once he had learned to read, he became enchanted with tales of
travel and adventure, and indeed with the very power of words themselves, but there
was also a worldly and earthy element to his character. At the age of eight he had
some vague appreciation for the bawdy rhymes and crude jokes that were current

among older boys; he could also recall the blunt racial slurs that were routinely used by those in his neighborhood. Beyond that, however, there was a contemplative and inward-looking aspect to his cast of mind. He could remember that before he was ten years old he would brood upon what seemed to be tantalizingly unanswerable contradictions that went to the very nature of the human spirit.

Various themes and motifs seem to characterize Eugene's adolescent years. He has a literary curiosity of prodigious proportions, and he reads books of all sorts by shelf-loads at a time. He has great energy and considerable zest for sports, even though he is awkward and ungainly on the baseball diamond. An imaginative boy, he is prone to indulge in vividly embroidered daydreams which cast an idealized counterpart of himself as an invincible hero. He has some awkward misadventures with women, which seem later to arouse further longings in him. During this period there occur some richly comic episodes, as when Eugene's father prepares an elegant stone angel as a burial monument for a deceased prostitute. There are also some hints of events in the wider world beyond them; on one occasion William Jennings Bryan visits the town and makes some suitably politic replies to questions from local admirers.

As the youngest member of his family, Eugene feels more closely drawn to his brother Ben than to others around him. Another brother, Steve, turns out to be a sort of ne'er-do-well, while their brother Luke has a particular talent for earning money from odd jobs of any kind but has little aptitude for academic work; after some study at a college and a technical school he becomes a worker in a boiler factory. Meanwhile, their father visibly has become sallow and aged; prostate cancer has set in, and his vigorous exuberant manner seems to have become subdued and petulant. In Eugene's life, a major change comes when he enrolls in the state university and for the first time lives away from home for extended periods. By this juncture it is recorded that, just short of the age of sixteen, he remains still very much a child at heart; great but vaguely felt ideals of beauty and order are still largely untempered by contact with the world beyond.

The university itself has a distinctive, unforgettable charm and resembles an oasis of learning in a provincial wilderness. Here Eugene's education begins in earnest; while previously he had been simply a precocious, somewhat pampered boy with vast and undefined ambitions, during his college work his impulse to read widely and in depth assumes somewhat clearer contours. At the outset he feels isolated and disoriented, but he eventually becomes initiated in college ways. He visits a prostitute in a neighboring city and comes down with a verminous affliction which must be cured by a local doctor when he returns home over Christmas. Later he feels stirred by impulses that are both romantic and erotic. During a summer period when he has moved back to Altamont, he meets Laura James. She is a pert, attractive woman five years older than Eugene, and she has already become engaged to another man; for the time being she has come to stay at the Gants' boarding house. Eugene has a brief but intense affair with her which, while loosely based on events in Wolfe's own life, seems here to have been reworked considerably in order to emphasize the romantic prowess of Wolfe's protagonist.

For a period during World War I, Eugene, who is too young for active service, goes to work at a Navy yard in Virginia, not too far from Laura James's original home; he is disappointed that, after their brief sojourn together, he does not hear anything further from her. Other and more distressing troubles soon confront Eugene and his family, for Ben, Eugene's favorite brother, who had defended him during family disputes, has been stricken with a fatal illness of the lungs; as his all-too-brief life draws to a close there are scenes that are alternately petty and poignant. At the hospital, their father suddenly begins complaining about medical costs, to the discomfiture of the others. On the other hand, Eugene, who has never been particularly religious, fervently begins to pray when it appears that Ben has passed beyond recovery. He reflects unhappily that somehow in death Ben has meant more to them than when he was alive. Toward the end, when Eugene has been graduated from college and is preparing to go on to Harvard University, it seems to him in some imagined way that out of the past Ben's ghost has come back and is asking him where he is going on his life's journey.

OF TIME AND THE RIVER

First published: 1935
Type of work: Novel

The adult years of Wolfe's fictional counterpart are depicted in this lengthy narrative of his quest for personal fulfillment in America and abroad.

In much of Wolfe's writing, lengthy descriptions of train journeys impart a sense of movement and change. In *Of Time and the River: A Legend of Man's Hunger in His Youth*, his hero, Eugene, embarks upon a trip northward. Having left college in his native state, he believes that he has become a witness to a vast and panoramic series of images which, taken together, reveal the many faces of America itself. There is to him a sensation of escape from the dark and mournful mystery of the South to the freedom and bright promise of the North, with its shining cities and extravagant hopes. The plains, peaks, and valleys that shape the landscape over which he passes, as well as the innumerable towns and cities along the way, bespeak to him the limitless diversity of the nation. Other images, mainly images from the past, are called up within Eugene when he stops in Baltimore to visit the hospital where, in his fatal illness, his father is being treated; the old man seems yellow, wan, and exhausted, and only the stonecutter's hands, of a massive size and grace, seem still to suggest the strength and dignity with which he had once carried out his chosen calling. Otherwise, old Gant appears to have wasted away, and his sullen self-pity indicates that little remains of his once vibrant spirit. Somewhat later, in some graphic passages, the old man is left drained and enfeebled by sudden and vast outpourings of blood; he dies in the midst of numerous relatives and friends who have come by during his last days.

Wolfe's second novel is divided into parts bearing allegorical allusions; the figure most readily identified with his fictional hero is portrayed in the second section as "young Faustus." At least as much as during earlier times, when he was a boy or an undergraduate student, Eugene Gant is propelled by an immense and boundless striving to read anything and everything he can and to encompass all known learning and literature in a self-imposed regimen that goes well beyond the limits of formal study. At Harvard's library he prowls about in the stacks, taking down volumes he has not seen before and timing with a watch how many seconds it takes to finish one page and read the next before moving on. Eugene also walks the streets alone, mainly for the sake of gathering in sights and sounds that are still new and not entirely familiar to him; he marvels at the lonely, tragic beauty of New England, which he has come to believe differs from his native South and yet resembles it in ways that distinguish both regions as essentially American.

Eugene, like Wolfe himself, for a time devotes unstinting energies to writing plays for a workshop which absorbs his energies, but later he recoils from such efforts as constraining and imposing limits upon his creative self. At times he expresses his disdain for productions that he thinks others had tried to make overly fashionable or artistic. Wolfe often was given to expressing his hero's observations and aspirations quantitatively, in large numbers, to suggest some great and unrealizable vision of the nation and of human culture, in its immeasurable richness: While at Harvard, Eugene yearns to read one million books, to possess ten thousand women, and to know something about fifty million of the American people. Such strivings convey the great elemental yearnings of Wolfe's protagonist, whose very being seems set upon not the satisfaction but the pursuit of his unending quest. For a time, however, he must provide for himself as best he can, and this he does by teaching college-level English courses in New York. All the while, the growing discontent fed by this routine breeds in him wants of another sort. As was the case with Wolfe himself, travel for Eugene seems to open vistas on several levels. One autumn he sets forth to see the great cities of the Old World.

In England, Eugene feels some affinity with a people who share with him a common language and literature; indeed, his admiration for British culture seems favorably to predispose him toward those he meets. Though England seems drab and colorless in some ways, and the cooking turns out to be for the most part bland and disappointing, at the end he senses a bond of affection has been established which transcends any outward differences. On the other hand—and in some respects it would seem that Wolfe regarded Europe as a measure by which those qualities most distinctive about America could be grasped anew—Eugene cannot but be struck by the atmosphere and attitudes which contrast with those of his own country. In France he feels overwhelmed by the Faustian urges that had beset him earlier; he wants to learn and read everything about Paris and its people. Not quite attracted or repelled, he becomes fascinated and at times awestruck by his surroundings.

Some episodes having less to do with cultural matters prove diverting and at times distressing. When he encounters a man he had known from his Harvard days and two American women, their brief camaraderie turns to bitterness and recrimination when Eugene, somewhat put out by what he regards as their affected Boston ways, becomes involved in a fight with his erstwhile friends; after some spirited quarrels, he leaves the others. Once out of Paris, he is befriended by some odd older women from noble families; in the end, as he has chronically been on the verge of exhausting his money altogether, his travels on the Continent must be brought to a close. Having traveled about at length, more and more he has become beset with a longing for home, and indeed he is eager for the sight of anything that might hint of America. When the journey of this modern Faust has been completed, he also—in a state of some wonderment—comes upon a woman for whom he has been longing, on the return voyage home.

THE WEB AND THE ROCK

First published: 1939
Type of work: Novel

In another retelling of events from the author's youth, the travails of love and creative writing are recounted at some length.

In the preface to this novel, written approximately four months before his death, Thomas Wolfe announced that he had turned away from the books he had written in the past; he had intended rather to create a hero whose discovery of life and the world takes place, by his standards, on a more objective plane. Other ways in which the pattern of his earlier works had been varied are evident. Although *The Web and the Rock* was based upon his early life and experiences, those portions dealing with childhood and adolescence were allotted comparatively less space. There is correspondingly more emphasis on events from the author's early adulthood that had not been discussed in the previous novels. The protagonist and Wolfe's final hero, named George Webber, outwardly does not resemble the author to the same extent as does Eugene Gant, though there can be little doubt that, in the same way as Gant, he was meant to be the spokesman for Wolfe's own thoughts and ideas. In the first part of the novel, the style also is somewhat more terse and less free flowing, than had been the case in previous works, though later the narrative tends more to resemble that which had been used earlier. It should be mentioned as well that, while it has sometimes been asserted that Wolfe's last two books were to a significant extent adapted by (and indeed, partly written by) his second editor, Edward Aswell, specialists have found that in their essential features the works conformed in most ways to the form in which Wolfe originally had cast them.

The Web and the Rock begins in another fictional version of Wolfe's native city, this time named Libya Hill; his central character, George Webber, is the son of a stonecutter who had migrated to the South many years before. George's early life is described from about the age of twelve. Because of his short, stocky, crouched bearing, George has a vaguely simian appearance; he is called "monkey," or "Monk," but while physically he differs noticeably from his creator, he otherwise has much in common with Wolfe. In the early portions of the novel there is a great deal of attention paid to sports and games and other pastimes; friendships and confrontations with other boys occupy much of his time, and indeed those he had known from this period seemed destined later to appear in his life at unexpected junctures. On the other hand, the boy could not but be fascinated by the dark and violent underside of Southern small-town life. On one occasion, a black man he had come to know inexplicably has gone berserk and kills several people with a rifle before being brought down by a sheriff's posse; his bullet-riddled corpse is left on display at a local undertaker's establishment. Such incidents underscore the fragile balance between orderliness and destructive impulses.

When George is about sixteen, the reader learns that his father has died and that George has become a student at a state school named Pine Rock College, where he comes upon some quaint and rustic characters; nevertheless, he feels that even with its provincialism and its austerity, his school is more than a match for the renowned private institutions of northern states. The events of George's college years are set forth among some evocations of the atmosphere that pervades the campus; in classes there is an earnest, though at times not self-consciously serious, effort to appreciate the better works of literature.

Students also have time enough for carousing and wild sports rallies that seem to have a primitive earthy vitality of their own. The peculiar status of college football heroes, who appear to hold sway in a domain all their own, is depicted in some vignettes of George's friend Jim Randolph, who seems possessed of extraordinary powers on the playing field but later proves incapable of accomplishing great things in the wider world. For George, however, new and portentous changes are ushered in when he moves to New York; the contrast between his obscure provincial background and outlook and the grandeur and squalor of the great city, in its massive and manifold forms, is particularly striking to the young man.

After living with friends for a while, and after a lonely and desperate year spent by himself, George's inchoate quest and his innermost yearnings are answered, after a fashion, much as they were in Wolfe's own life. The remaining portions of the novel have to do largely with a prolonged love affair with takes place prior to the publication of his first book.

On a return trip from Europe he meets a certain Esther Jack (who has generally been regarded as a fictional rendition of Aline Bernstein), and quickly, in a mysterious way, he becomes infatuated with her. This strange and for a time overwhelming passion is described as the result of longing which had created in her an idealized form of woman—indeed, the embodiment of someone she never was or possibly could never have been. In one light she is described as middle aged, even matronly, though full of energy and still attractive. In his enamored vision, he regards her as the supremely beautiful and sublime embodiment of his desires, and when he perceives her later as falling short of this extravagantly conceived image, quarrels and differences arise. There are as well some remarks on her Jewish origins and on the clannish, insular, but also generous character of her people. On a directly personal level, he seems attracted to her because of her solicitude and sympathy during his travails as an aspiring but as yet unrecognized writer; her concern for his well being is quite touching and leads to some memorable scenes where their affection is expressed during the enjoyment of succulent meals she has prepared for him. She also lends her considerable moral support to his work on his first novel, a bulky manuscript ten inches thick which he has started showing to publishers in the city. After this work has been unceremoniously rejected by the satirically if infelicitously named firm of Rawng and Wright, she consoles him and encourages him to look elsewhere.

Soon thereafter, however, discord sets them apart. He suggests that she has a penchant for younger lovers and becomes tormented by jealousy and distrust. Her sophisticated urban mannerisms begin to grate harshly upon his rather less refined sensibilities; remonstrances and countercharges fly back and forth, and claims that Christians cannot tolerate Jewish ways, or the converse, are bandied about. George apparently resents his dependence upon Esther; for her part, stricken by his sudden outbursts of suspicion and hostility, she threatens to end her own life.

As the situation seemingly has become intractable, George finally sets off for Europe, thinking that she will write him or make some effort to settle their differences. He travels in England and on the Continent, increasingly troubled by loneliness and doubts; he feels that he is a foreigner in lands where even American tourists seem strange and out of place. He tells himself finally, when he is in a hospital in Munich recovering from wounds he received in a fight, that "you can't go home again"; this reflection sets the tone for the next and final series of his adventures and experiences.

YOU CAN'T GO HOME AGAIN

First published: 1940
Type of work: Novel

Triumphs and troubles in the later life of the author are set forth in a work which also depicts social and political turmoil, in America and abroad, during the 1930's.

From among the several million recorded words that Wolfe wrote during his career, the phrase that concludes one work and was chosen as the title for this novel has been probably the best known of all the expressions he ever used. The adage "you can't go home again" evidently was suggested first by Ella Winter, the widow of the writer Lincoln Steffens. This phrase seems apt not on the most obvious literal level, but rather in the sense that, in the flux of time and life, old ties and associations cannot remain the same, unchanged; once they have been outgrown or cast off, old ways must be set aside as part of a past which cannot easily again be recaptured. Wolfe's last novel opens with George Webber's return to New York, where Esther Jack receives him; he is apprised that his manuscript has been favorably reviewed by a well-known publishing house, which has sent an advance check for five hundred dollars. He also learns that his aged maiden aunt has died, and he travels southward, to return home for the first time in many years. On the way he meets Nebraska Crane, a friend and companion from his boyhood days who, though he has made a name for himself as a professional baseball player, feels that the best period of his career is behind him.

When George arrives in Libya Hill, he is treated by some as a visiting local celebrity; in newspapers, he is quoted with some inventiveness as expressing the fondest sentiments possible about his native city. Libya Hill itself has been overtaken by frenetic speculation in real estate and, in fact, in all realms of business, which temporarily has transformed it into a boom town. There is a pervasive atmosphere of change, both superficial and permanent; George, who feels oddly isolated even on native ground, comes to sense that his visit has been an act of farewell more than a homecoming. Somewhat later, after his novel has been published, George ruefully, but with some amusement, notes the reaction it has stirred up among local people. Because much of his book was essentially based upon real characters, he has received letters complaining with some vehemence of the shame and disgrace he has brought upon those who once were his neighbors and friends; one anonymous writer threatens to kill him. On the other hand, someone else has offered to provide him with even more salacious material should he care to inquire.

By this time, George's affair with Esther has run its course; after some oddly harrowing scenes at one of her social gatherings, he decides that he can turn away decisively from what he regards as her artificially cultivated, high-society circles and way of life. He turns instead to other women for short periods of time, but finds none of them particularly endearing or even compatible. All the while, he has also become aware of changing fortunes all around him, brought about by the onset of the Great Depression. He learns that in Libya Hill land values have collapsed suddenly, with resulting hardships and uncertainty. In much of New York, signs of destitution and desperation can be seen at first hand; some moving passages describe dejected homeless men and the discovery of a suicide victim in the street. In spite of the many signs of desolation around him, and despite recurrent brooding loneliness, Wolfe's hero is moved to reaffirm his faith in life and creation.

In describing the only enduring friendship from this period of his hero's life, Wolfe paid unusual tribute to his editor Maxwell Perkins, whom he recast here as Foxhall Edwards. George Webber, who much earlier had lost his own father, is described as benefiting from a sort of spiritual adoption that provides him with needed guidance. To be sure, the editor depicted here seems in some ways foppish and has some strangely idiosyncratic habits. He also has a knack for getting around problems that seems at once cunning and guileless, but he is portrayed as fundamentally tolerant and fair-minded in ways that others of his profession are not. Another fictional portrait from life of a well-known literary figure appears in the course of George's further travels.

During a visit to London he has the opportunity to meet the writer Lloyd McHarg, who was modeled upon Sinclair Lewis. When a newspaper story reports that McHarg has warmly praised George's work, the young author manages to arrange a meeting with the great man. Although McHarg receives George on friendly, even cordial, terms, the younger man is struck not merely by his unprepossessing, in some ways ugly, appearance: In McHarg, he also believes that he can detect the trials and disappointments of fame and recognition. The widespread acclaim that McHarg had earned seems only to demonstrate that writers could not be satisfied merely with public acceptance; McHarg, in the sheer surfeit of his triumphs, has taken to constant traveling and drinking to allay the numbing boredom and loneliness that have befallen him.

Earlier in his career, Wolfe had shown some fondness for Germany, where he had traveled and where his first book, in translation, had been favorably received. Later, however, much had changed, and a sizable portion from the last part of this novel has to do with some striking and rather horrifying impressions that were gathered during travels under the Nazi regime. Although George Webber, like Wolfe himself was, is treated as an eminent foreign writer, he feels a pronounced uneasiness which sets in almost as soon as he arrives in Berlin. The Olympic Games held in the German capital are flanked by regimented demonstrations of marching men which hint strongly of preparations for war. People George meets are curiously reticent on political matters, though dark and unseemly rumors surface from time to time. The atmosphere of fear and compulsion seems more ubiquitous and more oppressive than any of the killings, gangster plots, or other manifestations of hatred and violence that America had ever known.

During a train trip to the west, George and some other travelers meet a curiously nervous little man, who is afraid he will be detained for currency violations; he presses upon George and the others some coins he had hidden away. When they change trains at the frontier, they discover that the man, who is Jewish, is attempting to escape while smuggling much of his money out of the country; in a brutal, wrenching confrontation with Nazi police, he is apprehended. The others helplessly must leave him to his fate. The novel concludes with George's return to New York, where he writes a long letter to Foxhall Edwards, summarizing his beliefs and setting forth his artistic credo. Though he will work no longer under his former editor and friend, he believes that some explanation—and some exposition of the directions his life has taken—is required. At the end, George maintains that the forces of time and change cannot be resisted and that the past he had known must be put behind him.

Summary

The ability of Thomas Wolfe to present personal experiences and memories in a manner that has inspired many readers to identify with the fictional characterizations of the author has contributed much to the appeal of his major works. Although to some his approach has appeared overly centered on the self, indeed narcissistic, he was able to transform impressions and ideas into forms of expression that are broadly representative of the American ethos, both during his own day and for later generations. The continuing attraction of his writings has been derived partly from his powers of description and characterization, but perhaps more than that from the extent to which the personal and the specific were made to appear universal in his great novels.

Bibliography

Bloom, Harold, ed. *Thomas Wolfe*. New York: Chelsea House, 1987.

Donald, David Herbert. *Look Homeward: A Life of Thomas Wolfe*. Boston: Little, Brown, 1987.

Evans, Elizabeth. *Thomas Wolfe*. New York: Frederick Ungar, 1984.

Holman, C. Hugh. *The Loneliness at the Core: Studies in Thomas Wolfe*. Baton Rouge: Louisiana State University Press, 1975.

Idol, John Lane, Jr. *A Thomas Wolfe Companion*. New York: Greenwood Press, 1987.

Kennedy, Richard S. *The Window of Memory: The Literary Career of Thomas Wolfe*. Chapel Hill: University of North Carolina Press, 1962.

McElderry, Bruce R., Jr. *Thomas Wolfe*. New York: Twayne, 1964.

Phillipson, John S., ed. *Critical Essays on Thomas Wolfe*. Boston: G. K. Hall, 1985.

Rubin, Louis D., Jr., ed. *Thomas Wolfe: A Collection of Critical Essays*. Englewood Cliffs, N.J.: Prentice-Hall, 1973.

Turnbull, Andrew. *Thomas Wolfe*. New York: Charles Scribner's Sons, 1967.

J. R. Broadus

TOM WOLFE

Born: Richmond, Virginia
March 2, 1931

Principal Literary Achievement
A skilled satirist and social critic, Wolfe began his career as a journalist, was a founder of the new journalism movement, and later became a satirical novelist.

Biography

Thomas Kennerly Wolfe, Jr. was born on March 2, 1931, in Richmond, Virginia, to businessman and scientist Thomas Kennerly and Helen (Hughes) Wolfe. He was graduated cum laude from Washington and Lee University in 1951 and went on to earn a Ph.D. in American studies from Yale University in 1957. From 1956 until 1959 he was a reporter for *The Union* in Springfield, Massachusetts, then moved to *The Washington Post* from 1959 to 1962. During the 1960's, he began to chronicle the foibles of his generation in a breathless, exciting style that was exuberant and distinctively his own, working as contributing editor for two major magazines: *New York* and *Esquire*.

In 1978 he married Sheila Berger, the art director of *Harper's* magazine, where he has also worked as a contributing artist. His drawings and caricatures, some of which are reproduced in his first collection of essays, have been exhibited. Wolfe studied creative writing at Washington and Lee (a classmate has remembered Wolfe's then preference for writing baseball stories and a fascination with *Gray's Anatomy*) before turning to American studies at Yale.

Wolfe's involvement with the "new journalism" began in 1963, after he had been assigned to write a newspaper story on the Hot Rod and Custom Car Show at the coliseum in New York. *Esquire* later sent him to cover the custom car scene in California; the essay he wrote for *Esquire*, a benchmark for the new journalism, supplied the title for his first published collection of essays, *The Kandy-Kolored Tangerine-Flake Streamline Baby* (1965).

Other collections followed: *The Pump House Gang* and *The Electric Kool-Aid Acid Test* (both 1968) documented the excesses of the 1960's, which Wolfe aptly called "The Me Decade." Wolfe continued to produce essay anthologies with flamboyant titles—*Radical Chic & Mau-Mauing the Flak Catchers* (1970) and *Mauve Gloves & Madmen, Clutter & Vine* (1976). In 1973, along with E. W. Johnson, Wolfe edited an influential anthology entitled *The New Journalism*, published by

Harper & Row, in which he attempted to describe the style of the movement, which combined objective description with a sense of "the subjective or emotional life of the characters."

Wolfe has always been obsessed with the icons of wealth, power, status, and fashion. In two books, *The Painted Word* (1975) and *From Bauhaus to Our House* (1981), he examined examples from painting and architecture. His work covers social and political as well as cultural criticism—the government-sponsored poverty program criticized in "Mau-Mauing the Flak Catchers," for example. Wolfe has been criticized for writing such lightweight articles as "The Girl of the Year" while the Vietnam War was in full swing, but Wolfe finally caught up with Vietnam in "The Truest Sport: Jousting with Sam and Charlie," which concerned Navy pilots who flew missions over North Vietnam; it was first published in *Esquire* in October of 1975 and was later included in *Mauve Gloves & Madmen, Clutter & Vine.*

Wolfe's major achievement during the 1970's was *The Right Stuff* (1979), an animated history of the American space program and the esprit de corps of the first astronauts, which won both the Columbia Journalism Award and the American Book Award for 1980. This nonfiction achievement was later matched by his sprawling satirical novel *The Bonfire of the Vanities* (1987), which became a bestseller.

Analysis

Tom Wolfe is the ultimate decadent stylist of the latter twentieth century. He invented his psychedelic style as if by accident, as he explained in the introduction of *The Kandy-Colored Tangerine-Flake Baby*. As a reporter, he had covered the Hot Rod and Custom Car Show in New York for the *Herald Tribune* in a conventional newspaper story, yet he sensed that his coverage had somehow missed the spirit of the event. Customizing as a folk art form, he believed, was culturally important, yet conventional journalism could not describe it adequately. He agreed to do a longer piece for *Esquire*, and his editor sent him to California. Up against a deadline, Wolfe concluded that he could not write the piece but told *Esquire* he would pass on his notes to Bryon Dobell, the managing editor, so that other writers could shape them into a story. Dobell simply printed Wolfe's forty-nine pages of random notes under the title "The Kandy-Kolored Tangerine-Flake Baby," and Wolfe's career as a stylist and chronicler of popular culture and of what Wolfe himself called "Pop Society" was born.

Wolfe's natural exuberance became the lynchpin of his flamboyant style, which could be used for either satire or praise. In *The Right Stuff*, for example, Wolfe indulges in satire when he writes about President Lyndon Johnson and the foibles of the astronauts and the space program, but many of his most energetic and remarkable passages are obviously meant to celebrate the achievements of the program and to praise the raw courage and determination of America's pioneers in space. The book, then, becomes a celebration of patriotism, individuality, and heroism. The genius of this book is that it manages to humanize the technological achievements of contemporary American science while also fortifying the myth of American inventiveness and ingenuity through heroic examples of individual courage. The astronauts are made vividly distinct as Wolfe describes them as though they were characters in a novel, a grand national epic of daring discovery. *The Right Stuff* is history embellished with psychology, history wedded to journalism and creative writing, history made subjective and personal—it is history brought to life.

In *The Right Stuff*, Wolfe did for history what he had earlier done for journalism. The conventional historian, like the conventional journalist, traditionally works under the constraints of objectivity. Wolfe's contribution was that he brought to the task of writing history and journalism a unique voice and point of view. He invaded the minds of his subjects as if he were portraying fictional characters, applying new journalism techniques to history.

In *The Kandy-Kolored Tangerine-Flake Streamline Baby*, for example, Wolfe is especially effective when he writes about the South. One of the best profiles in this collection concerns the "legend" of North Carolina stock-car racer Junior Johnson, whom Wolfe characterizes as "The Last American Hero," much admired for his skill, courage, and recklessness, virtues similar to those of test pilot Chuck Yeager in *The Right Stuff*. This local hero is a risk taker who developed his driving skills while delivering moonshine and outrunning federal agents on the back roads of his native state. Heroes are rarely found in the writings of Tom Wolfe; Johnson and Yeager are among those few.

Wolfe is a master of hyperbole, which he uses more often to denigrate than to praise, as when he describes Baby Jane Holzer as "the most incredible socialite in history." Wolfe understands vanity and folly, ego and excess, image-making and fame, money and power, and the quest for status, which is a dominant motif in his writing.

Wolfe's 1987 novel, *The Bonfire of the Vanities*, which he describes as being "realistic" fiction, can and should be read as a sociological satire on status—how it is achieved and how it can be lost. It is also a treatise on power and politics, exposing the decadent and corrupt nature of New York City. Clearly Wolfe knows his territory, having lived there and having earned his own literary status in the nation's most brutally competitive city; curiously, the nightmare vision of New York exactly fits the stereotype of provincial America's most negative impression of New York as a corrupt dystopia, an alien territory populated by greedy, egocentric, materialistic monsters. Wolfe's antihero, Sherman McCoy, is too seriously flawed by arrogance, vanity, licentiousness, and craven fear to have much tragic dimension, though he does seem capable of learning from his misfortune at the end. In general, one looks in vain for admirable characters, finding only emblems and caricatures. Wolfe may consider his style "realistic," but it often appears rather to be symbolic, allegorical, and savagely satiric.

THE KANDY-KOLORED
TANGERINE-FLAKE STREAMLINE BABY

First published: 1965
Type of work: Essays

A collection of essays on cultural trends and figures, shaped by the new journalism to resemble short stories.

This pioneering anthology established a model for the personal, subjective style of the new journalism. The first essay attempts to capture the spirit of the city of Las Vegas and is typical of Wolfe's self-conscious satirical method. Fascinated by the vulgar spectacle of Las Vegas, Wolfe was able to fashion a verbal style to suit the substance, a style that is itself excessive and prolix, repeating key words and motifs. The essay herniates itself in the first paragraph, for example, where the word "hernia" is repeated fifty-seven times, catching the babble of a casino zombie at the craps table. Wolfe piles words on top of one another to create a verbal cascade; he fractures syntax for effect; he overpunctuates, overloading his sentences, as in the title of his lead essay, "Las Vegas (what?) Las Vegas (can't hear you! too noisy) Las Vegas!!!"

At the end of the book, Wolfe describes "The Big League Complex" of New Yorkers with the wonderment of an outsider. Years later, in *The Bonfire of the Vanities*, he reworks this theme from the vantage point of an insider who has achieved status and tasted its hollowness. Wolfe later coined the phrase "The Me Decade" to describe the 1960's, after having helped to create the style of that decade. Each tirade of excess, every verbal spasm of his decadent and psychedelic style is designed to capture the reader's attention with the unstated but insistent plea: Look at Me!

Throughout the book, Wolfe is fascinated by cultural eccentricity. In "Clean Fun at Riverhead," he profiles Lawrence Mendelsohn, who created and then promoted the notion of the demolition derby as a new "sport." Other selections reveal a fixation on automobiles and car culture. The title essay concerns customized cars and the celebrities of this subculture, such as Hollywood customizer George Barris, who paints his "creations" with "Kandy Kolors." One of the book's longest and most effective pieces, "The Last American Hero," profiles stock-car racing celebrity Junior Johnson, explaining the man, his sport, and its cultural context in such a way as to convince the reader that Johnson may be convincingly "heroic."

Junior Johnson is a regional celebrity. Elsewhere in the book, Wolfe profiles national celebrities: motion-picture star Cary Grant, in "Loverboy of the Bourgeoisie," for example, in which Wolfe contends that Grant is "an exciting bourgeois" rather than "an aristocratic motion picture figure," and heavyweight champion Cassius Clay (later Muhammad Ali), in "The Marvelous Mouth," famous for making vulgar and extravagant claims about other contenders such as Sonny Liston.

Most of the book concerns celebrities and status. Many of the celebrities have faded into obscurity, such as celebrity model Baby Jane Holzer, "The Girl of the Year," once the darling of New York café society, now hardly a pop-cultural footnote. Perhaps more enduring is celebrity disc jockey Murray the K, "The Fifth Beatle," the "king of the Hysterical Disc Jockeys," famous for inventing a much-imitated goofy announcing style, who managed to befriend the Beatles during their first American tour and gained a measure of immortality by fortunate association.

Wolfe is fascinated by the off-beat. In "Purveyor of the Public Life," he profiles Robert Harrison, the publisher of "the most scandalous scandal magazine in the history of the world," *Confidential* (1952-1958), and a specialist in what Wolfe calls the *"aesthetique du schlock."* Wolfe cheerfully explores culture, high and low. On the one hand, he treats rock-and-roll magnate Phil Spector ("The First Tycoon of Teen"); on the other, he takes on Huntington Hartford and his Gallery of Modern Art ("The Luther of Columbus Circle") and the Museum of Modern Art ("The New Art Gallery Society").

Emblems of status abound: an executive's brown Chesterfield and his "Madison Avenue crash helmet" (in "Putting Daddy On"), fashionable interior decorators ("The Woman Who Has Everything"), tailor-made suits ("The Secret Vice"), and exclusive neighborhoods ("The Big League Complex"). Like F. Scott Fitzgerald, Wolfe is fascinated by the rich and powerful. Only rarely does he pay attention to the underclass, the have-nots, as he does in "The Voices of Village Square." Those voices come from the Women's House of Detention at 10 Greenwich Avenue. This is the author's choice, and it is apparently even his fixation.

THE BONFIRE OF THE VANITIES

First published: 1987
Type of work: Novel

A Wall Street high roller is involved in a hit-and-run accident and is eventually brought to justice.

The Bonfire of the Vanities provides an interesting contrast to Wolfe's earlier work. It is a huge, sprawling novel that runs to more than 650 pages, yet it reveals the same fascination with wealth, power, and status that dominated *The Kandy-Kolored Tangerine-Flake Streamline Baby*, his first book. In the novel, which was a long time in the making, Wolfe skillfully introduces a large and diverse cast of characters representing many levels of New York society while setting multiple, intersecting plots in motion. It begins as a meticulously constructed work. It is entertaining as satire and fascinating because of the way it weaves multiple satiric sketches into a unified but cumbersome plot that gains momentum like a runaway train. When it finally grinds to a halt, it seems to have run out of steam, almost dying of exhaustion.

The plot is so densely textured that it resists easy summary. The main plot follows the fortunes of Sherman McCoy, a thirty-eight-year old Yale-educated bond dealer on Wall Street who considers himself a "Master of the Universe." He lives in the "right" neighborhood, in a tenth-floor duplex on Park Avenue. He has a perfect wife and child, as well as a Mercedes and a mistress. The latter two possessions serve to bring about his ultimate downfall and disgrace.

Maria, his mistress, is married to a very wealthy husband. She is a well-traveled, ill-bred, faithless cracker bimbo. Maria spends a week in Italy, and Sherman agrees to meet her return flight at Kennedy Airport. Driving back to Manhattan, Sherman makes a wrong turn and ends up in the South Bronx. He gets lost in the land of the have-nots and ends up in a blocked cul-de-sac. Getting out of the Mercedes to remove an obstacle, he notices two approaching black youths, one of whom offers help. Believing they are "setting him up," Sherman scuffles with them. In a state of panic, he then runs for the car to effect a getaway. Maria, who is now driving, is also in a state of panic. She crashes the car into the boys, who have retaliated to Sherman's attack. One of them, Henry Lamb, suffers a concussion and lapses into a coma. The muck-raking press describes Lamb as an "honor student" and screams for racial justice.

Eventually Sherman McCoy will find himself charged with hit-and-run manslaughter, though, realistically, the wheels of justice turn slowly. At first all that is known is that the boy was hit by a Mercedes registered in New York. The Reverend Reginald Bacon, an opportunist who chairs the "Harlem-based All Peoples's Solidarity" movement, makes the most of the incident's political implications.

The exploitive press, represented by a sleazy alcoholic British tabloid hack named Peter Fallow, thrives on the issue. Abe Weiss, a Jewish district attorney who is up for reelection and his deputy, Lawrence Kramer, have a political stake in bringing Sherman to justice. Wolfe follows these and other characters through the protracted investigation, while Sherman sweats. It was his Mercedes, and he knows that Maria cannot be trusted to support him or even tell the truth about what happened. In the end, Sherman loses everything—his wife and child, his job, his Park Avenue apartment, his money, his power, and his status.

The novel ends in an epilogue in the form of a feature in *The New York Times* thirteen months after the accident; it informs the reader that Henry Lamb died and McCoy was arraigned for manslaughter. Bronx District Attorney Richard A. Weiss gets reelected as a result of his "tenacious prosecution." Albert Vogel, a radical-chic lawyer representing the victim, wins a $12 million settlement against McCoy. The sleazy Peter Fallow wins a Pulitzer Prize for his coverage of the McCoy affair. In short, all the corrupt characters come out winners.

McCoy, who is technically innocent, gains dignity and human dimension through his tribulations, once his career and his ego have been demolished; the only other potentially decent character, Thomas Killian, McCoy's defense attorney, also finds himself the target of litigation and on the skids financially.

Lisa Grunwald, profiling Wolfe for *Esquire*, argued that the writer is more significant as a storyteller than as a social critic, but this is an arguable conclusion if one measures the achievement of *The Bonfire of the Vanities*. Wolfe sets a complicated plot in motion and sustains a heavily textured narrative for hundreds of pages, but the same skill and brilliance that is amply in evidence at the beginning is not sustained at the conclusion, which seems rushed, forced, and curiously flat. It is a well-designed first novel, but a truly outstanding storyteller might have provided a more effective conclusion.

Supremely self-confident, Wolfe sees himself as a writer of realist fiction and has dared to compare himself with novelists Honoré de Balzac, Émile Zola, and Charles Dickens. As a latter-day naturalist, he may be able to justify this claim to an extent, but the comparison with Dickens is questionable. Dickens could be a master of sentiment, but Wolfe's flair for satire does not allow for sentiment in this epic tale of greed, vanity, and folly in contemporary New York. Dickens could draw characters that touched the hearts of his readers, but it is difficult to find characters in Wolfe's novel who are sympathetic or even likable; his characters are consistently deeply flawed. Rather than Dickens, Wolfe is closer in tone and spirit to Henry Fielding, whom he might begin to rival as a satirist. Even Fielding, however, was able to create the formidable Parson Adams—flawed, perhaps, by vanity, but essentially an honorable and honest man—in the novel *Joseph Andrews* (1742). There is no character of his dimension of humanity in *Bonfire of the Vanities*.

The novel quickly became a best-seller and was hugely successful. It was not without its critics, however. Reviewing Wolfe's novel for *The Nation*, John Leonard wrote that "only Tom Wolfe could descend into the sewers of our criminal justice system and find for his hero a white victim in a city where Bernie Goetz gets six months [for shooting a black youth he thought was threatening him in the New York subway]. . . . Only Wolfe could want to be our Balzac and yet not notice the real-estate hucksters and the homeless." Nevertheless, whatever its limitations, *Bonfire of the Vanities* is an intricately plotted work of social observation, and as Wolfe's first foray into full-length fiction, it is an impressive achievement.

Summary

Tom Wolfe revitalized American journalism with his first collections of essays. With *Bonfire of the Vanities*, he attempted to reform postmodern fiction by imitating the nineteenth century realist masters in a manner that has more in common with eighteenth century satire. Like his earlier essays, Wolfe's novel is fascinated with what he has called "status details," but the result of accumulating such details in a "realistic" setting is finally a novelistic comedy of manners pushed to the threshold of bitter satire. Though skilled as a storyteller, Wolfe's major contribution to American letters is that of a supreme stylist and satirist.

Bibliography

Bellamy, Joe David. Introduction to *Tom Wolfe: The Purple Decades*. New York:

Farrar, Straus & Giroux, 1982.

Eason, David L. "New Journalism, Metaphor, and Culture." *Journal of Popular Culture* 15 (Spring, 1982): 142-149.

Edwards, Thomas R. "The Bonfire of the Vanities." *The New York Review of Books* 35 (February 4, 1988): 8-9.

Grunwald, Lisa. "Aloft in the Status Sphere." *Esquire* 114 (October, 1990): 146-160.

Johnson, Michael L. *The New Journalism: The Underground Press, the Artists of Nonfiction, and Changes in the Established Media.* Lawrence: University Press of Kansas, 1971.

Leonard, John. "Delirious New York." *The Nation* 245 (November 28, 1987): 636-640.

Powers, Thomas. "The Lives of Writers." *Commonweal* 105 (March 3, 1978): 142-143, 147-148.

Wolfe, Tom, and E. W. Johnson, eds. *The New Journalism*. New York: Harper & Row, 1973.

James M. Welsh

RICHARD WRIGHT

Born: Roxie, Mississippi
September 4, 1908
Died: Paris, France
November 28, 1960

Principal Literary Achievement

Wright, one of the first African Americans to win a large white as well as black readership, indicted racism and wedded his protest against social injustice to an existentialist philosophy and a championing of the Third World against colonialism.

Biography

Richard Wright was the first of two sons born to sharecropper Nathan Wright and former schoolteacher Ella Wilson Wright in a village outside Natchez, Mississippi; all four of his grandparents had been slaves. After a move to Memphis, Tennessee, and Nathan's desertion before Richard was five, the family's circumstances became increasingly difficult as their poverty deepened. When in 1915 Ella became unable to support her sons, they were temporarily placed in the Memphis Settlement House, a Methodist orphanage.

Subsequent relocations moved Richard back and forth between the rural and urban South. In Elaine, Arkansas, in 1917, he encountered firsthand the virulence of Southern racism when his uncle was lynched. His mother experienced her first stroke when Richard was ten, and the crisis precipitated their removal to her parents' home in Jackson, Mississippi, where Richard chafed under the strict constraints placed on his behavior by the fundamentalism of his grandmother. Richard set out on his own in 1925, upon being graduated as valedictorian from the ninth grade. Heading first to Memphis, he spent two years saving the funds to move his family to Chicago.

Wright lived in Chicago from 1927 to 1937 and held a number of jobs, ranging from busboy to insurance salesman to youth counselor to day laborer. In 1935, he secured a position with the Illinois Federal Writers Project, where he worked with other literary apprentices such as Margaret Walker, Nelson Algren, and Arna Bontemps. While working at the post office in Chicago, Wright befriended several Communists and was recruited in 1933 for the John Reed Club, a leftist organization with a literary as well as political emphasis. The fellowship Wright found there provided his first sense of shared purpose with like-minded individuals; moreover, he found

in Marxism a systematic explanation for the oppressive circumstances that had defined his own experience.

In late 1933 Wright joined the Communist Party, and he became an eloquent spokesman for its attacks on racial and class injustice. For almost a decade, the Party's doctrines and aims provided the theoretical skeleton upon which Wright's fiction and journalism were built; he sought to arouse white readers to a fuller awareness of the degradation caused by institutionalized bigotry and to awaken the black masses to their own revolutionary potential. The effect of Wright's Party affiliation upon his creative work is debated among critics, some arguing that it subjected his writing to a doctrinal straitjacket, and others pointing to the coherence that Communist doctrine gave to his perceptions of reality. Wright privately broke with the Party in 1942, disillusioned with its attempts to curtail the individual freedom of the artist and its criticism of his novel *Native Son* (1940) as a counterrevolutionary work.

His more public renunciation in 1944 resulted from the Party's wartime compromise on the question of civil rights. For the rest of his life, Wright was attacked by the international Communist press. He conceded, nevertheless, that the Party's teachings had encouraged him to envision a wholesale reconfiguration of the social order, fueling a passionate idealism about the purposes of his writing. Moreover, through the Party he met both of his wives: Dmihah Rose Meadman, whom Wright married in 1939 and divorced soon after, and Ellen Poplar, to whom he was married in 1941 and by whom he had two daughters, Julia and Rachel.

The decade between 1935 and 1945 was the most productive period in Wright's creative career. His dedication to nurturing black aesthetic expression prompted his founding of the South Side Writers Group in 1936. Wright moved to New York City in 1937, where he was soon employed as editor for the Harlem bureau of the Communist *Daily Worker*. In 1938, he published a collection of short fiction about Southern racism entitled *Uncle Tom's Children* and won first prize in a Works Progress Administration (WPA) competition. He soon completed *Lawd Today*, his first effort to mine the autobiographical experience of Southern black migrants in Chicago, published posthumously in 1963. After receiving a Guggenheim Fellowship in 1939, Wright completed *Native Son* and in 1941 was awarded the prestigious Spingarn Medal of the National Association for the Advancement of Colored People (NAACP). *Twelve Million Black Voices*, a nonfictional "folk history" of black America composed in collaboration with photographer Edward Rosskam, appeared in that same year, as did a successful stage adaptation of *Native Son*. The publication of *Black Boy* (1945) cemented Wright's international celebrity as the preeminent black author of the decade.

Along with Wright's increasing literary reputation grew his sense of besieged isolation as an intellectual black artist at odds with factions that sought either to coopt or silence him. He eagerly accepted a 1946 invitation from the French government to visit that country under the sponsorship of his good friend Gertrude Stein. In Paris he exulted in the freedom from racist categorization that had plagued him in the United States, and with a second trip to France in 1947, he became an expatriate.

There Wright immersed himself in existentialism, befriending Jean-Paul Sartre, Simone de Beauvoir, and Albert Camus, and committed himself to a humanistic politics. The primary literary result of this philosophical odyssey was the novel *The Outsider* (1953).

Wright's expanded metaphysical concerns matched his political preoccupations with the efforts of Third World peoples to throw off colonial domination. The rationale for his support lay in his discovery of an intellectual and spiritual affinity with nonwhites; they alone, he argued, possessed the moral force to resurrect the West from the soullessness of modern industrialism and totalitarianism. Wright devoted considerable energy during the 1950's to the encouragement of black solidarity in the arts as well as politics. He became involved in the "negritude" movement exploring the black aesthetic sensibility, and in 1952 he helped organize the First Congress of Negro Artists and Writers. Similarly, he attended and reported upon conferences on Third World liberation and social reconstruction in such works as *Black Power* (1954), *The Color Curtain* (1956), *White Man, Listen!* (1957) and *Pagan Spain* (1957).

Wright's creative efforts also continued during this time, although critics concede that they lack the power of his earlier fiction. In addition to *The Outsider*, Wright published *Savage Holiday* (1954) and *The Long Dream* (1958). Shortly before his death he published *Eight Men*, a collection of short fiction that appeared in the United States in 1961. In addition, he became deeply involved in a 1951 film adaptation of *Native Son*, for which he wrote the screenplay and in which he played Bigger Thomas.

The events surrounding Wright's sudden death in 1960 have received considerable investigation. As an expatriate, he suffered harassment by the U.S. State Department, CIA, and FBI as a result of his former Communist membership, his outspoken critiques of American foreign policy during the Cold War, and the hysteria of the McCarthy era. The stresses of a faltering publishing career, financial difficulties, internal hostilities within the African-American community abroad, and recurrent health problems had put Wright in the hospital for extensive tests when a heart attack killed him on November 28, 1960. Conspiracy theories have surfaced, but biographers conclude that while the American government bears responsibility for intensifying the strains on Wright's health, no evidence of foul play exists.

Analysis

Wright's most significant achievement as a writer was his ability to render the particulars of American racism from the point of view of its victims. He powerfully chronicles the historical injustices that black Americans have suffered: physical abuse and emotional degradation; the denial of meaningful opportunities to cultivate and benefit from their native abilities, stifling living conditions dictated by segregation and poverty, and a compromised legal system. In his fiction as in his own life, characters respond to such outrages first with rebellion and finally with flight, since escape alone seems to offer a real alternative. Yet his depictions of the northern migration undertaken by thousands of Southern blacks in the twentieth century always include the disorientation and rootlessness they suffer in their new urban milieu, and his expatriates continue to struggle with the psychological wounds—rage, anxiety, and self-doubt—engendered by earlier bigotry.

The various philosophical positions Wright assumes in his work spring from his hunger to see the African American's experience as a metaphor for the modern human condition. Having learned to interpret the world through a deterministic lens, he finds in literary naturalism a congenial intellectual apparatus upon which to build the compelling logic of his narratives. The antidote to naturalistic despair in Wright's early fiction is provided by Communism, which explains the degradation of racism as part of a worldwide pattern of class exploitation whose remedy is assured through the historical inevitability of revolution: The Marxist hopefulness of *Uncle Tom's Children* and Max's anguished social protest in *Native Son* reflect this orientation. Even in *Native Son*, however, Wright is straining toward a less mechanistic interpretation of the black man's universality—one which equates the negation of self experienced under racism with a cosmic spiritual alienation that is humanity's existential fate.

The black man's symbolic import rests on his outcast status in relation to the dominant white culture. Denied his own identity by the racist premises determining his life and precluded from entering the culture on any other terms, he becomes a metaphysical outlaw estranged from the moral codes of his society and continually testing the limits of individual moral freedom in search of self-definition. Wright's fictions, from *Native Son* to *The Long Dream*, employ criminal melodrama not only because of the taste he developed for it as a boy but also because tales of violent crime dramatize his vision of modern man's existence in a godless universe. Wright's protagonists regularly find themselves faced with choosing between affirmation of their bond with others and assertion of their own egotism at the expense of such ties. This equation mirrors Wright's intellectual contradictions as well, for while he espouses a belief in Enlightenment rationalism (embodied first in Marxism and later in a committed existentialist individualism), his creative energies are most engaged when examining the psyche's dark, demoniac side. Wright demonstrates a fascination with psychoanalytic theory that takes a variety of forms.

Such interests explain Wright's increasing resistance later in his career to being categorized as a writer of racial themes—the troubled sensibility of *The Outsider's* Cross Damon, for example, is attributed to something other than his race. Ironically, a crucial source of Wright's outcast sensibility lay in his hostility to the Southern black community from which he had sprung, and much of his work indicts the elements therein which stifle rational thinking and thwart personal aspiration toward a better way of life. As Wright's international experience grew, he became aware of the presence of intellectuals such as himself in preindustrial societies worldwide.

While his fiction explores the tragic condition of these "marginal men" caught between cultures, his political writings of the 1950's charge them with the responsibility for transforming their homelands into modern industrial societies and insist that Western nations responsible for the colonization of the Third World materially assist them to that end. Wright also recorded his own divided responses to black cultures in Africa and the Caribbean, revealing an emotional empathy for the spiritual cohesiveness of such communities as well as a deep skepticism of the tribal and religious traditionalism that hampered what the West would term "progress." His report from Ghana in *Black Power* reflects that tension, which leads him to concede that history has transformed the African American into a Westerner. Wright's overarching literary vision springs from a philosophical extrapolation of that fact; he considered himself a cosmopolitan humanist grounded in secular rationalism but was convinced that only the non-white peoples of the Third World could redeem Western civilization. This view explains his willingness to devote so much energy in the last decade of his life to documenting the Third World's potential.

NATIVE SON

First published: 1940
Type of work: Novel

An angry black teenager in the Chicago ghetto commits two murders that liberate him from his own victimized mindset at the same time they feed the societal racism that has defined his life.

Native Son triggered Wright's emergence into the foreground of contemporary American literature; the book became a best-seller and was selected as the first Book of the Month Club offering by an African American. It immediately initiated controversy: Many within the black bourgeoisie condemned its depiction of a violent, white-hating black youth as the embodiment of white racist fantasies about the Negro "threat"; Wright's fellow Communists disliked its racial preoccupations and reactionary emphasis upon the misdirected rebellion of a lone individual. Yet the novel also garnered high praise, often from those same audiences: The NAACP awarded Wright the Spingarn Medal, and critic Irving Howe suggested that Wright had transcended strictly aesthetic evaluations, saying, "The day *Native Son* appeared, American culture was changed forever." Wright's avowed intention was to force readers to confront the full "moral horror" of American racism.

In the essay "How Bigger Was Born," Wright explains that his protagonist, Bigger Thomas, is the composite of innumerable young black men he had encountered throughout his life; their rebellious outrage at being denied entry into the American Dream explodes into unfocused violence that is as much a consequence of modern America's urban industrial rootlessness as it is their racial grievances. Wright's perspective rests on the Marxist tenet that the race question is intimately linked to the class exploitation at the heart of capitalism. Chicago's notorious 1938 Nixon case, in which a black teenager was tried for the robbery and murder of a white mother of two and which influenced Wright in some of his fictional choices, provided topical validity for a story whose larger truths Wright had been pondering for years.

The novel rests upon elaborate philosophical and aesthetic underpinnings. Wright composed *Native Son* in three "acts," entitled "Fear," "Flight," and "Fate," each of which blends naturalism, symbolism, and ideology. "Fear" deals with Bigger's circumstances as the eldest son in a fatherless household dependent on government assistance; it also depicts the emotional volatility with which he responds to the grinding poverty of their lives, his mother's expectations of rescue through accommodation to the system, and the repeated evidence of the futility of his ambitions in a racist culture. Among Wright's influences was Theodore Dreiser's *An American Tragedy* (1925), with which *Native Son* shares a bleak naturalism: The biological and environmental factors propelling Bigger's actions as a human "organism" subject him to the machinery of impersonal cosmic and societal forces poised to crush those who misstep. Bigger's automatic impulse is a chilling propensity for violence; the opening scene functions both as naturalistic parable and symbolic forecast. While trying to rescue his terrified family from a rat, his fear energizes him to an instinctual assault on the animal, which responds with equal fierceness until it is killed with a frying pan. The boy gloats over his kill, enjoying an efficacy denied him in daily life: To kill, he intuits, is paradoxically to live.

To placate his desperate mother, Bigger grudgingly takes a chauffeur's job with the wealthy Dalton family and is immediately thrown into a setting that arouses his deepest fears by putting him into constant, unpredictable contact with whites. When he is befriended by the Daltons' daughter Mary, whose political sensibility reflects that of her Communist boyfriend Jan Erlone, he is both attracted and repelled. He hates the danger in which she so unthinkingly puts him, for he knows the cultural taboos their contact violates, yet he is imaginatively and erotically fascinated by her for the same reason. He has no illusions concerning Mary and Jan's idealistic but implausible claims of solidarity with his race; they know nothing of his life and only compound his anxiety by their naïve efforts at egalitarianism. They tragically place Bigger in the most compromising position possible to a black man: He finds himself alone with a drunken white woman, responding tentatively to her vague sexual invitation. When he hears someone outside her bedroom door, his terror prompts him to suffocate her, after which he disposes of her body by decapitating and burning her in the basement furnace; such lurid details transform the realistic façade of the narrative into something surreal.

In "Flight," Bigger's efforts to deflect his own guilt serve only to ensure his entrapment. He concocts a scheme to disguise the crime as a kidnapping and ransom committed by Communists, but the black idiom of the ransom note betrays the killer's race. Media attention leads to his exposure when a reporter camped out at the house discovers Mary's bones as he stokes the furnace. Bigger's decision to seek the help of his girlfriend Bessie backfires when she reveals her inability to handle such pressure, and Bigger decides—this time quite cold-bloodedly—to kill her as well. With this second act, which Wright included despite friends' urgings to omit it, Bigger moves beyond the naturalism defining the first section of the novel and into the existential realm of moral experimentation reminiscent of another of Wright's literary influences, Russian novelist Fyodor Dostoevski's *Prestupleniye i nakazaniye* (1866; *Crime and Punishment*, 1886).

Ironically, while Bigger is far more responsible for Bessie's murder than for Mary's arguably accidental death, it is of virtually no importance to the white society that will eventually put him on trial. It becomes a footnote in his prosecution, the real target of which is his presumed violation of white womanhood. Yet Bigger's killing of Bessie does contribute to the chain of events springing his trap: It not only costs him the ransom money but also moves him steadily toward capture as the police dragnet confines him to the ghetto and finally isolates him on a rooftop water tower, in a scene recalling the rat episode.

"Fate" deals with Bigger's trial and his yearning to know what his life has meant before he dies. Wright uses verbatim Chicago newspaper accounts of the Nixon trial to demonstrate the inflammatory racist lens through which a crime such as Bigger's is projected before the public. This effort at sociological verisimilitude gives way to competing ideological analyses of Bigger's situation, the tensions between them indicative of the struggle within Wright himself between Communist Party doctrine and existentialist individualism.

The speech of Bigger's eloquent lawyer, Max, argues that the jury recognize the moral culpability of a society that produces boys filled with such hate and violence. Max also follows Marxist doctrine in pointing out the inevitable collision between classes in an exploitive capitalist system that pits haves against have-nots. Max's defense, while unheeded by the jury, which sentences Bigger to death, has a profoundly liberating effect on Bigger himself, who is stunned into recognizing that his humanity is confirmed, not denied, by his acts, which alone can define him: He declares, "What I killed for, I am!"

Bigger refuses to subordinate his identity to ideological symbolism and instead embraces his outlaw behavior as evidence of his vitality, not victimization. One might also argue that he is severing meaningful connection to collective societal values when he celebrates his act of murder as life-affirming. As the jail door swings shut on the doomed youth, Wright transforms Bigger from racial icon to representative existential man, responsible for determining the meaning of his own life in a cosmic void where death is the only absolute.

BLACK BOY

First published: 1945
Type of work: Autobiography

A sensitive and rebellious black American youth survives a life of poverty, familial strife, and Southern bigotry to pursue his goal of becoming a writer in the North.

Black Boy, which was another immediate best-seller, is often considered Wright's most fully realized work. Ostensibly a description of the first twenty-one years of his life, the book derives its aesthetic design from two distinct but interwoven narrative skeins: the African-American exodus motif, in which a character's movement from South to North suggests a flight from oppression to freedom, and the *Künstlerroman*, or novelistic account of the birth of the artist—in this case, a "portrait of the artist as a young black American." In the process, Wright analyzes how poverty, intolerance, and racism shaped his personality but also fed his creativity, enabling him to view his pain as an embodiment of the existential human condition.

As a chronicle of family life, *Black Boy* presents a grim portrait of violence, suffering, and disintegration. While the facticity of all the events related in the text is questionable, one cannot deny the authenticity with which Wright has documented the emotional truths of his childhood and their devastating psychological consequences. The central motif of the work is the gnawing hunger defining every facet of Richard's existence: physical hunger born of his family's worsening poverty after his father's abandonment; emotional hunger rooted in that abandonment, compounded by his mother's prolonged illnesses, and resulting in his alienation from other blacks; and intellectual hunger exacerbated by his limited formal schooling and the repressive religious fundamentalism of his maternal relatives. Wright had initially chosen "American Hunger" as his title, and it was later applied to the second volume of his autobiographical writings, published posthumously in 1977.

Richard's responses to the conditions of his life are from the first a volatile combination of rebellion, anger, and fear. *Black Boy* opens with a bored and peevish four-year-old Richard retaliating against his mother's demand for quiet by experimenting with fire until he sets the house ablaze; he then hides under the burning structure until he is pulled free by his enraged father and beaten unconscious. The episode provides a paradigm for Richard's young life: willful self-assertion repeatedly produces self-destructive consequences and crushing rejection by those closest to him. His renegade or outlaw sensibility is in dangerous conflict with the arbitrary tyranny of the authority figures dominating his youth, particularly males. Rather than offering a buffer against the injustices of the Jim Crow South, Richard's home is the crucible of his lifelong estrangement from the human community.

In childhood, Richard learns that the essential law of existence is struggle against forces deterministically operating to extinguish the weak; this view explains the pervasive naturalism of *Black Boy*. The lesson remains the same whether he is observing the casual violence of nature, confronting street urchins, or battling wits with prejudiced whites. Surrounded by hostility directed at him from all quarters, including the supposedly Christian adults who regularly beat and humiliate him, Richard rejects religion as fraudulent in its premises and hypocritical in its practices. He allows himself to be baptized only because of the emotional blackmail of his abject mother and the friends whose camaraderie he desperately seeks; he craves an analytic vantage point that will illuminate the random pointlessness of experience.

After he is graduated from the ninth grade and begins working in Memphis, he finds in writers such as H. L. Mencken, Theodore Dreiser, and Sinclair Lewis evidence not only that his own insights into the brutal nature of existence are valid but also that they are potentially the stuff of serious literature. Years earlier, he had discovered the explosive power of language and the raw emotional energy generated by melodramatic narrative, and he had vowed to become a writer. As a young man, he becomes consumed with literature's promise to give him a voice in counterpoise to all those forces that have worked so systematically to silence him, and he finds therein the purpose that will save and direct his life after the nightmare of his Southern childhood. Wright's naturalism, Marxism, and existentialism coalesce in *Black Boy*, particularly in his analysis of American racism.

On the most basic level, Wright depicts the situation confronting the African-American male in the first quarter of the twentieth century as literally life-threatening: by the age of fifteen, he had had an uncle lynched for being too successful and knew of a black youth murdered for forgetting the strict sexual taboos surrounding interchanges between black men and white women. He had been personally assaulted without provocation by white youths and had participated in street battles between white and black adolescents. His insistent pursuit of a way out of the South is thus a reaction to the physical terrorism exercised against the black community; it is also a repudiation of the psychological condition that racism fosters in its victims.

Richard has already suffered for years from the debilitating anxiety caused by trying to predict the behavior of whites, and he has often felt the impact of their displeasure, repeatedly losing jobs when they resent his manner or ambition. He chafes under the dehumanizing stereotypes they superimpose on him: "The White South said that it knew 'niggers,' and I was what the white South called 'nigger.' Well, the white South had never known me—never known what I thought, what I felt." Richard's exodus from the South is triggered as much by a spiritual hunger to define his own personhood, free of racist categorizations, as it is by a pursuit of greater material opportunity. Wright asserts that his personality bears permanent scars as a Southern black man—scars that explain his emotional and philosophical alienation as well as his unresolved anger. Significantly, however, they also serve as the creative wellspring of his powerful artistry.

Wright leaves no doubt about his resentment of the white racist social order that defined his youth; what is more difficult to resolve is the ambivalence toward blacks themselves which permeates *Black Boy*. By the time he reaches adulthood, Wright finds himself estranged from the black community by his dismissal of religion, his resistance to strategies for manipulating whites behind the mask of stereotype, and his contempt for passive acquiescence in response to white terrorism. That estrangement becomes central to his depiction of blacks and explains his vacillation between analytic detachment and deeply personal condemnation. Nevertheless, a key source of *Black Boy*'s narrative tension—and its author's positioning of himself as existential outcast—lies in his antipathy to the world that failed to nourish him. One might also argue that Wright's impulse to repudiate the past is very much in keeping with the American literary paradigm of "making oneself" anew in a new world. Richard sets out to define himself according to his own proclivities and talents in the unknown future of Chicago, toward which he is rushing by train at the close of the book.

Summary

Richard Wright's career marked the first time that an African American's work so forcefully commanded the attention of the American literary establishment; it did so through uncompromising depictions of the social and moral crisis that racism had precipitated in the United States. In harnessing his anger and alienation into creative channels and giving the oppressed a voice, Wright inspired the next generation of black writers, including Ralph Ellison, Chester Himes, and James Baldwin. Ironically, the militant racial activism of the 1960's led to a temporary rejection of Wright's achievement, despite his courageous political stances. More recently, however, contemporary black writers and critics are recovering Wright's legacy and recognizing him as a man ahead of his time.

Bibliography

Fabre, Michel. *The Unfinished Quest of Richard Wright*. New York: William Morrow, 1973.

Hakutani, Yoshinobu, ed. *Critical Essays on Richard Wright*. Boston: G. K. Hall, 1982.

Joyce, Joyce Ann. *Richard Wright's Art of Tragedy*. Iowa City: University of Iowa Press, 1986.

Kinnamon, Keneth. *The Emergence of Richard Wright: A Study in Literature and Society*. Urbana: University of Illinois Press, 1972.

Macksey, Richard, and Frank E. Moorer. *Richard Wright: A Collection of Critical Essays*. Englewood Cliffs, New Jersey: Prentice-Hall, 1984.

Walker, Margaret. *Richard Wright: Daemonic Genius*. New York: Warner Books, 1988.

Barbara Kitt Seidman

PAUL ZINDEL

Born: Staten Island, New York
May 15, 1936

Principal Literary Achievement
Widely recognized for his plays, Zindel is also credited with pioneering a new kind of fiction for young adults in which the crises of adolescence are portrayed with seriousness and candor.

Biography

Paul Zindel was born in Staten Island, New York, on May 15, 1936, the son of Paul and Beatrice Mary Frank Zindel. His father, a policeman, deserted his family when Paul was two years old, leaving Beatrice Zindel with the responsibility of rearing Paul and his sister, Betty, who was two years older. The breakup of the family left Paul with a deep-seated feeling of resentment toward his father, who ignored his children and failed to make any financial contribution to their support.

Following her husband's desertion, Zindel's mother worked in a variety of jobs, supplementing her salary at times by stealing small items from her clients. Since many of these jobs were short-term practical nursing assignments, the family moved frequently. As a result, Zindel's childhood was rootless and lonely. This loneliness was intensified when he developed tuberculosis at age fifteen and was forced to spend eighteen months in a sanatorium, where most of the patients were adults.

After his recovery and return to high school, Zindel, who had shown an interest in writing plays, entered a playwriting contest sponsored by the American Cancer Society. He was awarded a silver ballpoint pen for his drama about a pianist who recovers from a serious illness to play Chopin's *Warsaw Concerto* at Carnegie Hall.

During his senior year in high school, feeling what he has called a "teenaged angst," Zindel dropped out of school and traveled to Miami, Florida, where he tried unsuccessfully to find a job. After two weeks and the total exhaustion of his financial resources, Zendel returned to New York, where he finished high school in 1954, one year late. He then applied to five colleges, without any clear idea of what he wanted to do. He was accepted by several prestigious schools but decided to attend Wagner College on Staten Island, a move he believes was prompted by low self-esteem and social insecurity, legacies he attributes to his mother.

Zindel majored in chemistry at Wagner but maintained his interest in writing. He served as editor for the school newspaper and wrote an original play as his term pa-

Bonnie and Paul Zindel

per for a continental drama course. During a visit to New York to cover a writers' conference (an assignment he had given himself), Zindel came under the spell of Edward Albee, a playwright best known for his play *Who's Afraid of Virginia Woolf?* (1962). He signed up for a course taught by Albee and under his famous teacher's direction completed a play, *Dimensions of Peacocks* (unpublished). Produced in 1959, the play, about a disturbed teenager whose domineering mother is a practical nurse who steals from her patients, anticipates much of Zindel's later work.

Zindel was still uncertain about a career when he graduated from Wagner College. He needed a job, but he wanted to write, and he compromised by accepting a technical writing position with Allied Chemical. Six months later, bored and tired of commuting, he returned to Wagner to complete a master's program in education. In the fall of 1959, he was hired to teach physics and chemistry at Staten Island's Tottenville High School. He continued at Totenville High School until 1969, spending his summers writing plays. His second play, *Euthanasia and the Endless Hearts* (unpublished) was produced in 1960 and was followed in 1962 by *A Dream of Swallows* (unpublished). Neither play attracted critical attention.

During the summer of 1963, Zindel wrote *The Effect of Gamma Rays on Man-in-the-Moon Marigolds*, a play inspired by Zindel's memories of his mother. The play, which won the Pulitzer Prize in 1971, was first produced in 1965 by Houston's Alley Theater. A year later, Zindel took a one-year leave of absence from teaching to accept a Ford Foundation playwright-in-residence award at Alley Theater.

When he returned from Houston, Zindel became discouraged with teaching and resigned so that he could spend more time writing. Encouraged by Charlotte Zolotow, a children's book editor at Harper & Row who had been impressed with teenagers Ruth and Tillie in *The Effect of Gamma Rays on Man-in-the-Moon Marigolds*, Zindel began exploring the possibility of writing a young adult novel. After careful research, Zindel decided he wanted to attempt a novel of this type. *The Pigman*, which many consider a ground-breaking novel, was published in 1968 and was followed quickly by a second young adult novel, *My Darling, My Hamburger* (1969).

Zindel's third novel, *I Never Loved Your Mind*, was published in 1970, a year that marked the beginning of one of the most intense periods in his life. By 1973, he had completed three plays, *And Miss Reardon Drinks a Little* (1967), *The Secret Affairs of Mildred Wild* (1972), and *The Ladies Should Be in Bed* (1973), besides working on several screenplays. Two of Zindel's plays, *Let Me Hear You Whisper* (1970) and a shortened version of *The Effect of Gamma Rays on Man-in-the-Moon Marigolds*, were produced by National Education Television (NET) during this period. Shortly after this flurry of activity, Zindel had a breakdown and entered psycholanalysis.

On October 25, 1973, Zindel married Bonnie Hildebrand, who had helped in his recovery from his breakdown, and the couple moved to New York. The Zindels' first child, David, was born in 1974, and their second, Lizabeth, was born in 1976. The arrival of children may have prompted Zindel to write a children's picture book, *I Love My Mother* (1975). This was followed by three more young adult novels, *Pardon Me, You're Stepping on My Eyeball!* (1976), *Confessions of a Teenage Baboon*

(1977), and *The Undertaker's Gone Bananas* (1978). A play, *Ladies at the Alamo*, was produced in 1975.

In 1978, Zindel, seeking to earn more money, moved to Beverly Hills, California. By his own admission, money was Zindel's main motivation for writing during his California period. After writing three "potboilers"—*The Pigman's Legacy* (1980), *The Girl Who Wanted a Boy* (1981), and *When a Darkness Falls* (1984)—Zindel returned to the style of writing found in his earlier novels. *Harry and Hortense at Hormone High* (1984) and *A Begonia for Miss Applebaum* (1989) are both in *The Pigman* tradition of Zindel fiction. In 1985 Zindel, feeling that he was losing both artistic and moral perspective, moved his family back to New York.

Analysis

To understand the themes that preoccupy Paul Zindel, one must have a working knowledge of his personal life, since it infuses most of what he writes. His plays, for example, reflect his "virtually desperate" search for meaning in life. His young adult novels, on the other hand, reflect an attempt to resolve, through the creative process, problems left unresolved by an adolescence interrupted by a number of events.

The relationship between Zindel's personal life and his writing may also be seen in the way he works when writing. He usually begins by creating what he calls an "inspirational homunculus." This is a basic idea for a character, which is always based on a "life model" or "living image" (a real person Zindel has known). As his characters develop, Zindel identifies closely with them as he places them in situations in which they must resolve one or more of his own unresolved conflicts. Every situation is based on Zindel's own experience. His young adult novels are usually constructed around what he considers four fundamental themes of adolescence: the search for identity and meaning, the youthful questioning of traditional values, the loneliness of an individual in a crowd, and the difficulty of communication.

With minor variations, Zindel's stories follow an established formula. There is a principal protagonist, usually a dominant, wise-cracking male, who is joined by a second teenager, always of the opposite sex. The second character may also bear part of the responsibility for telling the story, as he/she does in *The Pigman* and *A Begonia for Miss Applebaum*. The couple are usually drawn together as a result of their own isolation. They are basically two people who are lonely because they are unable to communicate with their parents, their teachers, and, sometimes, with their peers. In some instances, their isolation is a result of their instinctive, superior, youthful wisdom which makes them oddities at home, at school, and in the community. Thus thrown together, the two proceed to wrestle with the problems associated with growing up. In the process, they learn valuable lessons and gain new insights.

Zindel's novels are written in a style which has been praised by some as "the authentic voice of the modern teenager." To others, Zindel's teenagers sound like Holden Caulfield, in J. D. Salinger's *The Catcher in the Rye* (1951). They acknowledge that the style is entertaining and suitable to the situations Zindel creates, but question whether anyone actually talks like a Zindel character.

Unlike the novels, Zindel's plays are written for adult audiences and feature few non-adult characters (*The Effect of Gamma Rays on Man-in-the-Moon Marigolds* is an exception). They are mostly about troubled women who do not seem to have Zindel's teenagers' knack for resolving their problems. The plays tend to exaggerate and embellish the themes of the novels. Many of the plays' female characters resemble the parental authority figures in the novels, but in the plays the women are more likely to be perversely crazy or mindlessly destructive to those around them. They often repeat the strange behavior of the adults in the novels; in the plays there is something bizarre about the way they act. For example, both Lorraine Jensen (*The Pigman*) and Tillie Frank (*The Effect of Gamma Rays on Man-in-the-Moon Marigolds*) are kept out of school to do housework, but when the demand is made by Tillie's mother it is tinged with an element of lunacy. Mrs. Jensen's excuse is simply that she needs Lorraine's help. She "can't go out and earn a living" and keep house, too. Betty Frank, however, manages to encapsulate into her demands frustrations and hatreds dating back to her own high school days. Like the novels, Zindel's plays are related to his personal life. Each play is, in a sense, a result of his search for "some sign, for any bit of hope, or reason, to make being a human sensible."

During an interview, Zindel once said that remembering that he was composed of matter which came from the sun a long time ago was a thrilling experience. "The idea of being linked to the universe by these atoms," he said, gave him a "feeling of meaning." This discovery of a form of cosmic resolution, arrived at through a knowledge of science, is frequently echoed in Zindel's plays and novels. *Pardon Me, You're Stepping on My Eyeball!*, for example, ends with the words, "At last there were the stars set in place." This sentiment is repeated in *Confessions of a Teenage Baboon*, which concludes: "I began to look past the moon, past all the great satellites of Jupiter, and dream upon the stars." It is in the conclusion of *The Effect of Gamma Rays on Man-in-the-Moon Marigolds* that Zindel makes his strongest statement about the value of science as a solution to the meaninglessness of being human. In a speech that shows the close relationship between Zindel's personal life and his writing, Tillie Frank says that the most important benefit of her experimentation is that it has made her feel important. "Every atom in me," she says, "has come from the sun—from places beyond our dreams."

THE EFFECT OF GAMMA RAYS ON MAN-IN-THE-MOON MARIGOLDS

First produced: 1965 (first published, 1971)
Type of work: Play

An alcoholic single parent, a teenaged daughter subject to seizures, and another daughter interested in science attempt to find meaning in life.

The Effect of Gamma Rays on Man-in-the-Moon Marigolds, which won a Pulitzer Prize in 1971, was inspired by Zindel's memories of his mother's "charmingly frantic" get-rich-quick schemes. In its focus on the crazy world of a severely troubled woman, and in its resolution in one of the characters' discovery of self-importance through science, *The Effect of Gamma Rays on Man-in-the Moon Marigolds* anticipates both the plays and young adult novels that Zindel would later write.

The Effect of Gamma Rays on Man-in-the-Moon Marigolds, like most of Zindel's plays, intensifies the themes and characters that appear in his young adult novels. Two teenagers, Ruth and Tillie, live in a world dominated by a single parent whose life has been a tragic disappointment. Like Zindel's mother, Beatrice Mary Frank Zindel, Betty Frank has been left with two children to support. She does this by providing nursing care in her home for elderly clients such as the ancient "Nanny," who is a resident at the time the play takes place.

Betty Frank, who was known as "Betty the Loon" during her high school career, is an unsympathetic exaggeration of some of the parents in Zindel's novels. Selfishly preoccupied, slightly alcoholic, and frequently lost in a dream world of preposterous schemes to make money and fantasies about what she might have been if she had not made the mistake of marrying and getting saddled with two kids, Betty Frank is capable of mindlessly destroying both her own and her daughters' worlds. With Ruth, who is subject to convulsions, Betty Frank is at times carelessly indulgent, at times a skillful nurse capable of talking Ruth out of an attack, and at times the most diabolically destructive force in Ruth's life. Her chloroforming of the girls' rabbit appears to be a calculated attack on Ruth's sanity.

With Tillie, on the other hand, Betty Frank exhibits none of the careless indulgences afforded Ruth. Tillie's passion is learning, and her mother, like some of the mothers in Zindel's novels, places a very low value on education. Since Ruth's ability to learn is limited, Betty Frank is content to allow her to attend regularly, but Tillie's interest seems to challenge her mother to find ways of placing stumbling blocks in the way of Tillie's education. Cleaning up rabbit droppings, to Betty Frank's thinking, is far more important than anything Tillie might discover at school. The final expression of her disapproval of education comes at the end of the play, when she refuses to attend an awards night event after Tillie wins the science competition for her experimentation with seeds exposed to radiation.

Underlying the action of the play is Zindel's "virtually desperate" search for something to "hang onto," something "to make being a human sensible." Unfolding against the backdrop of a senseless world like the Franks', Zindel attempts to find the "grain of truth" which will make it sensible. In *The Effect of Gamma Rays on Man-in-the-Moon Marigolds*, it is science that provides the "grain of truth" for Tillie.

Zindel often uses science as a metaphor for or a source of meaning and harmony, but it should be noted that his respect for science and for scientific experimentation is a qualified one. He disapproves of the use of animals for scientific research, and this disapproval is reflected in Ruth's indignation over Janice Vickery's boiling a live cat to study its anatomy. Zindel expanded on this theme later in *Let Me Hear You*

Whisper (1970), a play about a dolphin who refuses to talk when he learns the purpose of the experiment in which he is involved.

Nevertheless, as Tillie says at the close of her awards night presentation, science can give both a sense of meaning and a feeling of importance. Her experiment, she says, has made her curious about the universe. More important, working with seeds exposed to radiation has made her feel important, because she is made up of atoms that have come from space—from places "beyond our dreams."

THE PIGMAN

First published: 1968
Type of work: Novel

Two high school sophomores, a boy and a girl, learn a valuable lesson through their experiences with a lonely old man.

The Pigman, Zindel's first young adult novel, has been called a ground-breaking work. Zindel's portrayal of high school students struggling with their own problems in their own environments introduced a new type of adolescent fiction. *The Pigman* was revolutionary in that Zindel moved away from more cautious traditional juvenile fiction to a kind of writing which depicted teenagers and their problems with candor and seriousness. *The Pigman* established a style of writing for young adults which became almost a formula for teen novels (including Zindel's own) after 1968.

The Pigman records the adventures of two high school students whose search for fun leads to the death of a lonely old man. Like the novels which follow, it is written in a style which has been described as an accurate capturing of the "bright, hyperbolic sheen of teen-age language." The two teenagers who tell the story, John Conlan and Lorraine Jensen, assume responsibility for alternating chapters in what they call an "epic." Characteristically, John is the dominant personality. As in most of his novels, the principal characters are two teenagers of opposite sex, with the male typically taking the leading role. In novels such as *My Darling, My Hamburger* the boy serves as narrator, but in *The Pigman* and *A Begonia for Miss Applebaum* the task is shared, with each narrator responsible for alternating chapters. Notes, drawings, and reproductions of clippings are interspersed throughout the text, a device which Zindel uses less than successfully in some of his later novels.

The adults in *The Pigman* are treated unsympathetically, as they are in Zindel's plays. They are frequently unable to establish an adequate home environment, and they find most of the interests of the young either uninteresting or unimportant. Even school is categorized as unimportant. Lorraine's mother, like Betty Frank, often attempts to keep Lorraine at home to clean house, since she sees no practical advantage in an education. When Lorraine says that a Latin test is important, her mother responds by saying she is sure that later in life Lorraine will be using Latin daily. Parents are referred to derisively and in most instances are portrayed as being far less astute than their children, who, unlike their parents, are able to perceive the sources of problems, solve them, and in the process gain new insights hidden from their parents and other adults in the stories. Perhaps because of his own experience, Zindel sometimes appears unable to appreciate parental effort. In an introduction to *The Effect of Gamma Rays on Man-in-the-Moon Marigolds*, Zindel refers to his mother's efforts to support her family as "an endless series of preposterous undertakings." John Conlan reflects Zindel's attitude when he refers to his father as "the Bore" and assumes that Mr. Conlan is interested only in stocks.

The boys in Zindel's novels often follow John's practice of referring to their parents only by a derogatory nickname. In *I Never Loved Your Mind*, for example, Dewey Daniels refers to his parents as "the Engineer" and "the Librarian." The use of sobriquets underscores Zindel's portrayal of adults as one-dimensional, monomanic figures; it explains why teenagers such as John and Lorraine must seek their fun outside the family circle. Excitement may be found only among their peers, or in the company of adults such as Mr. Pignati, who is capable of varying from dull routine and can find fun in doing simple things.

Following his habit of using "life models" for the characters in his novels and plays, the characters in *The Pigman* are based on people Zindel has known. Lorraine's mother, like Betty Frank in *The Effect of Gamma Rays on Man-in-the-Moon Marigolds*, is modeled after Zindel's mother. Like Beatrice Zindel, Mrs. Jensen is a single parent working as a practical nurse, and like Zindel's mother Mrs. Jensen restocks her kitchen and bathroom shelves with items stolen from her clients.

Zindel has admitted that it was his own "interrupted adolescence" that prompted him to write for young adults and that his stories in the main are his own attempt to resolve problems left over from those years. As a result of this compulsion to solve problems, Zindel's novels always place the main characters in situations requiring the solution of a major youth-related problem. As the problem is solved, Zindel's teenagers (and Zindel himself) learn lessons and gain new insights. When the lesson does not seem obvious, Zindel may spell it out at the end of the novel, as he does in *The Pigman*. Speaking through John Conlan, Zindel says that life is what the individual makes it. Ultimately, there is "no one else to blame." People, like baboons, "build their own cages."

MY DARLING, MY HAMBURGER

First published: 1969
Type of work: Novel

Four high school seniors struggle with issues such as casual sex, contraceptives, and abortion.

My Darling, My Hamburger, Zindel's second young adult novel, was the first to use the type of offbeat title which would become a kind of Zindel trademark. Eventually, the Zindel bibliography would grow to include titles such as *Pardon Me, You're Stepping on My Eyeball!*, *Harry and Hortense at Hormone High*, and *The Amazing and Death Defying Diary of Eugene Dingman* (1987). Zindel is again concerned with four basic themes—identity and meaning, the questioning of traditional values, the loneliness of the individual, and the difficulty of communication. *My Darling, My Hamburger* goes beyond these concerns to deal with subjects such as casual sex, the use of contraceptives, and abortion as an alternative to unwanted pregnancies. These subjects are dealt with realistically and with candor.

Zindel departs from the format used in *The Pigman* and other novels by focusing on four teenagers rather then his usual two. These four, like the young people in the other novels, learn through their own experiences, without much help from adults. In *My Darling, My Hamburger*, the lesson appears to be that carefree living has risks and that people must account for their actions. Zindel also departs from *The Pigman* formula by using a third-person omniscient narrator to tell the story; the language used in the dialogue is similar to that used in his other novels. As in *The Pigman*, Zindel accompanies the text with facsimiles of letters and announcements, reproductions of lesson assignments, and copies of surreptitious notes, allowing for a more personal treatment of the characters.

As *My Darling, My Hamburger* develops it becomes apparent that Zindel believes that at least a part of the cynicism expressed by his teenaged characters must be attributed to their sense of having been betrayed by adults. These adults might have provided something for young people to fall back on at critical times in their lives. Instead, as Miss Fanuzzi does, they give "dumb" and impotent advice. Miss Fanuzzi, for example, recommends suggesting going for a hamburger when a boy is pressuring a girl to "go all the way." Her students realize that this advice is useless, and there is a sense of frustration, as well as betrayal, in the observation that "she needs a little more experience with men."

One of the strengths of *My Darling, My Hamburger* is Zindel's realistic portrayal of the pressures faced by adolescents. The impotence of adult advice in the face of this pressure is dramatized by his division of the book into two parts. Each of the divisions is given half the book's title, which is based on Miss Fanuzzi's advice for handling sexual stimulation. The first part, "The Darling," deals primarily with the pressures to yield to the male's sexual advances, and it ends with one of the main characters, Liz, yielding. The second part, "The Hamburger," is primarily concerned with the consequences; the title is ironic, since Miss Fanuzzi's advice has failed.

In most of his novels, Zindel's characters gain new insights and learn lessons as a result of their experiences. In *My Darling, My Hamburger*, the lessons are obvious to the reader, but many readers believe that Zindel diluted the impact of the novel by concluding with a weak ending. After all has been said and done, the novel ends in some commencement address platitudes. There is a hint that, when it comes to problems related to casual sex, contraceptives, and abortion, Zindel has little more to offer than Miss Fanuzzi.

I NEVER LOVED YOUR MIND

First published: 1970
Type of work: Novel

A teenaged high school dropout discovers the value of education as a result of a disappointing romance with a hippie-type coworker.

I Never Loved Your Mind, Zindel's third young adult novel, was written after Zindel had spent six months in Taos, New Mexico, following his decision to quit teaching. Zindel had taken a leave of absence from teaching to spend a year as playwright-in-residence at Houston's Alley Theater, and when he returned to the classroom he quickly became disillusioned with teaching. After his resignation, he went to Taos, where he lived in a house given him by a friend. When he returned from Taos and had to have an appendectomy, he commented that he was grateful to have a "traditional doctor . . . rather than someone at Hot Springs commune."

True to form, *I Never Loved Your Mind* is essentially a summarization of Zindel's own experiences, with characters drawn from life models. The model for Dewey Daniels was a "nasty and a little preppy" student of Zindel's, while Yvette Goethals is a composite. The primary model for Yvette was an orphan Zindel had befriended, but Zindel's mother may be seen in Yvette's habit of stealing something at the end of each shift she works.

After using the third-person omniscient narrator format in *My Darling, My Hamburger*, Zindel returned to first-person narrative in *I Never Loved Your Mind*. He also returned to the style of writing that characterizes the John Conlan chapters of *The Pigman*. Some readers, however, feel that Zindel places too much reliance on hyperbole in constructing Dewey's narratives. They point out that at times Zindel seems to arbitrarily opt for exotic, grotesque, or ridiculous imagery when plain language would serve. Dewey's description of Yvette provides one example of Zindel language excesses. Dewey begins by saying simply that Yvette's shape is "not too fat, not too slim." He then adds, "Best of all was a commendable frontal insulation of the respiratory cage." This description is followed by an asterisk, which points to a footnote explaining that Yvette "had some pair of peaches." The footnotes, intended as comic devices, tend to intensify a labored quality of the writing, giving many readers the impression that Zindel is trying too hard.

The story that Dewey Daniels sets out to tell is a variation on the old boy-meets-girl theme. Dewey is a high school dropout who works as an inhalation therapist in a local hospital. One of his coworkers is Yvette Goethals, a hippie type who is also a high school dropout. Yvette is a vegetarian and lives with a rock band. Dewey manages to convince himself he is in love with Yvette; it is Yvette's disclaimer that she never loved his mind after she and Dewey have slept together that provides the title for the novel. His brief, one-sided, and disillusioning love affair eventually leads

Dewey to a decision to return to school. Yvette, significantly, moves on to a hippie commune near Taos, New Mexico.

In most of Zindel's young adult novels, his characters are searching for answers to disturbing questions or are seeking resolution of some of the disturbing problems of adolescence. *I Never Loved Your Mind* touches on these problems—Dewey is confronted with the need for an education—but the novel is primarily an expression of Zindel's frustrations with teaching and of his distaste for the hippie subculture of the 1960's. Neither the hippies nor the students in Zindel's science classes were interested in things of the mind, and Yvette's parting words to Dewey become, for Zindel, the distasteful motto for the world he re-creates in the novel. Society, as a whole, appears to be saying to scientist and educator alike, "I never loved your mind."

For Zindel, who often uses science as a metaphor for harmony and meaning, this is a particularly tragic situation, as his reproduction of Yvette's illiterate letter at the end of the novel shows. The letter is symbolic of what society can expect from those who do not love the mind. Fortunately, Dewey comes to his senses, and his understanding of the need for the mind is reflected in his concluding words. While he has no idea what he is going to do, he is sure it is not going to be Yvette's "Love Land crap." Neither is he "going to give civilization a kick in the behind." Like the author, John realizes that he "might need an appendectomy sometime."

Summary

"Whatever I do," Paul Zindel once said, "becomes summarized in my writing." The result of this summarization is a series of plays and novels constructed around Zindel's own search for meaning and the resolution of problems left over from an adolescence interrupted by illness. The plays, which are written for an adult audience, are most often about troubled women, and they contain some attempt to find a reason behind a seemingly senseless life. The novels, on the other hand, are directed toward a young adult audience and are designed to provide both entertainment and insight. In each of Zindel's novels his characters, and perhaps his readers, learn a lesson.

Bibliography

Commire, Ann, ed. *Something About the Author.* Detroit: Gale Research, 1979.

Donelson, Kenneth, and Alleen Pace Nilsen. *Literature for Today's Young Adults.* Glenview, Ill.: Scott, Foresman, 1980.

Forman, Jack Jacob. *Presenting Paul Zindel.* Boston: Twayne, 1988.

"Paul Zindel." In *Twentieth Century American Dramatists*, edited by John MacNicholas. Vol. 7 in *Dictionary of Literary Biography.* Detroit: Gale Research, 1981.

Rees, David. *The Marble in the Water: Essays on Contemporary Writers of Fiction for Children and Young Adults.* Boston: Horn Book Press, 1980.

Chandice M. Johnson, Jr.

MAGILL'S
SURVEY
OF
AMERICAN
LITERATURE

GLOSSARY

Absurdism: A philosophical attitude underlining the alienation that humans experience in what absurdists see as a universe devoid of meaning; literature of the absurd often purposely lacks logic, coherence, and intelligibility.

Act: One of the major divisions of a play or opera; the typical number of acts in a play ranges from one to four.

Agrarianism: A movement of the 1920's and 1930's in which John Crowe Ransom, Allen Tate, Robert Penn Warren, and other Southern writers championed the agrarian society of their region against the industrialized society of the North.

Allegory: A literary mode in which a second level of meaning (wherein characters, events, and settings represent abstractions) is encoded within the narrative.

Alliteration: The repetition of consonant sounds focused at the beginning of syllables, as in: "Large *m*annered *m*otions of his *m*ythy *m*ind."

Allusion: A reference to a historical event or to another literary text that adds dimension or meaning to a literary work.

Alter ego: A character's other self—sometimes a double, sometimes another side of the character's personality, sometimes a dear and constant companion.

Ambiguity: The capacity of language to sustain multiple meanings; ambiguity can add to both the richness and the concentration of literary language.

Angst: A pervasive feeling of anxiety and depression, often associated with the moral and spiritual uncertainties of the twentieth century.

Antagonist: The major character or force in opposition to the protagonist or hero.

Antihero: A fictional figure who tries to define himself and to establish his own codes, or a protagonist who simply lacks traditional heroic qualities.

Apostrophe: A poetic device in which the speaker addresses either someone not physically present or something not physically capable of hearing the words addressed.

Aside: A short passage generally spoken by one dramatic character in an undertone, or directed to the audience, so as not to be heard by the other characters onstage.

Assonance: A term for the association of words with identical vowel sounds but different consonants; "stars," "arms," and "park," for example, all contain identical "a" (and "ar") sounds.

Atmosphere: The general mood or tone of a work; it is often associated with setting, but can also be established by action or dialogue.

Autobiography: A form of nonfiction writing in which the author narrates events of his or her own life.

Avant-garde: A term describing works intended to expand the conventions of a genre through the experimental treatment of form and/or content.

Bardic voice: A passionate poetic voice modeled after that of a bard, or tribal poet/singer, who composed lyric or epic poetry to honor a chief or recite tribal history.

Bildungsroman: Sometimes called the "novel of education," the *Bildungsroman* focuses on the growth of a young protagonist who is learning about the world and finding his place in life; typical examples are James Joyce's *A Portrait of the Artist as a Young Man* (1916) and Thomas Wolfe's *Look Homeward, Angel* (1929).

Biography: Nonfiction that details the events of a particular individual's life.

Black humor: A general term of modern origin that refers to a form of "sick humor" that is intended to produce laughter out of the morbid and the taboo.

Blank verse: Lines of unrhymed iambic pentameter; it is a poetic form that allows much flexibility, and it has been used since the Elizabethan era.

Caesura: A pause or break in a poem; it is most commonly indicated by a punctuation mark such as a comma, dash, semicolon, or period.

Canon: A generally accepted list of literary works; it may refer to works by a single author or works in a genre. The literary canon often refers to the texts that are thought to belong on university reading lists.

Catharsis: A term from Aristotle's *Poetics* referring to the purgation of the spectators' emotions of pity and fear as aroused by the actions of the tragic hero.

Character: A personage appearing in any literary or dramatic work.

Chorus: An individual or group sometimes used in drama to comment on the action; the chorus was used extensively in classical Greek drama.

Classicism: A literary stance or value system consciously based on classical Greek and Roman literature; it generally denotes a cluster of values including formal discipline, restrained expression, reverence for tradition, and an objective rather than a subjective orientation.

Climax: The moment in a work of fiction or drama at which the action reaches its highest intensity and is resolved.

Comedy: A lighter form of drama that aims chiefly to amuse and that ends happily; comedic forms range from physical (slapstick) humor to subtle intellectual humor.

Comedy of manners: A type of drama which treats humorously, and often satirically, the behavior within an artificial, highly sophisticated society.

Comic relief: A humorous incident or scene in an otherwise serious or tragic work intended to release the reader's or audience's tensions through laughter without detracting from the serious material.

Conceit: One type of metaphor, the conceit is used for comparisons which are highly intellectualized. When T. S. Eliot, for example, says that winding streets are like a tedious argument of insidious intent, there is no clear connection between the two, so the reader must apply abstract logic to fill in the missing links.

Confessional poetry: Autobiographical poetry in which personal revelation provides a basis for the intellectual or theoretical study of moral, religious, or aesthetic concerns.

Conflation: The fusion of variant readings of a text into a composite whole.

Conflict: The struggle that develops as a result of the opposition between the protagonist and another person, the natural world, society, or some force within the self.

Connotation: A type of meaning that depends on the associative meanings of a word beyond its formal definition. (*See also* Denotation.)

Conventions: All those devices of stylization, compression, and selection that constitute the necessary differences between art and life.

Counterplot: A secondary action coincident with the major action of a fictional or dramatic work. The counterplot is generally a reflection on or variation of the main action and is strongly integrated into the whole of the work.

Couplet: Any two succeeding lines of poetry that rhyme.

Cubism: In literature, a style of poetry, such as that of E. E. Cummings and Archibald MacLeish, which first fragments an experience, then rearranges its elements into some new artistic entity.

Dactyl: A metrical foot in which a stressed syllable is followed by two unstressed syllables; an example of a dactyllic line is "After the pangs of a desperate lover."

Deconstruction: An extremely influential contemporary school of criticism based on the works of the French philosopher Jacques Derrida. Deconstruction treats literary works as unconscious reflections of the myths of Western culture; the primary myth is that there is a meaningful world which language signifies or represents. The Deconstructionist critic is often concerned with showing how a literary text tacitly subverts the very assumptions or myths on which it ostensibly rests.

Denotation: The explicit, formal definition of a word, exclusive of its implications and emotional associations. (*See also* Connotation.)

Denouement: Originally French, this word literally means "unknotting" or "untying" and is another term for the catastrophe or resolution of a dramatic action, the solution or clarification of a plot.

Detective story: In the so-called "classic" detective story, the focus is on a crime solved by a detective through interpretation of evidence and clever reasoning. Many modern practitioners of the genre, however, have deemphasized the puzzle-like qualities, stressing instead characterization, theme, and other elements of mainstream fiction.

Determinism: The belief that a person's actions are essentially determined by biological and environmental factors, with free will playing a negligible role. (*See also* Naturalism.)

Deus ex machina: Latin, meaning "god out of a machine." In the Greek theater, it referred to the use of a god lowered by means of a mechanism onto the stage to untangle the plot or save the hero. It has come to signify any artificial device for the easy resolution of dramatic difficulties.

Dialogue: Speech exchanged between characters or even, in a looser sense, the thoughts of a single character.

Dime novel: A type of inexpensive book very popular in the late nineteenth century that told a formulaic tale of war, adventure, or romance.

Domestic tragedy: A serious and usually realistic play with lower-class or middle-class characters and milieu, typically dealing with personal or domestic concerns.

Donnée: From the French verb meaning "to give," the term refers to the premise or the given set of circumstances from which the plot will proceed.

Drama: Any work designed to be represented on a stage by actors. More specifically, the term has come to signify a play of a serious nature and intent which may end either happily (comedy) or unhappily (tragedy).

Dramatic irony: A form of irony that most typically occurs when the spoken lines of a character are perceived by the audience to have a double meaning or when the audience knows more about a situation than the character knows.

Dramatic monologue: A poem in which the narrator addresses a silent persona whose presence greatly influences what the narrator tells the reader.

Dramatis personae: The characters in a play; often it refers to a printed list defining the characters and their relationships.

Dramaturgy: The composition of plays; the term is occasionally used to refer to the performance or acting of plays.

Dream vision: A poem presented as a dream in which the poet-dreamer envisions people and events that frequently have allegorical overtones.

Dualism: A theory that the universe is explicable in terms of two basic, conflicting entities, such as good and evil, mind and matter, or the physical and the spiritual.

Elegy: The elegy and pastoral elegy are distinguishable by their subject matter, not their form. The elegy is usually a long, rhymed, strophic poem whose subject is meditation upon death or a lamentable theme; the pastoral elegy uses a pastoral scene to sing of death or love.

Elizabethan: Of or referring to the reign of Queen Elizabeth I of England, lasting from 1558 to 1603, a period of important artistic achievements; William Shakespeare was an Elizabethan playwright.

End-stop: When a punctuated pause occurs at the end of a line of poetry, the line is said to be end-stopped.

Enjambment: When a line of poetry is not end-stopped and instead carries over to the next line, the line is said to be enjambed.

Epic: This term usually refers to a long narrative poem which presents the exploits of a central figure of high position; it is also used to designate a long novel that has the style or structure usually associated with an epic.

Epilogue: A closing section or speech at the end of a play or other literary work that makes some reflection on the preceding action.

Episodic narrative: A work that is held together primarily by a loose connection of self-sufficient episodes. Picaresque novels often have an episodic structure.

Epithalamion: A bridal song or poem, a genre deriving from the poets of antiquity.

Essay: A nonfiction work, usually short, that analyzes or interprets a particular subject or idea; it is often written from a personal point of view.

Existentialism: A philosophical and literary term for a group of attitudes surrounding the idea that existence precedes essence; according to Jean-Paul Sartre, "man is nothing else but what he makes himself." Existential literature exhibits an awareness of the absurdity of the universe and is preoccupied with the single ethical choice that determines the meaning of a person's existence.

Expressionism: A movement in the arts, especially in German painting, dominant in the decade following World War I; external reality is consciously distorted in order to portray the world as it is "viewed emotionally."

Fabulation: The act of lying to invent or tell a fable, sometimes used to designate the fable itself.

Fantastic: The fantastic has been defined as a genre that lies between the "uncanny" and the "marvelous." All three genres embody the familiar world but present an event that cannot be explained by the laws of the familiar world.

Farce: A play that evokes laughter through such low-comedy devices as physical humor, rough wit, and ridiculous and improbable situations and characters.

First person: A point of view in which the narrator of a story or poem addresses the reader directly, often using the pronoun "I," thereby allowing the reader direct access to the narrator's thoughts.

Flashback: A scene in a fictional or dramatic work depicting events that occurred at an earlier time.

Foot: A rhythmic unit of poetry consisting of two or three syllables grouped together; the most common foot in English is the iamb, composed of one unstressed syllable attached to one stressed syllable.

Foreshadowing: A device used to create suspense or dramatic irony by indicating through suggestion what will take place in the future.

Formalism: A school of literary criticism which particularly emphasizes the form of the work of art—that is, the type or genre to which it belongs.

Frame story: A story that provides a framework for another story (or stories) told within it.

Free verse: A poem that does not conform to such traditional conventions as meter or rhyme, and that does not establish any pattern within itself, is said to be a "free verse" poem.

Genre: A type or category of literature, such as tragedy, novel, memoir, poem, or essay; a genre has a particular set of conventions and expectations.

Genre fiction: Categories of popular fiction such as the mystery, the romance, and the Western; although the term can be used in a neutral sense, "genre fiction" is often used dismissively to refer to fiction in which the writer is bound by more or less rigid conventions.

Gothic novel: A form of fiction developed in the eighteenth century that focuses on horror and the supernatural.

Grotesque: Characterized by a breakup of the everyday world by mysterious forces, the form differs from fantasy in that the reader is not sure whether to react with humor or with horror.

Half rhyme. *See* Slant rhyme.

Hamartia. *See* Tragic flaw.

Harlem Renaissance: A flowering of black American writing, in all literary genres, in the 1930's and 1940's.

Hero/Heroine: The most important character in a drama or other literary work. Popularly, the term has come to refer to a character who possesses extraordinary prowess or virtue, but as a technical term it simply indicates the central participant in a dramatic action. (*See also* Protagonist.)

Heroic couplet: A pair of rhyming iambic pentameter lines traditionally used in epic poetry; a heroic couplet often serves as a self-contained witticism or pithy observation.

Historical novel: A novel that depicts past events, usually public in nature, and that features real as well as fictional people; the relationship between fiction and history in the form varies greatly depending on the author.

Hubris: Excessive pride, the characteristic in tragic heroes such as Oedipus, Doctor Faustus, and Macbeth that leads them to transgress moral codes or ignore warnings. (*See also* Tragic flaw.)

Humanism: A man-centered rather than god-centered view of the universe that usually stresses reason, restraint, and human values; in the Renaissance, humanism devoted itself to the revival of the life, thought, language, and literature of ancient Greece and Rome.

Hyperbole: The use of gross exaggeration for rhetorical effect, based upon the assumption that the reader will not respond to the exaggeration literally.

Iamb: The basic metric foot of the English language, the iamb associates one unstressed syllable with one stressed syllable. The line "So long as men can breathe or eyes can see" is composed of five iambs (a form called iambic pentameter).

Imagery: The simulation of sensory perception through figurative language; imagery can be controlled to create emotional or intellectual effects.

Imagism: A school of poetry prominent in Great Britain and North America between 1909 and 1918. The objectives of Imagism were accurate description, objective presentation, concentration and economy, new rhythms, freedom of choice in subject matter, and suggestion rather than explanation.

Interior monologue: The speech of a character designed to introduce the reader directly to the character's internal life; it differs from other monologues in that it attempts to reproduce thought before logical organization is imposed upon it.

Irony: An effect that occurs when a writer's or a character's real meaning is different from (and frequently opposite to) his or her apparent meaning. (*See also* Dramatic irony.)

Jazz Age: The 1920's, a period of prosperity, sweeping social change, frequent excess, and youthful rebellion, for which F. Scott Fitzgerald is the acknowledged spokesman.

Künstlerroman: An apprenticeship novel in which the protagonist, a young artist, faces the conflicts of growing up and coming to understand the purpose of his life and art.

Leitmotif: The repetition in a work of literature of a word, phrase, or image which serves to establish the tone or otherwise unify the piece.

Line: A rhythmical unit within a poem between the foot and the poem's larger structural units; the words or feet in a line are usually in a single row.

Lyric poetry: Poetry that is generally short, adaptable to metrical variation, and personal in theme; it may explore deeply personal feelings about life.

Magical realism: Imaginary or fantastic scenes and occurrences presented in a meticulously realistic style.

Melodrama: A play in which characters are clearly either virtuous or evil and are pitted against one another in suspenseful, often sensational situations.

Memoir: A piece of autobiographical writing which emphasizes important events in which the author has participated and prominent people whom the author has known.

Metafiction: Fiction that manifests a reflexive tendency and shows a consciousness of itself as an artificial creation; such terms as "postmodernist fiction," "antifiction," and "surfiction" also refer to this type of fiction.

Metaphor: A figure of speech in which two different things are identified with each other, as in the T. S. Eliot line, "The whole earth is our hospital"; the term is also widely used to identify many kinds of analogies.

Metaphysical poetry: A type of poetry that stresses the intellectual over the emotional; it is marked by irony, paradox, and striking comparisons of dissimilar things, the latter frequently being farfetched to the point of eccentricity.

Meter: The rhythmic pattern of language when it is formed into lines of poetry; when the rhythm of language is organized and regulated so as to affect the meaning and emotional response to the words, the rhythm has been refined into meter.

Mise-en-scène: The staging of a drama, including scenery, costumes, movable furniture (properties), and, by extension, the positions (blocking) and gestures of the actors.

Mock-heroic style: A form of burlesque in which a trivial subject is absurdly elevated through use of the meter, diction, and familiar devices of the epic poem.

Modernism: An international movement in the arts which began in the early years of the twentieth century; modernism in general was characterized by its international idiom, by its interest in cultures distant in space or time, by its emphasis on formal experimentation, and by its sense of dislocation and radical change.

Monologue: An extended speech by one character in a drama. If the character is alone onstage, unheard by other characters, the monologue is more specifically referred to as a soliloquy.

Musical comedy: A theatrical form mingling song, dance, and spoken dialogue which was developed in the United States in the twentieth century; it was derived from vaudeville and operetta.

Myth: Anonymous traditional stories dealing with basic human concepts and fundamentally opposing principles; a myth is often constructed as a story that tells of supposedly historical events.

Narrator: The character who recounts the story in a work of fiction.

Naturalism: The application of the principles of scientific determinism to fiction. Although it usually refers more to the choice of subject matter than to technical conventions, conventions associated with the movement center on the author's attempt to be precise and objective in description and detail, regardless of whether the events described are sordid or shocking. (*See also* Determinism.)

Neoclassicism: The type of classicism that dominated English literature from the Restoration to the late eighteenth century. Modeling itself on the literature of ancient Greece and Rome, neoclassicism exalts the virtues of proportion, unity, harmony, grace, decorum, taste, manners, and restraint; it values realism and reason.

New Criticism: A reaction against the "old criticism" that either saw art as self-expression, applied extrinsic criteria of morality and value, or gave credence to the professed intentions of the author. The New Criticism regards a work of art as an autonomous object, a self-contained universe. It holds that a close reading of literary texts will reveal their meanings and the complexities of their verbal texture as well as the oppositions and tensions balanced in the text.

New journalism: Writing that largely abandons the traditional objectivity of journalism in order to express the subjective response of the observer.

Nonfiction novel: A novel such as Truman Capote's *In Cold Blood*, which, though taking actual people and events as its subject matter, uses fictional techniques to develop the narrative.

Novel: A long fictional form that is generally concerned with individual characterization and with presenting a social world and a detailed environment.

Novel of ideas: A novel in which the characters, plot, and dialogue serve to develop some controlling idea or to present the clash of ideas.

Novel of manners: The classic example of the form might be the novels of Jane Austen, wherein the customs and conventions of a social group of a particular time and place are realistically, and often satirically, portrayed.

Novella, novelle, nouvelle, novelette: These terms usually refer to that form of fiction which is said to be longer than a short story and shorter than a novel; "novella" is the term usually used to refer to American works in this genre.

Ode: A lyric poem that treats a unified subject with elevated emotion and seriousness of purpose, usually ending with a satisfactory resolution.

Old Criticism: Criticism predating the New Criticism and bringing extrinsic criteria to bear on the analysis of literature as authorial self-expression (Romanticism), critical self-expression (Impressionism), or work that is dependent upon moral or ethical absolutes (new humanism).

Omniscient narration: A godlike point of view from which the narrator sees all and knows everything there is to know about the story and its characters.

One-act play: A short, unified dramatic work, the one-act play is usually quite limited in number of characters and scene changes; the action often revolves around a single incident or event.

Opera: A complex combination of various art forms, opera is a form of dramatic entertainment consisting of a play set to music.

Original Sin: A concept of the innate depravity of man's nature resulting from Adam's sin and fall from grace.

Paradox: A statement that initially seems to be illogical or self-contradictory yet eventually proves to embody a complex truth.

Parataxis: The placing of clauses or phrases in a series without the use of coordinating or subordinating terms.

Pathos: The quality in a character that evokes pity or sorrow from the observer.

Pentameter: A line of poetry consisting of five recognizable rhythmic units called feet.

Picaresque novel: A form of fiction that involves a central rogue figure, or picaro, who usually tells his own story. The plot structure is normally episodic, and the episodes usually focus on how the picaro lives by his wits.

Plot: The sequence of the occurrence of events in a dramatic action. A plot may be unified around a single action, but it may also consist of a series of disconnected incidents; it is then referred to as "episodic."

Poem: A unified composition that uses the rhythms and sounds of language, as well as devices such as metaphor, to communicate emotions and experiences to the reader or hearer.

Point of view: The perspective from which a story is presented to the reader. In simplest terms, it refers to whether narration is first-person (directly addressed to the reader as if told by one involved in the narrative) or third-person (usually a more objective, distanced perspective).

Postmodernism: The term is loosely applied to various artistic movements which have followed so-called high modernism, represented by such giants as James Joyce and Pablo Picasso. The term is frequently applied to the works of writers (such as Thomas Pynchon and John Barth) who exhibit a self-conscious awareness of their predecessors as well as a reflexive treatment of fictional form.

Prose poem: A type of poem, usually less than a page in length, that appears on the page like prose; there is great stylistic and thematic variety within the genre.

Protagonist: Originally, in the Greek drama, the "first actor," who played the leading role. The term has come to signify the most important character in a drama or story. It is not unusual for there to be more than one protagonist in a work. (*See also* Hero/Heroine.)

Psychoanalytic theory: A tremendously influential theory of the unconscious developed by Sigmund Freud, it divides the human psyche into three components—the id, the ego, and the superego. In this theory, the psyche represses instinctual and sexual desires, and channels (sublimates) those desires into socially acceptable behavior.

Psychological novel: A form of fiction in which character, especially the inner life of characters, is the primary focus. The form has characterized much of the work of James Joyce, Virginia Woolf, and William Faulkner.

Psychological realism: A type of realism that tries to reproduce the complex psychological motivations behind human behavior; writers in the late nineteenth and early twentieth centuries were particularly influenced by Sigmund Freud's theories. (*See also* Psychoanalytic theory.)

Pun: A pun occurs when words which have similar pronunciations have entirely different meanings; a pun can establish a connection between two meanings or contexts that the reader would not ordinarily make. The result may be a striking connection or simply a humorously accidental connection.

Quatrain: Any four-line stanza is a quatrain; other than the couplet, the quatrain is the most common type of stanza.

Rationalism: A system of thought which seeks truth through the exercise of reason rather than by means of emotional response or revelation.

Realism: A literary technique in which the primary convention is to render an illusion of fidelity to external reality. Realism is often identified as the primary method of the novel form; the realist movement in the late nineteenth century coincided with the full development of the novel form.

Regional novel: Any novel in which the character of a given geographical region plays a decisive role; the Southern United States, for example, has fostered a strong regional tradition.

Representationalism: An approach to drama that seeks to create the illusion of reality onstage through realistic characters, situations, and settings.

Revue: A theatrical production, typically consisting of sketches, song, and dance, which often comments satirically upon personalities and events of the day; generally there is no plot involved.

Rhyme: A full rhyme comprises two or more words that have the same vowel sound and that end with the same consonant sound: "Hat" and "cat" is a full rhyme, as is "laughter" and "after." Rhyme is also used more broadly as a term for any correspondence in sound between syllables in poetry. (*See also* Slant rhyme.)

Rhyme scheme: Poems which establish a pattern of rhyme have a "rhyme scheme," designated by lowercase letters; the rhyme scheme of ottava rima, for example, is abababcc. Traditional stanza forms are categorized by their rhyme scheme and base meter.

GLOSSARY

Roman à clef: A fiction wherein actual persons, often celebrities of some sort, are thinly disguised.

Romance: The romance usually differs from the novel form in that the focus is on symbolic events and representational characters rather than on "as-if-real" characters and events. Character is often highly stylized, serving as a function of the plot.

Romantic comedy: A play in which love is the central motive of the dramatic action. The term often refers to plays of the Elizabethan period, such as William Shakespeare's *As You Like It* and *A Midsummer Night's Dream*, but it has also been applied to any modern work that contains similar features.

Romanticism: A widespread cultural movement in the late-eighteenth and early-nineteenth centuries, Romanticism is frequently contrasted with classicism. The term generally suggests primitivism, an interest in folklore, a reverence for nature, a fascination with the demoniac and the macabre, and an assertion of the preeminence of the imagination.

Satire: Satire employs the comedic devices of wit, irony, and exaggeration to expose and condemn human folly, vice, and stupidity.

Scene: In drama, a division of action within an act (some plays are divided only into scenes instead of acts). Sometimes scene division indicates a change of setting or locale; sometimes it simply indicates the entrances and exits of characters.

Science fiction: Fiction in which real or imagined scientific developments or certain givens (such as physical laws, psychological principles, or social conditions) form the basis of an imaginative projection, frequently into the future.

Sentimental novel: A form of fiction popular in the eighteenth century in which emotionalism and optimism are the primary characteristics. The best-known examples are Samuel Richardson's *Pamela* (1740-1741) and Oliver Goldsmith's *The Vicar of Wakefield* (1766).

Sentimentalism: A term used to describe any emotional response that is excessive and disproportionate to its impetus or occasion. It also refers to the eighteenth century idea that human beings are essentially benevolent, devoid of Original Sin and basic depravity.

Setting: The time and place in which the action of a literary work happens. The term also applies to the physical elements of a theatrical production, such as scenery and properties.

Short story: A concise work of fiction, shorter than a novella, that is usually more concerned with mood, effect, or a single event than with plot or extensive characterization.

Simile: Loosely defined, a simile is a type of metaphor which signals a comparison by the use of the words "like" or "as." Shakespeare's line, "My mistress' eyes are nothing like the sun," establishes a comparison between the woman's eyes and the sun, and is a simile.

Slant rhyme: A slant rhyme, or half rhyme, occurs when words with identical consonants but different vowel sounds are associated; "fall" and "well," and "table" and "bauble" are slant rhymes.

Slapstick: Low comedy in which physical action (such as a kick in the rear, tripping, and knocking over people or objects) evokes laughter.

Social realism: A type of realism in which the social and economic conditions in which characters live figure prominently in their situations, actions, and outlooks.

Soliloquy: An extended speech delivered by a character alone onstage, unheard by other characters. Soliloquy is a form of monologue, and it typically reveals the intimate thoughts and emotions of the speaker.

Sonnet: A traditional poetic form that is almost always composed of fourteen lines of rhymed iambic pentameter; a turning point usually divides the poem into two parts, with the first part presenting a situation and the second part reflecting on it.

Southern Gothic: A term applied to the scenes of decay, incest, madness, and violence often found in the fiction of William Faulkner, Erskine Caldwell, and other Southern writers.

Speaker: The voice which speaks the words of a poem—sometimes a fictional character in an invented situation, sometimes the author speaking directly to the reader, sometimes the author speaking from behind the disguise of a persona.

Stanza: When lines of poetry are meant to be taken as a unit, and the unit recurs throughout the poem, that unit is called a stanza; a four-line unit is one common stanza.

Stream of consciousness: The depiction of the thought processes of a character, insofar as this is possible, without any mediating structures. The metaphor of consciousness as a "stream" suggests a rush of thoughts and images governed by free association rather than by strictly rational development; the term is often used loosely as a synonym for interior monologue.

Stress: When more emphasis is placed on one syllable in a line of poetry than on another syllable, that syllable is said to be stressed.

Subplot: A secondary action coincident with the main action of a fictional or dramatic work. A subplot may be a reflection upon the main action, but it may also be largely unrelated. (*See also* Counterplot.)

Surrealism: An approach to literature and art that startlingly combines seemingly incompatible elements; surrealist writing usually has a bizarre, dreamlike, or nightmarish quality.

Symbol: A literary symbol is an image that stands for something else; it may evoke a cluster of meanings rather than a single specific meaning.

Symbolism: A literary movement encompassing the work of a group of French writers in the latter half of the nineteenth century, a group that included Charles Baudelaire, Stéphane Mallarmé, and Paul Verlaine. According to Symbolism, there is a mystical correspondence between the natural and spiritual worlds.

Syntax: A linguistic term used to describe the study of the ways in which words are arranged sequentially to produce grammatical units such as phrases, clauses, and sentences.

Tableau: A silent, stationary grouping of performers in a theatrical performance.

Terza rima: A rhyming three-line stanza form in which the middle line of one stanza rhymes with the first line of the following stanza.

Tetrameter: A line of poetry consisting of four recognizable rhythmic units called feet.

Theater of the absurd: The general name given to plays that express a basic belief that life is illogical, irrational, formless, and contradictory and that man is without meaning or purpose. This perspective often leads to the abandonment of traditional theatrical forms and coherent dialogue.

Theme: Loosely defined as what a literary work means. The theme of W. B. Yeats's poem "Sailing to Byzantium," for example, might be interpreted as the failure of man's attempt to isolate himself within the world of art.

Thespian: Another term for an actor; also, of or relating to the theater. The word derives from Thespis, by tradition the first actor of the Greek theater.

Third person: Third-person narration is related from a point of view more distant from the story than first-person narration; the narrator is not an identifiable "I" persona. A third-person point of view may be limited or omniscient ("all-knowing").

Three unities. *See* Unities.

Tone: Tone usually refers to the dominant mood of a work. (*See also* Atmosphere.)

Tragedy: A form of drama that is serious in action and intent and that involves disastrous events and death; classical Greek drama observed specific guidelines for tragedy, but the term is now sometimes applied to a range of dramatic or fictional situations.

Tragic flaw: Also known as hamartia, it is the weakness or error in judgment in a tragic hero or protagonist that causes the character's downfall; it may proceed from ignorance or a moral fault. Excessive pride (hubris) is one traditional tragic flaw.

Travel literature: Writing which emphasizes the author's subjective response to places visited, especially faraway, exotic, and culturally different locales.

Trimeter: A line of poetry consisting of three recognizable rhythmic units called feet.

Trochee: One of the most common feet in English poetry, the trochee associates one stressed syllable with one unstressed syllable, as in the line, "Double, double, toil and trouble."

Unities: A set of rules for proper dramatic construction formulated by European Renaissance drama critics and derived from classical Greek concepts: A play should have no scenes or subplots irrelevant to the central action, should not cover a period of more than twenty-four hours, and should not occur in more than one place.

Verisimilitude: The attempt to have the readers of a literary work believe that it conforms to reality rather than to its own laws.

Verse: A generic term for poetry; verse also refers in a narrower sense to poetry that is humorous or merely superficial, as in "greeting-card verse."

Verse paragraph: A division within a poem that is created by logic or syntax rather than by form; verse paragraphs are important for determining the movement of a poem and the logical association between ideas.

Victorian novel: Although the Victorian period extended from 1837 to 1901, the term "Victorian novel" does not include works from the later decades of Queen Victoria's reign. The term loosely refers to the sprawling works of novelists such as Charles Dickens and William Makepeace Thackeray, which are characterized by a broad social canvas.

Villanelle: The villanelle is a French verse form assimilated by English prosody. It is usually composed of nineteen lines divided into five tercets and a quatrain, rhyming aba, bba, aba, aba, abaa.

Well-made play: A type of play constructed according to a nineteenth century French formula; the plot often revolves around a secret (revealed at the end) known only to some of the characters. Misunderstanding, suspense, and coincidence are among the devices used.

Western novel: The Western novel is defined by a relatively predictable combination of conventions and recurring themes. These predictable elements, familiar from television and film Westerns, differentiate the Western from historical novels and other works which may be set in the Old West.

Worldview: Frequently rendered as the German *weltanschauung*, it is a comprehensive set of beliefs or assumptions by means of which one interprets what goes on in the world.

AUTHOR INDEX

TITLE INDEX

AGAINST DEMOCRACY

JASON BRENNAN

PRINCETON UNIVERSITY PRESS
Princeton and Oxford

Copyright © 2016 by Princeton University Press

Published by Princeton University Press
41 William Street, Princeton, New Jersey 08540

In the United Kingdom: Princeton University Press
6 Oxford Street, Woodstock, Oxfordshire OX20 1TR

press.princeton.edu

Jacket design by Faceout Studio.

All Rights Reserved

Library of Congress Cataloging-in-Publication Data

Names: Brennan, Jason, 1979– author.
Title: Against democracy / Jason Brennan.
Description: Princeton : Princeton University Press, [2016] | Includes bibliographical
  references and index.
Identifiers: LCCN 2016001826 | ISBN 9780691162607 (hardcover : acid-free paper)
Subjects: LCSH: Democracy—Philosophy. | Knowledge, Theory of—Political aspects. |
  Expertise—Political aspects.
Classification: LCC JC423 .B7834 2016 | DDC 321.8—dc23
LC record available at http://lccn.loc.gov/2016001826

British Library Cataloging-in-Publication Data is available

This book has been composed in Sabon Next LT Pro and Univers LT Std

Printed on acid-free paper. ∞

Printed in the United States of America

10 9 8 7 6 5 4 3 2

CONTENTS